XDoclet in Action

XDoclet in Action

CRAIG WALLS
NORMAN RICHARDS

MANNING

Greenwich
(74° w. long.)

For online information and ordering of this and other Manning books, go to www.manning.com. The publisher offers discounts on this book when ordered in quantity. For more information, please contact:

Special Sales Department
Manning Publications Co.
209 Bruce Park Avenue
Greenwich, CT 06830

Fax: (203) 661-9018
email: orders@manning.com

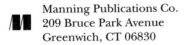

Manning Publications Co.
209 Bruce Park Avenue
Greenwich, CT 06830

Copyeditor: Tiffany Taylor
Typesetter: Denis Dalinnik
Cover designer: Leslie Haimes

ISBN 1-932394-05-2

Printed in the United States of America
1 2 3 4 5 6 7 8 9 10 – VHG – 07 06 05 04 03

For my wife, Raymie
C.W.

For Vincent
N.R.

brief contents

contents

ix

foreword

Let's face it: We're all lazy. At least, most of us are. Some of us have come up with rationalizations for this laziness, such as, "I get more done if I do less," or "By reducing complexity, I can build more complex systems," or the ever-popular "I just want to get the job done so I can go home." No matter which rationalization you choose, the concept of code generation and using metadata is probably appealing to you—if you're a programmer.

The story of XDoclet began a couple of years ago when I was involved in building the EJB container for the JBoss application server. Being the lazy programmer that I am, I found it a burden to write all those interfaces and XML descriptors related to EJB components. The editing slowed me down and made it difficult to manage a large application. But what really ticked me off was how punishing the whole process became when I wanted to change something! A simple change to a method meant editing many source files, as well as the XML descriptor containing the metadata for that method. There had to be a better way!

And there was. *JavaWorld*, which at the time was the leading online Java magazine, published an article about how to use the javadoc API to write custom doclets in order to create custom HTML documentation. I thought "Hey, that's a neat idea, but I'm not really interested in writing HTML: I want it to generate code!" A little tinkering told me this was a great approach for solving most of my problems. I could create custom javadoc tags and run the javadoc tool on my sources, and the doclet I wrote generated both source code and XML instead of HTML. Now all information about a component was centralized in a single file: the EJB bean code, from which I could generate everything else. Neat! I called the tool EJBDoclet and published it on my homepage using an open-source license. I knew other lazy programmers would be interested.

It is now a couple of years later, and XDoclet has evolved from its initial specialized EJBDoclet incarnation to a highly customizable generic tool that can help generate almost anything from your source code. It's also used for, among others, servlets, tag libraries, as well as WebWork and Struts actions, and it supports a number of server-specific XML descriptors for EJB. It has better documentation, a fairly large user base, and a thriving community built around it. There are even tools whose purpose is to create source code that contains XDoclet tags. In short, XDoclet has become a standard tool that can help most programmers become more productive.

If we take a step back and look at the bigger picture, we see that XDoclet combines two main points: code generation and code metadata. The last couple of years have seen an explosion of new standards, each of which mandates that a particular API be exposed by the components which implement it. Design patterns have also become more popular. These two factors provide good reasons for code generation because it is easy to create templates for both. If all you have to do to expose a standard API or use a particular design pattern is create source code that contains all the base information, and then use a code generation tool like XDoclet, which creates the artifacts required by those standards and design patterns, then it becomes significantly easier to perform those tasks. One of the main problems in software engineering is knowledge—actually, lack of knowledge. Both design patterns and standard APIs require that programmers know them well in order to create code that implements them. By using code generation based on templates, such as with XDoclet, it becomes easier to capture and reuse such knowledge, making it available to programmers who lack these skills.

XDoclet is great out of the box, but what's even more interesting is the support for custom modules that you can add to it. This lets you capture your own framework and design pattern standards, which is very helpful in a large company or team.

XDoclet is an open-source project with an active and responsive community of users and developers. You should feel free to contribute your ideas and code to it. As long as new standards, products, and best practices emerge, XDoclet will need to keep evolving in order to help developers where it matters the most. Our opportunity to be lazy depends on other developers' willingness to be creative.

The book you are now reading has been written by two developers who clearly understand all of the above ideas and principles. Through their concise writing they will show you how to apply XDoclet as efficiently as possible in your own projects, and will help you understand everything from the basics of XDoclet to how to expand it with your own plugins. No matter whether you choose to use XDoclet as a lazy developer or as a creative plugin writer, this book is your essential guide.

—Rickard Öberg
Creator of XDoclet

preface

When I first heard of XDoclet (then it was called *EJBDoclet*), I thought the whole idea was nonsense. The comment blocks in my Java code were for documentation, not for programming. Why would I ever put anything in a comment block that impacted the functionality of my program? How absurd! Besides, at the time I wasn't doing much with EJBs, so what use did I have for XDoclet?

But XDoclet wouldn't leave me alone. It kept crossing my path, with its name mentioned in web-logs, presentations, and mailing lists. I was being haunted by XDoclet.

Finally I gave in to those ghosts and gave XDoclet another look. And I'm glad I did. I found out that XDoclet was for more than just EJBs and that it addressed many of the code maintenance headaches I dealt with every day. It freed me from Deployment Descriptor Hell.

I eventually got past my hang-up with putting code in comment blocks. After all, javadoc comments aren't the real documentation—they're merely metadata used to generate the real documentation. In that light, metadata used to generate deployment descriptors and interfaces is just as appropriate in comment blocks as javadoc documentation.

Newly enlightened, I dove in head first to learn as much as possible about XDoclet. I sought out every book and every article I could find. But in my quest for XDoclet knowledge, I came up short. Unfortunately, very little had been written about XDoclet. Even XDoclet's own documentation was sparse (and, in some cases, inaccurate).

I decided to remedy that problem by writing an article documenting everything I learned about XDoclet. It wasn't long before I was commissioned by a prominent Java development magazine to write an article on XDoclet.

I shared my excitement over this new writing opportunity with my friend, Norman Richards. Much to my surprise, he informed me that he had just been commissioned to write an XDoclet article for the same magazine. Upon comparing notes, we learned that our articles[1] covered two sides of the same XDoclet coin. Moreover, we discovered that between the two of us, we probably had enough content to produce an entire book on XDoclet.

Several months and many sleepless nights later, the book you're now reading is the book we were looking for when we started learning XDoclet. We wrote this book for ourselves. We'll refer to it often as we get stuck working with XDoclet. Even as we were writing it, we were wishing we had a book like this to guide us.

We also wrote this book for you. Perhaps you've heard of XDoclet and wondered what it's all about and how you can apply it in your projects. Maybe you're a skeptic, and you're looking for evidence that XDoclet is as useful as is claimed. Or maybe your projects are already successfully employing XDoclet and you just need a reference to this wonderful tool. Whatever the case, this book is for you.

—Craig Walls

---

[1] Due to various reasons, including a huge book-writing project, neither of our articles were ever published.

acknowledgments

This book is more than a collection of words penned by two authors. In addition to those whose names are on the cover, there are many others who played very important roles and deserve credit for this book's existence.

First and foremost, we'd like to acknowledge the fine group of people we've worked with at Manning Publications. The professionalism of each and every one of you has made this project a true pleasure. Many thanks to Marjan Bace for believing in this project and giving us this awesome opportunity. And to everyone else we've worked with at Manning: Susan Capparelle, Denis Dalinnik, Lee Fitzpatrick, Leslie Haimes, Ted Kennedy (in memoriam), Mary Piergies, David Roberson, Iain Shigeoka, Marilyn Smith, Tiffany Taylor, and Helen Trimes.

We'd also like to acknowledge the reviewers who gave us the criticism we needed to shape the book: Dan Bereczki, Ryan Breidenbach, Daniel Brookshier, Kevin Curley, Ryan Daigle, Jeff Duska, Nathan Egge, Erik Hatcher, Jack Herrington, Ernest Hill, David Loeffler, Rickard Öberg, David Paine, Ben Sullins, and Michael Yuan.

A huge high-five to everyone in the XDoclet community for continuing to make XDoclet such a great tool. So many people have contributed in one way or another that it would be difficult to list them all here. But, to everyone who has written a module, addressed an issue in JIRA, or just answered a question on the mailing lists, our appreciation for everything you do.

Finally, we'd like to give special thanks to Rickard Öberg for his vision, for creating XDoclet in the first place, and for contributing to our book with his feedback and foreword.

CRAIG WALLS   I wish to especially thank my beautiful and loving wife, Raymie, for her encouragement and patience during this very long project. I can't believe how fortunate I am to have you in my life. I love you more than you can possibly know or than I can possibly express. Can you believe that I'm *finally* finished with this thing?

I extend my gratitude to Norm for being such a great co-author. There's no way I could've written all of this myself.

Much appreciation to Erik Hatcher for convincing me early on that I could do this and for answering tons of e-mails and questions along the way.

Many thanks to my team at Michaels: Ryan Breidenbach, Marianna Krupin, Van Panyanouvong, and Tonji Zimmerman. I couldn't imagine working with a more talented bunch of developers. You continue to challenge me every day.

Head scratches and belly rubs are owed to the furry and feathered friends who surrounded me during many of my writing sessions: Buster, Max, Frasier, Dodger, Caesar, Hamlet, Echo, Squit, Scuttle, Faith, Cricket, Othello, and especially Juliette, who watched over my shoulder while I banged away at the keyboard.

I wish to express my gratitude to my parents, who instilled in me a desire to learn and who got me started tinkering with computers way back when they bought me that Commodore VIC-20. (Fortunately, my programming activities have advanced beyond BASIC!)

Finally, I'd like to acknowledge a mixed group of people who have inspired me in one way or another throughout my life. Most of you probably don't even know it, but you've had a profound impact on my life: James Bell, Frank Cavallito, Bob Drummond, Jamie Duke, Robert Gleaton, Carolyn Gunn, Gary and Pat Henderson, Brad Lartigue, Hue McCoy, and Hubert Smith.

NORMAN RICHARDS   would like to thank…

Vincent, for not complaining too much when your dad's idea of quality time together for the last six months has been taking the laptop to Chuck E. Cheese's and working on the book while you played. I hope I can give you all the opportunities my parents gave me.

Michael Yuan, for showing me that writing a book wasn't such a far-out dream. I hope Enterprise J2ME does well.

Julie, for hope, dreams, and encouragement. 28-34-13-9-21-11-4. I hope you finally win.

All my friends, who shared my excitement about the book: Vedran, Pyoung Gyu, Sunny, Cinderella, Eriko, Thebes, Jessica, Kevlyn, and Devin.

Greg Lavender, for giving me my first chance; and Risto Miikkulainen, for helping me believe I had something valuable to say.

XML Austin, AustinJUG, and Capital Macintosh users groups, for making Austin such a wonderful place for techies. Thanks to the local nerds who inspire me, particularly Stu, Sam, Eitan, Damon, and Brent.

The core dump, for not picking on me about my inflated ego while I was in the room (that's what AIM is for). May you always know the joy of the ServiceLocator.

Schlotzsky's, Texspresso, Mozart's, and the Alamo Drafthouse, for all the free wireless I consumed while working on the book.

Chango's, for the Maximo Burrito. If you had wireless, I'd live there.

Xi, for the 999 chain. Alea Jacta Est!

Megatokyo, Homestar Runner, and Mr. Sinus, for reminding me to laugh every now and then.

Manning Publications, for giving me this page to ramble semi-coherently on.

about this book

XDoclet in Action is a complete resource for applying XDoclet code generation to your Java development process. XDoclet spans a wide range of Java technologies, and we'll show practical examples of XDoclet with each of the major technologies. Throughout the book, we'll build a simple web application that demonstrates how you can use XDoclet across multiple subsystems to build complete applications.

Our goal in each chapter is not to teach the technology we're looking at but to demonstrate how you can apply XDoclet code generation to that technology. However, you don't need to be an expert in any of the technologies. For example, you don't need to be an Enterprise JavaBeans guru to tackle the EJB chapter, but we'll assume some basic familiarity with EJB concepts. We've tried not to assume more than is necessary to understand how to apply XDoclet, and we've provided pointers to learning resources for the technologies we touch if you want to explore them further.

How to read this book

Whether you're completely new to XDoclet or you're an experienced XDoclet user, we recommend reading part 1. Regardless of which technologies you'll be using XDoclet with, the first section provides valuable background information that will help you better understand code generation with XDoclet.

XDoclet generates code for a wide range of domains. We don't expect that you'll use every type of code generation that XDoclet provides. The best place to start using XDoclet is with the systems you are already working with. The chapters can be used independently and in any order. Many of the chapters build on the web-log application we develop in this book. Our goal is simply to show how XDoclet can be used across multiple technologies, not to suggest that you should design an application using all of them. You can pick and choose among the various applications of XDoclet that are relevant to your own development needs.

Experienced XDoclet users will find value in part 4, which covers custom code generation and higher-level tools. The appendixes also provide the most complete XDoclet reference material available for the more advanced or obscure XDoclet options.

Part 1: The basics

Chapter 1 presents the basic concepts of code generation and shows where XDoclet fits in the bigger picture of code generation.

Chapter 2 gets you started with XDoclet and introduces the core XDoclet concepts you'll see throughout the book.

Part 2: Using XDoclet with Enterprise Java

Chapter 3 starts our look at J2EE with the premier application of XDoclet, generating code for EJBs. This chapter shows how XDoclet lets you generate a bean's interfaces, helper classes, and deployment information directly from the bean class.

Chapter 4 moves to the web-layer, showing XDoclet generation for servlets, filters, tag libraries, and listeners. This chapter explains how XDoclet can be applied to all the core Java web technologies.

Chapter 5 explores code generation for Struts and WebWork, two popular web frameworks.

Chapter 6 completes our look at enterprise technologies by showing how XDoclet can help manage the deployment descriptors you need to deploy your application in a J2EE application server. We look at deploying applications on both JBoss and WebLogic

Part 3: Other XDoclet applications

Chapter 7 examines data persistence frameworks. You'll see how XDoclet can be used with Hibernate, JDO, and Castor.

Chapter 8 jumps to web services. This chapter shows how to use XDoclet with Apache SOAP and its successor, Axis.

Chapter 9 introduces XDoclet code generation for JMX, including MBean interfaces and mlets. This chapter also explains how to generate JBoss-specific JMX deployment files.

Chapter 10 shows you how to us XDoclet to generate mock objects to help you unit-test your code.

Chapter 11 rounds out our look at the standard XDoclet generation tasks by showing how you can use XDoclet when developing portlet applications.

Part 4: Extending XDoclet

Chapter 12 digs deep into the internals of XDoclet and demonstrates how to extend XDoclet with custom templates and tasks. If you're thinking about generating code on your own, this chapter will show you how XDoclet can help.

Chapter 13 shows how to configure the popular Eclipse and IntelliJ IDEs for use with XDoclet. This chapter also shows higher-level code generation environments like AndroMDA and Middlegen, which use XDoclet code generation.

Appendixes

Appendix A details how to install XDoclet, including some common pitfalls that you may encounter along the way.

Appendixes B, C, and D give the most complete reference to XDoclet's tasks, subtasks, merge points, metadata tags, and template tags anywhere.

Appendix E looks at the future of XDoclet and tells you how you can help shape that future by getting involved in the XDoclet project.

Source code

The source code for the examples in this book is available for download at http://www.manning.com/walls.

Typographical conventions

The following conventions are used throughout the book:

- *Italic* typeface is used to introduce new terms.
- **Bold type** indicates text that you should enter.
- `Courier` typeface is used to denote code samples, as well as elements and attributes, method names, classes, interfaces, and other identifiers.

- Bold face `Courier` identifies sections of code that differ from previous, similar code sections.
- Code annotations accompany many segments of code. Certain annotations are marked with bullets such as ❶. These annotations have further explanations that follow the code.
- The ® symbol is used to indicate menu items that should be selected in sequence.
- Code line continuations use the ➡ symbol.

Author online

Purchase of *XDoclet in Action* includes free access to a private web forum run by Manning Publications where you can make comments about the book, ask technical questions, and receive help from the author and from other users. To access the forum and subscribe to it, point your web browser to http://www.manning.com/walls. This page provides information on how to get on the forum once you are registered, what kind of help is available, and the rules of conduct on the forum.

Manning's commitment to our readers is to provide a venue where a meaningful dialog between individual readers and between readers and the authors can take place. It is not a commitment to any specific amount of participation on the part of the authors, whose contribution to the AO remains voluntary (and unpaid). We suggest you try asking the authors some challenging questions lest their interest stray!

The Author Online forum and the archives of previous discussions will be accessible from the publisher's web site as long as the book is in print.

About the authors

Craig Walls, an XDoclet project committer, has been a software developer since 1994 and a Java fanatic since 1996. He lives in Dallas, Texas.

Norman Richards has developed software for a decade and has been working with code generation techniques for much of that time. He is an avid XDoclet user and evangelist. Norman lives in Austin, Texas.

about the title

Manning's *in Action* books combine an overview with how-to examples to encourage learning *and* remembering. Cognitive science tells us that we remember best through discovery and exploration. At Manning, we think of exploration as "playing." Every time computer scientists build a new application, we believe they play with new concepts and new techniques—to see if they can make the next program better than the one before. An essential element of an *in Action* book is that it is example-driven. *In Action* books encourage the reader to play with new code and explore new ideas. At Manning, we are convinced that permanent learning comes through exploring, playing, and most importantly, *sharing* what we have discovered with others. People learn best *in action*.

There is another, more mundane, reason for the title of this book: Our readers are busy. They use books to do a job or solve a problem. They need books that allow them to jump in and jump out easily—books that will help them *in action*. The books in this series are designed for these "impatient" readers. You can start reading an *in Action* book at any point, to learn just what you need just when you need it.

about the cover illustration

The figure on the cover of *XDoclet in Action* is an "Aldeano de la China que recoge la basura para los campus," a Chinese villager who collects odds and ends, a more discreet way of saying that he was the trash collector in his village. Perhaps the young man with the basket over his shoulder was a tinker or scavenger—looking to make a living from what others had discarded—rather than a man designated by the village to keep it clean. We do not know enough about village customs in China two hundred years ago to come up with a more accurate description of his function.

The illustration is taken from a Spanish compendium of regional dress customs first published in Madrid in 1799. The book's title page states:

Coleccion general de los Trages que usan actualmente todas las Nacionas del Mundo desubierto, dibujados y grabados con la mayor exactitud por R.M.V.A.R. Obra muy util y en special para los que tienen la del viajero universal.

which we translate, as literally as possible, thus:

General collection of costumes currently used in the nations of the known world, designed and printed with great exactitude by R.M.V.A.R. This work is very useful especially for those who hold themselves to be universal travelers

Although nothing is known of the designers, engravers, and workers who colored this illustration by hand, the "exactitude" of their execution is evident in this drawing. The "Aldeano de la China que recoge la basura para los campus" is just one of many figures in this colorful collection. Their diversity speaks vividly of the uniqueness and individuality of the world's towns and regions just 200 years ago. This was a time when the dress codes of two regions separated by a few dozen miles identified people uniquely as belonging to one or the other. The collection brings to life a sense of isolation and distance of that period and of every other historic period except our own hyperkinetic present.

Dress codes have changed since then and the diversity by region, so rich at the time, has faded away. It is now often hard to tell the inhabitant of one continent from another. Perhaps, trying to view it optimistically, we have traded a cultural and visual diversity for a more varied personal life. Or a more varied and interesting intellectual and technical life.

We at Manning celebrate the inventiveness, the initiative, and, yes, the fun of the computer business with book covers based on the rich diversity of regional life of two centuries ago brought back to life by the pictures from this collection.

Part 1

The basics

In part 1, you'll be introduced to the basic concepts of code generation, beginning with chapter 1, "A gentle introduction to code generation." You'll see several styles of code generation and learn where XDoclet fits into the overall code generation landscape. This chapter explains when code generation with XDoclet makes sense and provides advice for successfully integrating code generation into your projects.

Chapter 2, "Getting started with XDoclet," helps you take your first steps with XDoclet. It demonstrates the basics of XDoclet and shows you how to begin working with XDoclet generation. You'll learn how to infuse XDoclet metadata into your source code and invoke XDoclet code generation tasks. This chapter provides all the background you'll need to tackle the code generation tasks found throughout the book.

A gentle introduction to code generation

Any intelligent fool can make things bigger, more complex, and more violent. It takes a touch of genius—and a lot of courage—to move in the opposite direction.

—Albert Einstein (1879–1955)

Have you ever asked yourself why you have to write so much code to perform simple development tasks? Do you find yourself wishing you could focus on the code for your application domain instead of all the glue code that binds your system together? Do you ever wish you had a tool that was smart enough to examine your code and write your deployment descriptors for you? Almost every Java developer has at one time or another wished for a simpler way to do development, a mechanism to eliminate the tedious parts of application development so we can focus on the interesting problems we are trying to solve.

If that sounds appealing, then XDoclet is the tool you've been looking for. XDoclet is a code generation framework that can write large portions of your application for you, allowing you to focus on the code that matters most, instead of spending time writing glue code.

In this book, you'll discover what XDoclet can do for you, ranging from handling your EJBs to generating custom in-house code. This chapter gets you started with an introduction to XDoclet, as well as the basic concepts of code generation. With this foundation, you'll be able to determine when code generation is appropriate for your projects and when XDoclet is the right choice for you.

1.1   What is XDoclet?

XDoclet is an extensible, metadata-driven, attribute-oriented framework to generate Java code. Unless you're an alpha geek, that might not seem too exciting at first. So, let's rephrase: XDoclet is a tool that will write your code for you. No, it can't write all of it—but it can write some of the more mundane, repetitive parts, leaving you to focus on the important parts of your application.

The thought of having a computer program write our code for us is definitely exciting, but XDoclet isn't the only tool that makes this promise. Code wizards are a common feature in IDEs, particularly in GUI development. The RMI compiler, rmic, generates stub and skeleton classes for remote objects. XML has reduced the need for custom data formats and custom languages, but parser generators such as JavaCC are still in widespread use. And, the ever-popular JavaServer Pages technology is nothing more than a code generation framework that generates servlets from JSP files.

With all these options, why choose XDoclet for code generation? This is a trick question because code generation is a very broad umbrella under which the numerous flavors sit. XDoclet is no more a replacement for JavaCC than JSP is for rmic. These code generation tools operate in vastly different domains; the only thing they have in common is that they all generate code for you based on the data fed to them.

The questions we really need to ask are, what types of tasks is XDoclet suited for, and when should we choose XDoclet over other code generation options for those tasks? (Or should we use code generation at all?) We'll address these questions throughout the rest of this chapter.

1.2 *Types of code generation*

First, let's make it clear which type of code generation tasks we're talking about. The Java compiler can be considered a code generator. It generates Java bytecode from Java language source code. Some types of code generation happen at runtime. For example, the dynamic proxy, introduced in Java 1.3, is a form of code generation. At runtime, it dynamically generates a Java class based on a set of Java interfaces. Internally, the system generates a Java class file in memory, but there's no reason, performance aside, that it couldn't generate the Java source code and compile it into a class. This is exactly the approach that JavaServer Pages takes: JSP files are fed to a processor, which generates Java language source files. The resulting classes are compiled and loaded into memory.

Compilation and dynamic (runtime) code generation are both fascinating code generation tasks, but they represent a very different flavor of code generation than we'll look at in this book. We'll be examining systems that generate high-level source code that would normally be written by the developer during the development process (before the system is deployed or run). We normally think of this as source code written in the programming language in which the system is developed, but we'll include related files such as SQL database schema, deployment/configuration files, and internationalization resource files. Even though they aren't strictly source-code files, they are files created during the development process that define the behavior of the deployed system. We'll often refer to these generated files as *artifacts* of code generation; this term is slightly awkward, but it serves its purpose.

At the highest level, techniques to generate source code can be divided into two styles: *active* and *passive* code generation. The distinction is the role code generation plays in the development process.

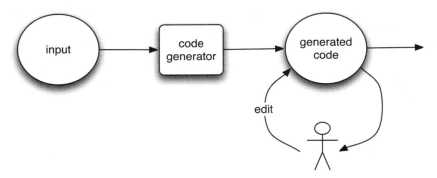

Figure 1.1 **In passive code generation, code is generated once and then modified by the developer.**

1.2.1 *Passive style: one-time code generation*

Passive code generation refers to code generation that is done once up front. The generated code is imported into the project and edited by the developer just like hand-written code. Figure 1.1 shows how the developer works in a passive generation system.

The generated code is meant to be a starting point only—an aid to give structure to the final class but not necessarily to produce the complete class. In passive generation, the developer makes changes to the generated code only and doesn't need to revisit the data that is input to the code generator. In many passive code generation systems (IDE code wizards in particular), the input to the code generator isn't even saved. If something changes and the code generator needs to be run again, reproducing the original input may be an error-prone task. Additionally, regenerating the code in a passive generation system typically requires writing over the generated code and losing any hand-coded changes.

Passive code generation has its uses, but the value provided by a passive generation system is inherently limited. The generator runs only once and then moves out of the picture, putting an upper bound on the total value provided by the generator.

1.2.2 *Active style: integrated code generation*

Active code generation, on the other hand, is integrated much more tightly into the development cycle. In an active generation system, the developer affects the generated code only by modifying the input to the code generator. Figure 1.2 shows the role the developer plays in an active code generation system.

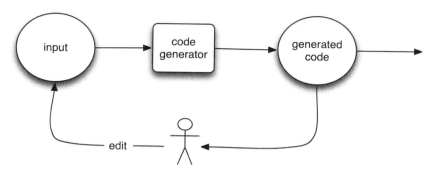

Figure 1.2   With active code generation, the developer edits only the input to the generator, not the generated code.

In an active generation system, the code is considered only a by-product of the build process and is never meant to be edited. In fact, the generated code should not even be checked in the revision-control system. Instead, the input data files are the revision-controlled components that the development process manages.

Active code generation provides significantly larger returns than passive generation at the expense of a little more complexity and up-front effort. The reward comes from being able to affect changes in large code bases with only small changes to the input.

Consider a parser generator. It takes an input file that describes the grammar of a language to be parsed and produces code that does that parsing. Parsing code can be very complex and error prone; small changes in the grammar to be parsed may require significant code changes in the parser. Fortunately, as a developer, you can simply edit the grammar file to make the changes you need. The code generator manages the complexity of the parser code. This process can be repeated throughout development as the grammar changes.

1.3   *Code generation input sources*

Even among active code generation systems, a wide variety of options are available. Looking back at figure 1.2, we didn't specify the input source the developer works with. The nature of the input distinguishes the type of code generation system perhaps even more than the nature of the code being generated. So, let's look at a few of the more common inputs to active code generation systems: model-driven generation, data-file input, and source-file input.

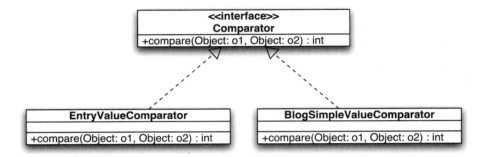

Figure 1.3   A simple UML class diagram showing an interface and two concrete subclasses.

1.3.1 *Models as an input source*

The Unified Modeling Language (UML) has taken a prominent role in application design in recent years. UML provides a standard way to diagram class hierarchies, object interaction, system architectures, and more. Almost every aspect of a system can be modeled using UML. Although proficiency in the full range of UML models requires training and study, most engineers are familiar enough to be productive with the more basic diagrams such as class diagrams and sequence diagrams. Figure 1.3 shows a very simple UML class model.

UML class models such as this one are an interesting input source for active code generators. Some modeling tools offer only passive generation; but many offer active generation by placing special markers in the generated files clearly delineating the parts of the file the developer can change and the parts the code generator owns (which may be overwritten by the code generator when the code is regenerated). Model-driven code generation is very good at generating basic class hierarchies and common access patterns such as getter and setter methods and GUI listener stubs, but it tends to fall flat when it comes to generating classes that provide specific functionality.

Look back at figure 1.3. Using only that model, with no knowledge of how an EntryValueComparator or a BlogSimpleValueComparator works, what could a real human programmer write?

```
public class EntryValueComparator
    implements Comparator
{
    public int compare(Object o1, Object o2) {
        throw new RuntimeException("not yet implemented");
    }
}
```

If your organization requires a specific copyright header or requires every class to have basic logging or version attributes, those could be added. But these are generic features common to every class. There's no way for programmers to provide any additional functionality without going beyond the model and utilizing their own knowledge of the domain or design documentation outside of the class model.

And that turns out to be the limit of code generators based on models, at least without tools capable of modeling implementation details. Modeling tools are good at specifying design but poor at specifying implementation details necessary for code generation.

It might sound like model-driven generation is not very useful, but this isn't true. Model-driven generation is quite a powerful technique, but it falls short mainly due to problems related to tools. Model-driven generation requires buy-in to a (typically proprietary) modeling tool, and modeled data relevant to code generation isn't easily exported to other modeling tools. Model-driven code generation can be difficult to fit into the build process. Modeling tools are very slow to launch, because they aren't designed to be part of an automated build system. In addition, proprietary modeling tools are notoriously strict when it comes to licensing, making it expensive to perform code generation as a part of each developer's build. As model-driven code generation becomes more popular, we hope the tools will improve to make the technique more accessible.

1.3.2 *Data files as input*

Data files are another common source of input. Input data files can take many forms, from simple tabular CSV (comma separated values) files to XML files that describe rich relations between logical entities that are to be generated. Pure data-driven code generation adds a powerful layer of abstraction to the system. Instead of working with code, the developer works with concepts expressed as raw data. This data can be manipulated, visualized, and duplicated without requiring expensive tools.

Consider a simple XML representation of the comparator classes we just looked at. With a small amount of data, you can represent the key features of the classes and their implementations:

```
<comparators>
    <comparator name="EntryValueComparator"
            type="EntryValue">
        <attribute>createdDate</attribute>
    </comparator>
    <comparator name="BlogSimpleValueComparator"
```

```
                    type="BlogSimpleValue">
            <attribute>name</attribute>
        </comparator>
    </comparators>
```

With a custom generator, you could easily generate an implementation class from this data:

```
public class EntryValueComparator
    implements Comparator
{
    public EntryValueComparator() {
    }

    public int compare(Object o1, Object o2) {
        EntryValue entry1 = (EntryValue) o1;
        EntryValue entry2 = (EntryValue) o2;

        return entry1.getCreatedDate()
                    .compareTo(entry2.getCreatedDate());
    }
}
```

On the other side of the spectrum from raw data files are custom data formats and languages. Parser generators often work this way, providing a notation to express the grammar of the language to generate a parser for. In some sense, these data files can be thought of as higher-level programming languages, but typically they don't really provide a programming language. Instead, they provide a data representation with hooks to embed programming fragments written in the language that is the target of the code generator.

1.3.3 *Source files as input*

The input data for code generation can be embedded in the source files themselves. This might resemble preprocessing instructions that are run through a highly specialized pre-processor before compilation. In other cases, instructions for code generation are embedded in comments in the source code. In some highly specialized cases (RMI compilation, for example), the original source code provides all the information needed for code generation.

1.4 *How XDoclet fits in*

XDoclet's approach is a fairly unique blend of several of the styles we've seen so far. XDoclet provides data-driven code generation based on metadata that is placed in javadoc comment blocks in the developer source file. The best way to see what this means is to look at a class that contains XDoclet code generation comments:

```
package com.xdocletbook.jmx;

/**
 * @jmx.mbean
 *     name="Memory:name=memoryMonitor"
 *     description="Memory Monitor MBean"
 *
 * @jmx.mlet-entry
 *     archive="MemoryMonitorMBean.jar"
 *
 * @jboss.service servicefile="jboss"
 *
 * @jboss.xmbean
 */
public class MemoryMonitor
    implements MemoryMonitorMBean
{
  public MemoryMonitor() {
  }

  /**
   * @jmx.managed-attribute
   *     description="Amount of free memory available"
   *     access="read-only"
   */
  public long getAvailableMemory() {
    return Runtime.getRuntime().freeMemory();
  }

  /**
   * @jmx.managed-attribute
   *     access="read-only"
   */
  public long getTotalMemory() {
    return Runtime.getRuntime().totalMemory();
  }

  /**
   * @jmx.managed-attribute
   *     access="read-only"
   */
  public long getMaxMemory() {
    return Runtime.getRuntime().maxMemory();
  }

}
```

XDoclet metadata is placed in special comment blocks in the class

Metadata can also be specified for individual methods

This is an ordinary Java source file. The metadata required for XDoclet to generate code is placed in comment blocks. Placing the code generation input data in comment blocks provides several key advantages:

- *Metadata is related to the code.*   In XDoclet, all generated code is related to existing classes. You can't instruct XDoclet to, for example, generate an interface class completely in isolation. You can, however, provide a class related to the interface (a concrete subclass, perhaps) and ask XDoclet to generate the interface. The requirement to have a related context from which to generate code greatly affects the tasks that are compatible with XDoclet. Not all generation tasks can be easily expressed in terms of a relationship with other classes in the project. However, for the tasks that can be (you'll see many examples throughout the book), having clear relationships to existing classes brings much of the power of model-driven code generation to XDoclet.

- *Metadata and the code are never separated.*   In any code generation system, you can gain understanding of what is being generated by looking at the generated code. However, it gives only part of the picture. Many times, the higher-level view provided in the input source is more meaningful. Storing metadata inside the source files means the metadata is always visible to anyone viewing the code. If the metadata were stored separately, then you would have to consult those files, in addition to the source code, to understand the system. In some cases the added burden is minor, but it is usually good to group related pieces of information together.

- *Metadata is human readable and computer readable.*   In order to get information from the input data, the developer needs to be able to view it. If heavyweight standalone tools are required to view the input data, then you increase the burden and place barriers between the developers and their code. If a tool provides expressive and powerful views of the input data, then crossing those barriers becomes a profitable investment. However, many code generation tools provide most of their value in manipulating the input data and are less useful when trying to visualize the data. Even when a code generation tool provides productive views, what you see is often only a view of the input data. Important details frequently are hidden behind menus and lost in the imprecision of the user interface.

- *No special tools are required to view XDoclet code generation input data.*   (A code editor that understands javadoc comment blocks and tags is helpful). The same data that is used by the XDoclet engine is visible and meaningful to the developer. Even if you don't understand XDoclet, it is possible to understand many of the details of the generated code just by looking at the data. In fact, we've seen projects where developers with no XDoclet training were able to create data for code generation by copying definitions from other files in the project. Although we certainly don't advocate blind development, these cases are a testament to the power of human-readable metadata.

- *Metadata can be shared between tasks.* A final, and less obvious, advantage is that by placing all the code generation input data in the source files, the data can be shared between tasks. As you'll see later in the book, many XDoclet projects apply more than one task inside the project. These tasks are usually loosely related and have some overlap in terms of the data required. With XDoclet, you can share the common data rather than having to duplicate the input data for each code generation task. A side benefit is that the metadata can also be extracted and used by other applications.

1.5 Deciding when to use XDoclet

You've seen how XDoclet fits into the overall landscape of techniques that generate code, but the question still remains: Why choose XDoclet? We've presented some of the reasons that make XDoclet an interesting approach to code generation, but the most compelling reason to use XDoclet is that *it works*. XDoclet can simplify and speed up the development process.

In the end, this is the only answer that matters; but arriving at that end requires a bit more justification. So, we'll approach the issue from a more pragmatic approach. First, we'll look at whether you should generate code at all. Assuming code generation fits into the picture, should you do the code generation by hand or use a tool? Finally, when you do use a tool, when should you choose XDoclet?

1.5.1 Should you generate code?

All other things being equal, the choice to generate or not generate code should be simple—why write code by hand when you can delegate the work to a code generator? But, unfortunately, all other things aren't always equal. One of the biggest obstacles to code generation occurs when the code you're working on doesn't abstract well for code generation purposes. Or, perhaps the parts of your system that might be targets for code generation are too small to be worth the investment it takes to get a code generator up and running.

Fortunately, most Java developers face tasks that are amenable to code generation. EJB development and web development, arguably the most common Java development tasks, both present numerous opportunities for code generation. Detecting tasks that provide opportunities for code generation is a skill that requires experience to develop.

Repetition is a key attribute of systems that are good targets for code generation. Any time the same piece of information is repeated in a system, an opportunity for code generation exists. Sometimes you can eliminate the repetition by refactoring the code and improving the design, but often the repetition is required as part of interfacing with other parts of the system. Let's look at a few common types of repetition that are good targets for code generation:

- *Deployment and configuration files*—Deployment and configuration files let you isolate application decisions concerning a specific instance of a running system and defer the specification of configuration to deployment time. However, this information is, by its very nature, directly related to the code base. It's usually possible to derive the structure of the configuration file, if not the actual values, from the system and reduce the need to manually keep the configuration files in sync with the code.

- *Systems built around business models*—It's highly desirable for all business objects in a business-model-oriented system to have a high degree of consistency both in terms of interface and implementation. Each business object should look and work like the other business objects in the system. Naming conventions, object-creation policies, logging, configuration, and interfaces to other components and back-end systems should be uniform. Code generation is one way to ensure consistency throughout a business model system. Code generation pays off particularly as the business model evolves. Manually updating all the business-object code by hand makes even small changes costly. If the bulk of the business-object system is generated, then business model changes are less costly to implement.

- *Multitier systems*—In addition to the repetition within each tier, multitier systems have repetition at the interfaces between tiers. This repetition is necessary to keep systems from becoming too tightly coupled. Business delegates and service locators are examples of common patterns in multitier systems that introduce repetition. These bridge components are good targets for code generation.

- *Interface oriented components*—Interfaces and implementation classes are obvious repetition points. Code generation can often be used to generate concrete implementation classes for interfaces, or interfaces for concrete implementations. If you're really lucky, a code generator will be able to generate both of these classes.

Repetition is not difficult to spot, and doing so gets easier as you become more experienced with code generation. Fortunately, there are even easier ways to know if code generation fits: Look at what the code generation tools support.

1.5.2 *Should you use a tool or build the generator yourself?*

Writing a code generator from scratch is a difficult and time-consuming task that shouldn't be undertaken lightly. We strongly recommend using code generation tools whenever they are available. Code generation tools represent tested, proven code generation that doesn't require much up-front development investment. Of course, tools come at a cost. Potential licensing costs aside, learning a tool takes time and energy that could otherwise be applied to the project. It's important to weigh the costs and benefits; but we've found that in most cases, when a tool is available, it provides the best overall value.

If no tools exist to generate the code you want, a code generation framework is the next best choice. A code generation framework provides the basic tools necessary for code generation but requires the developer to provide code to do the actual generation for a given domain. This could be as simple as writing a code template or as complicated as creating code in a high-level programming language to print out the generated code line by line. The nature of the framework dictates the difficulty, but the development costs are non-trivial even for the simplest frameworks.

If no suitable tools or frameworks exist, then as a last resort you can write the entire code generator from scratch. This is the most costly and difficult path, but the rewards of code generation are so compelling that even if you decide to write a code generator by hand, the investment can pay off quickly. Although we've made it sound like writing a code generator from scratch is a monumental task, it isn't so difficult that you should avoid it entirely. We recommend that you look at *Code Generation in Action* to better understand the costs and rewards of hand-written code generators.[1]

---

[1] Jack Herrington, *Code Generation in Action* (Greenwich, CT: Manning, 2003).

1.5.3 *Should you choose XDoclet?*

We wouldn't be writing this book if we didn't think XDoclet was a great code generation tool. If XDoclet has a solution for a domain you are working in, we highly recommend giving it a try. Some applications are more compelling than others (for example, there's no reason you should ever have to write a complete deployment descriptor by hand again), but the core XDoclet tasks covered in this book all provide significant value to the developer.

If none of the core tasks solve your problem, then you may still want to consider developing your code generation tasks on the XDoclet framework. Chapter 12 explains in detail how to apply XDoclet to in-house code generation tasks.

1.6 *Code generation wisdom*

We hope you're convinced that code generation is a good idea and are intrigued by XDoclet's inline metadata approach. In the following chapters, we'll dive into XDoclet to see specifically what it can do for you; but before we do that, we want to take a final look at code generation in general and provide some hints and tips that will help when you're trying to integrate XDoclet code generation into your development process.

1.6.1 *Don't generate what you don't understand*

This is the prime directive of code generation. Code generation is a tool to make good developers better. It should never be used as a crutch by developers who don't understand the technologies they are working with. Sadly, many developers prematurely begin using time-saving tools before they understand the domain they are working with. IDEs are notorious for helping untrained developers jump into deep water without first learning to swim. But applying code generation to a domain you don't understand is like tying a cement block to your leg before jumping in. When problems arise, you won't be able to distinguish between problems with the design and problems with the code generator.

Before you consider code generation, make sure you thoroughly understand the technologies you're working with. It's better to apply code generation after you have developed several applications using the technologies for which you're generating code. If you're new to a technology, develop at least a few portions of your application by hand before considering code generation. Don't use generated code that you couldn't have written by hand.

Beyond this, it's important that you understand the purpose of every line being generated. A code generator may use techniques or features you haven't encountered before or don't have much experience with. When you first generate code for a system, inspect it carefully. Make sure you understand everything that is generated. Don't wait until a problem arises to discover what the code is really doing.

1.6.2 Test the generated code

Even in organizations with a strong commitment to testing, there is often reluctance to write unit tests for generated code. Perhaps it stems from placing too much trust in the code generator. You can certainly place a lot of faith in the code produced by a mature code generation system; the generated code has probably been used enough times and viewed by enough eyes that even small problems have been detected. (Finding bugs is another reason we stress that you should thoroughly read and understand any code generated.) But code generators are not perfect. Each use of a code generator is different, and nobody but you can test the input you give to the generator.

Even if you could count on the generated code being completely bug-free, code generators aren't static. The generated code may be changed and refined over time. Even if these changes are also completely bug-free, the assumptions and intentions of the generator may evolve. Having a test suite in place will help make sure the generated code does what you intend it to do and that it will continue doing it the same way in the future.

1.6.3 Don't be afraid to change your design to accommodate generation

As developers, we strive to maximize code quality while minimizing development costs. Code generation aims to both increase quality and reduce costs, so you should naturally look for any opportunities to generate code. However, when you're looking at a system and discover that you can't employ code generation, the tendency in many projects is to give up on code generation and not consider it further.

What's often missed is the fact that with some minor changes to the system design, code generation might be a perfect fit. In that case, why not consider making those changes? Many times, the necessary changes are purely cosmetic— class names or method names might need to be changed for consistency, or maybe you need to change your object hierarchy slightly to accommodate the needs of the generator.

Whenever you discover that code generation isn't a fit for your task, look at what you would need to change to make it a better fit. You might find that the benefit of being able to generate code far outweighs the cost of making the changes.

An example we see often with XDoclet is deploying the same class (an EJB, servlet, filter, or some other standard component) multiple times with slightly different parameters. Doing so requires only a few lines in the deployment descriptor and is good way to reuse existing code. However, XDoclet doesn't work well with this type of reuse; it likes a one-to-one correlation between classes and deployed entities. If you use this technique, you might be tempted to give up on XDoclet as a potential tool. But before you do, you should consider the cost of creating unique subclasses for XDoclet to work with. You may find that your system is so dynamic that you can't anticipate the deployed entities at development time, or you may discover that the change would make the design of the system less interesting, in which case making the change doesn't make sense. On the other hand, perhaps with only a tiny change to the code base you can enable code generation and simplify the overall system greatly.

1.6.4 *Generate layer by layer, piece by piece*

When you decide to apply code generation to an existing system, don't convert the entire application in one shot. We recommend isolating individual subsystems and converting the system layer by layer. In a J2EE application, you might start with the EJB layer. Once you're confident that the generated code is working, then consider the web tier. Isolating the layers gives you more control and keeps the migration process more manageable.

Within the layer, move into code generation one subtask at a time. The deployment descriptor is a good place to start. After the metadata is in place for the deployment information, add in the new data for each of the other tasks.

Figure 1.4 shows a simple J2EE application with an EJB tier and a web tier. Within the EJB tier, you use entity beans and session beans; in the web tier, you use Struts, servlets, and tag libraries. If this were an existing project, you would start integrating XDoclet in each tier separately. The EJB tier is a good place to start. Within the EJB tier, you can generate the EJB deployment descriptors and then generate the code for the beans. You can even separate out the beans by first converting the session beans and then the entity beans.

After you're happy with the EJB tier generation, you can move on and do code generation in the web tier, moving one task at a time. At each step, you have a running system that you can test, thus making sure your code generation efforts haven't introduced any bugs in the system.

This is absolutely critical when introducing XDoclet into an existing project. When you're starting a project from scratch, you may want to jump in and apply all the code generation at once—but if you're bringing XDoclet into an existing

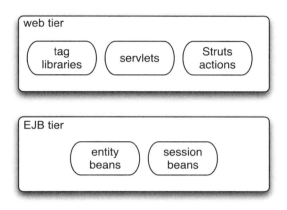

Figure 1.4
A typical J2EE application with web and EJB tiers. Each tier contains several types of components.

system, doing so isn't prudent. Take it slowly, and make sure the system works correctly after each step.

1.6.5 *Keep generated files out of the code repository*

Generated files are by-products of the build process. There is a natural desire to place generated source code with the hand-written code in the repository, but don't do it. You should run code generation at each and every build and discard the results when you're done. Keep in mind that just like the compiled class files, generated source files can be reproduced from the input files whenever you desire. Tracking them in the repository is redundant. The place to store generated files, if needed, is in your official build archive. When you archive your build results (classes, jars, javadocs, and so on), add the generated code for reference.

A practice that will help enforce the idea that generated and hand-written code are different is to generate code into a different location from your hand-written code. If the generated code is in a separate directory, you'll be less tempted to mistakenly check generated code into the source repository. This approach also makes it much easier to clean your build (remove all the contents not in the source repository) and to locate the generated files for archival purposes.

In the examples in this book, we place our source code in the standard src directory and place the generated source code in a directory named gensrc right next to it. (The names of the directories aren't significant, but if you're looking for names, src and gensrc are good conventions to follow.)

1.6.6 *Look for repetition*

A final piece of advice is to keep an eye out for repetition. Whenever information is repeated in the system, you're doing more work than you have to. Good programmers never write more code than they need to perform a task. Some types of repetition, like name repetition (having classes, methods, or properties with names derived from each other) or implementation repetition (having the same code in multiple places) are obvious. Good object-oriented design techniques teach you to minimize these types of repetition.

Common design patterns are a type of repetition that is normally considered good design. We aren't suggesting that factories, facades, or decorators are bad by any means. However, repetition of design by applying design patterns is a form of repetition that can often be eliminated by applying code generation.

Code generation is one way to eliminate repetition, but it is not always the easiest or the best way. As you get more experienced with code generation, you will begin to notice repetition and get a feel for when code generation is the right answer. But you won't see it unless you look for it.

1.7 *Summary*

Code generation is the process of letting a computer program write portions of your code for you. Code generation captures knowledge about how to code a particular task and allows you to reuse that logic in ways that wouldn't otherwise be possible. Many styles of code generation are available, and no one method can solve all the code generation problems that exist. Nonetheless, XDoclet is applicable to a wide variety of tasks that Java developers see on a daily basis. XDoclet can help you deliver these systems more quickly and reliably than by coding the entire system by hand.

In the next chapter, we will get started with XDoclet. We'll look at the fundamentals of code generation with XDoclet and give you your first glimpses of XDoclet in action.

Getting started
with XDoclet

This chapter covers

- Generating a todo list
- Using XDoclet with Ant
- Core XDoclet concepts
- Code generation patterns

> *The beginning of knowledge is the discovery of something we do not understand.*
>
> —Frank Herbert (1920–1986)

XDoclet is a code generation tool that promises amazing benefits for some of the most common Java development tasks. XDoclet can help you produce applications faster and with less effort. You'll eliminate redundancies and write less code. You'll escape "deployment descriptor hell" and improve the manageability of your applications. That's a pretty tall order for a few javadoc-inspired attributes to fill. But as you'll see, XDoclet does an astonishing amount of work.

One of the difficulties in talking about XDoclet is that XDoclet is both a framework and a diverse set of code generation applications. Although the details of each application are different (EJB code generation is different than Struts code generation, both of which are different from JMX code generation), the core concepts and usages have a lot in common.

In this chapter, we'll look at the basic XDoclet framework concepts that permeate all XDoclet applications. But before we do that, let's jump right in and see XDoclet in action.

2.1 XDoclet in action

Every programmer knows that code is never finished. There's always another feature to add, a refactoring to apply, or a bug to fix. It's common for programmers to comment on these issues in the code to remind themselves (or other programmers) of an action that needs to be taken.

How do you keep track of those tasks to complete? Ideally, you compose a tidy todo list. XDoclet provides an extremely useful (and often overlooked) todo generator that can handle this task. This is a perfect, noncommittal opportunity to get started with XDoclet and introduce XDoclet into a project.

2.1.1 A common issue

Suppose you are developing a class for an application involving spoons:

```
public class Matrix {
    // TODO - need to handle the case where there is no spoon
    public void reload() {
        // ...
        Spoon spoon = getSpoon();
        // ...
    }
}
```

Ideally, the next time you visit this code, you will be able to handle the null spoon problem. But what if you don't revisit this code any time soon? How will you remember that you still have some work you want to do in this class? You could search through all of your source files looking for the text *TODO*. Unless your IDE has built-in todo list support, that is far from an ideal solution. XDoclet has a better alternative: If you mark issues on classes and method using the @todo tag, XDoclet can generate a todo report for your project.

2.1.2 Adding an XDoclet tag

The following code shows the trivial modification needed to convert your ad hoc todo item into something a bit more formal:

```
public class Matrix {
    /**  @todo need to handle the case where there is no spoon */
    public void reload() {
        // …
    }
}
```

This simple javadoc-inspired tag is all the metadata XDoclet needs. XDoclet will use the information in the tag, including its relationship to the class and the method in question, to produce a todo report.

2.1.3 Integrating with Ant

To generate your todo list, you need to make sure XDoclet is properly installed. If you don't have XDoclet installed yet, see the instructions in appendix A. Make sure you have an init target that is modeled after the one in the appendix. At the bare minimum, your init target should contain the following task definition for the <documentdoclet> task:

```
<taskdef name="documentdoclet"
        classname="xdoclet.modules.doc.DocumentDocletTask"
        classpathref="xdoclet.lib.path" />
```

The <documentdoclet> task is one of the core XDoclet applications. You'll see quite a few others as you go on.

Now you can add a todo target to the Ant build file that invokes the todo list task:

```
<target name="todo"
        depends="init">
    <documentdoclet destdir="todo">

        <fileset dir="${dir.src}">
            <include name="**/*.java" />
```

**Start <documentdoclet>
task context; output goes
to todo directory**

```
        </fileset>

        <info />    <⎯    <info> subtask does all the work
      </documentdoclet>
    </target>
```

The code uses the `<info>` subtask to look for `todo` attributes in all your source files. HTML summaries are placed in the `todo` directory.

NOTE   XDoclet makes extensive use of Ant. Although you don't need to be an Ant master to use XDoclet, you need at least a basic working knowledge of Ant. We'll point out any tricky usages of Ant as we go, but if you need a refresher, we recommend *Java Development with Ant*.[1]

2.1.4 *Generating a professional-looking todo list*

The todo summary pages that XDoclet creates are very professional looking. Using the summary pages, you can see at a glance which packages and classes have outstanding todo items (along with count information). Todo items can be associated with methods, classes, and fields, and the report clearly distinguishes between them. Class-level todo items are marked with the word *class*, and method-level todo items are marked with an *M* and the signature of the related method. Constructor and field-related todo items are similarly marked.

Figure 2.1 shows a todo list generated by XDoclet. This todo list is for the 1.2b2 release of XDoclet (generating a todo list for the single class we just looked at wouldn't make a terribly compelling example) and is distributed with XDoclet. XDoclet's todo list is distributed in the `doc/todo` directory. Not only is todo information useful for the XDoclet development team, but it can also play a role as part of the documentation of the system.

This may not seem like a huge task at first, but consider for a moment that the only effort expended here was to add machine-readable `@todo` tags to the source files instead of free-form comments that can only be recognized by a human reader. The output produced is easier to read and more useful to programmers than that produced by many commercial issue-tracking systems.

---

[1]   Erik Hatcher and Steve Loughran, *Java Development with Ant* (Greenwich, CT: Manning, 2002).

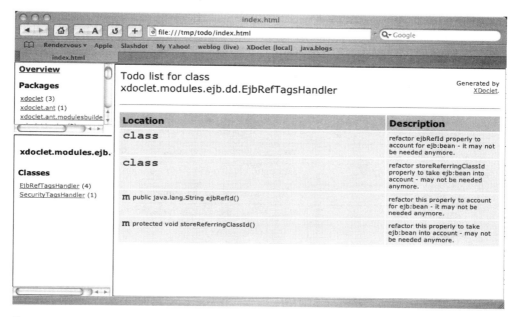

Figure 2.1   The todo list for the XDoclet source tree

2.2   *Tasks and subtasks*

XDoclet does much more than produce variations on the javadoc inline documentation theme. XDoclet is best known as a tool for generating Enterprise JavaBean (EJB) interfaces and deployment descriptors. However, XDoclet is actually a full-featured, attribute-oriented code generation framework. J2EE code generation is the showcase application of XDoclet, but as you will see throughout this book, XDoclet's usefulness extends far beyond J2EE and project documentation.

2.2.1   *XDoclet tasks*

Although we'll talk about using XDoclet to generate code, it's more correct to say that you use a specific XDoclet task, such as `<ejbdoclet>`, to generate code. Each XDoclet task focuses on a single domain and provides a spectrum of code generation options within that domain.

DEFINITION   *Tasks* are the high-level code generation applications available in XDoclet.

Table 2.1 shows the seven core XDoclet tasks and the space of code generation tasks they address. The core tasks ship with XDoclet and are available for use out of the box.

Table 2.1   The seven core XDoclet tasks and their scopes

Task	Scope
`<ejbdoclet>`	EJBs—enterprise beans, utility classes, deployment descriptors
`<webdoclet>`	Web development—servlets, filters, taglibs, web frameworks
`<hibernatedoclet>`	Hibernate persistence—configuration, Mbeans
`<jdodoclet>`	JDO—metadata, vendor configuration
`<jmxdoclet>`	JMX—MBean interfaces, mlets, configuration files
`<doclet>`	Custom templates for ad hoc code generation
`<documentdoclet>`	Project documentation like the todo list

`<ejbdoclet>` is by far the most developed XDoclet task and the most widely used. Many projects using XDoclet only make use of EJB code generation; however, EJBs and web development typically go hand in hand, and `<webdoclet>` is the next most popular XDoclet task. Of course, it is possible (and highly desirable) for a single development project to use more than one XDoclet task, but each XDoclet task exists separately from the others and doesn't interact directly with them.

2.2.2   XDoclet subtasks

One aspect of XDoclet sets it apart from single-purpose code generation tools: XDoclet tasks are collections of fine-grained subtasks that perform very narrow types of code generation within the domain of the task.

DEFINITION   *Subtasks* are the single-purpose code generation procedures provided by a task.

Tasks provide a context and grouping to manage related subtasks (see figure 2.2). The subtasks are responsible for performing the code generation. It's not uncommon for a task to invoke multiple subtasks to perform various aspects of a larger code generation task. For example, when working with EJBs, you might want to generate a home interface for each bean, a remote interface for each bean, and

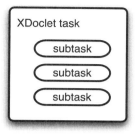

**Figure 2.2
Tasks are groups of
related code
generation subtasks
that work together.**

the `ejb-jar.xml` deployment descriptor. These are three separate code generation subtasks in the context of the `<ejbdoclet>` task.

Subtasks can be invoked in any combination and in any order to provide exactly the level of code generation needed on any project. Subtasks within a single XDoclet task often share functionality and use the same XDoclet tags in the source files. This means that once you get started with a task, it's usually easy to leverage your work by using related subtasks.

Subtask interaction

Let's get an idea of how subtasks relate by looking at the subtasks for `<ejbdoclet>`. Suppose you're creating a CMP (container managed persistence) entity bean. You'll want to use several `<ejbdoclet>` subtasks:

- `<deploymentdescriptor>`—To generate the `ejb-jar.xml` deployment descriptor
- `<localhomeinterface>`—To generate the local home interface
- `<localinterface>`—To generate the local interface

In the process of doing so, you'll mark some basic information about your entity bean's CMP fields. When you deploy your bean, you may want to provide basic mapping information that specifies table and column names in a relational database using vendor-specific deployment descriptors. XDoclet lets you leverage your existing CMP XDoclet attributes and add relational mapping attributes. With just a few additions, you can now invoke, for example, both the `<jboss>` subtask and the `<weblogic>` subtask to generate deployment descriptors for those application servers. XDoclet provides varying levels of support for almost a dozen application servers, multiplying your initial effort greatly.

But that's only the tip of the iceberg. You could also use the `<entitycmp>` subtask to generate a subclass of your bean that provides a concrete implementation of the entity bean interface methods you aren't interested in implementing yourself.

If you've also used the `<valueobject>` subtask to generate a value object for your bean, then the `<entitycmp>` subtask will generate methods to construct your value object for you.

Feeling dizzy yet? Unfortunately, the `<cupofcoffee>` subtask hasn't made it into XDoclet (yet), so we'll take a rest.

The point here isn't to explain all the `<ejbdoclet>` subtasks (and we've barely scratched the surface) or overwhelm you with the possibilities but to show how a task's many subtasks can work together. Once you've overcome the initial effort to get started with an XDoclet task, it pays handsomely to explore the related subtasks—the development costs are considerably cheaper and the rewards significantly higher than approaching a subtask in isolation.

2.3 Invoking tasks from Ant

XDoclet is married to Ant. XDoclet tasks are exposed as Ant build tasks, and there is no other supported way to invoke XDoclet. Ant is the de facto Java build tool, so this isn't much of a limitation. In fact, quite the opposite is true—the close relationship with Ant makes XDoclet a perfect fit in almost any Ant build process.

Figure 2.3 shows the XDoclet task from figure 2.2 in the context of Ant. XDoclet tasks are not merely exposed in Ant, they are actually Ant tasks. For this reason, XDoclet is only accessible from within Ant.

2.3.1 Declaring tasks

XDoclet isn't distributed with Ant, so you have to download and install XDoclet to be able to use it (see appendix A for installation instructions). Each XDoclet task

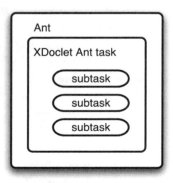

**Figure 2.3
XDoclet tasks are Ant
tasks and are only
accessible from
within Ant.**

you use must be declared using Ant's `<taskdef>` task. If you follow the instructions in appendix A, you should have the following task definition:

```
<taskdef name="ejbdoclet"
        classname="xdoclet.modules.ejb.EjbDocletTask"
        classpathref="xdoclet.lib.path"/>
```

If you aren't familiar with Ant, this code tells Ant to load the `<ejbdoclet>` task definition. You could name the task anything you like, but it's better to stick with the standard naming conventions to avoid confusion. The `classname` and `classpathref` attributes tell Ant where to locate the XDoclet classes that implement this task. If you want to use other XDoclet tasks, you must include `<taskdef>` declarations for those tasks as well.

It's common to wrap all the XDoclet task definitions in a single Ant target than can be added as a dependency to any targets that need to use them. You probably already have an `init` target in your build file, which is the perfect place to add your XDoclet task definitions (and if you don't, you can create one). Here's an `init` target that declares both the `<ejbdoclet>` and `<webdoclet>` tasks in addition to the `<documentdoclet>` task you used earlier:

```
<target name="init">
    <taskdef name="documentdoclet"
            classname="xdoclet.modules.doc.DocumentDocletTask"
            classpathref="xdoclet.lib.path" />
    <taskdef name="ejbdoclet"
            classname="xdoclet.modules.ejb.EjbDocletTask"
            classpathref="xdoclet.lib.path"/>
    <taskdef name="webdoclet"
            classname="xdoclet.modules.web.WebDocletTask"
            classpathref="xdoclet.lib.path"/>
</target>
```

Now that the tasks are defined, XDoclet is ready to go.

2.3.2 *Using tasks*

You can use declared tasks inside any target. Within the context of a task, you can invoke subtasks. Let's jump straight into a target that invokes the `<ejbdoclet>` task. Don't worry about the specifics of the syntax; at this point you should just note the basic concepts:

```
<target name="generateEjb" depends="init">

    <ejbdoclet destdir="${gen.src.dir}">            ⟵┐  <ejbdoclet> task;
                                                      │  everything takes place
        <fileset dir="${src.dir}">                    │  in this context
```

```
            <include name="**/*Bean.java"/>
        </fileset>

        <deploymentdescriptor                          Subtask that overrides destdir
            destdir="${ejb.deployment.dir}"/>          attribute on <ejbdoclet>


        <homeinterface />                   Subtasks that inherit
        <remoteinterface />                 context defined by
        <localinterface />                  <ejbdoclet>
        <localhomeinterface />
    </ejbdoclet>
</target>
```

Think of the task as providing a configuration context in which the subtasks operate (remember that the subtasks do the code generation work). When you invoke a subtask, you inherit the context of the task, but you are free to override those values if it makes sense. You override the `destdir` property in this example because two different types of generation are going on: the `<deploymentdescriptor>` subtask, which is a task that creates a deployment descriptor, and the various interface generation subtasks that generate Java source code. The deployment descriptor needs to be placed in a location convenient for inclusion in your EJB JAR file, but the generated code should be placed where you can invoke the Java compiler. Even though the subtasks are closely related, the nature of the tasks are different enough that you want different defaults.

The `<fileset>` attribute also applies to all the subtasks. Because it's a complex Ant type (a set of files) as opposed to a simple text or numeric value, you have to declare it as a sub-element of the task (don't confuse these configuration elements with subtasks). Of course, if you wanted to give a different input file set to any of your subtasks, you could place another `<fileset>` sub-element inside those subtasks.

Many more configuration options are available. We'll introduce the most useful ones as we cover each task and subtask in later chapters. The appendixes provide a more complete reference to the various configuration options available in each task and subtask.

2.4 *Tagging your code with attributes*

Reusable code generation systems need input to produce interesting output. A parser generator needs a description of the language to parse in order to generate the parser. A business object code generator needs a domain model to know which business objects to generate. XDoclet takes as its input Java source files and generates related classes or deployment/configuration files.

However, the information needed to generate code isn't always available in the original source files. Consider a servlet-based application where you want to generate a web.xml file. The servlet source file only contains the class name and the appropriate servlet interface methods. It doesn't contain any information about how to map the servlet to a URI pattern or what initialization parameters the servlet needs. Of course, this makes sense—if the class told you those details, you would hardly need to place that information in the web.xml file in the first place.

XDoclet doesn't know this information either. Fortunately, the solution is simple. If the information isn't available in the source files, you can put it there in the form of XDoclet attributes. XDoclet parses the source files, extracts the attributes, and passes them along to the templates to provide the critical data needed to generate code.

2.4.1 *The anatomy of an attribute*

XDoclet attributes are nothing more than javadoc extensions. They look and work just like javadoc attributes and can be placed inside javadoc documentation comments. Documentation comments are simple; they begin with /** and end with */. Here's a quick example:

```
/**
 * This is a javadoc comment. Comments can span multiple
 * lines and each line can start with an asterisk ('*'), which
 * will be ignored in parsing.
 */
```

Any text between the comment markers is a javadoc comment and will be visible to XDoclet. Comment blocks are always associated with an entity in the Java source file and are placed immediately before the element they are associated with; comment blocks not immediately preceding a commentable entity are ignored. Classes (and interfaces) can have comment blocks, as can methods and fields:

```
/**
 *   a class comment
 */
public class SomeClass
{
    /** a field comment */
    private int id;
```

```
/**
 * constructors can have comments
 */
public SomeClass() {
    // ...
}

/**
 *  and so can methods
 */
public int getId() {
    return id;
}
}
```

Comment blocks have two sections: the description section and the tag section.
The tag section begins when the first javadoc @tag is seen. Javadoc tags have two
components: the tag name and the tag description. The tag description is
optional and can span multiple lines:

```
/**
 *  This is the description section.
 *  @tag1 the tag section begins here
 *  @tag2
 *  @tag3 the previous tag had no tag description. This
 *  one has a multi-line description
 */
```

XDoclet adds a layer of expressiveness to javadoc tags by adding parameterized
tags. With XDoclet, you can add *name*="*value*" parameters in the description portion of the javadoc tag. This minor change drastically increases the expressiveness
of javadoc tags and makes it much easier to expose rich metadata. The following
is an entity bean method with XDoclet attributes:

```
/**
 * @ejb.interface-method
 * @ejb.relation
 *     name="blog-entries"
 *     role-name="blog-has-entries"
 * @ejb.value-object
 *     compose="com.xdocletbook.blog.value.EntryValue"
 *     compose-name="Entry"
 *     members="com.xdocletbook.blog.interfaces.EntryLocal"
 *     members-name="Entries"
 *     relation="external"
 *     type="java.util.Set"
 */
public abstract Set getEntries();
```

Parameterized tags allow for logical groupings of related attributes. You can express meta-information about the class that is rich enough to generate code from, yet readable enough that a programmer who is familiar with the tags can quickly understand how the class is used. (If it's not clear what is being expressed here, don't worry; you'll see what these specific tags mean when we look at EJBs in chapter 4.)

Note that the tag names here start with `ejb`. XDoclet follows the convention of tag names of the form *namespace.tagname*. This ensures that XDoclet tags are not confused with javadoc tags, and that tags related to one task do not conflict with tags from another task.

NOTE   For a more technical review of javadoc comments, see chapter 18 of the Java Language Specification (http://java.sun.com/docs/books/jls/).

2.5 *Code generation patterns*

XDoclet is a template-based code generation engine. At a high level, output files are generated by evaluating templates in varying contexts. The expressiveness of the templates and the nature of the contexts in which they are evaluated determine exactly what XDoclet can and can't generate. If you are evaluating the XDoclet platform, it's very important to understand these concepts. Otherwise you may miss out on some of the power of XDoclet or, worse, be caught by surprise by its limitations.

XDoclet runs in the context of the Ant build tool. XDoclet provides Ant tasks and subtasks that you use to interact with the XDoclet engine. Tasks act as containers for the subtasks, which are responsible for performing the code generation. Subtasks perform their work by invoking templates. A template provides a cookie-cutter image of the code you will generate. The template can draw on the input source files, including the metadata attributes in those source files, to provide data to drive the template. Additionally, templates may provide merge points that allow the user to plug in template fragments (merge files) to further customize the generated code.

Figure 2.4 shows the flow of information in an XDoclet task. We'll look more closely at each of these components in the following sections.

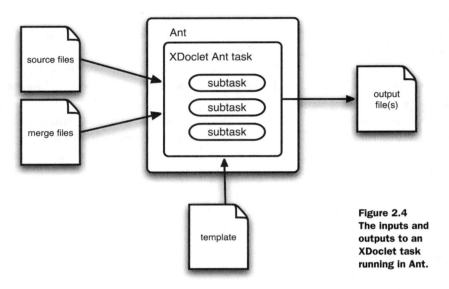

Figure 2.4
The inputs and outputs to an XDoclet task running in Ant.

2.5.1 *Template basics*

XDoclet generates code using code templates. A *template* is a prototypical version of the file you want to generate. The template is marked up using XML tags that instruct the template engine how to adjust the generated code based on the input classes and their metadata.

DEFINITION *Templates* are generic cookie-cutter images of code or descriptors to be generated. When the template is evaluated, the specific details are filled in.

Templates are always applied in some context. A template may be applied in the context of one class (*transform generation*), or it may be applied in a global context (*aggregate generation*). Understanding the difference is critical to understanding the types of tasks to which XDoclet can be applied.

When you use XDoclet to generate deployment descriptors, you are using aggregate generation. A deployment descriptor isn't related to any one class; instead, it aggregates information about multiple classes into one output file. Figure 2.5 shows the how aggregate generation looks. In this model, the template is evaluated once and generates one output file, regardless of how many input files you have.

In transform generation, the template is evaluated once for each source file, with that input class as the context. The template generates one output file for each input file (see figure 2.6).

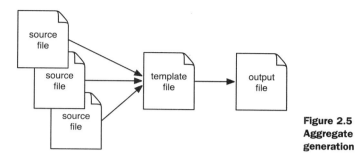

**Figure 2.5
Aggregate
generation**

Generating local and remote interfaces for an EJB is a good example of transform generation. It's obvious that the interface has a one-to-one correspondence with the bean class. You transform the bean into its interface using information about the class (its methods, fields, interfaces, and so on) and its XDoclet attributes. There's no other information you need.

It might seem backward to generate the interface from the implementation. If you were writing the code by hand, you would likely write the interface first and develop your implementation class based on that interface. XDoclet doesn't work well in this model because it can't generate the business logic to fill in the methods declared in the interface. If the business logic could be described using XDoclet attributes or could be derived from naming conventions (JavaBean accessors such as setName and getName, for example), then it would be possible to generate code from the interface. However, in general, it isn't realistic to work in this direction. It's much simpler to provide the implementation and describe how the interface methods relate to it.[2]

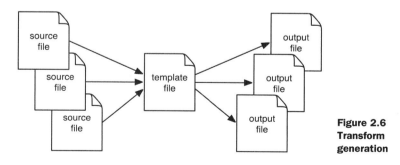

**Figure 2.6
Transform
generation**

---

[2] A notable exception is mock objects, where you generate a mock object implementation class from an interface. We'll look at mock objects in chapter 10.

The key difference between aggregate and transform generation is the context information. Even in a code generation task that involves generating only a single Java file as output, aggregate generation is not normally used because the context can provide vital information such as the package in which you should generate the class and the name of the class. Without context information, these details must be configured separately.

2.5.2 *Template tags*

We've gone into quite a bit of depth about templates without showing you what one looks like. Template files are like JSP files. They contain text and XML tags, which are evaluated to produce text that is copied directly to the output file. Only XML tags that are in a namespace beginning with XDt are XDoclet template tags; other XML tags are not treated with any significance by XDoclet. The following fragment is typical of XDoclet templates:

```
public class
    <XDtClass:classOf><XDtEjbFacade:remoteFacadeClass
      /></XDtClass:classOf>
    extends Observable
{
    static <XDtClass:classOf><XDtEjbFacade:remoteFacadeClass
        /></XDtClass:classOf> _instance = null;
    public static
      <XDtClass:classOf><XDtEjbFacade:remoteFacadeClass
        /></XDtClass:classOf> getInstance() {
      if (_instance == null) {
        _instance = new
              <XDtClass:classOf><XDtEjbFacade:remoteFacadeClass
              /></XDtClass:classOf>();
      }
      return _instance;
    }
}
```

Looking at the template, you can see that it generates a basic class definition with a static field instance and a static method getInstance that controls access to the instance. Thinking about Java syntax, you can easily deduce that the XDoclet template tags are intended to produce the name of the class you are generating, although it probably isn't obvious how the tags work.

Even if you'll never write a template, it's important to understand how templates are evaluated. Sooner or later, you'll invoke an XDoclet task that fails or that doesn't produce the output you expect it to, and the fastest course of action may be to look at the template to figure out what's wrong.

Let's look at the static field declaration:

```
static <XDtClass:classOf><XDtEjbFacade:remoteFacadeClass
             /></XDtClass:classOf> _instance = null;
```

To XDoclet, this template fragment looks much simpler:

```
static <tag /> _instance = null;
```

XDoclet evaluates `tag` and places the output of the tag, if any, back into the document. Some tags perform a computation and place the output back into the stream. These tags are called *content tags*, because they produce content.

The other type of tag is the *body tag*. Body tags have text between their begin and end tags. What makes a body tag particularly interesting is that this text can itself be a template fragment, which the enclosing tag can evaluate. In the case of the `XDtClass:classOf` tag we just looked at, its body is a template that consists of a single tag:

```
<XDtEjbFacade:remoteFacadeClass />
```

The `classOf` tag evaluates this template, which happens to produce a fully qualified class name as its output, and chops off the package name, leaving only the class name. Body tags don't necessarily have to evaluate their bodies—they can choose whether to do so based on external conditions they check (they might check whether you're generating an interface instead of a class, for example). These are *conditional tags*. Other body tags provide iterator type functionality, evaluating their body multiple times. An example might be a tag that evaluates its body once for each method in a class.

XDoclet tags provide high-level code generation functions, but they can be somewhat inflexible and less expressive than you want. Rather than trying to provide a general-purpose template engine, XDoclet instead has focused on creating an extensible template engine. It's easy to write your own tags using the full expressiveness and capabilities of the Java platform. You'll see how to do this in chapter 11.

2.6 *Customizing through merging*

Code generation systems are often rejected because they are perceived as producing rigid, inflexible code. Most code generation systems don't let you edit the generated code; so, if the system isn't flexible enough, your best bet for extensibility is to use inheritance to extend the generated classes or to apply common design patterns like Proxy and Adaptor to achieve the desired behavior. These are all heavy alternatives to generating the code you want. Given the WYGIWYG (what you generate is what you get) nature of code generation and the high cost of working with code that doesn't function the way you want, it's highly desirable for a code generation system to be customizable enough that you can generate the best code possible up front.

XDoclet offers customization through *merge points*—points in a template file where the template designer allows you to insert code at runtime. Sometimes a merge point covers an entire region of the generation template, allowing you to not only add to the template, but also fundamentally change what is generated. Merge points are a cooperative effort between the creator of the code generation task and the user. If the creator of the task doesn't give you adequate merge points, you might not be able to customize the code the way you like. However, the core XDoclet tasks have very well-defined merge points.

DEFINITION   *Merge points* are predefined extension points in templates that allow you to customize the generated code at runtime.

Let's look at a few quick examples from the XDoclet source tree. At the end of the template for generating primary keys for entity beans, the code defines the following merge point:

```
<XDtMerge:merge file="entitypk-custom.xdt"></XDtMerge:merge>
```

If you create a merge file named `entitypk-custom.xdt` in your `merge` directory, then the contents of that template will be included at the merge point. Your customizations have all the power of top-level templates and can perform any computation a template can (including defining custom tags and defining their own merge points).

In this case, the merge point uses the same file for each class context the template is run in. It's also possible for the merge file to use a unique merge file for every class context. This is useful when you want to customize only a small number of classes or when you don't want to write a template and would instead prefer to write the customization for each target. Regardless of the motivation, per-class merge points are easy to recognize: They have the standard XDoclet per-class marker, {0}, in their name. Here is a larger example for generating security role references in `ejb-jar.xml`:

```
<XDtMerge:merge file="ejb-sec-rolerefs-{0}.xml">
 <XDtClass:forAllClassTags tagName="ejb:security-role-ref">
```

```
        <security-role-ref>
            <role-name><XDtClass:classTagValue
                         tagName="ejb:security-roleref"
                         paramName="role-name"/></role-name>
            <role-link><XDtClass:classTagValue
                         tagName="ejb:security-roleref"
                         paramName="role-link"/></role-link>
        </security-role-ref>
    </XDtClass:forAllClassTags>
</XDtMerge:merge>
```

This part of the template is executed inside a tag that iterates over the beans in the project. For each bean, XDoclet looks for a merge file specific to that bean by substituting the symbolic name of the current class context for the {0} in the merge file name. For example, for the BlogFacadeBean you will develop later in this book, XDoclet would try to load the merge file ejb-sec-rolerefs-BlogFacade.xml.

If the merge file is not present, then the template code inside the merge tag is evaluated. This means that merge points not only can provide customizable additions to a generated file, but also can define replacements for portions of a template. Not all XDoclet tasks provide replacement merge points, preferring instead to provide additive merge points only. It is up to the task creator to decide what types of merge points are appropriate for the task they are providing.

The only missing detail is how XDoclet locates your merge files. Each XDoclet task or subtask provides a mergeDir attribute that allows you to specify the directory where you place your merge files.

NOTE Throughout the book, we will identify important merge points. However, for more complete documentation on merge points, see appendix B. If you want to learn how to write XDoclet templates for merge points, see chapter 11.

2.7 *The big picture*

Although they are never explicitly stated, two principles run throughout the design of XDoclet:

- Every piece of information in the system should have a single authoritative source, and every use of the information should derive from that one source.

- Information about a class should be kept with that class.

Information is easier to deal with when it isn't replicated and when the distance between it and related information is minimized. It's hard to argue with this as an abstract concept, but the application to your code might be less clear.

These principles can be seen clearly in Enterprise JavaBeans. In fact, it was the messy world of EJBs that inspired the writing of EjbDoclet (the predecessor of XDoclet). To create a single EJB, multiple classes must be written. Of course, there is the bean itself, but you also need to be concerned with the home interface and the local and/or remote interfaces to the bean. In the case of an entity bean, you may have value objects to pass data to the outside world and data access objects to retrieve data from the database. If your entity bean has a name field, how many times is this piece of information repeated? The bean will have get and set accessor methods on it. These methods will likely be on the local/remote interfaces, or on a value object if that pattern is employed. Adding a new field could require you to touch a half dozen (or more) classes.

Using XDoclet, you can capture the information about the attribute in a single location, the bean implementation class. To expose the accessor methods in the local or remote interface, you can insert metadata in the source, along with all the other information needed to derive those classes. But you can do more than that. You can mark the attribute as persistent and have XDoclet generate the appropriate lines in the deployment descriptor. You can even specify the column name you want to map to in your database, to be placed in the application server–specific deployment descriptor. In other words, you can capture all the information about a class in the class itself and derive the related information from it.

Eliminating redundancy is important, as is keeping related information together. Think about the problem with software documentation. It can be incredibly difficult to keep the documentation in sync with the code. It's tempting to change the code and then decide to update the documentation "tomorrow." But one type of documentation has proven relatively easy to keep in sync: javadoc.

With javadoc, API documentation is kept in the same file as the code. When the documentation is sitting in the same file as the source, it's hard to not take the extra bit of time to update the documentation. This is the principal of *locality*: The closer information is, the easier it is to update. And the easier it is to update, the more likely the developer is to update it.

This principal isn't limited to documentation. Java developers face scattered systems all the time. Classes use resource bundles defined in separate files. Servlets and EJBs have deployment information in far away deployment descriptors. Keeping these information sources up to date is just plain difficult. Although XDoclet won't magically make your entire application stay in sync, it does provide tools to eliminate a lot of the effort that would otherwise be wasted on managing application information across multiple files.

It's important to understand these two ideas because they are the problems that XDoclet solves best. If your development suffers from redundancy and excessively spread-out information, you will find that XDoclet does particularly well at solving your problems.

2.8 Summary

Each XDoclet code generation task is different. The tasks are configured differently, use different tags, and produce different code. However, despite these differences, they all rely on the same core concepts. Once you understand the mechanics of XDoclet code generation, jumping from generating EJB data objects to generating servlet deployment information is relatively straightforward. If you find yourself confused about how some part of XDoclet works, take a step back from the specific task you're working in and look at the core XDoclet concepts involved. Chances are, the problem will be much clearer when you remove the details of the domain you're working in.

Part 2

Using XDoclet with Enterprise Java

In part 1, you got a taste of code generation and how to get started with XDoclet. With this groundwork laid, you are ready to look at some practical applications of XDoclet. In part 2, you'll explore the XDoclet modules that work with J2EE technologies and related frameworks.

Chapter 3, "XDoclet and Enterprise JavaBeans," covers the original XDoclet module. In this chapter, you'll learn how to use XDoclet to generate deployment descriptors, interfaces, and other artifacts associated with EJB development.

Chapter 4, "XDoclet and the web-layer," looks at how XDoclet can help with web-layer J2EE technologies. In this chapter, you'll learn how to generate deployment descriptor files for servlets and JSP tag libraries.

Chapter 5, "XDoclet and web frameworks," moves beyond the core web technologies and looks at the XDoclet modules that work with Jakarta Struts and OpenSymphony's WebWork, two popular web-layer frameworks.

Chapter 6, "XDoclet and application servers," takes a step back and reveals how to use XDoclet to generate vendor-specific deployment descriptors for a variety of application servers.

3
XDoclet and
Enterprise JavaBeans

This chapter covers
- Generating EJB deployment descriptors
- Generating EJB interfaces
- Utility and value objects
- Working with transactions
- Message-driven beans

> *Don't worry, head. The computer will do all the thinking from now on.*
>
> —Homer Simpson

Enterprise JavaBeans (EJBs) are difficult. Anyone who tells you otherwise is trying to sell you something. Although XDoclet can't make your work with EJBs easy, it does make EJB development a little less complicated and error prone.

EJBs are the server-side enterprise components that sit at the heart of many J2EE applications. *Entity beans* are the components that represent enterprise data, typically critical business records stored in a relational database. *Session beans* encapsulate the details of the business logic, the rules and procedures governing the use of the enterprise data in the entity beans. Like session beans, *message-driven beans* often encapsulate complex business logic and provide business services, but they are different from session beans because they are invoked via asynchronous messaging.

Enterprise components have to deal with transaction integrity, security, reliability, and a host of other enterprise concerns. These are hard concepts to start with. EJBs, as part of the J2EE platform, are designed to be able to deal with these enterprise concerns, but the price is complexity. Just think of all the work you must do to write a single EJB. Writing the simplest of EJBs involves at least four files: the implementation class, a home interface, a business method interface, and a deployment descriptor. EJBs that are more complex may include additional interfaces, value objects, utility classes, and container-specific deployment files. Creating these classes and deployment files for each EJB can be tedious, and somehow managing to keep everything in sync can be maddening.

XDoclet was originally created (as EjbDoclet) to address this madness. Because XDoclet's original mission was to assist with development of EJBs, it is no surprise that XDoclet comes with a rich set of code generation tasks for EJBs. In this chapter, we'll explore how applying XDoclet to EJB development can save time, simplify development, and perhaps even salvage your sanity.

3.1 Building the web-log application

To demonstrate XDoclet's EJB code generation capabilities, you'll build the EJB layer of a web-log application. In doing so, you'll hand off as much of the work as possible to XDoclet and see many ways that XDoclet can assume the burden of EJB development.

3.1.1 *The web-log component model*

The web-log application is composed of three entity components: a `blog` object that represents an individual web-log within the system, a `topic` object that is an organizational unit within each web-log, and an `entry` object that represents individual entries with a web-log. You'll implement these objects as container-managed persistence (CMP) 2.0 entity beans.

In addition to these entity objects, you'll write a stateless session bean called `BlogFacade` that serves as a session façade for the entity beans. All operations against blogs, topics, and entries will be conducted through `BlogFacade`.

Figure 3.1 shows how these components are related to each other. You'll code these components to use XDoclet so that it does a lot of the work for you. (For a preview of the bean code, turn to section 3.6.1 later in this chapter.)

Before you begin writing the code for these components, however, you must create a sub-build file (to be called from `build.xml`) including XDoclet instructions that will save you from having to write all the code yourself.

3.1.2 *Creating the EJB code generation build file*

The `<ejbdoclet>` Ant task is the XDoclet task responsible for generating various artifacts associated with EJB development. `<ejbdoclet>` works with XDoclet meta-information tags placed in EJB implementation classes to generate many different types of artifacts associated with the EJBs, including:

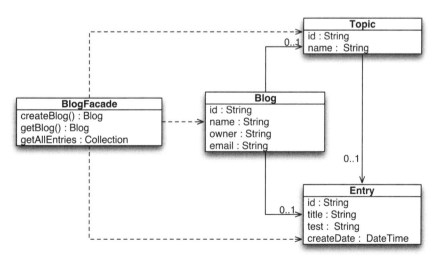

Figure 3.1   The web-log application consists of three entity beans and a session façade.

- `ejb-jar.xml`
- Home and remote interfaces
- Local home and local interfaces
- Utility classes
- Concrete bean implementation classes
- Primary key classes
- Value object classes
- Data Access Object (DAO) interfaces
- Vendor-specific deployment descriptors

Normally, you'd have to write these files and classes by hand. Instead, you'll use the `<ejbdoclet>` task in the Ant build file to generate artifacts associated with your EJBs. `<ejbdoclet>` takes advantage of information already coded in the EJB implementation classes, along with XDoclet tagging, to generate these files and classes automatically.

Within the `<ejbdoclet>` task, you'll place several subtasks that tell XDoclet what types of artifacts you want to be generated for your EJBs. Table 3.1 highlights some of the most common subtasks of `<ejbdoclet>`.

Table 3.1   Most commonly used subtasks of `<ejbdoclet>` and the types of files they generate

Subtask	Description
`<dao>`	Generates DAO interfaces for BMP entity beans
`<deploymentdescriptor>`	Generates the `ejb-jar.xml` deployment descriptor
`<entitybmp>`, `<entitycmp>`, and `<session>`	Generates concrete implementation classes for BMP, CMP, and session beans
`<entitypk>`	Generates primary key classes for entity beans
`<homeinterface>` and `<localhomeinterface>`	Generates home interfaces
`<remoteinterface>` and `<localinterface>`	Generates business method interfaces
`<utilobject>`	Generates utility object classes
`<valueobject>`	Generates value object classes for entity beans
`<easerver>`, `<jboss>`, `<jonas>`, `<jrun>`, `<orion>`, `<pramati>`, `<resin-ejb-xml>`, `<weblogic>`, and `<websphere>`	Generates vendor-specific deployment descriptors and other artifacts

NOTE	See appendix B for a reference to the attributes of the `<ejbdoclet>` task and its subtasks covered in this chapter. Appendix C provides a reference to the XDoclet tags.

Listing 3.1 shows `build-ejbgen.xml`, the sub-build file called from the `generate` target in `build.xml` that uses `<ejbdoclet>` to generate EJB deployment descriptors and other artifacts.

Listing 3.1   build-ejbgen.xml

```xml
<?xml version="1.0" encoding="UTF-8"?>
<project name="Blog" default="generateEjb" basedir=".">
  <path id="xdoclet.lib.path">
    <fileset dir="${lib.dir}" includes="*.jar"/>
    <fileset dir="${xdoclet.lib.dir}" includes="*.jar"/>
  </path>

  <target name="generate-ejb">
    <taskdef name="ejbdoclet"
        classname="xdoclet.modules.ejb.EjbDocletTask"
        classpathref="xdoclet.lib.path"/>

    <ejbdoclet destdir="${gen.src.dir}">
      <packageSubstitution packages="ejb"
          substituteWith="interfaces"/>

      <fileset dir="${src.dir}">
        <include name="**/*Bean.java"/>
      </fileset>

      <deploymentdescriptor
          destdir="${ejb.deployment.dir}"/>              Generate ejb-jar.xml
                                                         deployment descriptor

      <homeinterface/>
      <remoteinterface/>                Generate EJB
      <localinterface/>                 interfaces
      <localhomeinterface/>

      <valueobject>
        <packageSubstitution
            packages="ejb" substituteWith="value"/>       Generate
      </valueobject>                                       value objects
                                                           and utility
      <utilobject includeGUID="true" cacheHomes="true">    classes for
        <packageSubstitution                               beans
            packages="ejb" substituteWith="util"/>
      </utilobject>
```

```
              <entitycmp/>          Generate concrete
              <session/>            implementation classes
            </ejbdoclet>
          </target>
        </project>
```

3.2 Defining the EJBs

The subtasks in table 3.1 tell `<ejbdoclet>` generically what types of EJB artifacts you want XDoclet to generate. But each bean must be tagged with meta-information to tell XDoclet details about how to generate the artifacts.

The most basic information about a bean is communicated to XDoclet through the class-level `@ejb.bean` tag. XDoclet provides reasonable default values for many of the attributes on `@ejb.bean`, but we recommend that you always tag each of your beans with this tag to precisely define how XDoclet generates code for your EJBs.

The following code excerpt from the `BlogFacadeBean` session bean demonstrates how you use `@ejb.bean` to define a stateless session bean:

```
/**
 * @ejb.bean
 *      name="BlogFacade"
 *      type="Stateless"
 *      view-type="remote"
 */
public abstract class BlogFacadeBean implements SessionBean {
...
}
```

It's clear here that the session bean is known as `BlogFacade` and that it is a stateless session bean. The `view-type` attribute is important because it restricts XDoclet from generating local interfaces for the session bean.

The `name` attribute of `@ejb.bean` is optional, but we've specified it in our examples for clarity. If it isn't specified, then the bean's name is derived from the class name by removing a `Bean`, an `EJB`, or an `Ejb` suffix.[1] In this case, had you not specified `name`, the name would have defaulted to `BlogFacade` anyway.

Using `@ejb.bean` with entity beans isn't much different from using it with session beans. This code excerpt from the `BlogBean` entity bean shows that you have to add only a few more attributes for an entity bean (the new attributes are shown in bold):

---

[1] Or any suffix listed in the `ejbClassNameSuffix` attribute of `<ejbdoclet>`.

```
/**
 * @ejb.bean
 *     name="Blog"
 *     type="CMP"

 *     primkey-field="id"
 *     view-type="local"
 */
public abstract class BlogBean implements EntityBean {
 ...
}
```

The `type` attribute is very important here. The container managed persistence (CMP) and bean managed persistence (BMP) models are different, so you need to tell XDoclet which you're using. The choice of models is entirely a local architecture decision; however, we recommend using EJB 2.0 CMP for new projects, as we've done here, by setting `type` to CMP. By default, XDoclet assumes CMP 2.x, but if you want to use CMP 1.1, you can set the `cmp-version` attribute of `@ejb.bean` to 1.x.

Entity beans must be uniquely identified with a primary key—a field containing a value that is different for every entity bean. You use the `primkey-field` attribute to indicate that the `id` field will be the primary key field.

Because `BlogFacade` is the only client of the entity beans and because all the EJBs will be deployed in the same container, you set `view-type` to local so that only local interfaces will be generated. This helps limit network overhead in the communications between the EJBs.

Now that you've defined the EJB-layer of the web-log application and incorporated XDoclet into the build, let's look at the types of code artifacts you'll let XDoclet generate for you.

3.3 *Adding the subtasks for the EJB application*

The web-log application takes advantage of many of `<ejbdoclet>`'s subtasks to generate code for the application:

- The `ejb-jar` deployment descriptor
- Home and remote interfaces (for the `BlogFacade` session bean)
- Local home and local interfaces (for each of the `Blog`, `Topic`, and `Entry` entity beans)
- `Utility` objects (one for each of the EJBs)

- Concrete implementation classes (one for each of the EJBs)
- Value object classes (one for each of the entity beans)

Note that the web-log application doesn't require all of the types of artifacts that can be generated by XDoclet. Some artifacts, such as DAO classes and those associated with message-driven beans, will be discussed later in this chapter.

3.3.1 *Letting XDoclet write deployment descriptors*

Regardless of the type of bean you're writing or how it fits within your application, all EJBs must be configured in a deployment descriptor file. The standard deployment descriptor file as defined in the EJB specification is `ejb-jar.xml`. The structure of `ejb-jar.xml` is complex and building it by hand is an unfulfilling job reserved only for those who enjoy frustration. Unless this describes you, you should consider allowing XDoclet to write `ejb-jar.xml` for you.

The `<deploymentdescriptor>` subtask of `<ejbdoclet>` is responsible for generating `ejb-jar.xml`. To keep the generated `ejb-jar.xml` file in a location convenient for inclusion in the EJB JAR file, you set the `destDir` attribute to the EJB deployment directory (where it will later be picked up by the `<ejbjar>` Ant task):

```
<deploymentdescriptor destDir="${ejb.deployment.dir}"/>
```

3.3.2 *Generating home and local home interfaces*

EJB clients create and locate instances of EJBs using an EJB's home and/or local home interface. You use the `<homeinterface>` and `<localhomeinterface>` subtasks of `<ejbdoclet>` to let XDoclet generate these interfaces for you:

```
<homeinterface/>
<localhomeinterface/>
```

Each EJB's `view-type` governs which one of these interfaces (if not both) is generated for the bean. If the `view-type` is unset or set to both, then both interfaces are generated. If `view-type` is local, then only the local home interface is generated. Conversely, only the standard (remote) home interface is generated if the bean's `view-type` is remote.

Although these subtasks have several attributes to alter their behavior (described in appendix A), usually you don't need to set any attributes for them.

What goes into the home and local home interfaces?

Two types of methods are part of the home and local home interfaces: `create` methods and `finder` methods. (`Finder` methods are discussed later in section 3.5.1.)

Clients of session and entity EJBs use one or more `create` methods in the EJB home and/or local home interfaces to instantiate the EJB. The `create` methods correspond to `ejbCreate` methods in the bean's implementation class that initialize the state of the bean.

When you write the implementation of `ejbCreate` in your bean implementation classes, you can have XDoclet include a corresponding `create` method in the home and/or local home interfaces by tagging the `ejbCreate` method with `@ejb.create-method`.

The following code excerpt from `TopicBean.java` shows how you use `@ejb.create-method` to instruct XDoclet to write `create` methods into the local home interface that is generated:

```
/** @ejb.create-method */
public String ejbCreate(String name, String blogId)
    throws CreateException {
  this.setId(BlogUtil.generateGUID(this));
  this.setName(name);

  return null;
}
```

Now that you've had XDoclet generate home interfaces for your beans, let's have it generate the business method interfaces as well.

3.3.3 *Generating remote and local interfaces*

Once a client has obtained an EJB reference through the home interface, it makes use of the bean by calling business methods declared in the bean's remote and/or local interfaces. You use the `<remoteinterface>` and `<localinterface>` subtasks of `<ejbdoclet>` to tell XDoclet to generate the remote and local interfaces:

```
<remoteinterface/>
<localinterface/>
```

Again, the value of each EJB's `view-type` attribute governs which interface is generated for the bean.

Adding methods to the remote and local interfaces

Methods in an EJB's implementation class are exposed in the remote and/or local interfaces using the method-level `@ejb.interface-method` tag. The following code excerpt from `BlogBean.java` demonstrates how you use `@ejb.interface-method` to tell XDoclet to include a method in the generated local interface for `BlogBean`:

```
/**
 * @ejb.interface-method
```

```
    */
    public abstract String getId();
    public abstract void setId(String id);
```

Notice that you don't use `@ejb.interface-method` on the `setId` method. Not all methods necessarily need to be exposed to the client through the remote and/or local interfaces. In this case, you don't expose `setId` because as the primary key of the entity bean, the `id` field is considered immutable. Exposing `setId` to `Blog-Bean`'s client would break the immutability of `id`.

3.3.4 *Generating utility objects*

One of the most useful classes that XDoclet can generate is a utility object. Utility objects offer convenient methods that simplify the work of looking up a bean's home interface and generating unique ID values for the beans.

The `<utilobject>` subtask of `<ejbdoclet>` does the work of generating a utility object class for each of your EJBs. The following excerpt from `build-ejbgen.xml` shows how you use `<utilobject>` to generate utility objects for your EJBs:

```
<utilobject
    kind="physical"
    cacheHomes="true"
    includeGUID="true">
  <packageSubstitution
      packages="ejb" substituteWith="util"/>
</utilobject>
```

It's a good idea to keep the client-related classes, such as these utility classes, in a separate package from the actual bean classes. Therefore, you apply package substitution to ask XDoclet to place the utility classes for the EJBs in a separate `util` package.

Looking up the home interface

Before you can access any EJB object, regardless of type, you first have to get the bean's home interface. This requires a JNDI lookup using a JNDI name you have to remember and, for remote EJBs, a narrowing operation. That's a lot of work just for an object that is only an interface to the objects you really want. The utility objects can wrap all the ugly lookup code and provide simple lookup methods for your local and remote home interfaces.

All your entity beans were marked with a `view-type` of local, so they will all have `getLocalHome` methods included in their utility objects. The `BlogFacade` session bean will have `getHome` included in its utility object because it has a `view-type` of remote.

According to the `kind` attribute you've specified, the utility objects for all beans should look up the home interfaces using the bean's physical name in JNDI. However, you can control the lookup method on a bean-by-bean basis by using the `@ejb.util` tag and its `generate` attribute at the class level of your beans.

The `generate` attribute of `@ejb.util` can be set to one of three values: logical, physical, or no. Setting `generate` to logical or physical overrides the `kind` attribute of `<utilobject>`. A `generate` value of no instructs XDoclet to not generate a utility object at all.

Looking up a home interface can be a costly operation, especially for remote home interfaces where the lookup involves a network access. The utility objects can cache the home interface after it's initially retrieved to save the overhead of redundant JNDI calls. The `cacheHomes` attribute tells XDoclet to write code into the generated utility object class that caches a home or local home interface after initial lookup and to return the cached copy upon successive calls to `getHome` or `getLocalHome`.

Utility objects are good for more than just looking up home interfaces, though. They're also useful for generating unique values for primary keys.

Globally unique ID generators

The `includeGUID` attribute indicates that XDoclet should include a `generateGUID` method in the generated utility object class. This method takes an `Object` and returns a 32-character `String` that is:

- Unique to the millisecond
- Unique to the server's IP address
- Unique to the home interface instance
- Unique to a `SecureRandom`

In other words, it's very unique!

This method is handy if the primary key field of your entity bean is a `String` and you need to set it to a unique value. In fact, you use the `generateGUID` method in the web-log application to set the `id` field of the entity beans. For example, the `ejbCreate` method in `BlogBean` uses the `generateGUID` method like this:

```
public String ejbCreate(String name, String owner, String email)
    throws CreateException {
  this.setId(BlogUtil.generateGUID(this));
  this.setName(name);
  this.setOwner(owner);
```

```
    this.setEmail(email);

    return null;
}
```

The XDoclet-generated GUIDs aren't compatible with GUIDs generated by other applications, and usage should not be mixed with them. And, although they are unique, they don't offer the uniqueness guarantees that standard GUIDs offer. Nonetheless, if you need a quick way to generate unique identifiers, the XDoclet GUID method can be handy.

3.3.5 *Generating concrete EJB implementation classes*

If generating utility objects for EJBs is the handiest feature of <ejbdoclet>, then generating concrete implementation classes comes in a close second. Session and entity beans all have several life cycle methods that allow you to write code to hook into the various lifecycle events of a bean. These methods include ejbActivate, ejb-Passivate, ejbRemove, and (for entity beans) ejbLoad and ejbStore.

Most applications don't need to hook into their EJBs' life cycle events. The web-log application is no different. Nevertheless, because these methods are declared in interfaces (javax.ejb.SessionBean and javax.ejb.EntityBean), you're *required* to implement them in your EJBs—even if you only write empty implementations.

Fortunately, XDoclet saves you from this nonsense with the <session>, <entitybmp>, and <entitycmp> subtasks of <ejbdoclet>. As their names imply, <session> is used to generate concrete session bean classes, <entitybmp> is used to generate concrete BMP entity bean classes, and <entitycmp> is used to generate concrete CMP entity bean classes.

There are two steps to using these subtasks:

1 *Declare classes abstract.* As you write EJB implementation classes, you'll declare them to be abstract. Because they are abstract, you won't be required to implement the required interface methods. The generated concrete implementation classes will subclass your abstract classes and include default (no-op) implementations of the lifecycle methods.

2 *Include EJB subtasks.* Include one or more of the <session>, <entitybmp>, and <entitycmp> subtasks in your build file. For your purposes, these subtasks do not require any attributes to be set.

The web-log application doesn't include any BMP entity beans, so you only use <session> and <entitycmp> in your build:

```
<session/>
<entitycmp/>
```

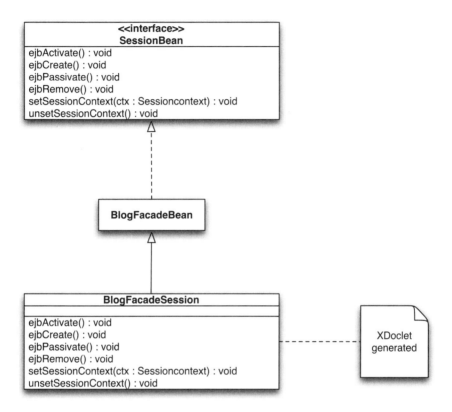

Figure 3.2 `BlogFacadeSession`, **a generated concrete subclass of** `BlogFacadeBean`, **implements** `SessionBean` **life cycle methods.**

These subtasks instruct XDoclet to generate classes that extend the abstract EJB implementation classes, including empty implementations of the methods required by the EJB interfaces.

Figure 3.2 shows how a generated concrete implementation class, `Blog-FacadeSession`, relates to its abstract implementation class, `BlogFacadeBean`.

But what if you *want* to hook into a bean's lifecycle events? Well, go ahead and write the life cycle methods you need in your abstract implementation classes—XDoclet won't override them in the concrete implementation.

Value object assembler methods

Aside from implementing no-op life cycle methods for you, concrete implementations can also contain methods to help with value objects. If you're planning to let XDoclet generate value objects for you (see section 3.3.9), XDoclet will also write value object assembler methods in your entity bean's concrete implementation classes. These assembler methods construct and return instances of value objects, pre-populated with your entity bean's state information.

You don't have to do anything special to have XDoclet write the value object assembler methods. As long as you're already having XDoclet generate value objects and concrete bean implementation classes, the assembler methods are part of the deal.

Even though XDoclet will generate these assembler methods in the concrete EJB class for you, you must explicitly tell XDoclet to expose them through the bean's remote and/or local interfaces using the `@ejb.interface-method` tag. To do so, declare an abstract method with the same signature as the assembler method in the bean's abstract implementation class and tag it with `@ejb.interface-method`. For example, `TopicBean.java` from the web-log example has the following declaration in its abstract implementation class:

```
/**
 * @ejb.interface-method
 */
public abstract TopicValue getTopicValue();
```

Because `TopicBean`'s `view-type` is local, a local interface is generated, and this method will be available only locally.

3.3.6 Including EJB references

As you saw in figure 3.1, the `BlogFacade` session bean is a client of the `Blog`, `Topic`, and `Entry` entity beans. `BlogFacade` looks up the local home interfaces for those entity beans in JNDI with a nickname defined in `ejb-jar.xml` using `<ejb-local-ref>` elements. How can you get XDoclet to include `<ejb-local-ref>` elements in `ejb-jar.xml`?

The class-level `@ejb-ref` tag is the answer. You have tagged the `BlogFacade` class with `@ejb-ref` so that XDoclet will write the appropriate `<ejb-local-ref>` elements into `ejb-jar.xml`:

```
/**
 ...
 *
 * @ejb.ejb-ref
 *     ejb-name="Blog"              Define reference
 *     view-type="local"           to Blog bean
 *     ref-name="ejb/BlogLocal"
 *
```

```
 * @ejb.ejb-ref
 *     ejb-name="Entry"          Define reference
 *     view-type="local"         to Entry bean
 *     ref-name="ejb/EntryLocal"
 *
 * @ejb.ejb-ref
 *     ejb-name="Topic"          Define reference
 *     view-type="local"         to Topic bean
 *     ref-name="ejb/TopicLocal"
 */
public abstract class BlogFacadeBean implements SessionBean {

  /** @ejb.interface-method */
  public BlogValue createBlog(String name, String owner,
      String email) throws ApplicationException {
    try {
      BlogLocalHome home = BlogUtil.getLocalHome();
      BlogLocal blog = home.create(name, owner, email);    createBlog
      return blog.getBlogValue();                          method uses
    } catch (NamingException e) {                           referenced
      throw new ApplicationException(e);                    Blog bean
    } catch (CreateException e) {
      throw new ApplicationException(e);
    }
  }
}
```

The `@ejb-ref` tag works with the `<deploymentdescriptor>` subtask to include `<ejb-ref>` and `<ejb-local-ref>` elements in `ejb-jar.xml`. The `ejb-name` attribute is the name of the EJB being referenced. `ref-name` is the JNDI name of the referenced bean's home or local home interface. The `view-type` attribute indicates whether the bean is remote or local. We recommend against setting `view-type` to remote when using `@ejb.ejb-ref` and deploying to an EJB 2.0-compliant container—it's more efficient to have EJBs reference each other locally when they're running within the same container.

3.3.7 *Including container-managed persistent fields*

Container-managed persistence entity beans, as their name suggests, are entity beans whose persistence is handled by the EJB container. In the EJB 2.0 specification, CMP fields are defined in an entity bean by including abstract getter and setter methods for the field and including a corresponding `<cmp-field>` element in `ejb-jar.xml`.

In your entity beans, you use the method-level `@ejb.persistence` tag on the fields' getter methods to tell XDoclet which fields are to be CMP fields. For example, the following code excerpt shows how the getter method of the `title` field of the `Entry` entity bean is declared:

```
/**
 * @ejb.persistence
 */
public abstract String getTitle();
```

The `@ejb.persistence` tag works with the `<deploymentdescriptor>` subtask to include `<cmp-field>` elements within the `<entity>` element in `ejb-jar.xml`.

3.3.8 *Declaring relationships*

As of the EJB 2.0 specification, CMP entity beans not only can have their field persistence handled by the container, but also can have the container manage their relationships with other entity beans. The web-log application has three relationships that tie all three entity beans together. A `Blog` has zero or more topics and zero or more entries. Furthermore, topics have zero or more entries. All of these are one-to-many relationships.

As an example of how you define relationships using XDoclet, let's look at how you relate entries to blogs. The `BlogBean` class includes the following code:

```
/**
 * @ejb.relation
 *     name="blog-entries"
 *     role-name="blog-has-entries"
 */
public abstract Set getEntries();
```

On the other side of the relationship, in the `EntryBean` class, you have the following:

```
/**
 * @ejb.interface-method
 *
 * @ejb.relation
 *     name="blog-entries"
 *     role-name="entry-belongs-to-blog"
 *     cascade-delete="yes"
 */
public abstract BlogLocal getBlog();
```

Declaring `getEntries` and `getBlog` as abstract is typical of how you declare container-managed relationship fields in EJB 2.0. But the `@ejb.relation` tag does the job of defining the nature of the relationship in `ejb-jar.xml`. The `@ejb.relation` tag works with the `<deploymentdescriptor>` subtask to include `<ejb-relation>` elements in `ejb-jar.xml`.

The `name` and `role-name` attributes map directly to the `<ejb-relation-name>` and `<ejb-relationship-role-name>` elements in `ejb-jar.xml`'s `<ejb-relation>` block. To keep things tidy, you also apply a cascade delete rule to the entry side of the relationship so that if a blog is removed, all of its entries are also removed.

The two previous blocks of code result in the following being written to the generated `ejb-jar.xml` file:

```
<ejb-relation >
  <ejb-relation-name>blog-entries</ejb-relation-name>
  <ejb-relationship-role >
    <ejb-relationship-role-name>
      entry-belongs_to-blog
    </ejb-relationship-role-name>
    <multiplicity>Many</multiplicity>
    <cascade-delete/>
    <relationship-role-source >
      <ejb-name>Entry</ejb-name>
    </relationship-role-source>
    <cmr-field >
      <cmr-field-name>blog</cmr-field-name>
    </cmr-field>
  </ejb-relationship-role>
  <ejb-relationship-role >
    <ejb-relationship-role-name>
      blog-has-entries
    </ejb-relationship-role-name>
    <multiplicity>One</multiplicity>
     <relationship-role-source >
       <ejb-name>Blog</ejb-name>
     </relationship-role-source>
    <cmr-field >
      <cmr-field-name>entries</cmr-field-name>
      <cmr-field-type>java.util.Set</cmr-field-type>
    </cmr-field>
  </ejb-relationship-role>
</ejb-relation>
```

3.3.9 *Generating value objects*

Each call to a method on a remote EJB may go across the network, implying a performance penalty. The performance penalty adds up with every call to the EJB's methods. It can be especially brutal if the bean's client is accessing the bean's state through the getter and setter methods.

Putting this in perspective, consider what would happen if the client of your web-log EJBs were to use references to an `Entry` entity bean when displaying a list of web-log entries. To display the name and text of the entry, the client would have to make calls to getName and getText on each of these references. If the list consists of 50 entries, then 50 calls to getName and 50 calls to getText must be made—100 remote calls over the network. Ouch!

To the rescue comes the *value object* (or *data transfer object*) design pattern. A value object is a POJO (plain old Java object) that mirrors entity beans' properties or a subset thereof. Using a value object, the entire state of an entity bean can be set or retrieved in a single call, instead of requiring multiple calls to the attribute getter and setter methods. For more about value objects and other solutions to other common EJB problems, see *Bitter EJB*.[2]

The <valueobject> subtask of <ejbdoclet> is responsible for generating value object classes. It doesn't require any parameters, but you use a <packageSubstitution> to package the generated value objects appropriately:

```
<valueobject>
  <packageSubstitution packages="ejb" substituteWith="value"/>
</valueobject>
```

To indicate the entity beans for which you want a value object generated, you tag the class level of the beans with @ejb.value-object. In the web-log application, you want value objects for all your entity beans, so BlogBean, TopicBean, and EntryBean are all tagged with @ejb.value-object.

When no attributes of @ejb.value-object are specified, a default value object class is generated that includes all the persistent fields of the entity bean. For example, consider how you apply @ejb.value-object in EntryBean.java:

```
/**
...
 * @ejb.value-object
...
 */
public abstract class EntryBean implements EntityBean {
...
}
```

Used this way, a default EntryValue class is generated that includes all of Entry-Bean's persistent fields. Furthermore, because you're letting XDoclet generate a concrete implementation class for EntryBean, XDoclet also includes a getEntry-Value method in the concrete implementation class. Figure 3.3 shows how the EntryValue class relates to EntryBean and the concrete bean implementation class, EntryCMP.

---

[2] Bruce Tate, Mike Clark, Bob Lee, and Patrick Linskey, *Bitter EJB* (Greenwich, CT: Manning, 2003).

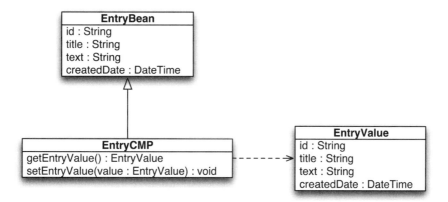

Figure 3.3 The `EntryValue` value object contains all the fields from `EntryBean`.

`EntryBean`, like the other entity beans in the web-log application, is already fairly simple. Therefore, it's fine to include all the persistent fields in the bean's value object class. But there are times when you may want a value object that contains only a subset of the entity bean's fields.

Generating multiple value objects

Suppose you have a use-case where you only want to list the IDs and titles of web-log entries. The `EntryValue` value object created earlier will certainly work, but it's a waste of resources to generate a value object class that carries around the extra information that won't be used—especially considering that an entry's `text` field could contain a lengthy bit of data.

XDoclet can generate more than one value object for each entity bean, each containing a different subset of the entity bean's properties. That's where the `name` and `match` attributes come into play.

There are two steps to generating a subset value object:

1   *Declare the value object.* You tag the class level of the entity bean with `@ejb.value-object`, setting the `name` and `match` attributes. The `name` attribute can be anything—it's used to name the generated value object class. The `match` attribute can also be anything you want—it's merely used to reference the fields you want included in the value object.

2   *Map bean attributes to value objects.* You tag the getter method of each persistent field you want included in the value object with `@ejb.value-object`, setting the `match` parameter to the same value you chose for the class-level `@ejb.value-object` tag.

(Optionally, you can set the class-level `@ejb.value-object`'s match attribute to * and skip step 2 to include all persistent fields in the generated value object class.)

The following code excerpt from `EntityBean.java` shows how you add additional `@ejb.value-object` tags in order to have a simpler value object class generated (containing only `id` and `title` fields):

```
/**
...
 * @ejb.value-object         ◁──   Generate default value object
 *                                  containing all persistent fields
 * @ejb.value-object
 *      name="EntrySimple"         Generate second value
 *      match="simple"             object containing only
...                                matched persistent fields
 */
public abstract class EntryBean implements EntityBean {
...
   /**
    * @ejb.value-object match="simple"
    */
   public abstract String getId();
...
   /**
    * @ejb.value-object match="simple"
    */
   public abstract String getTitle();
...
}
```

Using `@ejb.value-object` as you have in the previous example, a value object class named `EntrySimpleValue.java` is generated. You may have also noticed the two class-level `@ejb.value-object` tags. The first indicates that you still want to generate the default value object class that includes all fields of `EntryBean`.

Value objects and container-managed relationships

What if your entity beans are related using container-managed relationships? Are those relationships mirrored in the generated value object classes? Yes, they can be, if you want.

Any relationship is considered to be either aggregate or composite. An *aggregate* relationship is one in which each end of the relationship can exist without the other end. For example, consider a baseball team and its players—although related, each entity's existence is not dependent on the other. In a *composite* relationship, on the other hand, one or both ends of the relationship are dependent on the other end for their existence. An example might be a purchase order and its line items; the line items have no meaning outside of the context of their purchase order.

The `aggregate/aggregate-name` and `compose/compose-name` attributes of `@ejb.value-object` are used to indicate aggregate and composite relationships, respectively, within generated value objects. You may wonder what difference it makes. Primarily, it's in the way the members of the relationship come into existence. In an aggregate relationship, existing entity beans are looked up before their value object is added to the aggregate collection. With composite relationships, entity beans are created anew before their value object is added to the composite collection.

For example, consider the relationship between topics and entries in the weblog application. The following code excerpt shows how you indicate that you want this relationship reflected in the `TopicBean`'s value object:

```
/**
 * @ejb.interface-method
 *
 * @ejb.relation                              Define relationship
 *     name="topic-entries"                    between topics and
 *     role-name="topic-has-entries"           entries
 *
 * @ejb.value-object
 *     aggregate="com.xdocletbook.blog.value.EntryValue"    Include
 *     aggregate-name="Entry"                               relationship
 *     members="com.xdocletbook.blog.interfaces.EntryLocal" in Topic
 *     members-name="Entries"                               value object
 *     relation="external"
 *     type="java.util.Set"
 */
public abstract Set getEntries();
```

This is a one-to-many relationship, with each topic containing zero or more entries. This relationship is considered an aggregate relationship because topics are not directly responsible for creating entries.

The `members` attribute indicates the bean-level interface that makes up the members of the aggregation (or composition). In the previous example, it's the `EntryLocal` interface. XDoclet uses the `members-name` attribute to name methods generated in the concrete bean class for adding and removing aggregation elements. For instance, given the previous example, XDoclet will write `addEntries` and `removeEntries` methods in `BlogCMP.java`.

3.4 Managing EJB security

Suppose you want to restrict access to some methods of your EJBs. How can you disallow the use of certain methods except to those users who are authorized to use them?

The EJB specification allows for two types of authorization: container-managed and bean-managed. *Container-managed authorization* is declarative, with security roles and permissions defined in `ejb-jar.xml`. *Bean-managed authorization* is programmatic; security roles are still defined in `ejb-jar.xml`, but permission control is left up to you to write within your EJB's methods.

3.4.1 Container-managed authorization

The method-level `@ejb.permission` tag works with the `<deploymentdescriptor>` subtask to include security-role and method-permission constraints in the generated `ejb-jar.xml` file. This tag is applicable for all methods tagged with either `@ejb.create-method` or `@ejb.interface-method`.

You use the `@ejb.permission` tag in the web-log application to limit access to certain administration methods. For example, only the administrator of the web-log application should be able to delete a blog from the system. Therefore, the `deleteBlog` method in `BlogFacade` is tagged as follows:

```
/**
 * @ejb.interface-method
 * @ejb.permission
 *     role-name="Administrator"
 */
public void deleteBlog(String blogId) {
 ...
}
```

This simple tag results in many lines being added to `ejb-jar.xml`. Within the `<assembly-descriptor>` block, a `<security-role>` is defined for `Administrator`. Also, within the `<assembly-descriptor>` block, a `<method-permission>` block is written to only allow administrators to use the `deleteBlog` method.

Container-managed authorization is fine for most situations, but it's inadequate when your authorization scheme requires instance-level security. Let's look at how bean-managed authorization can help in those cases.

3.4.2 Bean-managed authorization

Suppose that, to completely secure the web-log application, you want to restrict creation of entries in a blog to that blog's owner. You could tag `BlogFacade`'s createEntry method with @ejb.permission and specify a role-name of Owner, but doing so would not prevent a web-log owner from posting to a web-log they don't own.

It isn't enough to know that a user owns any web-log; you also must know that they own the web-log they are posting to. In other words, you must take into account some instance-specific information when deciding whether to allow a web-log entry to be created.

Unfortunately, XDoclet can't help you write the code that defines the business rules surrounding instance-level security. It can, however, assist in defining security roles in the deployment descriptor file. The @ejb.security-role-ref tag is used to add <security-role-ref> elements to ejb-jar.xml.

There are two steps to implementing bean-managed authorization for a method:

1 Tag the bean with @ejb.security-role-ref at the class level to define the abstract security role and link it to a real security role.

2 Write your own security-checking mechanism into the method.

For example, consider the following excerpt of createEntry from BlogFacade-Bean.java:

```java
/**
 * @ejb.interface-method
 * @ejb.security-role-ref
 *      role-name="Owner"
 *      role-link="blogowners"
 */
public EntryValue
    createEntry(String title, String text, String blogId,
    String topicId) throws ApplicationException {

  try {
    String userName = ctx.getCallerPrincipal().getName();

    BlogLocalHome blogHome = BlogUtil.getLocalHome();
    BlogLocal blogLocal = blogHome.findByPrimaryKey(blogId);

    if(!ctx.isCallerInRole("Owner") ||
        !userName.equals(blogLocal.getOwner())) {
      throw new SecurityException("Not blog owner");
    }
...
    // Create the blog entry
  } catch (SecurityException e) {
    throw new ApplicationException(e);
  }
}
```

The `role-link` attribute of `@ejb.security-role-ref`, as used here, ties the abstract `role-name` of `Owner` to the real `security-role` of `blogowners`. Because `role-name` is abstract and only relevant within the context of the `BlogFacade` bean, this mechanism allows you to arbitrarily choose a role-name for your bean without having to worry about a collision with another role of the same name in the same container.

The real security check is done by first checking that the caller to this method is an `Owner` and then verifying that the caller's name is equal to the blog owner's name. If either of these checks fails, then the caller must not be the blog's owner, and a security exception is thrown.

3.4.3 *Identity propagation*

When an EJB is the client of another EJB, how is security identity propagated between the two beans? An EJB that invokes a method on another EJB can identify itself in one of two ways: It can assume the identity of its own caller or take on another role.

If you're letting XDoclet generate the deployment descriptor for you, you can also tell XDoclet how you want an EJB to identify itself when calling other EJBs. The class-level `@ejb.security-identity` tag is used to specify an EJB's security identity.

When you want your bean to identify itself as its own caller's identity, set the `use-caller-identity` attribute to true. To have your bean assume another identity, set the `run-as` attribute to the role-name you want the EJB to take on.

It is important to note that `use-caller-identity` and `run-as` are mutually exclusive parameters. You should use one or the other, but not both.

3.5 *Using query methods with entity beans*

Suppose you want to look up instances of an entity bean that match certain criteria. Or, suppose your entity bean needs to query individual fields of other instances of the bean. Query methods and EJB-QL (EJB query language) enable you to query entity beans.

Two types of query methods are available to entity beans. *Find* methods are used to find an entity bean or a collection of entity beans that match a set of criteria. *Select* methods are more versatile; they're able to return individual CMP field values.

3.5.1 *Find methods*

Find methods are made available in an entity bean's home and/or local home interface and are used to look up an entity bean (or collection of entity beans) given some criteria. With CMP entity beans, the container implements the find methods for you based on a definition in `ejb-jar.xml`. Use the class-level `@ejb.finder` tag on your entity beans to have XDoclet generate find methods in the generated `ejb-jar.xml` and include the method in the generated home and/or local home interfaces.

For example, you need a way to retrieve all the entries in a blog for a given date. To accomplish this, you write the `findByBlogWithinDateRange` find method for the `Entry` bean:

```
/**
 ...
 *
 * @ejb.finder
 *     signature="java.util.Collection findByBlogWithinDateRange(
 *         com.xdocletbook.blog.interfaces.BlogLocal blog,
 *         java.util.Date startDate, java.util.Date endDate )"
 *     query="SELECT OBJECT(e) FROM Entry AS e WHERE e.blog = ?1 AND
 *         e.createdDate > ?2 AND e.createdDate < ?3"
 ...
 */
public abstract class EntryBean implements EntityBean {
 ...
}
```

The `signature` attribute specifies the Java signature of the method that is to be created. The `query` attribute defines the EJB-QL query used to look up the entries for `findByBlogWithinDateRange`.

If you're working with BMP entity beans, you must write the `ejbFindByXXX` methods yourself. But you can still have XDoclet include the method in the generated home and/or local home interfaces by using `@ejb.finder` and only specifying the `signature` attribute.

3.5.2 *Select methods*

Select methods are similar to find methods, except that instead of returning an entire entity bean reference, select methods return values from a single CMP field (which may itself be a reference to another entity bean). Select methods are limited to being used internally by the bean, however. In other words, they aren't exposed to the entity bean's clients in the home or local home interface. To define a select method, declare an abstract `ejbSelectXXX` method in your bean implementation class and tag it with the `@ejb.select` tag.

For example, suppose you need a way to obtain a count of the number of entries within a topic. Unfortunately, there's no clean way of pulling this off. It would be nice if EJB-QL had a `count` function like SQL, but it doesn't.

Instead, you can define two methods within `TopicBean`. The first is a select method that selects all the `Entry` IDs for entries contained within a specific topic:

```
/**
 * @ejb.select
 *      query="SELECT e.id FROM Topic AS t IN(t.entries) e
 *          WHERE t.id = ?1"
 */
public abstract Set ejbSelectTopicEntryIds(String topicId);
```

The second method, which is exposed in the bean's local interface, calls the select method and returns the size of the `Set` containing the entry IDs:

```
/** @ejb.interface-method */
public int getEntryCount() {
  Set entrySet = ejbSelectTopicEntryIds(this.getId());
  return entrySet.size();
}
```

By default, any EJB references returned from a select method are local. You can override this behavior by specifying a value for `@ejb.select`'s `result-type-mapping` attribute. The valid values are Local and Remote.

3.6 *How you've benefitted from XDoclet so far*

You've seen a lot of ways that XDoclet can assist with EJB development. We're not done yet—XDoclet still has a few more EJB tricks up its sleeve. But before we move on, let's stop and look at how you've used XDoclet so far in the web-log application, and see how much XDoclet has done for you.

Table 3.2 shows how you've profited from using XDoclet. You've written only four Java classes[3] by hand—XDoclet has generated everything else you need. Because you wrote the EJB layer of the web-log application, you have added <ejb-doclet> and several of its subtasks to the build file (see listing 3.1) to have XDoclet generate EJB artifacts as part of the build process.

---

[3] The complete source code for the examples in this chapter and the rest of the book can be downloaded from the book's web site at http://www.manning.com/walls.

Table 3.2   The web-log application development demonstrates the number of items XDoclet can generate for you. For this application, you wrote only four files, and XDoclet did the rest.

What you wrote	What XDoclet generated

`BlogBean.java`
`TopicBean.java`
`EntryBean.java`
`BlogFacadeBean.java`
	The `ejb-jar.xml` deployment descriptor

	A concrete implementation class for each EJB: ■ `BlogCMP.java` ■ `EntryCMP.java` ■ `TopicCMP.java` ■ `BlogFacadeSession.java`
	Home and remote interfaces for the `BlogFacade` bean: ■ `BlogFacade.java` ■ `BlogFacadeHome.java`
	Local home and local interfaces for each of the entity beans: ■ `BlogLocal.java` ■ `BlogLocalHome.java` ■ `EntryLocal.java` ■ `EntryLocalHome.java` ■ `TopicLocal.java` ■ `TopicLocalHome.java`
	A utility object class for each EJB: ■ `BlogFacadeUtil.java` ■ `BlogUtil.java` ■ `EntryUtil.java` ■ `TopicUtil.java`

So, your contribution to this project has been only 5 files (the 4 Java files and the build file), whereas XDoclet's contribution has been to generate 17 different files. Furthermore, XDoclet has made sure that all the code is in sync. It almost seems unfair to make XDoclet do most of the work (but you'll never hear it complain).

Now let's look at some EJB uses of XDoclet that you weren't able to use in the web-log application.

3.7   *Managing transactions*

Transactions can make an application more robust by providing all-or-nothing operations. Within a transaction, if any operation fails, then the entire transaction fails; all work is rolled back as if it never happened.

The way that transactions are handled with an EJB can either be bean-managed or container-managed. Container-managed transactions are declared in `ejb-jar.xml` and handled automatically by the container. Bean-managed

transactions give you more control, but you're required to implement the transaction code yourself.

3.7.1 *Container-managed transactions*

To illustrate how to use the `@ejb.transaction` tag, consider a `RobinHood` bean that
does all the things the legendary Robin Hood and his merry men might do. The
following excerpt from `RobinHoodBean.java` shows how one of the transactional
methods might be defined:

```
/**
 * @ejb.bean
 *     name="RobinHood"
 *     type="Session"
 *     transaction-type="Container"
 */
public class RobinHoodBean implements javax.ejb.SessionBean {
  ...
  /**
   * @ejb.transaction type="RequiresNew"
   */
  public void performMission() throws PlansFoiledException {
    try {
      float loot = robFromTheRich();
      giveToThePoor(loot);
      dance();
    } catch (Exception e) {
      throw new PlansFoiledException();
    }
  }
  ...
}
```

By default, XDoclet assumes container-managed transactions for your EJBs and
includes a `<transaction-type>` element to that effect in `ejb-jar.xml`. (If you'd
like, you can explicitly specify container-managed transactions by setting the
`transaction-type` attribute of `@ejb-bean` to Container.)

Using container-managed transactions, you can specify transaction rules for
each of your EJB's methods using the `@ejb.transaction` tag. `@ejb.transaction` has
a single attribute, `type`, which can be set to one of the values listed in table 3.3. This
tag is both a class-level tag and a method-level tag. When applied at the class level,
it sets a transaction rule for all methods in the EJB. At the method level, it specifies
the transaction rule for the method to which it's applied.

At the method level, `@ejb.transaction` can be applied to any method that is
also tagged with either `@ejb.interface-method` or `@ejb.create-method`. This

makes sense when you consider that any method that isn't tagged with these methods won't be exposed to the EJB's client.

Table 3.3   Valid values for @ejb.transaction's type attribute

Value	Description
Required	The method should always run within a transaction. If no transaction is already started, the EJB container starts one for this invocation.
RequiresNew	The method should always run within a new transaction. If a transaction is already started, that transaction is suspended and a new transaction is started.
Supports	The method runs within a transaction only if the client had one running already. Otherwise, the invocation will not run within a transaction.
Mandatory	A transaction must already be running when the bean is invoked. If no transaction is running, `javax.ejb.TransactionRequiredException` is thrown.
NotSupported	The bean will not be run within a transaction. If the client is running a transaction, it is suspended for the duration of this method.
Never	The bean cannot be run within a transaction. If the client is running a transaction, an exception is thrown (`javax.ejb.RemoteException` for remote calls or `javax.ejb.EjbException` for local calls).

The `@ejb.transaction` tag, as used in the `RobinHood` bean example, results in the following being written to `ejb-jar.xml`:

```
<container-transaction >
  <method >
    <ejb-name>RobinHood</ejb-name>
    <method-intf>Remote</method-intf>
    <method-name>performMission</method-name>
  </method>
  <trans-attribute>RequiresNew</trans-attribute>
</container-transaction>
```

By setting the transaction type to RequiresNew, the `performMission` method always executes within a new transaction. If any of the steps fails (`robFromTheRich`, `giveToThePoor`, or `dance`), then the entire method is considered to have failed and everything is rolled back as though it never happened.

Container-managed transactions are fine for most cases, but what if you need more control over transactional boundaries? What if you need transaction boundaries to be independent of method boundaries? Let's look at how bean-managed transactions can help in these situations.

3.7.2 *Bean-managed transactions*

Suppose you decide that the dance method should not be considered part of the transaction. Let's say Robin Hood can't dance this time for some reason (perhaps he shot himself in the foot with an arrow). Just because he can't dance, doesn't mean the loot should be taken away from the poor and given back to the rich.

With bean-managed transactions, you're required to use the Java Transaction API (JTA) to control your own transactions within the bean's code. But in doing so, you can exclude the dance method from the transaction:

```
/**
 * @ejb.bean
 *     name="RobinHood"
 *     type="Session"
 *     transaction-type="Bean"
 */
public class RobinHoodBean implements javax.ejb.SessionBean {
 ...
  public void performMission() throws PlansFoiledException {
    javax.transaction.UserTransaction transaction = null;
    try {
      java.util.Properties env = ...
      Context ctx = new InitialContext(env);
      transaction = (javax.transaction.UserTransaction)
        ctx.lookup("java:comp/UserTransaction");

      transaction.begin();    ◁— Begin transaction

      float loot = robFromTheRich();
      giveToThePoor(loot);

      transaction.commit();    ◁— End transaction
                                                          ⎫ Roll back
      dance();                                            ⎪ transaction if
    } catch (Exception e) {                               ⎬ anything goes
      if(transaction != null) transaction.rollback();  ◁—⎭ wrong
      throw new PlansFoiledException();
    }
  }
 ...
}
```

By specifying a transaction type of Bean, you're given more control of transaction boundaries, but you're forced to handle transaction scope for yourself.[4]

---

[4] To learn more about bean-managed transactions in EJBs, read *EJB Cookbook* by Ben Sullins and Mark Whipple (Greenwich, CT: Manning, 2003) or *Mastering Enterprise JavaBeans*, 2nd ed. by Ed Roman, Scott Ambler, and Tyler Jewell (New York: John Wiley, 2002).

3.8 *Working with Data Access Objects*

When you're writing BMP entity beans, it's a bad practice to put the persistence code in the bean itself. Instead, we recommend that BMP entity beans be used with a Data Access Object (DAO). The DAO will be used any time `ejbCreate`, `ejb-Load`, `ejbStore`, or `ejbRemove` is called on the entity bean to perform the persistence work on behalf of the entity bean.

XDoclet can't write the DAO persistence code for you. However, it can include calls in the generated concrete bean implementation class to a DAO that you write.[5]

3.8.1 *Generating DAO interfaces*

To make it possible for the concrete bean implementation class to make calls to your DAO class, your DAO class must implement an interface generated by XDoclet. There are two steps to have XDoclet generate DAO interfaces and the calls to them:

1 Add the `<dao>` subtask of `<ejbdoclet>` to the build file. This subtask does not require any parameters, although you may want to include a `<package-Substitution>` to place the generated interfaces in a more appropriate package. For example:

```
<dao>
  <packageSubstitution packages="ejb" substituteWith="dao"/>
</dao>
```

2 Tag each of your BMP entity beans with the class-level `@ejb.dao` tag. `@ejb.dao` has two mutually exclusive attributes: `impl-class` and `impl-jndi`. The `impl-class` attribute indicates the fully qualified name of a class that implements the generated DAO interface. Similarly, the `impl-jndi` attribute specifies a JDNI name that can be used to look up a class that implements the DAO interface.

The generated DAO interface includes a `load` method, a `store` method, a `remove` method, and one or more `create` methods. These methods are called from the bean's concrete implementation class in the `ejbLoad`, `ejbStore`, `ejbRemove`, and `ejbCreate` methods, respectively.

---

[5] For more information on the Data Access Object pattern or other enterprise design patterns, see *Patterns of Enterprise Application Architecture* by Martin Fowler (Boston: Addison-Wesley, 2003) or *Core J2EE Patterns: Best Practices and Design Strategies*, 2nd ed. by Deepak Alur, John Crupi, and Dan Malks (Upper Saddle River, NJ: Prentice Hall PTR, 2003).

The web-log application didn't use any BMP entity beans. However, for illustration's sake, let's rewrite `TopicBean` to be a BMP entity bean and let XDoclet generate a DAO interface. Here's what the BMP version of `TopicBean.java` might look like:

```
/**
 * @ejb.bean
 *     name="Topic"
 *     type="BMP"          <─── Mark bean as BMP entity bean
 *     primkey-field="id"
 *     view-type="local"
 *
 * @ejb.dao
 *     impl-class="com.xdocletbook.blog.dao.TopicDaoImpl"   <─┐
 */                                                XDoclet can't generate
public abstract class TopicBean                    DAO implementation class
     implements EntityBean
{
  private String id;
  private String name;

  /** @ejb.create-method */
  public String ejbCreate(String name)
      throws CreateException
  {

    this.setId(TopicUtil.generateGUID(this));   <─┐ Use GUID generation
    this.setName(name);                            in the utility object
                                                   XDoclet generates
    return null;
  }

  /**
   * @ejb.interface-method
   * @ejb.persistence
   */
  public String getId() {
    return id;
  }

  public void setId(String id) {
    this.id = id;
  }

  /**
   * @ejb.interface-method
   * @ejb.persistence
   */
  public String getName() {
    return name;
  }
}
```

```
  /**
   * @ejb.interface-method
   */
  public void setName(String name) {
    this.name = name;
  }
}
```

This BMP version of `TopicBean` is only slightly more complex than the CMP version. Thanks to XDoclet, most of the complexity is in the generated concrete implementation class, `TopicBMP`.

The main thing to pay attention to here is the class-level `@ejb.dao` tag. This simple tag does two things. First, it generates a `TopicDAO` interface as described earlier. Second, it writes the `ejbCreate`, `ejbStore`, `ejbLoad`, and `ejbRemove` methods in `TopicBMP` such that they make calls to the `create`, `store`, `load`, and `remove` methods in an implementation of `TopicDAO`.

So, where does the implementation of `TopicDAO` come from? As great as XDoclet is, it doesn't know how you want to handle persistence in your DAO. (Besides, if you want something to automatically figure out persistence for you, then you shouldn't be using BMP—CMP is what you're looking for.) Therefore, you're left to write the DAO implementation.

3.8.2 Adding methods to the DAO interface

What if your BMP entity bean has methods aside from the standard entity bean persistence methods that you want delegated to the DAO? How can they be included in the generated DAO interface?

The method-level `@dao.call` tag enables you to add any method you want to the DAO interface. Suppose, for example, that you have written a finder method for your BMP entity bean and want to delegate the database query to the DAO class. Tag the finder method in the BMP class with `@dao.call`:

```
  /**
   * @dao.call
   */
  public abstract findByName(String name);
```

XDoclet will include the `findByName` method in the generated DAO interface (thereby requiring you to implement it in the DAO class) and implement a concrete implementation of `findByName` in the concrete implementation class that calls the DAO class.

3.9 *Working with message-driven beans*

Up until now, we have focused most of our attention on how XDoclet can help with session and entity beans. Before we end our discussion of XDoclet and EJBs, let's examine how XDoclet can help with the other EJB—message-driven beans.

Message-driven beans (MDBs) are significantly simpler components than either session beans or entity beans. Because JMS is the API for accessing MDBs, they don't have home or local home interfaces for XDoclet to generate. MDBs have only a single business method called `onMessage`; therefore, remote and local interfaces are unnecessary. And, they are stateless in nature, so they need no persistence logic or value objects. In fact, except for their dependence on an EJB container, MDBs only vaguely resemble EJBs.

MDBs do, however, have a small number of deployment descriptor elements in `ejb-jar.xml`. This is where XDoclet steps in. When you write your MDB implementation class, tag it with MDB-specific attributes, and XDoclet will generate the appropriate deployment descriptor definitions in `ejb-jar.xml`.

Using XDoclet with MDBs is remarkably simple. Only one XDoclet tag is used, and it's one you already know—the `@ejb.bean` tag. The `@ejb.bean` tag has four attributes that correspond to MDBs: `message-selector`, `acknowledge-mode`, `destination-type`, and `subscription-durability`.

Also, as with other types of EJBs, you can use the `type` attribute of `@ejb.bean` to tell XDoclet that the bean is a message-driven bean by setting the attribute to MDB. However, with message-driven beans, the `type` attribute is optional—XDoclet can easily figure out that a bean is an MDB, because it implements `javax.ejb.MessageDrivenBean`.

Let's look at how the MDB-specific attributes of `@ejb.bean` help when you're developing message-driven beans.

3.9.1 *Defining message selectors*

Message selectors are a great way to increase overall performance of your MDB. An MDB may not necessarily be interested in acting on every message that is delivered to it. To eliminate the noise, an MDB can use a message selector, declared in the deployment descriptor, that tells the container how to filter out unwanted messages.

A *message selector* is a query that is not too dissimilar from an SQL query. For example, if a JMS client sets a header property called `batchCode` on its messages (perhaps using `message.setStringProperty`), an MDB might filter out all messages except for those matching a given batch code by specifying the following in the deployment descriptor:

```
<message-selector>batchCode='BC123'</message-selector>
```

Using the `message-selector` attribute of the `@ejb.bean` tag, you can specify the message selector in your bean's source code as follows:

```
/**
 * @ejb.bean
 *     name="Logger"
 *     type="MDB"
 *     message-selector="batchCode='BC123'"
 */
public class LogBean implements MessageDrivenBean, MessageListener {
...
}
```

It's important to note that the value of `message-selector` is written directly into the deployment descriptor. Therefore, it may be necessary to wrap the value within an XML CDATA block. For example:

```
message-selector="<![CDATA[itemAge < 500]]>"
```

Using the CDATA block ensures that the `ejb-jar.xml` file will be parsed correctly if the `message-selector` has less-than (<) or greater-than (>) signs.

3.9.2 *Setting an acknowledge mode*

When you're using container-managed transactions in an MDB, messages are automatically put back on the message queue if a transaction is rolled back. Therefore, message acknowledgment is unnecessary.

However, if you choose to program your own transactions (bean-managed transactions), the transaction ends after the message has been delivered. That means the message consumption occurs outside of the transaction. In this case, you need to tell the container to acknowledge the messages for you.

There are two types of acknowledgments: automatic and delayed. *Automatic acknowledgment* tells the container to immediately acknowledge a message upon delivery to the MDB. *Delayed acknowledgment* tells the container to acknowledge the message as soon as it gets a chance—but not necessarily immediately. Because there may be a delay between message delivery and acknowledgment, it's possible that a message may be delivered more than once.

To specify an acknowledgment mode for your bean-managed transaction MDB, use the `acknowledge-mode` attribute of `@ejb.bean`. For example:

```
/**
 * @ejb.bean
 *     name="Logger"
 *     type="MDB"
 *     transaction-type="Bean"
 *     acknowledge-mode="Dups-ok-acknowledge"
 */
public class LogBean implements MessageDrivenBean, MessageListener {
 ...
}
```

The valid values for `acknowledge-mode` are Auto-acknowledge for automatic acknowledgment and Dups-ok-acknowledge for delayed acknowledgment. Notice that you also set the `transaction-type` attribute to Bean to indicate that this MDB will handle its own transactions.

Now let's wrap up our discussion of XDoclet and MDB by looking at the two ways that MDBs can consume messages.

3.9.3 *Specifying destinations*

MDBs consume messages from two messaging domains: publish/subscribe and point-to-point. In the publish/subscribe domain, publishers produce a message to be consumed by many subscribers to a *topic* (not to be confused with a topic in the context of the web-log application). As the name implies, this model is analogous to a magazine publisher and the subscribers to the magazine.

In the point-to-point domain, exactly one listener consumes each message, pulling the message from a *queue*. Think of point-to-point as a bunch of people playing a card game where, with each turn, a player draws a card from the top of the deck.

The destination type is specified in `ejb-jar.xml` with the `<destination-type>` element. The valid values are javax.jms.Topic for publish/subscribe and javax.jms.Queue for point-to-point messaging.

The `destination-type` attribute of `@ejb.bean` tells XDoclet how to set the destination type in `ejb-jar.xml`. For example:

```
/**
 * @ejb.bean
 *     name="CardPlayer"
 *     type="MDB"
 *     destination-type="javax.jms.Queue"
 */
public class CardPlayerBean
    implements MessageDrivenBean, MessageListener {
 ...
}
```

Here the `CardPlayer` bean will pull the next message off of the queue (or the next card from the deck), and no other listeners to the queue will ever see that message.

3.9.4 *Setting subscription durability*

In the publish/subscribe domain, there's also a notion of *subscription durability*. If an MDB topic subscriber is durable, then message delivery is guaranteed—even if the MDB isn't running when the message is first delivered. Think of durable messages the same way you think of email messages. Even if your email client isn't running when the email is sent, you'll still receive the email eventually, once you start your email client.

If it is nondurable, the messages delivered while the MDB isn't running are discarded. Think of nondurable messages as you would a vacuum-cleaner salesperson who rings your doorbell. If you're not there to answer the door when they arrive, they'll eventually go away (which, in my experience, is definitely *not* what happens if you do answer the door).

You specify subscription durability for an MDB through the `subscription-durability` attribute of the `@ejb.bean` tag. For example:

```
/**
 * @ejb.bean
 *      name="Homeowner"
 *      type="MDB"
 *      destination-type="javax.jms.Topic"
 *      subscription-durability="NonDurable"
 */
public class HomeownerBean
     implements MessageDrivenBean, MessageListener {
...
}
```

If you set `subscription-durability` to NonDurable, the `Homeowner` bean will never be bothered with messages that are sent while the `Homeowner` bean is not available (perhaps those messages are from a pesky vacuum-cleaner salesman).

The valid values for `subscription-durability` are Durable and NonDurable. Again, subscription durability is applicable only in the publish/subscribe domain.

3.10 *Summary*

We've covered a lot of ground in this chapter. You've seen how XDoclet can tackle much of the work required in EJB development. By appropriately tagging the source of an EJB's implementation class, you can make XDoclet generate deployment descriptors, home and local home interfaces, remote and local interfaces, utility objects, value objects, and many other EJB artifacts. XDoclet even helps when you're developing message-driven beans.

You also built the EJB layer of a web-log application. In the coming chapters, you'll build the web-layer that is the client of `BlogFacade` and presents the web-log to a web-user.[6]

---

[6] For more information about working with EJBs, see *EJB Cookbook*, which provides a number of recipes that will help you overcome common EJB development problems.

XDoclet and the web-layer

This chapter covers

- Generating `web.xml` deployment descriptors for servlets, filters, and listeners
- Working with web security
- Referencing EJBs
- Generating tag library descriptor (TLD) files

We've heard that a million monkeys at a million keyboards could produce the complete works of Shakespeare; now, thanks to the Internet, we know that is not true.

—Robert Wilensky

More and more applications today expose their functionality to the end-user through the Web. Whether it is an e-commerce Internet site, a vendor-relations extranet application, or a human resources intranet application, web-based applications are now the norm rather than the exception.

Servlets and JSPs are two Java-based technologies geared toward the web user interface. Although much simpler than EJBs, servlets and JSP tag libraries have their respective deployment descriptor files. Servlets are configured within an application server using web.xml to describe the servlets and map them to URL patterns. JSP tag libraries are described in tag library descriptor (TLD) files. Even though these descriptor files are fairly simple, they still duplicate much information from the application source code and declare details separate from the problem domain.

In this chapter, we turn our attention to the web-layer and explore how XDoclet can be used to generate deployment descriptors for servlets and JSP tag libraries. As we do, we'll begin developing the web user interface for the web-log application.

4.1 *Adding web-layer generation to the build file*

The `<webdoclet>` task is the web-layer's answer to `<ejbdoclet>`. Whereas `<ejbdoclet>` generated artifacts associated with the EJB layer, `<webdoclet>` is responsible for generating the deployment descriptor files for servlets and JSP tag libraries.

As you did with `<ejbdoclet>`, you'll use subtasks within `<webdoclet>` to indicate what types of web artifacts you want generated. Table 4.1 highlights the subtasks of `<webdoclet>`.

Table 4.1   Subtasks of `<webdoclet>` and the types of files they generate

Subtask	Description
`<deploymentdescriptor>`	Generates the web.xml deployment descriptor
`<jsptaglib>`	Generates TLD deployment descriptors for JSP tag libraries
`<strutsconfigxml>`	Generates struts-config.xml for Jakarta Struts applications
`<strutsvalidationxml>`	Generates validation.xml for Jakarta Struts applications

continued on next page

Table 4.1 Subtasks of `<webdoclet>` and the types of files they generate *(continued)*

Subtask	Description
`<webworkactiondocs>`	Generates WebWork action documentation
`<webworkconfigproperties>`	Generates the `views.properties` file for WebWork actions
`<jbosswebxml>`, `<jonaswebxml>`, `<jrunwebxml>`, `<resin-web-xml>`, `<weblogicwebxml>`, `<webspherewebxml>`	Generates vendor-specific web deployment descriptors and other artifacts

In this chapter, we're only going to work with the `<deploymentdescriptor>` and `<jsptaglib>` subtasks. We'll look at the Struts and WebWork tasks when we discuss web frameworks in chapter 5, and in chapter 6 we'll explore the application server-specific uses of `<webdoclet>`.

We've chosen to separate the web-layer build tasks from the rest of the application in a subordinate build file. Listing 4.1 shows this sub-build file, build-webgen.xml. The web-layer build file is invoked from the `generate` target in the main application build file. Using separate build files for each component of the system makes the build files smaller and easier to understand, but it also means that you need to take care to properly define the task definitions and XDoclet classpath.

Listing 4.1 build-webgen.xml

```xml
<?xml version="1.0" encoding="UTF-8"?>

<project name="Blog" default="generateWeb" basedir=".">
  <path id="xdoclet.lib.path">
    <fileset dir="${lib.dir}" includes="*.jar"/>
    <fileset dir="${xdoclet.lib.dir}" includes="*.jar"/>
  </path>

  <target name="generate-web">
    <taskdef name="webdoclet"
        classname="xdoclet.modules.web.WebDocletTask"
        classpathref="xdoclet.lib.path"/>

    <!-- Generate servlet and JSP Tag "stuff" -->
    <webdoclet destdir="${gen.src.dir}"
            mergeDir="${merge.dir}">
      <fileset dir="${src.dir}">
        <include name="**/*Servlet.java" />
        <include name="**/*Filter.java" />
```

```
            <include name="**/*Listener.java" />
            <include name="**/*Tag.java" />
        </fileset>

        <deploymentdescriptor
            destdir="${web.deployment.dir}"
            distributable="false" />

        <jsptaglib filename="blogtags.tld"
            shortname="blog"
            destDir="${web.deployment.dir}" />
      </webdoclet>
    </target>
</project>
```

The `<webdoclet>` task contains the `<deploymentdescriptor>` and `<jsptaglib>` sub-tasks, which generate the `web.xml` and taglib TLD files, respectively. Now let's look at the XDoclet tags that drive the results of these subtasks.

4.2 *Working with servlets*

Unlike EJBs, which have dozens of artifacts to be managed, servlets have only one: `web.xml`. The `web.xml` file is a deployment descriptor for a web application. When a web application is deployed, this file instructs the application server how web components (servlets, servlet filters, listeners) are to be configured within the web container. Among the declarations in `web.xml` are servlet and filter initialization parameters, servlet-to-URL mappings, and references to EJBs.

Even though there's only one file to manage in addition to an application's implementation code, it's still one file too many. It's one more file that must be kept in sync with the application code, or the web application won't work (anyone who has ever renamed a servlet and forgotten to change `web.xml` will attest to this).

Every web application starts with the proverbial home page. The home page for the Blog-o-matic application (figure 4.1) is simple, displaying only a welcome message and links for navigating to other parts of the application.

The Blog-o-matic home page is served via `HomePageServlet` (listing 4.2). `Home-PageServlet` is extremely simple—so simple that it doesn't contain any real logic and merely dispatches to a JSP that makes up the home page. Nevertheless, it's a good example of how to use XDoclet's servlet tags to write servlet declarations into `web.xml`.

Figure 4.1   The home page for the Blog-o-matic application

Listing 4.2   HomePageServlet.java

```java
package com.xdocletbook.blog.servlet;

import java.io.IOException;
import javax.servlet.ServletConfig;
import javax.servlet.ServletException;
import javax.servlet.http.HttpServlet;
import javax.servlet.http.HttpServletRequest;
import javax.servlet.http.HttpServletResponse;
import org.apache.log4j.Level;
import org.apache.log4j.Logger;

/**
 * @web.servlet
 *     name="HomePage"
 *
 * @web.servlet-init-param
 *     name="LogLevel"
 *     value="${LOG_LEVEL}"
 *
 * @web.servlet-mapping
 *     url-pattern="/home"
```

Define servlet named HomePage

Set LogLevel initialization parameter to value of ${LOG_LEVEL} Ant property

Map servlet to /home URL pattern

```
    */
public class HomePageServlet extends HttpServlet {
  private static Logger LOGGER =
      Logger.getLogger(HomePageServlet.class);

  public void init() throws ServletException {
    String logLevel = getInitParameter("LogLevel");

    if(logLevel != null && logLevel.length() > 0) {
      LOGGER.setLevel(Level.toLevel(logLevel));
    }
  }

  public void service(HttpServletRequest request,
      HttpServletResponse response)
      throws ServletException, IOException {

    LOGGER.debug("Displaying home page");
    request.getRequestDispatcher(
        "jsp/home.jsp").forward(request, response);
  }
}
```

As you can see, this code takes advantage of some XDoclet @web tags. These tags give <webdoclet> meta-information it needs to register deployment information for HomePageServlet in web.xml. Let's look at how these tags translate to web.xml declarations.

4.2.1 *Configuring servlets in web.xml*

The first and most basic tag used with servlets is @web.servlet. This tag instructs XDoclet to write a <servlet> configuration block in web.xml.

Using @web.servlet is straightforward. The name attribute gives the servlet a reference name to be used in web.xml. For HomePageServlet, you give the servlet HomePage as its reference name. When you're generating the web.xml from XDoclet, the name you use isn't important—you just need to choose a name that is unique within the application:

```
/**
 * @web.servlet
 *      name="HomePage"
 */
public class HomePageServlet extends HttpServlet {
  ...
}
```

This translates to the following `<servlet>` entry being written to `web.xml`:

```
<servlet>
  <servlet-name>HomePage</servlet-name>
  <servlet-class>
      com.xdocletbook.blog.servlet.HomePageServlet
  </servlet-class>
</servlet>
```

As you'll see later, when we discuss security, `@web.servlet` also has a `run-as` attribute that is useful for specifying a security identity for a servlet. But for now, let's look at how XDoclet can help you write servlet initialization parameters.

Defining servlet initialization parameters

Suppose that in the test environment, you want the logging level for `HomePage-Servlet` to always be at debug, but for the production environment, you'll use the default logging level. How can you set the logging to be different for the production build than it is for the test build?

Servlets can have initialization parameters defined in `web.xml` to set initial values or to customize the servlet's behavior in some way. `HomePageServlet` uses an initialization parameter called `LogLevel` to override the default logging level for this servlet:

```
/**
 * @web.servlet-init-param
 *      name="LogLevel"
 *      value="${LOG_LEVEL}
 */
public class HomePageServlet extends HttpServlet {
...
}
```

The `@web.servlet-init-param` tag enables you to define servlet initialization parameters in the servlet code for XDoclet to include when it writes `web.xml`. But wait—how is defining servlet parameters directly in the servlet source code any different than hard-coding the values in the servlet?

If you set the `value` attribute of `@web.servlet-init-param` to some static value, then you're limiting yourself to modifying the value at deployment by editing `web.xml` by hand (or, if you're lucky, with a tool). If your deployment activities are strongly separated from development activities, you may already work this way, delivering an application that needs further deployment-time configuration. However, even in this case, you may want to go beyond the limitations of static parameters.

Fortunately, tag attribute values can reference Ant properties as well as static values. The ability to set attribute values to Ant properties gives this tag purpose—you might have some servlet initialization parameters that vary across environments (test versus production, for example).

To set the logging level at build time, you can either define the LogLevel property in the Ant build script or specify it on the command line when you run Ant:

```
ant -DLogLevel=debug
```

When run with the LogLevel property set to debug, the web.xml entry for Home-PageServlet looks like this:

```
<servlet>
  <servlet-name>HomePage</servlet-name>
  <servlet-class>
      com.xdocletbook.blog.servlet.HomePageServlet
  </servlet-class>

  <init-param>
    <param-name>LogLevel</param-name>
    <param-value>debug</param-value>
  </init-param>
</servlet>
```

Now let's look at how you can map a URL to HomePageServlet.

Mapping servlets to URLs

HomePageServlet is of little use unless you map it to a URL pattern. The @web.servlet-mapping tag is used to map a servlet to one or more URL patterns. You tag HomePageServlet as follows:

```
/**
 * @web.servlet
 *       name="HomePage"
 *
 * @web.servlet-mapping
 *       url-pattern="/home"
 */
public class HomePageServlet extends HttpServlet {
...
}
```

This results in the following being written to web.xml:

```
<servlet-mapping>
  <servlet-name>HomePage</servlet-name>
  <url-pattern>/home</url-pattern>
</servlet-mapping>
```

Given this definition, `HomePageServlet` is accessible via a URL that looks like http://{*server-name*}/blog/home.

4.3 Referencing EJBs

Good design and best practice dictate that servlets should limit their responsibility with regard to business logic and should delegate responsibility for business logic to some other entity. It's common for a servlet to be the client to an EJB that handles the business logic. `ListEntriesServlet` (listing 4.3) is an example of such a servlet.

Listing 4.3   ListEntriesServlet.java

```
package com.xdocletbook.blog.servlet;

import java.io.IOException;
import javax.servlet.ServletException;
import javax.servlet.http.HttpServlet;
import javax.servlet.http.HttpServletRequest;
import javax.servlet.http.HttpServletResponse;
import com.xdocletbook.blog.exception.ApplicationException;
import com.xdocletbook.blog.interfaces.BlogFacade;
import com.xdocletbook.blog.interfaces.BlogFacadeHome;
import com.xdocletbook.blog.util.BlogFacadeUtil;

/**
 * @web.servlet
 *     name="ListEntries"
 *
 * @web.servlet-mapping
 *     url-pattern="/listEntries"
 *
 * @web.ejb-ref
 *     name="ejb/BlogFacade"
 *     type="session"
 *     home="com.xdoclet.blog.interfaces.BlogFacadeHome"
 *     remote="com.xdoclet.blog.interfaces.BlogFacade"
 *     link="BlogFacade"
 */
public class ListEntriesServlet extends HttpServlet {
  public void service(HttpServletRequest request,
      HttpServletResponse response)
      throws ServletException, IOException {

    try {
      String blogId = request.getParameter("blogId");
      String name = request.getParameter("name");
```

Declare reference to BlogFacade session bean

```
    BlogFacadeHome home = BlogFacadeUtil.getHome();
    BlogFacade facade = home.create();

    request.setAttribute("blog", facade.getBlogSimple(blogId));
    request.setAttribute("entries",
        facade.getRecentEntries(blogId, 10));
    request.getRequestDispatcher(
        "jsp/entryList.jsp").forward(request, response);
} catch (Exception e) {
    request.setAttribute("appException",
        new ApplicationException(e));
    request.getRequestDispatcher(
        "jsp/error.jsp").forward(request, response);
    }
  }
}
```

Look up the bean linked to using the generated utility class

As shown in figure 4.2, `ListEntriesServlet` is a client of `BlogFacade`, using the EJB to retrieve a list of recently created entries to be displayed.

So that `ListEntriesServlet` can look up `BlogFacade`'s home interface, you need to define a reference to the `BlogFacade` bean for `ListEntriesServlet`:

```
/**
 * @web.ejb-ref
 *     name="ejb/BlogFacade"
 *     type="session"
 *     home="com.xdoclet.blog.interfaces.BlogFacadeHome"
 *     remote="com.xdoclet.blog.interfaces.BlogFacade"
 *     link="BlogFacade"
 */
public class ListEntriesServlet extends HttpServlet {
...
}
```

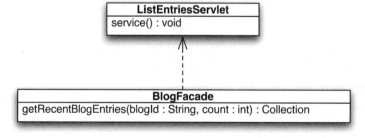

Figure 4.2
`ListEntriesServlet` depends on the `BlogFacade` bean to do its bidding.

As you'll recall from chapter 3, the `@ejb.ejb-ref` tag helped you set up EJB references for `BlogFacade` to the entity beans. The `@web.ejb-ref` tag does for servlets what `@ejb.ejb-ref` does for EJBs. The `@web.ejb-ref` tag in `ListEntriesServlet` instructs XDoclet to write the following EJB reference in `web.xml`:

```
<ejb-ref >
  <ejb-ref-name>ejb/BlogFacade</ejb-ref-name>
  <ejb-ref-type>session</ejb-ref-type>
  <home>com.xdoclet.blog.interfaces.BlogFacadeHome</home>
  <remote>com.xdoclet.blog.interfaces.BlogFacade</remote>
  <ejb-link>BlogFacade</ejb-link>
</ejb-ref>
```

Unlike `@ejb.ejb-ref`, `@web.ejb-ref` has no `view-type` parameter to specify whether the reference should be local or remote. Instead, a separate tag, `@web.ejb-local-ref`, specifies local EJB references. Using `@web.ejb-local-ref` differs from using `@web.ejb-ref` only in that instead of a `remote` attribute, a `local` attribute serves to specify the local interface.

For example, if you wanted to create a local EJB reference to the `BlogFacade` bean, you'd tag `ListEntriesServlet` as follows:

```
/**
 * @web.ejb-local-ref
 *     name="ejb/BlogFacade"
 *     type="session"
 *     home="com.xdoclet.blog.interfaces.BlogFacadeHome"
 *     local="com.xdoclet.blog.interfaces.BlogFacade"
 *     link="BlogFacade"
 */
public class ListEntriesServlet extends HttpServlet {
...
}
```

NOTE   EJB references are defined at the web application level in `web.xml`. This is different than EJB references in `ejb-jar.xml`, where each EJB has its own set of references to other EJBs. Because web EJB references are at the application level, it's not necessary to tag all servlets that are clients for a particular EJB. In fact, tagging more than one servlet to reference the same EJB will produce warning messages during the build. Even so, we recommend that you ignore the warnings and tag all servlets that are clients of the EJB. That way, even if one of the servlets is removed, you can be assured that the references will be written to `web.xml`.

4.4 *Configuring servlet security*

Most non-trivial applications require some form of security. The web-log application, for example, requires that a user be logged in (authentication) and be a blog owner (access control) before creating new topics or entries. In addition, the user must be the owner of the particular blog to which they are attempting to add entries or topics.

The Servlet specification addresses access control directly through `<security-role>` declarations in `web.xml`. Fine-grained access control ("Is this user the blog owner?") is indirectly addressed with a `java.security.Principal` object placed in the servlet request.

The web-log application uses `CreateTopicServlet` (listing 4.4) to add new topics to a blog. But you don't want just anyone adding new entries to a blog—the user must be the owner of the blog in question.

Listing 4.4   CreateTopicServlet.java

```
package com.xdocletbook.blog.servlet;

import java.io.IOException;
import javax.servlet.ServletException;
import javax.servlet.http.HttpServlet;
import javax.servlet.http.HttpServletRequest;
import javax.servlet.http.HttpServletResponse;
import com.xdocletbook.blog.exception.ApplicationException;
import com.xdocletbook.blog.exception.InvalidUserException;
import com.xdocletbook.blog.interfaces.BlogFacade;
import com.xdocletbook.blog.interfaces.BlogFacadeHome;
import com.xdocletbook.blog.util.BlogFacadeUtil;
import com.xdocletbook.blog.value.BlogSimpleValue;

/**
 * @web.servlet
 *     name="CreateTopic"
 *
 * @web.servlet-mapping
 *     url-pattern="/createTopic"
 *
 * @web.ejb-ref
 *     name="ejb/BlogFacade"
 *     type="session"
 *     home="com.xdoclet.blog.interfaces.BlogFacadeHome"
 *     remote="com.xdoclet.blog.interfaces.BlogFacade"
 *     link="BlogFacade"
 *
```

```
 * @web.security-role                          Set up security role named from
 *      role-name="${OwnerRole}"               ${OwnerRole} Ant property
 *
 * @web.security-role-ref                       Declare blogowner
 *      role-name="blogowner"                   nickname for
 *      role-link="${OwnerRole}"                ${OwnerRole} role
 */
public class CreateTopicServlet extends HttpServlet {
  public void service(HttpServletRequest request,
      HttpServletResponse response)
      throws ServletException, IOException {

    String blogId = request.getParameter("blogId");
    String name = request.getParameter("name");

    try {
      BlogFacadeHome home = BlogFacadeUtil.getHome();
      BlogFacade blogFacade = home.create();

      BlogSimpleValue blog = blogFacade.getBlogSimple(blogId);
      String userName = request.getUserPrincipal().getName();
      String blogOwner = blog.getOwner();
      if(request.isUserInRole("blogowner") &&         Verify that user
          userName.equals(blogOwner)) {                is allowed to
        blogFacade.createTopic(name, blogId);          create a topic
      } else {                                         in this blog
        request.setAttribute("userException",
            new InvalidUserException(userName, blogOwner));
        request.getRequestDispatcher(
            "jsp/badUser.jsp").forward(request, response);
      }
    } catch (Exception e) {
      request.setAttribute("appException",
          new ApplicationException(e));
      request.getRequestDispatcher(
          "jsp/error.jsp").forward(request, response);
    }
  }
}
```

CreateTopicServlet is tagged with @web.security-role and @web.security-role-ref tags. Let's look at how XDoclet uses these tags to declare security roles in web.xml.

4.4.1 Declaring security roles

The Servlet specification allows you to declare security roles in a web application by placing a `<security-role>` element within the `<web-app>` element. The `@web.security-role` tag tells XDoclet to write this declaration into the generated `web.xml` file:

```
/**
...
 * @web.security-role
 *      role-name="${OwnerRole}"
...
 */
public class CreateTopicServlet extends HttpServlet {
...
}
```

A *role* is just a logical grouping of authenticated principals (or users). How principals are assigned to a role and how declarative security is administrated through that role are container-specific issues that are not directly addressed by the Servlet specification (and therefore are not directly addressed by any of XDoclet's @web tags).

The `@web.security-role` tag applied to `CreateTopicServlet` defines a role-name based on an Ant property called `OwnerRole`. Because security roles are created and assigned within the container, the actual role name may not be known at development time; even if it is known, it should not be hard-coded into the servlet code. Therefore, just as you did with initialization parameters, you specify the security role name at build time. Another key benefit here is that the same role may be used in multiple servlets. If you were to hard-code the tag reference in each servlet, you would have to update the role name in each servlet if it changed. By referring to an Ant property, you can ensure that the information is defined only once.

NOTE Security roles are defined at the web application level; but `@web.security-role` is a servlet-level tag. As such, you only need to add this tag to one servlet, even if it's intended for use by several servlets. But which servlet do you tag? Even though only one servlet needs to be tagged, we recommend that you tag all applicable servlets with `@web.security-role`. It won't hurt anything to do so, and if you end up eliminating any servlets, you won't lose the security role definition.

If the `OwnerRole` property in `build.xml` were set to WebLogOwner, then the generated `web.xml` file would include the following `<security-role>` declaration:

```
<security-role>
  <role-name>WebLogOwner</role-name>
</security-role>
```

4.4.2 *Programming security in servlets*

If the security role for blog owners is defined at build-time, then how can you know what role to check for in the security logic? Security role references bridge the gap between build-time role declarations and development-time security logic.

Here you create a mapping between the declared role name and `blogowner`, a name to be used within the servlet code. In effect, `blogowner` becomes a nickname for whatever role name is chosen at build-time:

```
/**
...
 * @web.security-role
 *     role-name="${OwnerRole}"
 *
 * @web.security-role-ref
 *     role-name="blogowner"
 *     role-link="${OwnerRole}"
 */
public class CreateTopicServlet extends HttpServlet {
...
}
```

For example, if `${OwnerRole}` is set to WebLogOwner, then `CreateTopicServlet`'s `<servlet>` declaration in `web.xml` is written as follows:

```
<servlet>
  <servlet-name>CreateTopic</servlet-name>
  <servlet-class>
    com.xdocletbook.blog.servlet.CreateTopicServlet
  </servlet-class>

  <security-role-ref>
    <role-name>blogowner</role-name>
    <role-link>WebLogOwner</role-link>
  </security-role-ref>
</servlet>
```

Figure 4.3 shows how the logical `blogowner` role reference you use in the servlet is mapped to the `WebLogOwner` role in the application server. (Keep in mind that, for this to work, it is your responsibility to define the meaning of this role in the application server.)

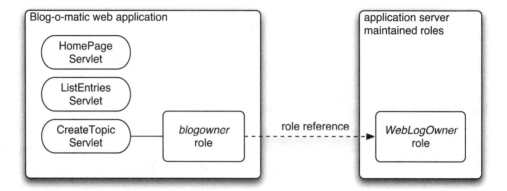

Figure 4.3 Security roles in the web application are logical names that map to a real security role configured in the application server.

Using the `blogowner` nickname, `CreateTopicServlet` can verify that the user is permitted to create a topic by using the following excerpt of code:

```
String userName = request.getUserPrincipal().getName();
String blogOwner = blog.getOwner();
if(request.isUserInRole("blogowner") &&
     userName.equals(blogOwner)) {
...
}
```

The first part of the `if` clause verifies that the user is in the `blogowner` role. The second part verifies that the user is the owner of the blog in question.

4.4.3 *Propagating security roles*

By default, when a servlet invokes methods on an EJB, the servlet is identified as being in the same role as its user. Suppose that you want `CreateTopicServlet` to always run as a `blogowner` user when it invokes methods on `BlogFacade`. To accomplish this, you tag `CreateTopicServlet` as follows:

```
/**
 * @web.servlet
 *       name="CreateTopic"
 *       run-as="blogowner"
 ...
 */
public class CreateTopicServlet extends HttpServlet {
...
}
```

Because you've added the `run-as` attribute to `@web.servlet`, the servlet's declaration in `web.xml` now looks like this:

```
<servlet>
  <servlet-name>CreateTopic</servlet-name>
  <servlet-class>
    com.xdocletbook.blog.servlet.CreateTopicServlet
  </servlet-class>

  <run-as>
    <role-name>blogowner</role-name>
  </run-as>

  <security-role-ref>
    <role-name>blogowner</role-name>
    <role-link>WebLogOwner</role-link>
  </security-role-ref>
</servlet>
```

Now, when `CreateTopic` makes calls to the `BlogFacade` bean, it will always identify itself as being in the `blogowner` role.

4.5 Working with servlet filters

You may have noticed in figure 4.1 that a list of blogs appears in the left-hand navigation. This list of blogs is available on the left side of every page of the web-log application. But, because you didn't write any code into `HomePageServlet` to retrieve a list of blogs, this list must have been hard-coded in the JSP, right?

Actually, the list is dynamically created every time the page is presented. If `HomePageServlet` doesn't retrieve the blog list, and if it's not hard-coded, then where does it come from?

The Servlet 2.3 specification introduced *servlet filters*—components that intercept requests to servlets, applying pre-processing logic (such as logging, user authentication, and so on) before sending the requests on to their intended recipients. Figure 4.4 shows how a filter can intercept a request before it's passed on to the servlet that would normally process it.

`BlogLoadFilter` (see listing 4.5) is a servlet filter that retrieves a list of all blogs (in the form of `blog` value objects) in the web-log application and places the list in request scope to be displayed on the application's left-hand navigation.

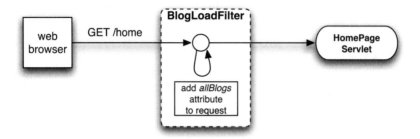

Figure 4.4 `BlogLoadFilter` **intercepts requests before they hit the**
`HomePageServlet` **and adds attributes on the requests.**

Listing 4.5   BlogLoadFilter.java

```java
package com.xdocletbook.blog.filter;

import java.io.IOException;
import javax.servlet.Filter;
import javax.servlet.FilterChain;
import javax.servlet.FilterConfig;
import javax.servlet.ServletException;
import javax.servlet.ServletRequest;
import javax.servlet.ServletResponse;
import com.xdocletbook.blog.interfaces.BlogFacade;
import com.xdocletbook.blog.util.BlogFacadeUtil;

/**
 * @web.filter
 *     name="BlogLoader"
 *
 * @web.filter-init-param
 *     name="LogLevel"
 *     value="${LogLevel}"
 *
 * @web.filter-mapping
 *     url-pattern="/*"
 */
public class BlogLoadFilter implements Filter{
  FilterConfig filterConfig;

  private static Logger LOGGER =
      Logger.getLogger(BlogLoadFilter.class);

  public void init(ServletConfig config)
      throws ServletException {
    String logLevel = config.getInitParameter("LogLevel");
    if(logLevel.equals("debug")) {
      LOGGER.setLevel(Level.DEBUG);
```

Annotations (in right margin):

Declare filter to be named BlogLoader (points to `@web.filter name="BlogLoader"`)

Set LogLevel initialization parameter to value of ${LOG_LEVEL} Ant property (points to `@web.filter-init-param name="LogLevel" value="${LogLevel}"`)

Apply filter to all pages in application (points to `@web.filter-mapping url-pattern="/*"`)

```java
      } else if(logLevel.equals("info")) {
        LOGGER.setLevel(Level.INFO);
      } else if(logLevel.equals("warn")) {
        LOGGER.setLevel(Level.WARN);
      }
    }

  public void init(FilterConfig filterConfig)
      throws ServletException {
    this.filterConfig = filterConfig;
  }

  public void doFilter(ServletRequest request,
      ServletResponse response, FilterChain chain)
      throws IOException, ServletException {

      try {
        LOGGER.debug("Getting reference to BlogFacade.");
        BlogFacade blogFacade = BlogFacadeUtil.getHome().create();

        LOGGER.debug("Putting blogs in request.");
        request.setAttribute("allBlogs", blogFacade.getAllBlogs());
      } catch (Exception e) {
        LOGGER.error(e);
        request.getRequestDispatcher("/jsp/error.jsp").
            forward(request, response);
      }

    chain.doFilter(request, response);
  }

  public void destroy() {
  }
}
```

XDoclet can write filter deployment information in web.xml just as it does for servlets (otherwise, there'd be very little point in bringing up filters in this book!). As you'll see, using XDoclet with filters isn't much different than using it with servlets.

4.5.1 *Configuring filters in web.xml*

The @web.filter tag is used to define a filter in web.xml. Although @web.filter has several attributes, the only one that is required is name. This attribute serves a purpose similar to that of @web.servlet's name attribute.

You use @web.filter with BlogLoadFilter to name the filter BlogLoader:

```
/**
 * @web.filter
 *      name="BlogLoader"
 */
public class BlogLoadFilter implements Filter{
...
}
```

This results in the following `<filter>` declaration being written to `web.xml`:

```
<filter>
  <filter-name>BlogLoader</filter-name>
  <filter-class>
      com.xdocletbook.blog.filter.BlogLoadFilter
  </filter-class>
</filter>
```

Feeling déjà vu yet? As we continue looking at the XDoclet filter tags, you'll probably feel like we've covered this material before. That's because the filter tags work in an almost identical way to the servlet tags.

Setting filter initialization parameters

You want to be able to configure the logging level of `BlogLoadFilter` the same as you did for `ListBlogsServlet`. To accomplish this, you tag `BlogLoadFilter` using the `@web.filter-init-param` tag. This tag is to filters what `@web.servlet-init-param` is to servlets:

```
/**
 * @web.filter
 *      name="BlogLoader"
 *
 * @web.filter-init-param
 *      name="LogLevel"
 *      value="${LogLevel}"
...
 */
public class BlogLoadFilter implements Filter {
...
}
```

Just as with servlets, setting the `LogLevel` variable to debug results in the following entry being written to `web.xml`:

```
<filter>
  <filter-name>BlogLoader</filter-name>
  <filter-class>
      com.xdocletbook.blog.filter.BlogLoadFilter
  </filter-class>
  <init-param>
```

```
      <param-name>LogLevel</param-name>
      <param-value>debug</param-value>
    </init-param>
  </filter>
```

At this point, you have only made the filter available from within the web application. You still need to specify which requests the filter applies to.

Mapping filters

Just as servlets can be mapped to URL patterns, so can filters. In order to intercept all requests to the web-log application, you map `BlogLoadFilter` to `/*`:

```
/**
 * @web.filter
 *     name="BlogLoader"
...
 * @web.filter-mapping
 *     url-pattern="/*"
 */
public class BlogLoadFilter implements Filter {
...
}
```

This results in the following `<filter-mapping>` entry being written to `web.xml`:

```
<filter-mapping>
  <filter-name>BlogLoader</filter-name>
  <url-pattern>/*</url-pattern>
</filter-mapping>
```

But now your encounter with déjà vu comes to an end, because although you can map filters to URLs (as you have done in the previous example), you can just as easily map a filter to a specific servlet.

Suppose, for instance, that you only want to log requests to `ListBlogsServlet`. Here's how you would map the filter to this specific servlet:

```
/**
 * @web.filter
 *     name="BlogLoader"
...
 * @web.filter-mapping
 *     servlet-name="ListBlogsServlet"
 */
public class BlogLoadFilter implements Filter {
...
}
```

A `Filter` class can contain multiple `@web.filter-mapping` attributes. So, if you want your filter to apply to more than one URL pattern or servlet, then you just need to add the extra definitions, and XDoclet will make it happen.

4.6 Applying XDoclet to listeners

In addition to filters, the Servlet 2.3 specification also introduced *listeners*—components that respond to events surrounding the creation and destruction of servlet contexts and sessions, as well as the creation and removal of context or session attributes.

Listing 4.6 shows `BlogContextListener`, a session context listener that listens for context initialization and destroy events. Upon context initialization, a database connection is created and placed into the context. When the context is destroyed, the database connection is closed. Although this particular listener serves little purpose in an application that relies solely on entity beans for persistence, it is nonetheless a practical use of a listener.

Listing 4.6   BlogContextListener.java

```java
package com.xdocletbook.blog.listener;

import java.sql.Connection;
import java.sql.DriverManager;

import javax.servlet.ServletContext;
import javax.servlet.ServletContextEvent;
import javax.servlet.ServletContextListener;

/**
 * @web.listener        <-- Configure listener in web.xml
 */
public class BlogContextListener implements ServletContextListener {
  private static final String DB_URL =
      "jdbc:mysql://127.0.0.1/blog";
  private static final String DB_DRIVER = "org.gjt.mm.mysql.Driver";

  public void contextDestroyed(ServletContextEvent contextEvent) {
    ServletContext context = contextEvent.getServletContext();
    Connection conn =
        (Connection)context.getAttribute("connection");

    try {
      conn.close();
    } catch (Exception e) {
      context.log("Error closing DB connection: " + e);
    }
  }

  public void contextInitialized(ServletContextEvent contextEvent) {
    ServletContext context = contextEvent.getServletContext();

    try {
```

```
        Class.forName(DB_DRIVER);
        Connection conn = DriverManager.getConnection(DB_URL);
        context.setAttribute("connection", conn);
      } catch (Exception e) {
        context.log("Error getting DB connection: " + e);
      }
    }
  }
}
```

As you can see from this example, listeners are remarkably simple to configure using XDoclet. In fact, the @web.listener tag is the only tag that is directly applicable to listeners. Furthermore, this tag doesn't have any attributes to set. Applying @web.listener to BlogContextListener registers the filter in web.xml as follows:

```
<listener>
  <listener-class>
    com.xdocletbook.blog.listener.BlogContextListener
  </listener-class>
</listener>
```

Believe it or not, that's all there is to using XDoclet with listeners. Now let's conclude our discussion of the core web technologies by looking at how XDoclet can be applied to JSP tag libraries.

4.7 *Writing custom JSP tags*

Custom tags, introduced in the JSP 1.2 specification, enable you to embed code in JSPs using HTML-like tags. They're great for reducing the amount of Java scriptlet code written directly in a JSP and for packaging repeatedly used display logic into reusable page components.

DateFormatTag (listing 4.7) defines a custom JSP tag that formats dates displayed in the web-log application. You tag it with some XDoclet tags that provide the <jsptaglib> subtask of <webdoclet> with meta-information to generate a tag library descriptor (TLD) file.

Listing 4.7   DateFormatTag.java

```
package com.xdocletbook.blog.tag;

import java.io.IOException;
import java.text.SimpleDateFormat;
import java.util.Date;
import javax.servlet.jsp.JspException;
import javax.servlet.jsp.tagext.TagSupport;

/**
```

```
 *  @jsp.tag
 *      name="formatdate"
 *      body-content="empty"
 */
public class DateFormatTag extends TagSupport {
  private static final String
      DEFAULT_FORMAT="EEEE, MMMM d yyyy; h:mm:ss aa-z";

  private String format = DEFAULT_FORMAT;
  private Date date;

  public int doEndTag() throws JspException {
    try {
      if(date != null) {
        SimpleDateFormat formatter = new SimpleDateFormat(format);
        pageContext.getOut().write(formatter.format(date));
      }
    } catch (IOException e) {
    }

    return EVAL_PAGE;
  }

  public Date getDate() {
    return date;
  }

  /**
   * @jsp.attribute
   *      required="true"
   *      rtexprvalue="true"
   *      type="java.util.Date"
   */
  public void setDate(Date date) {
    this.date = date;
  }

  public String getFormat() {
    return format;
  }

  /**
   * @jsp.attribute
   *      required="false"
   *      rtexprvalue="false"
   *      type="java.lang.String"
   */
  public void setFormat(String format) {
    this.format = format;
  }
}
```

❶ Declare dateformat tag as empty tag (no content)

❷ Date attribute is required and takes java.util.Date values

❸ Format attribute is optional

❶ At the class level, the `name` attribute of `@jsp.tag` tells XDoclet that this tag is to be named `formatdate`. The `body-content` attribute indicates that this is an empty tag (that is, it will contain no content). Defined this way, the `formatdate` tag can be used in a JSP as follows:

```
<blog:formatdate date="..." format="..."/>
```

The method-level `@jsp.attribute` tag used on each of the setter methods[1] defines the attributes of the JSP tag. In this case, the `formatdate` tag has two attributes: **❷** a required `date` attribute of type `java.util.Date` and **❸** a nonrequired `format` attribute of type `java.lang.String`.

By setting the `rtexprdate` attribute to true for the `date` field, you indicate that this attribute can be set to a value that is evaluated at runtime. For example, the following excerpt shows how `listEntries.jsp` uses the `formatdate` tag when it displays the creation date of blog entries:

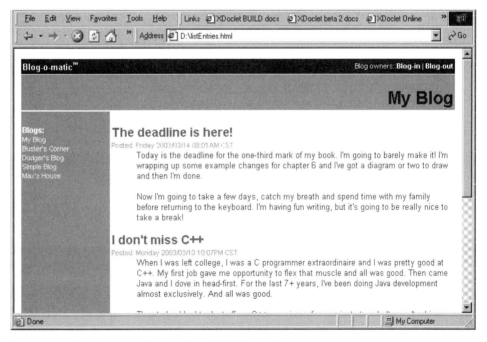

Figure 4.5 A blog's entries displayed by ListEntriesServlet

---

[1] The `@jsp.attribute` tag could be placed on either the setter or the getter method of an attribute. But it makes more sense to place it on the setter method because that is the one accessor method required for a JSP tag.

```
<span class="contentDetails">
Posted: <blog:formatdate
   date="<%= entryValue.getCreatedDate() %>"/>
</span>
```

Looking closely at the dates displayed in figure 4.5, you can see the results of the dateformat tag.

XDoclet doesn't make tag libraries simple, but it does help you eliminate the hassle of writing and maintaining tag library deployment descriptors. Thus you can focus on the real work: writing the tags.

4.8 *Summary*

Although servlets and JSP tag libraries are not nearly as complex as EJBs, keeping implementation and deployment files synchronized can be challenging. XDoclet steps up to the challenge by taking responsibility for writing deployment descriptor files based on implementation specifics.

A small portion of the web-layer of the web-log application has now been built. In chapter 5, we'll continue building the web-layer. But instead of using servlets directly, we'll use Jakarta Struts and OpenSymphony's WebWork, two servlet-based web frameworks. In doing so, we'll look at how XDoclet can be applied to those frameworks.

5

XDoclet and
web frameworks

If you have built castles in the air, your work need not be lost; that is where they should be. Now put the foundations under them.

—Henry David Thoreau (1817–1862)

In chapter 4, we looked at ways to apply XDoclet to generate deployment descriptor files for the standard web-layer technologies such as servlets, filters, and JSP tag libraries. These technologies are at the center of any Java-based web application, but they are really just the building blocks we use to construct web applications. Although it's possible to construct rich web applications using only these core technologies, most large-scale web applications are constructed at a higher level using a web framework.

The accepted best practice in web application development is the Model-View-Controller (MVC) architecture. Two very popular web frameworks are Struts from the Apache Jakarta project and WebWork from the OpenSymphony project. Both of these frameworks provide the controller logic, routing requests to the appropriate business logic and invoking the right presentation layer components to present the right page in the user's web browser.

In this chapter, we'll explore how XDoclet can be used to generate configuration files and other associated artifacts used by these frameworks. In doing so, we'll develop much of the web-layer of the web-log application.

5.1 Merging framework servlets into web.xml

Both Struts and WebWork work by registering a dispatcher servlet that is responsible for intercepting client HTTP requests and invoking the correct action in the framework. Before you can get very far with either framework, you need to register the framework's dispatcher servlet (`ActionServlet` for Struts or `Servlet-Dispatcher` for WebWork) in the `web.xml` file.

In chapter 4, you saw how to use XDoclet to generate `web.xml`, including registering servlets in `web.xml`. But there's a problem here: XDoclet requires source code with the appropriate XDoclet tags inserted. If you're using an external framework, you probably don't have the source code in the build tree, nor would you want to have to put it there.

There are several solutions. One popular solution is to create a servlet that extends the framework servlet and provides the needed XDoclet attributes. This simple solution works with both Struts and WebWork. However, it's somewhat unsatisfying to have to create a new class just for the purpose of embedding XDoclet attributes in it. If you aren't providing any new functionality in the extended class, a better approach is to take advantage of merge points for web.xml.

A *merge point* is a plugin point where XDoclet lets you insert your own code during code generation. You place the code to be merged into web.xml in specially named merge files in the merge directory, and XDoclet inserts the code at the right point. There are many web.xml merge points (see the reference in appendix B for a complete list), but for now, we'll only look at those that are necessary for including Struts and WebWork dispatcher servlets in the web.xml file.

We're interested in two merge points:

- servlets.xml—Contains external servlet definitions
- servlet-mappings.xml—Contains external servlet-mapping definitions

Figure 5.1 shows how the merge files are inserted into the generated web.xml file.

XDoclet doesn't impose any restrictions about the content of these merge files. You can place any content that would be valid (according to the web.xml DTD). However, it's better to stick to the intended usage of the merge files.

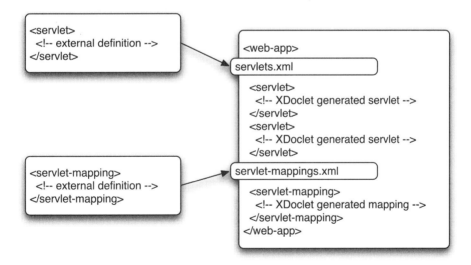

Figure 5.1 External definitions can be merged into the generated web.xml.

5.1.1 *Merging ActionServlet for Struts*

For Struts, you need to register the `ActionServlet`. To do that, place the code shown in listing 5.1 in your `servlets.xml` file.

Listing 5.1   servlets.xml merge file to include the Stuts ActionServlet definition

```
<servlet>
  <servlet-name>StrutsActionServlet</servlet-name>
  <servlet-class>
      org.apache.struts.action.ActionServlet
  </servlet-class>
</servlet>
```

As you can see, this merge file is simple, containing only the `<servlet>` definition for `ActionServlet` and setting the `application` parameter (to define the base name of the Struts properties file). If you have other external servlet definitions, they should be placed in this merge file.

In addition to the servlet definition, you also need a servlet mapping to map a URL pattern to `ActionServlet`. You map the `ActionServlet` to a URL pattern of `*.do` using the `servlet-mappings.xml` merge file, as shown in listing 5.2.

Listing 5.2   servlet-mappings.xml merge file maps a URL to ActionServlet

```
<servlet-mapping>
  <servlet-name>
      StrutsActionServlet
  </servlet-name>
  <url-pattern>*.do</url-pattern>
</servlet-mapping>
```

Clearly, writing these merge files is simply a matter of writing what you would have written in `web.xml` for `ActionServlet` yourself if XDoclet weren't writing `web.xml` for you.

5.1.2 *Merging ServletDispatcher for WebWork*

Merging WebWork's `ServletDispatcher` into `web.xml` is almost the same as merging in `ActionServlet`: create a `servlets.xml` merge with WebWork's dispatcher servlet, appropriately named `ServletDispatcher`, and map a URL to the `ServletDispatcher`.

Listing 5.3 shows a new `servlets.xml` merge file that includes the WebWork `ServletDispatcher` servlet.

Listing 5.3   servlets.xml merge file to include WebWork's ServletDispatcher

```
<servlet>
  <servlet-name>
    WebWorkServletDispatcher
  </servlet-name>
  <servlet-class>
    webwork.dispatcher.ServletDispatcher
  </servlet-class>
</servlet>
```

You also need to map a URL to the `ServletDispatcher`. For WebWork actions, you map `*.action`. Listing 5.4 shows the updated `servlet-mappings.xml` merge file that includes the new servlet mappings for `ServletDispatcher`.

Listing 5.4   servlet-mappings.xml merge file maps a URL to ServletDispatcher

```
<servlet-mapping>
  <servlet-name>
    WebWorkServletDispatcher
  </servlet-name>
  <url-pattern>*.action</url-pattern>
</servlet-mapping>
```

That's all there is to it. From now on, when XDoclet generates the `web.xml` file, it will merge the content of these files in with the generated entries. Now that you can be assured that the dispatcher servlets will be registered in `web.xml`, let's look at how you can use XDoclet when you're developing a Struts-based application.

5.2 Using XDoclet with Jakarta Struts

The Struts framework from Apache's Jakarta project is an implementation of the Model-View-Controller (MVC) architectural design pattern. More accurately, Struts is an implementation of the view and controller portions of MVC, leaving implementation of the model as an exercise for the developer.

The controller implementation in Struts is `ActionServlet`. Figure 5.2 illustrates the sequence of events that takes place when Struts handles a request:

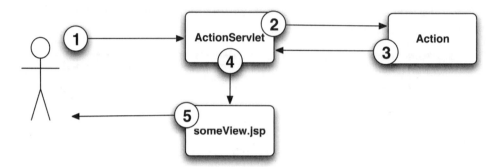

Figure 5.2   How requests are handled in a Struts application

① `ActionServlet` receives requests from the client.

② `ActionServlet` dispatches the request to an appropriate `Action`.

③ The `Action` performs the business logic that is being requested and returns the results to `ActionServlet`.

④ `ActionServlet` dispatches control to a view component (typically a JSP) to display the results of the `Action`.

⑤ View details are returned to the client (typically as HTML).

When the client request contains form data, this information is passed from `ActionServlet` to the `Action` in an `ActionForm` object. The `ActionForm` takes on the burden of mapping the client request data into something the `Action` can understand before the `Action` sees it. If the request data is found to be invalid, then `ActionServlet` can route the request away from the `Action`, perhaps to a page that explains the problem and asks the user to make a new request.

You'll use XDoclet to generate several Struts-related pieces for your applications. The first is the `struts-config.xml` file. This file tells Struts what `Actions` are available in the system and which URLs map to which `Actions`. It also tells Struts which view to send to the user after the `Action` has completed. In addition, you'll have XDoclet generate `ActionForm` classes and the `validation.xml` file.

5.2.1   Enabling Struts generation in the build files

The primary artifacts generated by XDoclet for Struts are two `.xml` files:

- The `struts-config.xml` file defines much of the structure of a Struts application, including `Actions`, `Action` form beans, and `Action`-to-view mappings.

- The `validation.xml` file defines rules that govern the validation of form beans.

Table 5.1 shows the subtasks associated with generating Struts artifacts and describes the type of artifacts they generate.

Table 5.1   Struts-related subtasks

Subtask	Description
`<strutsconfigxml>`	Generates the `struts-config.xml` file with `Action`, `Action-Form`, and action exception handler declarations (a subtask of `<webdoclet>`)
`<strutsvalidationxml>`	Generates the Struts Validator configuration file, `valida-tion.xml` (a subtask of `<webdoclet>`)
`<strutsform>`	Generates `ActionForm` implementations from entity EJBs and plain Java objects (a subtask of `<ejbdoclet>`)

You need to update two build files to enable Struts generation: the web build file (`build-webgen.xml`) and the EJB build file (`build-ejbgen.xml`).

Updating the build file

Update `build-webgen.xml` (listing 5.5) to include `<strutsconfigxml>` and `<strutsvalidationxml>` so that XDoclet will generate `struts-config.xml` and `val-idation.xml` for you.

Listing 5.5   New build-webgen.xml, including Struts configuration file generation

```
<?xml version="1.0" encoding="UTF-8"?>

<project name="Blog" default="generateWeb" basedir=".">
  <path id="xdoclet.lib.path">
    <fileset dir="${lib.dir}" includes="*.jar"/>
    <fileset dir="${xdoclet.lib.dir}" includes="*.jar"/>
  </path>

  <target name="generate-web">
    <taskdef name="webdoclet"
        classname="xdoclet.modules.web.WebDocletTask"
        classpathref="xdoclet.lib.path"/>

    <!-- Generate servlet and JSP Tag "stuff" -->
    <webdoclet destdir="${web.deployment.dir}"
        mergeDir="${merge.dir}">
      <fileset dir="${src.dir}">
        <include name="**/*Servlet.java" />
        <include name="**/*Filter.java" />
        <include name="**/*Listener.java" />
        <include name="**/*Tag.java" />
```

```
        <include name="**/*Action.java" />
        <include name="**/*Form.java" />
      </fileset>

      <fileset dir="${gen.src.dir}">
        <include name="**/*Form.java" />
      </fileset>

      <deploymentdescriptor

          distributable="false" />

      <jsptaglib filename="blogtags.tld"
          shortname="dateformat"/>

      <strutsconfigxml
          version="1.1" />

      <strutsvalidationxml />
    </webdoclet>
  </target>
</project>
```

Consider Action and Form classes when applying <webdoclet>

Also include Form classes in generated code directory

Generate Struts I.I-compatable struts-config.xml

Generate validation.xml to configure Struts validator

As you can see, you use the destDir attribute on both subtasks to indicate that struts-config.xml and validation.xml should be generated in the web deployment file directory.

Adding a subtask to the EJB build file

The other type of Struts artifact that can be generated is an ActionForm class. As you'll see later (in section 5.2.3), you can either write your own ActionForm classes or have XDoclet generate an ActionForm based on an EntityBean definition. To take advantage of ActionForm class generation, you use the <strutsform> subtask of <ejbdoclet>. Because this is a subtask of <ejbdoclet>, you need to add it to build-ejbgen.xml. Listing 5.6 shows the new build-ejbgen.xml that includes this subtask.

Listing 5.6 New build-ejbgen.xml, including the <strutsform> subtask

```
<?xml version="1.0" encoding="UTF-8"?>
<project name="Blog" default="generateEjb" basedir=".">
  <path id="xdoclet.lib.path">
    <fileset dir="${lib.dir}" includes="*.jar"/>
    <fileset dir="${xdoclet.lib.dir}" includes="*.jar"/>
  </path>

  <target name="generate-ejb">
    <taskdef name="ejbdoclet"
```

```
            classname="xdoclet.modules.ejb.EjbDocletTask"
            classpathref="xdoclet.lib.path"/>

    <ejbdoclet destdir="${gen.src.dir}">
      <packageSubstitution packages="ejb"
          substituteWith="interfaces"/>

      <fileset dir="${src.dir}">
        <include name="**/*Bean.java"/>
      </fileset>

      <deploymentdescriptor
          destdir="${ejb.deployment.dir}"/>

      <homeinterface/>
      <remoteinterface/>
      <localinterface/>
      <localhomeinterface/>

      <valueobject>
        <packageSubstitution
            packages="ejb" substituteWith="value"/>
      </valueobject>

      <utilobject includeGUID="true" cacheHomes="true">
        <packageSubstitution
            packages="ejb" substituteWith="util"/>
      </utilobject>

      <entitycmp/>
<session/>

      <strutsform>                                        Generate Struts
        <packageSubstitution                              ActionForm
            packages="ejb" substituteWith="form"/>         classes from
      </strutsform>                                        entity beans
    </ejbdoclet>
  </target>
</project>
```

Here you apply a package substitution so that generated `ActionForm` classes are placed in the `com.xdocletbook.blog.form` package (the original source package name with `form` substituted for `ejb`).

5.2.2 *Implementing an Action*

Web frameworks provide a lot of value in managing dynamic web interactions. In Struts, the unit of interaction is the `Action`. You'll implement an `Action` for creating a blog called, aptly enough, `CreateBlogAction`. Earlier you saw how `Actions`

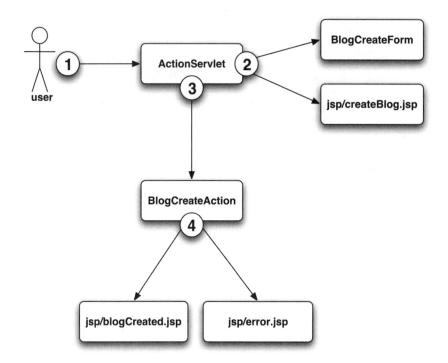

Figure 5.3 The workflow behind the `CreateBlogAction`

are invoked by the Struts `ActionServlet` at a high level. Figure 5.3 shows a more detailed view of `CreateBlogAction` and the control flow around it:

① The user makes a request to `/createBlog.do` by clicking a link in another web page. The request is routed to `ActionServlet` for handling. Remember that when you registered `ActonServlet` in the `web.xml` file, you told the web container to pass any `.do` requests to `ActionServlet`.

② `ActionServlet` creates a `BlogCreateForm` and populates any data from the input request. If the data is incomplete (as it will be the first time the user enters the page) or otherwise invalid, `ActionServlet` takes the user to your input page, which is `jsp/createBlog.jsp`.

③ If the `BlogCreateForm` is valid, `ActionServlet` passes the request (and the validated data) to `CreateBlogAction` for processing.

④ If `CreateBlogAction` is able to successfully create the blog as requested by the user, control is passed to the success page, `jsp/blogCreated.jsp`. If an application error occurs, control is passed to `jsp/error.jsp`.

With that in mind, let's get started by creating the `Action`.

5.2.3 Declaring the Struts Action

The web-log application uses `CreateBlogAction` (listing 5.7) to create new blogs within the web-log application. It's a client of the `BlogFacade` bean, and it uses `BlogFacade` to perform the actual act of creating a blog.

Listing 5.7   CreateBlogAction.java

```
package com.xdocletbook.blog.struts.action;

import javax.servlet.http.HttpServletRequest;
import javax.servlet.http.HttpServletResponse;
import org.apache.struts.action.Action;
import org.apache.struts.action.ActionForm;
import org.apache.struts.action.ActionForward;
import org.apache.struts.action.ActionMapping;
import com.xdocletbook.blog.exception.ApplicationException;
import com.xdocletbook.blog.form.BlogCreateForm;
import com.xdocletbook.blog.interfaces.BlogFacade;
import com.xdocletbook.blog.interfaces.BlogFacadeHome;
import com.xdocletbook.blog.util.BlogFacadeUtil;

/**
 * @struts.action
 *     name="blog.Create"                          Define
 *     path="/createBlog"                          Action
 *     input="jsp/createBlog.jsp"
 *
 * @struts.action-forward                          Upon success, go to
 *     name="success"                              jsp/blogCreated.jsp
 *     path="jsp/blogCreated.jsp"
 *
 * @struts.action-exception
 *     type="com.xdocletbook.blog.exception.ApplicationException"
 *     key="app.exception"                         Define what to do when
 *     path="jsp/error.jsp"                        ApplicationException
 */                                                is thrown
public class CreateBlogAction extends Action {
  public ActionForward execute(ActionMapping mapping,
      ActionForm form, HttpServletRequest request,
      HttpServletResponse response) throws Exception {

    BlogCreateForm blogForm = (BlogCreateForm)form;

    try {
      BlogFacadeHome home = BlogFacadeUtil.getHome();
      BlogFacade blogFacade = home.create();

      blogFacade.createBlog(
          blogForm.getName(), blogForm.getOwner(),
```

```
            blogForm.getEmail());
    } catch (Exception e) {
      throw new ApplicationException(e);
    }

    return mapping.findForward("success");
  }
}
```

The `@struts.action` tag used at the class level of `CreateBlogAction` defines the basic information about this action. This tag declares:

- The `ActionForm` bean can be found in request scope using `blog.Create` as the key.
- The context-relative URL path for `CreateBlogAction` is `/createBlog`.
- If validation fails, display the page defined by `jsp/createBlog.jsp`.

XDoclet translates these attributes into the following `<action>` declaration in `struts-config.xml`:

```
<action
  path="/createBlog"
  type="com.xdocletbook.blog.struts.action.CreateBlogAction"
  name="blog.Create"
  scope="request"
  input="jsp/error.jsp"
  unknown="false"
  validate="true"
>
</action>
```

Forwarding Action results

When `CreateBlogAction` has completed, you want it to go to a page indicating that the blog was successfully created. You use the `@struts.action-forward` tag to define a forward named `success` that maps to `jsp/blogCreated.jsp`.

XDoclet uses the attributes specified using the `@struts.action-forward` tag to write this `<forward>` definition into `struts-config.xml`:

```
<forward
    name="success"
    path="jsp/blogCreated.jsp"
    redirect="false"
/>
```

Handling Action exceptions

What if an error occurs while an `Action` is processing a request? In earlier versions of Struts, you had to write exception-handling code within your `Action` implementation. But as of Struts version 1.1, exceptions thrown from an Action's `execute` method can be handled by the framework. Declarations written in `struts-config.xml` define how the framework should handle the exception.

With XDoclet, you can tag the `Action` implementation classes with the `@struts.action-exception` tag to have XDoclet write the exception-handler declarations into the generated `struts-config.xml`. `CreateBlogAction.java` is tagged with one such tag:

```
/**
...
 * @struts.action-exception
 *     type="com.xdocletbook.blog.exception.ApplicationException"
 *     key="app.exception"
 *     path="jsp/error.jsp"
 */
public class CreateBlogAction extends Action {
...
}
```

These tags result in the following `<exception>` declaration being written to `struts-config.xml` with CreateBlogAction's `<action>` declaration:

```
<exception
    key="app.exception"
    type="com.xdocletbook.blog.exception.ApplicationException"
    path="jsp/error.jsp"
/>
```

The `@struts.action-exception` tag tells Struts to send the user to `jsp/error.jsp` when an `ApplicationException` is thrown. The `ActionError` created has a message found in a message resources file (the `ApplicationResources.properties` file) using `app.exception` as the key.

You've now seen how XDoclet can write `Action` declarations for you in `struts-config.xml`. Next let's look at how you can apply XDoclet to `ActionForm` beans.

5.2.4 Defining ActionForms

When a Struts `Action`'s execute method is called, it's passed a reference to the `HttpServletRequest` object. Certainly, just as with servlets, you could pull parameters out of the request by making calls to the request object's `getParameter` method. Then each `Action` implementation could perform any necessary validation on the parameters. But that technique would be awkward and could lead to redundant code if you had to pull and validate the same parameters in several actions.

The Struts framework offers an alternative to writing your own pull/validate code. In addition to the `HttpServletRequest` object passed in the call to `execute`, the framework also passes in an `ActionForm` object. A *form bean* is any subclass of `org.apache.struts.action.ActionForm` that, in typical JavaBean fashion, has one or more properties exposed with getter and setter methods. These properties are populated (and optionally validated) from parameters passed in on the request.

`CreateBlogAction` uses `BlogCreateForm` (listing 5.8) to retrieve request parameters.

Listing 5.8 BlogCreateForm.java

```
package com.xdocletbook.blog.form;

import java.io.Serializable;
import org.apache.struts.validator.ValidatorForm;

/**
 * @struts.form
 *      name="blog.Create"
 */
public class BlogCreateForm extends ValidatorForm
    implements Serializable {
  private String name;
  private String owner;
  private String email;

  public BlogCreateForm() {
  }

  public String getName() {
    return this.name;
  }

  /**
   * @struts.validator
   *      type="required"
   */
  public void setName(String name) {
    this.name = name;
  }

  public String getOwner() {
    return this.owner;
  }

  /**
   * @struts.validator
```

Fields marked as required must be present in the request

```
 *        type="required"
 */
public void setOwner(String owner) {
  this.owner = owner;
}

public String getEmail() {
  return this.email;
}

/**
 * @struts.validator
 *        type="required"
 *
 * @struts.validator
 *        type="email"
 */
public void setEmail(String email) {
  this.email = email;
}
}
```

> **This field is required and must be a properly formatted email address**

You use the `@struts.action-form` tag to tell XDoclet to include the following
`<form-bean>` definition in `struts-config.xml`:

```
<form-bean
    name="blog.Create"
    type="com.xdocletbook.blog.form.BlogCreateForm"
/>
```

The `name` attribute, `@struts.action-form`'s only attribute, gives the form bean a
logical name that's referenced in the `<action>` declaration of any action that uses
this form bean.

Now you've created a form bean and tagged it to be declared in `struts-config.xml`, but how can you have the framework perform validation on its fields?

Validating forms using the Struts Validator

You have two options for defining validation rules for the form bean: programmatic validation and declarative validation. *Programmatic validation* involves overriding `ActionForm`'s `validate` method and applying the validation rules in the Java code. This approach is great when the validation rules are complex, requiring more than simple type and format checking. Unfortunately, XDoclet can't help you write validation rules using this approach. Therefore, we won't go into any further detail about programmatic validation here; instead, we refer you to *Struts in Action* for more information.[1]

Declarative validation, as its name implies, involves writing the ActionForm as a sub-class of ValidatorForm instead of ActionForm and writing validation rules in a configuration file called validation.xml. A field is determined to be valid if its value "looks like" a valid value. Table 5.2 shows the 14 standard validators that come with Struts 1.1. These validations are perfectly adequate for most applications.

Table 5.2   The standard Struts 1.1 validators available to ValidatorForm

Validator	Definition
creditCard	Succeeds if the value is a valid credit card number
date	Succeeds if the value is a valid date
email	Succeeds if the value looks like an email address
mask	Succeeds if the value matches a pattern defined in the mask attribute
maxLength	Succeeds if the value's length is no greater than the value in the max-Length attribute
minLength	Succeeds if the value's length is no less than the value in the min-Length attribute
range	Succeeds if the value is within the range defined by the min and max Validator variables (inclusive)
required	Succeeds if the value is non-empty (whitespace ignored)
byte, short, integer, long, float, double	Succeeds if the value can be converted to the corresponding primitive type

BlogCreateForm subclasses ValidatorForm instead of ActionForm. This means you use declarative validation with this form bean.

BlogCreateForm requires two validation rules:

- All the fields are required and therefore must be sent as parameters to the request.
- The email field must *look like* an email address.

If these validation rules are broken, then the user should see an error message.

---

[1] Ted Husted, Cedric Dumoulin, George Franciscus, David Winterfeldt, and Craig R. McClanahan, *Struts in Action* (Greenwich, CT: Manning, 2003).

XDoclet comes with a few tags that help you define these validation rules in the validation.xml file. The following excerpt shows how you can update BlogCreate-Form.java, applying the @struts.validator tags to the setter methods:

```
/**
 * @struts.validator
 *      type="required"
 */
public void setName(String name) {
  this.name = name;
}
...
/**
 * @struts.validator
 *      type="required"
 */
public void setOwner(String owner) {
  this.owner = owner;
}
...
/**
 * @struts.validator
 *      type="required "
 *
 * @struts.validator
 *      type="email"
 */
public void setEmail(String email) {
  this.email = email;
}
```

For the name and owner fields, you set the validator type attribute to required. The type attribute maps to the depends attribute of the <field> element in validation.xml. In this case, it indicates that the fields are both required.

Because the email field is required and has a maximum length, you used two @struts.validator tags, setting the type attributes to required and email.

By tagging BlogCreateForm.java this way, you cause XDoclet to write the following validation rules into validation.xml:

```
<formset>
  <form name="blog.Create">
    <field property="owner"
        depends="required">

      <arg0 key="blog.Create.owner"/>
    </field>
    <field property="email"
        depends="required,email">
```

```
        <arg0 key="blog.Create.email"/>
      </field>
      <field property="name"
          depends="required">

        <arg0 key="blog.Create.name"/>
      </field>
    </form>
  </formset>
```

Now that you've seen how you can use XDoclet to declare the hand-written form beans in `struts-config.xml`, let's look at one of the more controversial uses of `@struts.form`.

Generating ActionForms from EJBs

Earlier, you applied the `@struts.form` tag to `BlogCreateForm` in order to have XDoclet register the form bean in `struts-config.xml`. But `@struts.form` has a slightly different use when it's used with entity EJBs. When it's applied at the class level of an entity EJB, it generates a form bean class based on the EJB's fields.

As a demonstration, let's tag `BlogBean.java` (from chapter 3) with the `@struts.form` tag:

```
/**
 ...
 *
 * @struts.form
 *      name="Everything"
 *      include-all="true"
 ...
 */
public abstract class BlogBean implements EntityBean {
 ...
}
```

You set the `include-all` attribute to true so that all of the EJB's persistent fields are included in the form bean. When you run the build, `BlogEverything-Form.java` is generated (see listing 5.9).

> **Listing 5.9 BlogEverythingForm.java: a form bean class generated from BlogBean.java**

```
package com.xdocletbook.blog.form;

/**
 * Generated by XDoclet/ejbdoclet/strutsform. This class
 * can be further processed with
 * XDoclet/webdoclet/strutsconfigxml.
 *
 * @struts.form name="blog.Everything"
```

Generated form bean class is tagged with @struts.form

```
 */
public class BlogEverythingForm
    extends    org.apache.struts.action.ActionForm
    implements java.io.Serializable
{
    protected java.lang.String id;
    protected java.lang.String name;
    protected java.lang.String owner;
    protected java.lang.String email;

    /** Default empty constructor. */
    public BlogEverythingForm() {}

    public java.lang.String getId()
    {
        return this.id;
    }

    public void setId( java.lang.String id )
    {
        this.id = id;
    }

    public java.lang.String getName()
    {
        return this.name;
    }

    public void setName( java.lang.String name )
    {
        this.name = name;
    }

    public java.lang.String getOwner()
    {
        return this.owner;
    }

    public void setOwner( java.lang.String owner )
    {
        this.owner = owner;
    }

    public java.lang.String getEmail()
    {
        return this.email;
    }

    public void setEmail( java.lang.String email )
    {
        this.email = email;
    }
}
```

A two-phase process is involved when you use `@struts.form` to generate form beans from entity beans:

1   The first phase occurs when the `<strutsform>` subtask of `<ejbdoclet>` processes `BlogBean.java` and generates `BlogEverythingForm.java`.

2   The second phase occurs when `<strutsconfigxml>` processes `BlogEverythingForm.java` and uses the `@struts.form` to add an entry for the form bean to `struts-config.xml`.

What if you have an action that doesn't need all the fields from `BlogBean`? Suppose you only need the `id` and `name` fields. Using the `@struts.form-field` tag, you can pick and choose which fields are included. To include only the `id` and `name` fields, you tag the getter methods for those fields with `@struts.form-field`:

```
/**
 ...
 * @struts.form
 *      name="Simple"
 */
public abstract class BlogBean implements EntityBean {
 ...
   /**
    ...
    * @struts.form-field form-name="Simple"
    */
   public abstract String getId();
 ...
   /**
    ...
    * @struts.form-field form-name="Simple"
    */
   public abstract String getName();
 ...
}
```

The `form-name` attribute maps back to the `name` attribute of the `@struts.form` tag. Tagging `BlogBean` in this way results in the generation of `BlogSimpleForm.java` (listing 5.10).

> **Listing 5.10   BlogSimpleForm.java generated by the <strutsform> subtask**

```
package com.xdocletbook.blog.form;

/**
 * Generated by XDoclet/ejbdoclet/strutsform. This class
 * can be further processed with
```

```
 * XDoclet/webdoclet/strutsconfigxml.
 *
 * @struts.form name="blog.Simple"
 */
public class BlogSimpleForm
    extends     org.apache.struts.action.ActionForm
    implements java.io.Serializable
{
    protected java.lang.String id;
    protected java.lang.String name;

    /** Default empty constructor. */
    public BlogSimpleForm() {}

    public java.lang.String getId()
    {
        return this.id;
    }

    public void setId( java.lang.String id )
    {
        this.id = id;
    }

    public java.lang.String getName()
    {
        return this.name;
    }

    public void setName( java.lang.String name )
    {
        this.name = name;
    }
}
```

You're probably wondering by now why we said earlier that using @struts.form with entity EJBs is controversial. At the center of the controversy is the question "Should view-layer objects be generated from model-layer entities?" Some believe that this is wrong and should never be done. Others see no problem with it. We're going to sit squarely in the middle of the fence on this issue. We agree that it is probably not a good idea to mix the model and the view in this way, but if having your form bean class generated for you makes things easier, then go for it.

5.3 Using XDoclet with WebWork

Another web-layer framework that is gaining in popularity is OpenSymphony's WebWork.[2] WebWork is a MVC framework, similar to Struts. In some ways, Web-Work is simpler than Struts. For example, whereas Struts has `Actions` to answer a request and separate `ActionForm` beans to carry the request parameters to the `Actions`, a WebWork `Action` is both the handler of the request and the carrier of request parameters.

As a result of its intentional simplicity, WebWork requires very little configuration and, therefore, very little for XDoclet to generate. WebWork needs only a single configuration file to operate. (Actually, there are two WebWork configuration files, but they're equivalent and you need only one of them.) Table 5.3 shows the WebWork-specific subtasks of `<webdoclet>` and what they generate.

Table 5.3 WebWork subtasks and what they generate

Subtask	Description
`<webworkconfigproperties>`	Generates the `views.properties` file for mapping Web-Work actions to views
`<webworkactionsxml>`	Generates the `actions.xml` file for mapping WebWork actions to views
`<webworkactiondocs>`	Generates HTML documentation for WebWork actions

The `views.properties` and `actions.xml` mapping files serve the same purpose, and you should use one exclusive of the other. We recommend that, if possible, you only work with the `actions.xml` file, because the `views.properties` file is being deprecated in newer versions of WebWork. However, in case you're using an older version of WebWork, we'll discuss how to generate `views.properties`. Finally, we'll cover how to use `<webworkactiondocs>` to create HTML documentation for the WebWork actions.

5.3.1 Configuring Actions in actions.xml

To have XDoclet generate `actions.xml` for you, add the following lines to `build-webgen.xml`:

```
<webworkactionsxml
    destDir="${web.deployment.dir}" />
```

---

[2] It may be interesting to note that Rickard Öberg, the creator of EjbDoclet (the forerunner to XDoclet), is also the creator of WebWork.

Let's build `CreateEntryAction.java` (listing 5.11) to demonstrate XDoclet's support for WebWork. `CreateEntryAction` is an `Action` that uses `BlogFacadeBean` to create a new entry within a blog.

Listing 5.11   CreateEntryAction.java

```
package com.xdocletbook.blog.webwork.action;

import webwork.action.ActionContext;
import webwork.action.ActionSupport;
import com.xdocletbook.blog.exception.InvalidUserException;
import com.xdocletbook.blog.interfaces.BlogFacade;
import com.xdocletbook.blog.interfaces.BlogFacadeHome;
import com.xdocletbook.blog.util.BlogFacadeUtil;

/**
 * Creates a web-log entry.            Declare name under
 *                                     which you're
 * @webwork.action              ❶      registering the action
 *     name="createEntry"     ◁┘
 *     success="jsp/entryCreated.jsp"    ❷  Declare
 *     login="jsp/badUser.jsp"              control flow
 *     error="jsp/error.jsp"                for the action
 */
public class CreateEntryAction extends ActionSupport {
  private String title;
  private String text;
  private String blogId;
  private String topicId;

  public String execute() throws Exception {

    ActionContext context = ActionContext.getContext();
    String userName =
        context.getContext().getPrincipal().getName();

    try {
    BlogFacadeHome home = BlogFacadeUtil.getHome();
    BlogFacade facade = home.create();

    facade.createEntry(title, text, blogId, topicId);
    } catch (InvalidUserException e) {
      return LOGIN;
    } catch (Exception e) {
      return ERROR;
    }

    return SUCCESS;
  }
}
```

```
public String getBlogId() {
  return blogId;
}

public String getText() {
  return text;
}

public String getTitle() {
  return title;
}

public String getTopicId() {
  return topicId;
}

public void setBlogId(String blogId) {
  this.blogId = blogId;
}

public void setText(String text) {
  this.text = text;
}

public void setTitle(String title) {
  this.title = title;
}

public void setTopicId(String topicId) {
  this.topicId = topicId;
}
}
```

The `@webwork.action` tag accomplishes two things:

1 The `name` attribute gives the action a name. The action is referenced on a URL using this name. In this case, the URL will look something like http://{*servername*}/blog/createEntry.action.

2 The `success`, `login`, and `error` attributes define the views to which the action will be sent, depending on the value returned from the `execute` method.

When the `@webwork.action` tag in `CreateEntryAction.java` is processed through the `<webworkactionsxml>` subtask, the following `actions.xml` file is generated:

```
<actions>
  <action
      name="com.xdocletbook.blog.webwork.action.CreateEntryAction"
      alias="createEntry">
```

```
        <view name="success">jsp/entryCreated.jsp</view>
    </action>
</actions>
```

5.3.2 *Configuring Actions in views.properties*

Even though it's being deprecated, many WebWork applications still use the older `views.properties` file instead of `actions.xml` for configuration. Although we recommend using `actions.xml` for new development, if you're porting a WebWork application that uses `views.properties`, it's better to let XDoclet generate `views.properties` first. Once you're satisfied that the move to XDoclet was successful, then consider having XDoclet generate `actions.xml` instead. This approach will help you eliminate risk and separate out XDoclet-related problems from WebWork migration problems.

In order to generate the `views.properties` file, you must use the `<webworkconfigproperties>` subtask instead of `<webworkactionsxml>`. Add the following lines to `build-webgen.xml`:

```
<webworkconfigproperties
    destDir="${web.deployment.dir}" />
```

You don't need to change `CreateEntryAction.java`. The `<webworkconfigproperties>` subtask works from the same tags as `<webworkactionsxml>` to generate `views.properties`.

5.3.3 *Documenting actions*

When you're creating a large web application using WebWork, you may get lost in all the action classes you create. The `<webworkactiondocs>` subtask creates HTML documentation for any WebWork actions it processes. To document your actions, add the following lines to `build-webgen.xml`:

```
<webworkactiondocs
    destDir="${webwork.actiondocs.dir}" />
```

By adding this subtask to the build, you'll make XDoclet create `actions.html`, documenting any WebWork action that it finds. Figure 5.4 shows what the documentation for `CreateEntryAction.java` looks like when viewed in a web browser.

5.4 *Summary*

Web frameworks such as Jakarta Struts and OpenSymphony's WebWork formalize Java web-layer development into a prescribed set of patterns and declarative definitions, removing some of the tedium and complexity of dealing with Java's core

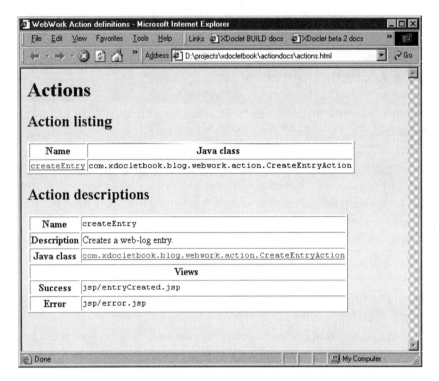

Figure 5.4   XDoclet can generate javadoc-inspired documentation for WebWork actions. This is the generated documentation for `CreateEntryAction`.

web technologies. However, managing the configuration files for these frameworks manually can be quite a chore. As you've seen in this chapter, XDoclet takes the fuss out of writing configuration files for Struts and WebWork.

We've now completed the web-layer of the web-log application. At this point, you've created a complete working application, using XDoclet as much as you possibly can. In the next chapter, we'll round out our discussion of using XDoclet with J2EE technologies by looking at how XDoclet can generate vendor-specific deployment descriptors.

6

XDoclet and
application servers

135

The essence of knowledge is, having it, to apply it; not having it, to confess your ignorance.

—Confucius

In the previous chapters, you used XDoclet to help you create a complete and functional J2EE application for managing web-logs. XDoclet generated code and deployment descriptors for the backend EJB layer and a front-end web-layer. XDoclet even came in handy when you were working with higher-level web development frameworks like Struts and WebWork. Yet, even though you've developed a complete application, you still have to cross one final hurdle: deployment to an application server. In this chapter, we'll look at why developers of supposedly portable, vendor-agnostic J2EE applications need to think about application servers. Then, we'll look at the code generation tasks XDoclet provides for deploying to J2EE application servers.

As you'll see, it's usually not difficult to deploy your application on an application server, but deployments can quickly become complicated. You may need to deploy your application for multiple customers or with multiple application servers. You'll probably have different deployment needs during development and testing than with a live deployment. XDoclet works well even for more complicated deployments, and we'll look at a few techniques that will help you leverage XDoclet for these scenarios.

6.1 *Why we need vendor-specific tasks*

J2EE application development is meant to provide solutions for large, complicated enterprise application development. You've already seen how J2EE provides solutions for transactions, security, robustness, and other enterprise development concerns. But J2EE goes beyond supporting enterprise technology needs; it also tries to provide an enterprise component development process.

6.1.1 *J2EE development roles*

J2EE development responsibilities are broken down into several important logical roles. For application development, the important roles are the application component provider, the application assembler, and the deployer. Figure 6.1 shows the various J2EE development roles. The application component provider creates the J2EE components: EJBs, servlets, JSPs, HTML pages, and so on. The application assembler takes the components created by the application assembler and combines them into a complete application. The application assembler manages all the internal dependencies of the application—resolving EJB references, for example. A

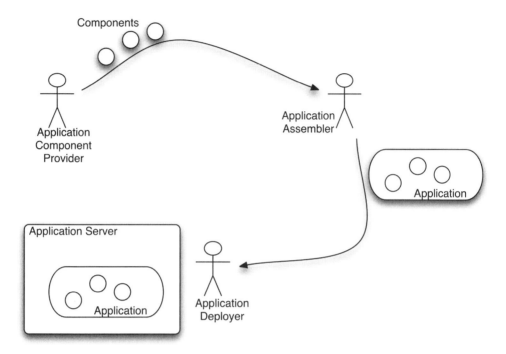

Figure 6.1 **The component provider, application assembler, and application deployer work together to create and deploy a J2EE application.**

J2EE application doesn't end there, though. Even though the application is complete, it may still have dependencies on resources external to the application, such as a relational database or a user management system. Resolving these roles is the job of the deployer.

If you have developed J2EE applications, you may be scratching your head a bit. The technical tasks should be familiar, but you probably don't structure development responsibilities along those lines. In most organizations, all three tasks are done by the same developers at the same time, although it isn't uncommon for parts of the deployer role to be broken out from the development team. There's nothing wrong with this approach; it just means that J2EE provides much more flexibility than any one project usually needs.

6.1.2 *J2EE application deployment*

No matter how you assign the application roles, you can't escape the deployment stage. A J2EE application isn't a standalone application—it has to be deployed within the context of an application server. So far you have used XDoclet to help with component development by generating interfaces and classes and with application assembly by creating deployment descriptors. (You might find it odd that most of the deployment descriptors are generated in the assembly phase, not the deployment phase, but try not to be too confused by the naming.) But, there is still a lot of work left to do to get a deployable application.

You still have to connect application datasources and user roles to resources configured in the application server. You may need to link to external EJBs, or perhaps provide a specific JNDI name for a bean to be looked up by. You might want to configure the database schema for your container managed persistence (CMP) beans. The application server itself determines what deployment-time aspects are configurable, but the things we just mentioned are very common.

There's no prescribed method that an application server must use to allow you to perform the deployment configuration. However, the major application servers provide powerful (but proprietary) deployment descriptors to use. Having different deployment descriptors for each application server makes J2EE development a bit more complicated than you might like, but fortunately XDoclet can help you with deployment descriptors.

6.1.3 *Generating application server deployment descriptors*

The process of generating application server deployment descriptors is typical for XDoclet. You add tags containing the new deployment metadata and then invoke the subtask appropriate to your application server. XDoclet supports many application servers to varying degrees, but some application servers are better supported than others.

The following are the more popular application servers supported by XDoclet:

- WebLogic
- JBoss
- WebSphere
- JRun
- Orion
- JOnAS

We'll only look at JBoss and WebLogic in depth. For details on generating for the other supported application servers, see the task and tag references in the appendixes. The good news is that for most of the deployment configuration you will need to do, the differences between application servers aren't that great.

Let's get started by deploying the web-log application on JBoss.

6.2 Deploying on JBoss

Blogomatic is packaged and deployed as an EAR file consisting of two modules: an EJB JAR file containing your beans and a WAR (web archive) file containing the web front end. You've used XDoclet to generate the standard deployment descriptors for these modules (`ejb-jar.xml` and `web.xml`, respectively). To deploy the application on JBoss, you need to supplement the standard descriptors with the JBoss deployment descriptors. We'll look at how to do this first for an EJB JAR and then for the WAR file.

Figure 6.2 shows how the final deployed EAR file will be organized on JBoss. Several new JBoss deployment descriptors are shown. You'll learn how XDoclet generates each of these files in the following sections.

As we look through these deployment issues, we'll touch on a number of advanced topics. For example, when deploying CMP entity beans, we'll hit a number of object relational mapping concepts. We'll assume a basic familiarity with these underlying deployment details. XDoclet can't shield you from needing to understand the details inherent in a J2EE deployment, but it can make those details easier to manage.

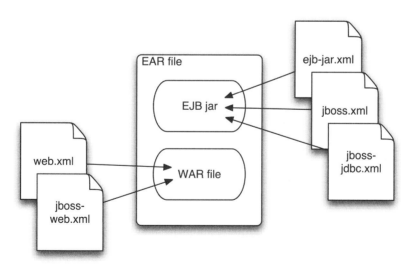

Figure 6.2   The EAR file consists of an EJB JAR file and a WAR file with the associated deployment descriptors.

6.2.1 *Deploying an EJB JAR on JBoss*

You'll begin by instructing XDoclet to generate the JBoss deployment descriptor.
You need to invoke the `<jboss>` subtask inside `<ejbdoclet>`:

```
<ejbdoclet destdir="${gen.src.dir}" mergeDir="${merge.dir}">
    <packageSubstitution packages="ejb"
                         substituteWith="interfaces"/>

    <fileset dir="${src.dir}">
        <include name="**/*Bean.java" />
        <include name="**/*Service.java" />
    </fileset>

    <deploymentdescriptor
            destdir="${ejb.deployment.dir}"/>

    <jboss destdir="${ejb.deployment.dir}"
           version="3.0" />
</ejbdoclet>
```

The `<jboss>` subtask works just like the other subtasks you've seen. Compare the
`<jboss>` subtask invocation with the deployment descriptor subtask invocation.
They both perform similar tasks and require similar attributes. The location of
the generated deployment descriptors is specified in the `destdir` attribute. You
place the JBoss descriptors in the same place you put the regular deployment
descriptors. All the descriptors eventually need to be placed in the `META-INF` directory of the EJB JAR file, so keeping them together is helpful.

You've also added a `version` attribute to specify that you want to generate JBoss
3.0–style deployment descriptors. XDoclet can also generate for JBoss 2.4 and has
some support for features in 3.2. XDoclet defaults to 2.4 if you don't specify anything, so it's important to make sure you specify the correct value.

The `<jboss>` subtask generates the `jboss.xml` deployment descriptor and also
generates the CMP deployment descriptor if needed. For JBoss 2.4, this is
`jaws.xml`. In 3.0 and up, the CMP descriptor is `jbosscmp-jdbc.xml`.

You haven't specified any deployment-related metadata, so the deployment
descriptors generated aren't useful yet. Next you'll see how to specify metadata to
drive the `<jboss>` subtask.

6.2.2 *Specifying database schema*

If you're using container managed persistence, the most important deployment
detail to configure is usually the database mapping. Just because you use CMP
doesn't mean you aren't concerned with how your beans map to your relational

database. Sometimes you're faced with the task of mapping beans onto existing relational tables. In other cases, you might need to lock in the database schema to simplify database access from outside the J2EE application.

We'll begin by looking at the `Blog` bean and declaring the table the bean should map to. The `@ejb.persistence` tag has a `table-name` attribute that allows you to specify table name you want JBoss to use:

```
/**
 * An entity bean representing a blog (weblog).
 * @ejb.bean name="Blog"
 *           local-jndi-name="blogamatic.Blog"
 *           type="CMP"
 *           cmp-version="2.x"
 *           primkey-field="id"
 *           view-type="local"
 * ...
 * @ejb.persistence table-name="blog"
 */

public abstract class BlogBean
    implements EntityBean
{
    // ...
}
```

With the table declared, the next step is to map your CMP fields to columns in your table. You use the `@ejb.persistence` tag again, but this time at the method level. Keep in mind that you need to place the attributes on the `get` method for the CMP field you're interested in (not the `set` method):

```
/**
 * Owner of the blog
 *
 * @ejb.persistence column_name="blog_owner"
 * ...
 */
public abstract String getOwner();
```

You can go one step further and specify the data type of the column in the database and the JDBC type mapping to use for this field using the `sql-type` and `jdbc-type` attributes. Suppose you knew that your usernames would never be longer than 32 characters. You could tell JBoss to use `varchar(32)` and get exactly the schema you want in the database. The declaration is simple:

```
/**
 * Owner of the blog
 *
```

```
 * @ejb.persistence column_name="blog_owner"
 *                  sql-type="varchar(32)"
 *                  jdbc-type="VARCHAR"
 *   ...
 */
public abstract String getOwner();
```

In general, JBoss does a very good job of mapping fields to the best datatype for the type of database being used, so you should rarely need to specify these values. Keep in mind that the sql-type value is needed only for table creation, so if JBoss isn't creating the tables for you, you don't need to bother defining a value for the type. However, when you're working with JBoss, you must specify both the sql-type and jdbc-type values together. If you specify one and not the other, the value will be ignored.

6.2.3 *Mapping foreign keys*

Finally, you need to declare how container-managed relations are mapped. Let's look at the Blog bean you developed in Chapter 3. Each Blog contains some number of Entry objects. This is a one-to-many relationship. Each Entry belongs to only one Blog, so you need to store the primary key of the Blog bean in the table for the Entry bean.

You don't need to add anything to the blog table, so your Blog bean stays the same:

```
/**
 *
 * @ejb.relation
 *     name="blog-entries"
 *     role-name="blog-has-entries"
 *
 *   ...
 */
public abstract Set getEntries();
```

You need to add a foreign key column to the table for the Entry bean using the @jboss.relation tag. This tag takes two parameters: the primary key field of the entity on the other side of the relationship and the column name you will use locally to store the value:

```
/**
 * @ejb.relation
 *     name="blog-entries"
 *     role-name="entry-belongs_to-blog"
 *     cascade-delete="yes"
```

```
   * @jboss.relation related-pk-field="id" fk-column="blog_id"
   */
  public abstract BlogLocal getBlog();
```

One interesting alternative would be to declare the relation mapping on the `Blog` side if you wanted to use the `@jboss-target-relation` tag. This declares values to apply to the other side of the relationship, not the current side. It's primarily useful for one-to-many relationships that can only be traversed from the one side to the many side. Imagine that the `Entry` bean didn't have a `getBlog` method. In that case, you'd have no place to hang the `@jboss.relation` tag, so you'd be forced to use `@jboss.target-relation` on the `Blog` side of the relationship:

```
  /**
   *
   * @ejb.relation
   *     name="blog-entries"
   *     role-name="blog-has-entries"
   * @jboss.target-relation related-pk-field="id"
   *                        fk-column="blog_id"
   */
```

6.2.4 *Handling relation tables*

One-to-one or one-to-many relations are easy to map. In a one-to-one relationship, the primary key of the related object needs to be stored in the row for the current object. This reference can be stored on either side of the relationship.

In a one-to-many relationship, things are slightly more complicated. We just looked at the case of one blog having many entries. You placed the primary key of the blog in the row of the related entry. Each entry belongs to one blog, so you can still map the one side of the relationship with a simple foreign key.

Suppose, however, that a single entry could belong to any number of blogs. Naturally, you don't want the overhead of storing a duplicate entry for each blog, so this many-to-many relationship will be of great value.

You have to change the beans such that an entry has a set of blogs, and doing so implies changes to your façade and possibly to your client code. Fortunately, those changes are easy to make. Mapping, on the other hand, isn't so easy any more—you can no longer store the primary key of the blog alongside the entry, because there is no longer a single value.

Although you can't store the relation information in either of the existing tables, nothing prevents you from creating a new table for this purpose. This is called a *mapping table*, and its sole purpose is to relate rows in one table to rows in another table. Take a step back and think about the many-to-many relationship

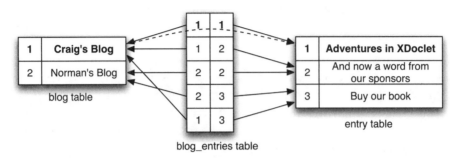

Figure 6.3 The `blog_entry` mapping table maps a `blog` ID to an `entry` ID, creating a connection between the rows in each table.

between a blog and an entry. You couldn't embed the information about the relationship in either object, so instead you created a new table with a row that represents the imaginary line connecting the two rows in the original tables. The only data required by this new table is the primary key information for both entities. Figure 6.3 shows how the `blog_entries` table connects a blog with an entry. The dotted line represents the implicit connection from one of the `blog` rows and one of the `entry` rows through `blog_entries` mapping table.

You can instruct JBoss how you would like this mapping table created by specifying the mapping table name and the column names for the keys of the objects on both sides. You'll place the relation table tags in `BlogBean`. You'll also add the information about how to map the primary key of the `entry` object, which you didn't need before:

```
/**
 *
 * @ejb.relation
 *     name="blog-entries"
 *     role-name="blog-has-entries"
 * @jboss.relation related-pk-field="id"
 *                 fk-column="entry_id"
 * @jboss.relation-table table-name="blog_entry"
 *  ...
 */
public abstract Set getEntries();
```

The mapping table is named `blog_entry`, and the ID of the related `entry` object is stored in the `entry_id` column. In the `Entry` bean, you need to change the method signature slightly to accommodate the fact that an entry is related to multiple blogs:

```
/**
 * @ejb.relation
 *     name="blog-entries"
 *     role-name="entry-has-blogs"
 * @jboss.relation related-pk-field="id" fk-column="blog_id"
 */
public abstract Set getBlogs();
```

The relation information looks exactly like it did before. The `role-name` has been modified to better describe the new relationship, and the `cascade-delete` directive was removed because the entry is no longer dependent on one blog to provide context.

6.2.5 *Creating database tables*

You've specified how you want to map your entity beans to a relational database, but the tables you're mapping to must be created in the databases. JBoss offers several basic database-management functions. It can create the database tables when the application starts up and can also remove the database tables when the application stops. That may not be the right solution for deploying a production system, but it definitely comes in handy during development:

```
/**
 * An entity bean representing a blog (weblog).
 *
 * @ejb.bean name="Blog"
 *           local-jndi-name="blogamatic.Blog"
 *           type="CMP"
 *           cmp-version="2.x"
 *           primkey-field="id"
 *           view-type="local"
 *
 * @ejb.persistence table-name="blog"
 *
 * @jboss.persistence create-table="true"
 *                    remove-table="true"
 *
 * ...
 */
```

The `create-table` and `remove-table` attributes for the `@jboss.persistence` tag control whether JBoss creates and removes the tables when the application is deployed and undeployed. You probably wouldn't want JBoss to delete a table if JBoss isn't creating the table for you. However, you might like JBoss to create the table (if it doesn't already exist) but not automatically delete it.

We looked at relation tables in the prior section. The `@jboss.relation-table` declaration also supports the `create-table` and `remove-table` attributes:

```
/**
 *
 * @ejb.relation
 *     name="blog-entries"
 *     role-name="blog-has-entries"
 * @jboss.relation related-pk-field="id"
 *                 fk-column="entry_id"
 * @jboss.relation-table table-name="blog_entries"
 *                       create-table="true"
 *                       remove-table="true"
 * ...
 */
public abstract Set getEntries();
```

If your table creation strategy doesn't vary between beans (and it probably shouldn't), then you should default the create-table and remove-table values to Ant properties. By using values specified in Ant properties, you can ensure that the values are consistent throughout your application:

```
/**
 * @jboss.persistence create-table="${table_create}"
 *                    remove-table="${table_remove}"
 */
```

Another way to achieve the same goal is to set a default value as a parameter to the <jboss> subtask in Ant:

```
<jboss destdir="${ejb.deployment.dir}"
       version="3.0"
       createTable="true"
       removeTable="true" />
```

This approach requires less effort, but it also removes valuable information from the source files. Keeping the table-creation details alongside the other XDoclet-managed metadata is very helpful. However, as with all design decisions, the best choice for you is entirely dependent on the nature of the project you're working on.

6.2.6 *Specifying physical JNDI names*

The home interface (local and/or remote) of each bean needs to be bound to a physical JNDI name at deployment. This name is a sort of global address for the bean. When you're referencing beans in the same EAR file, you don't need to worry much about the JNDI name, because the references will be resolved using the ejb-link values that XDoclet places in the ejb-jar.xml. However, if you will need to refer to the bean from another J2EE application (possibly in another server) or from code running in the same J2EE application that doesn't have the benefit of a declared `ejb-ref`, you should specify the JNDI name explicitly.

Here, you add a `jndi-name` attribute to the `BlogFacade` session bean:

```
/**
 * @ejb.bean
 *     name="BlogFacade"
 *     type="Stateless"
 *     view-type="remote"
 *     transaction-type="Container"
 *     jndi-name="blogamatic_BlogFacade"
 */
```

The JNDI namespace is global to the application server, not just to the J2EE application, so it's important to choose unique names. A common practice is to add the application name to the JNDI name, as in this example. If your session bean also had a local home interface, you could declare the JNDI name to bind the local home to using the `local-jndi-name` attribute.

If you use the application name in more than one place, you can declare it in an Ant property like `app.name` and then reference it as `jndi-name="${app. name}_BlogFacade"`. It's always a good idea to put shared data in a well-known location and reference it.

Specifying datasource mappings

One final deployment option you might want to set is the default datasource for CMP beans. If you don't specify a datasource, JBoss will use `java:/defaultDS`, which maps to the internal Hypersonic database (unless you change the definition). Relying on application server–wide defaults can be problematic, particularly when you're trying to deploy multiple applications. We recommend setting per-application defaults for the default datasource. There are two good ways to do this: specify the default datasource when you invoke the `<jboss>` subtask, or use a merge file to configure defaults.

It's simple to specify the default datasource when you invoke the `<jboss>` subtask in Ant:

```
<jboss destdir="${ejb.deployment.dir}/META-INF"
       version="3.0"
       datasource="java:/blogData"
       datasourceMapping="MS SQLSERVER2000" />
```

Unless you specify something different for a particular bean, the default datasource is `java:/blogData`, which is a Microsoft SQL Server 2000 database. We should point out that this doesn't define the datasource. XDoclet can't create the datasource definition XML files JBoss needs. It links to an existing datasource.

You can accomplish an equivalent task using merge files. XDoclet looks for the `jbosscmp-jdbc-defaults.xml` merge file to configure the CMP defaults. If you feel more comfortable working with the JBoss XML structure, then the merge file is a good option. To define a datasource, the `jbosscmp-jdbc-defaults.xml` file should contain the datasource configuration options:

```
<defaults>
    <datasource>java:/blogData</datasource>
    <datasource-mapping>MS SQLSERVER200</datasource-mapping>
</defaults>
```

NOTE If you use the merge file, the default values specified in the `<jboss>` sub-task are ignored. This includes the other CMP-related values such as `create-table` and `remove-table`.

To override the default datasource for a specific bean, `@jboss.persistence` accepts `datasource` and `datasource-mapping` attributes. The values apply only to the bean the tag is on:

```
/**
 * @jboss.persistence datasource="java:/someOtherDS"
 *                    datasource-mapping="MS SQLSERVER200"
 */
```

CMP isn't the only place a datasource reference is needed. Datasources may be required in BMP beans and session beans. You access datasources through logical resource references that you look up using JNDI names. To complete the deployment, you need to map the local logical name onto the physical JNDI name of the declared datasource:

```
/**
 * @ejb.resource-ref   res-ref-name="jdbc/blogData"
 *                     res-type="javax.sql.DataSource"
 *                     res-auth="Container"
 *
 * @jboss.resource-ref res-ref-name="jdbc/blogData"
 *                     jndi-name="java:/blogDS"
 *
 */
```

Of course, there are many more JBoss-specific EJB deployment options. These are the most common, but you'll undoubtedly need to go further eventually. See appendixes B and C for documentation of the more obscure options.

6.3 *Deploying a WAR file on JBoss*

Deploying a web application on a particular application server is less complicated than deploying an EJB JAR file. Far fewer deployment details are left for the application server to decide. Things are also made easier by the fact that the deployment details are related to the application as a whole and not to individual components as they are in EJBs.

You've used the `<webdoclet>` task to generate the `web.xml` file for the WAR file. JBoss uses the `jboss-web.xml` file, stored alongside `web.xml`, for the JBoss-specific application details. The `<jbosswebxml>` subtask generates this for you:

```
<webdoclet destdir="${gen.src.dir}" mergeDir="${merge.dir}">
  <jbosswebxml destdir="${web.deployment.dir}" />
</webdoclet>
```

The `destdir` attribute controls where the generated file goes. As with all the deployment descriptor tasks, you shouldn't place the generated deployment descriptors in the same place as the generated source files. You need to make sure the generated file is located where it will be picked up by your build system and placed into the WAR file.

6.3.1 *Setting a default web context*

Every J2EE web application services a unique context root. The *context root* is the first component of the path in a URL; all the content in the WAR file should be subordinate to it. For example, if your web application is deployed with a context root of /MyApplication on the host www.xdocletbook.com, then the servlets, JSPs, and static content for that web location are available at http://www.xdoclet-book.com/MyApplication/.

When you're deploying a full J2EE application in an EAR file, the context root of the WAR file is specified in the `application.xml` file. We strongly recommend the use of EAR files for J2EE applications, even if your application can be fully contained in a single WAR file.

If you plan to deploy a WAR file in isolation, JBoss sets the default context according to the base of the WAR filename. So, `blog.war` is assigned the context root /blog. This is a nice convenience, but maintaining specific filenames (especially considering the case of the filename) at deployment time is asking for trouble. The best option is to include the value in the `jboss-web.xml` file. You can specify the context root using the `contextroot` attribute:

```
<webdoclet destdir="${gen.src.dir}" mergeDir="${merge.dir}">
    <jbosswebxml destdir="${web.deployment.dir}"
                 contextroot="/blog" />
</webdoclet>
```

Again, if you're deploying a WAR file as part of an EAR file, it's better not to set this attribute. However, for a pure web application, setting the value here is good.

6.3.2 *Setting a security domain*

In the web application, you referenced certain users and groups without defining where this information should come from. JBoss uses the Java Authentication and Authorization Service (JAAS) to manage authentication and authorization. JAAS is an optional package in Java 1.3, but it has become a standard Java technology starting in Java 1.4.

JBoss provides a default JAAS domain if you don't specify one, but it's better to explicitly choose the JAAS domain for your application and not rely on default values for the whole server. JAAS domains are bound in the JNDI tree, and referencing one is as simple as setting the value of the securitydomain attribute of <jbosswebxml> to the correct domain:

```
<webdoclet destdir="${gen.src.dir}" mergeDir="${merge.dir}">
    <jbosswebxml destdir="${web.deployment.dir}"
                 securitydomain="java:/jaas/blogauth"
                 contextroot="/blog" />
</webdoclet>
```

It's your responsibility to configure the security domain you will be referencing. XDoclet can't add the security domain to the JBoss login-config.xml file, so you have to manage the configuration system by hand. XDoclet only provides a mechanism to link a JAAS domain you have already created.

6.3.3 *Setting a virtual host*

A single web container may be called to respond to requests for more than one hostname. These additional hosts are called *virtual hosts* because they don't correspond to real, unique machines on the network. Each virtual host may have its own set of J2EE applications, which you want to be visible only when connecting to that host.

The virtualhost attribute allows you to specify the virtual host on which this WAR file will be deployed:

```
<webdoclet destdir="${gen.src.dir}" mergeDir="${merge.dir}">
    <jbosswebxml destdir="${web.deployment.dir}"
```

```
                        securitydomain="java:/jaas/blogauth"
                        contextroot="/blog"
                        virtualhost="blogs.xdocletbook.com" />
    </webdoclet>
```

This setting makes sure your blog application only responds to requests addressed to http://blogs.xdocletbook.com/blog. Requests to http://www.xdocletbook.com/blog will not be serviced by this web application, even though the request goes to the same server on the same physical machine.

6.4 *Deploying on WebLogic*

One nice aspect of J2EE application development is portability. For the most part, all the major application servers offer a similar set of features, and thus the deployment-time options are similar. With a little deployment-time customization, you can move your application from one application server to another. However, the differences are great enough that it's worthwhile to examine how XDoclet operates with another application server.

You've already deployed your application on JBoss, so now we'll turn our attention to WebLogic. WebLogic is a popular application server developed by BEA Systems. Deploying on BEA WebLogic isn't conceptually any different than doing so on JBoss, and we'll examine it the same way. First we'll look at deploying an EJB JAR; then we'll look at deploying the web application.

6.4.1 *Deploying an EJB JAR on WebLogic*

As you did with JBoss, you'll begin by deploying an EJB JAR on WebLogic. You need to use the `<weblogic>` subtask of `<ejbdoclet>`:

```
<ejbdoclet destdir="${gen.src.dir}" mergeDir="${merge.dir}">
    <packageSubstitution packages="ejb"
                         substituteWith="interfaces"/>

    <fileset dir="${src.dir}">
        <include name="**/*Bean.java" />
        <include name="**/*Service.java" />
    </fileset>

    <deploymentdescriptor
            destdir="${ejb.deployment.dir}" />

    <weblogic destdir="${ejb.deployment.dir}"
              version="7.0" />
</ejbdoclet>
```

The <weblogic> subtask generates the two WebLogic EJB deployment descriptors you need: weblogic-ejb-jar.xml and weblogic-cmp-rdbms-jar.xml. These two files are similar in function to the JBoss EJB and CMP configuration files.

XDoclet generates deployment descriptors for versions 6 and 7 of WebLogic. You must specify the specific version to the subtask to make sure the generated files are appropriate for the version you're working on.

6.4.2 *Specifying database mapping*

The <weblogic> subtask supports the same basic functionality for CMP fields that you saw in the <jboss> subtask. @ejb.persistence is used to specify both the table name and column names for simple fields. However, you begin to see differences as you look at the database mappings for container-managed relationships. We looked at the relationship between blogs and entries earlier. Here's the way the mapping looks for WebLogic:

```
/**
 * @ejb.relation
 *      name="blog-entries"
 *      role-name="entry-belongs_to-blog"
 *      cascade-delete="yes"
 * @weblogic.relation key-column="blog_id"
 *                          foreign-key-column="blog_id"
 */
public abstract BlogLocal getBlog();
```

There's a subtle difference here between the @jboss.relation tag and the @weblogic.relation tag. JBoss maps the CMR field on the other bean to a foreign column in the current bean's table. WebLogic, on the other hand, maps a column in the other bean's table to a foreign key column on the current bean's table. Small differences like this drive the application server-specific tags.

You also have @weblogic.target-column-map to perform the mapping of a CMR relation from the opposite side of the relationship:

```
/**
 * @ejb.relation name="blog-entries"
 *               role-name="blog-has-entries"
 * @weblogic.target-column-map
 *          key-column="blog_id"
 *          foreign-key-column="blog_id"
 */
```

Finally, let's take a quick look at the mapping table example from section 6.2.4. For a mapping table, you need a table name and column names for the primary keys on both sides of the relation. Pay attention to the use of the key-column attribute for WebLogic instead of the `related-pk-field` attribute used with JBoss. This is the only significant difference between the two systems:

```
/**
 *
 * @ejb.relation
 *     name="blog-entries"
 *     role-name="blog-has-entries"
 * @weblogic.column-map key-column="entry_id"
 *                          foreign-key-column="entry_id"
 * @weblogic.relation join-table-name="blog_entries"
 * ...
 */
public abstract Set getEntries();
```

You still need to map the entry side of the relation:

```
/**
 * @ejb.relation name="blog-entries"
 *               role-name="entry-has-blogs"
 * @weblogic.column-map key-column="blog_id"
 *                          foreign-key-column="blog_id"
 */
public abstract Set getBlogs();
```

You could also use `@weblogic.target-column-map` to map both sides of the relation from the `Blog` bean.

6.4.3 Managing tables

WebLogic provides two interesting table-management functions. Like JBoss, WebLogic can create CMP tables for you when the application starts; but unlike JBoss, there's no option to remove tables when the application stops. However, WebLogic does provide a useful feature that JBoss lacks: the ability to test a CMP table to make sure it's valid. This validation is extremely useful, because it can quickly detect mismatches between the schema and the database that occur during development. You can set both these options at the application level as attributes to the `<weblogic>` subtask:

```
<weblogic destdir="${ejb.deployment.dir}"
                version="7.0"
                createtables="true"
                validateDbSchemaWith="MetaData" />
```

Here you validate the schema using JDBC metadata. You could also specify `Table-Query` (instead of `MetaData`) to use a query against the table to determine whether the tables are compatible.

6.4.4 Using WebLogic-specific features

As you can see, with some small exceptions, most of the features we covered in the JBoss section have equivalent settings in WebLogic. Rather than rehashing those examples, let's look at a couple of features that are specific to WebLogic: configuring the bean pool size and passing values by reference.

EJBs are normally pooled by the application server. The application server maintains a pool of beans to respond to requests. The application server can try to maintain an appropriately sized pool of beans, but performance is usually best when the deployer tunes the pool size. WebLogic allows the pool size for a bean to be configured for each bean. You use the `@weblogic.pool` tag to set the initial and maximum pool sizes:

```
/**
 * A session facade for managing a blog
 *
 * @ejb.bean
 *      name="BlogFacade"
 *      type="Stateless"
 *      view-type="remote"
 *
 * @weblogic.pool max-beans-in-free-pool="20"
 *                initial-beans-in-free-pool="5"
 */
public abstract class BlogFacadeBean
     implements SessionBean
{
     // ...
}
```

Another useful WebLogic deployment option is enabling call by reference. Access to remote beans is normally by value; this means each parameter passed into or out of a remote method invocation needs to be copied. This is the only option for a true remote operation, but if the client is in the same JVM, then this overhead is unnecessary. You can greatly improve performance by passing the values by reference (passing the objects directly without creating new objects). You do so by using the `@webogic.enable-call-by-reference` tag:

```
/**
 * A session facade for managing a blog
 *
 * @ejb.bean
 *      name="BlogFacade"
 *      type="Stateless"
 *      view-type="remote"
 *
```

```
 * @weblogic.enable-call-by-reference true
 */
public abstract class BlogFacadeBean
    implements SessionBean
{
    // ...
}
```

Of course, there are many more options for deploying EJB JARs on WebLogic—we haven't even scratched the surface here. These examples are meant to show the types of options available when you're working with EJB JARs on WebLogic. For a full list of generation options, see appendixes B and C.

6.4.5 Deploying a WAR file on WebLogic

The WebLogic deployment descriptor for a WAR file is `weblogic.xml`. It can be generated by the `<weblogicwebxml>` subtask of `<webdoclet>`:

```
<webdoclet destdir="${gen.src.dir}" mergeDir="${merge.dir}">
    <weblogicwebxml destdir="${web.deployment.dir}"
                    description="blogamatic web log app"
                    version="7.0"/>
</webdoclet>
```

The `destdir` attribute is important to make sure the deployment descriptors end up in the right location for inclusion in the WAR file. The `version` attribute here is the same as for the `<weblogic>` subtask for `<ejbdoclet>`. It's important to make sure the version corresponds to the version of WebLogic you'll be deploying to—otherwise, your deployment descriptors may end up with inappropriate settings.

The first thing you should set is the context root. The context root in WebLogic serves the same purpose as the context root in JBoss, setting the web context under which the WAR file will be accessible:

```
<webdoclet destdir="${gen.src.dir}" mergeDir="${merge.dir}">
    <weblogicwebxml destdir="${web.deployment.dir}"
                    description="blogamatic web log app"
                    version="7.0"
                    contextroot="/blog" />
</webdoclet>
```

The final setting we'll look at is the security context for the web application. Because this is an application-wide context, you can also set the value on the `<weblogicwebxml>` subtask:

```
<webdoclet destdir="${gen.src.dir}" mergeDir="${merge.dir}">
    <weblogicwebxml destdir="${web.deployment.dir}"
                    description="blogamatic web log app"
```

```
                              version="7.0"
                              contextroot="/blog"
                              securitydomain="blogdomain" />
        </webdoclet>
```

The security domain needs to be separately defined. XDoclet can't reach inside the application and create the security domain for you. The `securitydomain` attribute here is only a reference to an externally defined security domain.

Now that we've looked at application deployment on two types of application servers, let's see how XDoclet can help with more complex deployments that involve multiple servers.

6.5 *Working with multiple application servers*

A standards-based J2EE application should be deployable on any J2EE application server, regardless of the platform—at least, that's the theory. It doesn't always work out that way. Still, being able to move quickly from one application server to another is nice. As long as you're using application servers known to XDoclet, deploying on a new application server can be as simple as adding a few new tags and invoking the subtasks for that application server.

But don't think that XDoclet is limited to working with a single application server at a time. Provided you have defined any needed tags in the source files, XDoclet will happily generate deployment descriptors for any number of application servers.

Vendors have been very good about making sure the deployment descriptors for each application server are uniquely named. So, if you need to deploy on multiple application servers, you should be able to place all the vendor-specific deployment descriptors together and deploy your application directly on any of the servers.

If you run into a problem and need to create unique application EAR files for each application server, you can adjust the `destdir` attribute of each of the vendor subtasks to generate the vendor deployment descriptor in a place that makes sense for your project.

Inside XDoclet, you shouldn't need to worry about tags colliding. The vendor tags are all uniquely named. The `@jboss.persistence` tag, for example, would not be used by the `<weblogic>` subtask. The common tags, such as `@ejb.persistence`, normally contain the same values for each application server.

There are two ways to deal with common tags that need to vary from server to server. First, you can look for an application server equivalent for the common tag. In this chapter, you saw how to define a table name using `@ejb.persistence`:

```
/**
 * @ejb.persistence table-name="blog"
 */
```

However, if you want to override this value for JBoss, you can add the JBoss equivalent:

```
/**
 * @ejb.persistence table-name="blog"
 * @jboss.persistence table-name="jboss_blog"
 */
```

Not all common tags have vendor-specific equivalents. In fact, most don't. If you need to change a value that doesn't have a vendor equivalent, the next best option is to use Ant property substitution and run XDoclet once with each context. If your blog table name was stored in the `${blog_table}` property, the XDoclet tag would reference it as follows:

```
/**
 * @ejb.persistence table-name="${blog_table}"
 */
```

You'd then need to invoke XDoclet with the `${blog_table}` property set appropriately for each server instance:

```
<antcall target="xdoclet-server1">
    <param name="blog_table" value="server1_blog"/>
</antcall>
<antcall target="xdoclet-server2">
    <param name="blog_table" value="server2_blog"/>
</antcall>
```

In this example, `xdoclet-server1` and `xdoclet-server2` represent targets that invoke XDoclet in a way that's useful for a particular application server. You have to use the `<antcall>` command because in Ant, properties are normally immutable. Using `<antcall>` is the only way to invoke a target with a property value different from the current value. The new value is set only within the scope of the target invoked by `<antcall>`.

This is a slight oversimplification, because you probably wouldn't store the values in your Ant build file directly like this. The best solution is to store the values in a property file and pass the name of the property file to the target invoked by `<antcall>` for loading. You'll see an example of the property file approach in the next section.

6.6 *Working with multiple deployments*

Applications are rarely deployed in only one environment. Even for in-house applications where there is only one final deployment, an application normally needs to be deployed on development machines as well as testing machines. Database configurations are different in each of these contexts. Clustering is another setting that usually differs between deployment types.

To support multiple deployments, you need to select the XDoclet tag parameters that may vary and place the values in a property file. In section 6.2.5, we suggested using Ant properties to control the JBoss `create-table` and `remove-table` flags. This is a good example of a property that might require different settings for each deployment type.

Let's create a simple properties file, `deploy.properties`, that will contain property values that are appropriate for the deployment context. A developer might want both `create-table` and `remove-table` to be true, but when you're doing a testing or development build, these properties could be set to false. Your `deploy.properties` looks like this:

```
create-table=true
remove-table=true
```

Now you can refer to these values inside your tags:

```
/**
 * @jboss.persistence create-table="${create-table}"
 *                    remove-table="${remove-table}"
 */
```

You need to make sure Ant loads the appropriate property file. The simplest way is to load the properties as part of the `init` task:

```
<property file="deploy.properties" />
```

> **NOTE**   When you're working with properties files, you need a strong understanding of Ant if you want to do anything complicated. We recommend *Java Development with Ant* if you need to understand some of the more complicated Ant techniques.[1]

---

[1]   Erik Hatcher and Steve Loughran, *Java Development with Ant* (Greenwich, CT: Manning, 2002).

6.7 *Summary*

XDoclet can generate code for all the stages of J2EE application development, from component development to application assembly to deployment. At every stage of development, you need to decide whether XDoclet provides enough value to warrant using it on the project. For the earlier stages of development, the chances are very high that XDoclet will fit into your development process and provide substantial value. But when it comes to deployment, you need to carefully examine your deployment process and customer needs to make sure XDoclet is a good fit. XDoclet generally is useful, at least for local development deployments.

When it's time to deploy, you'll find that XDoclet provides very good support for creating deployable applications on all the major application servers Not only can you generate the application server–specific deployment descriptors, but by using XDoclet metadata you can also leverage existing deployment information to cross application server boundaries and deploy to new application servers more rapidly than was possible before. XDoclet helps take the J2EE promise of portability to an even higher level.

Part 3

Other XDoclet applications

In part 2, you saw how XDoclet can be used when you're developing J2EE applications. However, as you'll learn in part 3, there's more to XDoclet than EJBs and servlets. Many other XDoclet modules have been developed to provide code generation support for non-J2EE technologies.

Chapter 7, "XDoclet and data persistence," discusses the XDoclet modules related to some popular Java persistence frameworks. In this chapter, you'll learn how you can use XDoclet to generate object-relational mapping files for Hibernate, JDO, and Castor.

Chapter 8, "XDoclet and web services," looks at Apache SOAP and Apache Axis, two web services frameworks, and explains how XDoclet can generate deployment descriptors for these frameworks.

Chapter 9, "XDoclet and JMX," explores the various XDoclet tasks associated with Java Management Extensions. In addition to learning how to generate interfaces for standard MBeans, you'll see how XDoclet can be used to generate artifacts for deploying MBeans in JBossMX and MX4J.

Chapter 10, "XDoclet and mock objects," covers mock objects, a powerful technique for unit-testing and generating mock implementations of your interfaces with XDoclet.

Chapter 11, "XDoclet and portlets," concludes our discussion of the modules that come built in with XDoclet. In this chapter, you'll learn how to write portlets suitable for deployment within a JSR-168–compliant portlet container and discover how XDoclet can generate a `portlet.xml` deployment descriptor for your portlet applications.

7

XDoclet and
data persistence

This chapter covers

- Generating Hibernate mapping files
- XDoclet and JDO metadata
- Working with Castor JDO and Castor XML

A memory is what is left when something happens and does not completely unhappen.

—Edward de Bono

Most non-trivial applications process data that must be stored in a database or some other form of persistent storage. An address book application, for example, would be of little use if it didn't remember the addresses entered into it for later retrieval.

Although many Java applications utilize JDBC as their only means to access data persisted in a relational database, JDBC still leaves much to be desired. Specifically, much redundant code must be written to move data back and forth between a JDBC result set and the Java object that represents the data within a system.

Ideally, we'd like the means of persisting data to be transparent, freeing us to focus on the business logic that processes the data without concern for how it's stored. Many frameworks have been devised to hide the details of how data is stored, including entity EJBs.

Even though entity beans make for a fine object-relational persistence framework, they represent only one option for data persistence. Other frameworks challenge entity beans as the persistence framework of choice. Among the challengers are Hibernate, Castor, and Sun Microsystems' own Java Data Objects (JDO) specification.

In this chapter, we'll look at how XDoclet can be used to generate mapping files associated with these data persistence frameworks, starting with Hibernate, the newest of the challengers.

7.1 *Hibernating data*

Hibernate is a persistence framework that is gaining a lot of popularity. Using an XML mapping file to tie database tables and fields to Java classes and properties, Hibernate provides near-transparent persistence of Java objects. You can download and find more information about Hibernate from http://hibernate.source-forge.net.

The XML mapping file defines metadata separate from the application code, thereby requiring additional management responsibility. Keeping the mapping file synchronized with the application classes that it describes can be quite a chore.

This looks like a job for XDoclet. Using XDoclet tasks and tags for Hibernate, you can focus on writing the application code and leave the nuisance of managing Hibernate mapping files to XDoclet. Let's begin by adding the appropriate XDoclet tasks to build files.

7.1.1 *Preparing the build for Hibernate*

The first thing you need to do is prepare the build to generate Hibernate mapping files. To keep Hibernate generation tasks separate from the rest of your build, you'll create a new build-hibernate.xml file and call it from the main build.xml file. The following excerpt from build.xml shows how you add the call to build-hibernate.xml from the generate target:

```
<target name="generate">
  <ant antfile="build-ejbgen.xml" target="generate-ejb"/>
  <ant antfile="build-webgen.xml" target="generate-web"/>
  <ant antfile="build-hibernate.xml" target="generate-hibernate"/>
</target>
```

The <hibernatedoclet> XDoclet task is responsible for generating mapping files for Hibernate. Table 7.1 describes the subtasks of <hibernatedoclet>.

Table 7.1   <hibernatedoclet> subtasks and the types of files they generate

Subtask	Description
<hibernate>	Generates Hibernate object-relational mapping files
<jbossservice>	Generates a JBoss MBean descriptor for Hibernated classes

Add the <hibernatedoclet> task and the <hibernate> subtask to build-hibernate.xml (listing 7.1) to generate Hibernate mapping files.

Listing 7.1   build-hibernate.xml generates Hibernate mapping files.

```
<?xml version="1.0" encoding="UTF-8"?>

<project name="Blog" default="generate-hibernate" basedir=".">
  <path id="xdoclet.lib.path">
    <fileset dir="${lib.dir}" includes="*.jar"/>
    <fileset dir="${xdoclet.lib.dir}" includes="*.jar"/>
  </path>

  <target name="generate-hibernate">
    <taskdef name="hibernatedoclet"
        classname="xdoclet.modules.hibernate.HibernateDocletTask"
        classpathref="xdoclet.lib.path"/>

    <hibernatedoclet destdir="${generated.dir/hbm}"
        mergeDir="${merge.dir}">
      <fileset dir="${src.dir}">
        <include name="**/*.java" />
      </fileset>
```

Generate
Hibernate
artifact

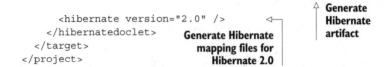

By default, the generated Hibernate mapping files target Hibernate version 1.1, but you set the `version` attribute of `<hibernate>` to "2.0" to indicate that you want mapping files appropriate for version 2.0 of Hibernate.

Now that the build file is ready, you can begin writing classes to be persisted by Hibernate.

7.1.2 *Tagging classes for Hibernation*

As an example of how you can use XDoclet to generate Hibernate mapping files, let's revisit the web-log application that you started in chapter 3. As you recall, three objects make up the object model for the web-log application: `Blog`, `Topic`, and `Entry`. For a refresher, the relationships between these objects are shown in figure 7.1.

Suppose you decide you don't want to define the objects in your web-log application using entity beans. Instead, let's try Hibernate as the persistence framework. You'll start by rewriting the web-log objects as POJOs (plain old Java objects)

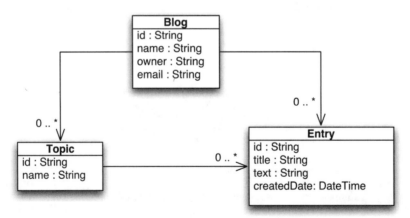

Figure 7.1 The three objects that make up the object model of the web-log application. A `Blog` represents an individual web-log in the system. The `Entry` and `Topic` classes represent, respectively, the entries in a web-log and the topics that organize the entries within the web-log.

instead of as entity beans and then tagging those classes with @hibernate tags. Listing 7.2 shows Blog.java, the new class that represents a Blog object.

Listing 7.2 Blog.java is a POJO persisted with Hibernate.

```
package com.xdocletbook.blog.pojo;

/**
 * @hibernate.class           This class is persisted
 *     table="Blog"           to the blog table
 */
public class Blog {
  private String id;
  private String name;
  private String owner;
  private String email;

  public Blog() {
  }

  /**
   * @hibernate.id             id is the ID field
   *     generator-class="uuid.string"   (primary key)
   */
  public String getId() {
    return id;
  }

  /**
   * @hibernate.property
   */
  public String getEmail() {
    return email;
  }

  /**
   * @hibernate.property       Persist
   */                          these
  public String getName() {    fields
    return name;
  }

  /**
   * @hibernate.property
   */
  public String getOwner() {
    return owner;
  }

  public void setEmail(String string) {
```

```
        email = string;
    }

    public void setId(String string) {
        id = string;
    }

    public void setName(String string) {
        name = string;
    }

    public void setOwner(String string) {
        owner = string;
    }
}
```

You tag `Blog.java` at the class level with `@hibernate.class` to tell XDoclet that `Blog.java` is a class to be persisted by Hibernate and that therefore XDoclet should generate a Hibernate mapping file. The `table` attribute specifies that instances of `Blog` are to be persisted to the `blog` relational database table.

The getter methods of `Blog.java` are tagged with `@hibernate.property` to indicate that these fields are the persistent fields of `Blog.java`. Every persisted object needs a primary key, so the `getId` method is tagged with `@hibernate.id` to indicate that the `id` field is the primary key for the `Blog` object. The `generator-class` attribute tells Hibernate how primary keys are to be generated for the persisted object. You set this attribute to "uuid.string" to generate a universally unique `String` value for the `id` field.

When the `<hibernate>` subtask processes `Blog.java`, it generates the following Hibernate mapping file, `Blog.hbm.xml`:

```xml
<?xml version="1.0"?>

<!DOCTYPE hibernate-mapping PUBLIC
    "-//Hibernate/Hibernate Mapping DTD 2.0//EN"
    "http://hibernate.sourceforge.net/hibernate-mapping-2.0.dtd">

<hibernate-mapping>
    <class
        name="com.xdocletbook.blog.pojo.Blog"
        table="Blog"
        dynamic-update="false"
    >

        <id
            name="id"
```

```
                column="id"
                type="java.lang.String"
                unsaved-value="any"
        >
                <generator class="uuid.string">
                </generator>
        </id>

        <property
            name="email"
            type="java.lang.String"
            update="true"
            insert="true"
            column="email"
        />

        <property
            name="name"
            type="java.lang.String"
            update="true"
            insert="true"
            column="name"
        />

        <property
            name="owner"
            type="java.lang.String"
            update="true"
            insert="true"
            column="owner"
        />

        <!--
            To add non XDoclet property mappings, create a file
            named hibernate-properties-Blog.xml containing the
            additional properties and place it in your merge dir.
        -->

    </class>
</hibernate-mapping>
```

To complete the object model of the application, you also write POJO implementations of `Entry.java` (listing 7.3) and `Topic.java` (listing 7.4), tagging them for Hibernate persistence the same way you did `Blog.java`.

Listing 7.3   Entry.java tagged to be persisted using Hibernate

```
package com.xdocletbook.blog.pojo;

import java.util.Date;

/**
```

```
 * @hibernate.class          Persist Entry objects
 *     table="Entry"          to Entry table
 */
public class Entry {
  private String id;
  private String text;
  private String title;
  private Date createdDate;

  public Entry() {
  }

  /**
   * @hibernate.id              Define primary
   *     generator-class="uuid.string"    key field
   */
  public String getId() {
    return id;
  }

  /**
   * @hibernate.property
   */
  public String getText() {
    return text;
  }

  /**                              Declare
   * @hibernate.property           persistent
   */                              fields
  public String getTitle() {
    return title;
  }

  /**
   * @hibernate.property
   */
  public Date getCreatedDate() {
    return createdDate;
  }

  public void setId(String string) {
    id = string;
  }

  public void setText(String string) {
    text = string;
  }

  public void setTitle(String string) {
    title = string;
```

```
  }

  public void setCreatedDate(Date date) {
    createdDate = date;
  }
}
```

Listing 7.4 Topic.java tagged for Hibernate persistence

```
package com.xdocletbook.blog.pojo;

/**
 * @hibernate.class              Persist Entry objects
 *      table="Topic"            to Topic table
 */
public class Topic {
  private String id;
  private String name;

  public Topic() {
  }

  /**
   * @hibernate.id                      <— Define primary key field
   *      generator-class="uuid.string"
   */
  public String getId() {
    return id;
  }

  /**
   * @hibernate.property   <— Declare persistent fields
   */
  public String getName() {
    return name;
  }

  public void setId(String string) {
    id = string;
  }

  public void setName(String string) {
    name = string;
  }
}
```

When these classes are processed by the <hibernate> subtask, the @hibernate tags guide <hibernate> in generating Entry.hbm.xml and Topic.hbm.xml mapping files. The generated Hibernate mapping files are almost ready for use in your application. But first, you must declare the relationships between your application objects.

Defining relationships

So far, the web-log classes have been rather simple, with only a handful of properties and a primary key. But the object model of the application is not quite so simple. Complex relationships exist between Blogs, Topics, and Entrys. How can XDoclet help you to define those relationships?

Let's consider the relationship between Blogs and Entrys. A Blog can have multiple Entrys, but each Entry belongs to only one Blog. From the perspective of a Blog, this is a one-to-many relationship. To define the Blog side of this relationship, you add a getEntries method and a setEntries method to Blog.java and tag it as shown in listing 7.5.

Listing 7.5   Changes to Blog.java defining the relationship to Entry.java

```
package com.xdocletbook.blog.pojo;

import java.util.Set;

/**
 * @hibernate.class
 */
public class Blog {
...
  private Set entries;

...

  /**
   * @hibernate.set
   *     lazy="true"
   *     cascade="all"
   *
   * @hibernate.collection-one-to-many
   *     class="com.xdocletbook.blog.pojo.Entry"
   *
   * @hibernate.collection-key
   *     column="blog"
   */
  public Set getEntries() {
    return entries;
  }
}
```

❶ Define Hibernate `<set>` collection

❷ Define one-to-many relationship between Blog and Entry

❸ Use blog field of Entry as collection key

```
    public void setEntries(Set set) {
        entries = set;
    }
}
```

❶ Use the `@hibernate.set` tag on `getEntries` to tell XDoclet to define a `<set>` definition in `Blog.hbm.xml` for the `Blog-Entry` relationship. By choosing a set as the collection type for the relationship, you're saying that each `Entry` within the relationship is unique.

❷ Because this relationship is a one-to-many relationship, you use the `@hibernate.collection-one-to-many` tag to define the nature of the relationship between `Blog` and `Entry`.

❸ You also tag the method with the `@hibernate.collection-key` tag to indicate that the `blog` field in an `Entry` is what links the `Entry` to a particular `Blog`. In database terms, the `blog` field is the foreign key on `Entry` to a `Blog`.

As a result of applying these changes to `Blog.java`, the following excerpt is added to `Blog.hbm.xml`:

```
<set
    name="entries"
    lazy="true"
    inverse="false"
    cascade="all"
    sort="unsorted"
>
  <key column="blog"/>

  <one-to-many
      class="com.xdocletbook.blog.pojo.Entry"/>
</set>
```

From the perspective of `Entry`, the relationship is many-to-one. To define this end of the relationship, you add a `blog` property to `Entry.java` and tag its getter method with `@hibernate.many-to-one`, as shown in listing 7.6.

Listing 7.6 Changes to Entry to define its relationship to Blog

```
package com.xdocletbook.blog.pojo;
import java.util.Date;

/**
 * @hibernate.class
 *     table="entry"
```

```
*/
public class Entry {
...
  private Blog blog;
...

  /**
   * @hibernate.many-to-one        ◁──❶   Define many-to-one
   */                                      relationship between
  public Blog getBlog() {                  Entry and Blog
    return blog;
  }

  public void setBlog(Blog blog) {
    this.blog = blog;
  }
}
```

❶ By tagging the getBlog method with @hibernate.many-to-one, you declare that this side of the relationship is many-to-one with Blog.

> **NOTE**   By default, Hibernate assumes that the foreign key is a field named the same as the type being returned; in this case, it expects the foreign key to be named blog. If the database column were named something else, you would use the column attribute of @hibernate.many-to-one to specify a different name.

When Entry.hbm.xml is generated, the following declaration is included as a result of the @hibernate.many-to-one tag:

```
<many-to-one
    name="blog"
    class="com.xdocletbook.blog.pojo.Blog"
    cascade="none"
    outer-join="auto"
    update="true"
    insert="true"
    column="blog"
/>
```

In addition to the Blog-Entry relationship, you can declare the Topic-Entry and Blog-Topic relationships in a similar fashion.

The mapping files are now complete. Let's look at how you can use the Hibernated classes in the web-log application.

7.1.3 *Using the Hibernated classes*

Everything in Hibernate works within the context of a Hibernate session (net.sf.hibernate.Session). A Session can be obtained from a SessionFactory (net.sf.hibernate.SessionFactory), which can be obtained from a Hibernate configuration (net.sf.hibernate.cfg.Configuration). The Session class has methods that allow you to create, load, delete, or update objects that are persisted using Hibernate.

As a demonstration of how to use these Hibernated objects, let's write Blog-FacadeHibernate.java (listing 7.7), a POJO version of the BlogFacadeBean.java that you wrote in chapter 3. This time, however, you use Hibernated classes instead of entity beans.

> **Listing 7.7   BlogFacadeHibernate.java uses Hibernated classes.**

```
package com.xdocletbook.blog.pojo;

import java.util.Collection;
import net.sf.hibernate.HibernateException;
import net.sf.hibernate.Session;
import net.sf.hibernate.cfg.Configuration;

import com.xdocletbook.blog.exception.ApplicationException;

public class BlogFacadeHibernate {
  private Session session;

  public BlogFacadeHibernate() throws ApplicationException {
    try {
      session =
          new Configuration().buildSessionFactory().openSession();   ← Set up Hibernate
    } catch (HibernateException e) {                                     session
      throw new ApplicationException(e);
    }
  }

  public Blog createBlog(String name, String owner, String email)
      throws ApplicationException {

    try {
      Blog blog = new Blog();
      blog.setName(name);
      blog.setOwner(owner);      ⎤ Create and
      blog.setEmail(email);      ⎥ save Blog
                                 ⎥ object
      session.save(blog);        ⎦
      return blog;
    } catch (HibernateException e) {
```

```
        throw new ApplicationException(e);
      }
    }

    public void deleteBlog(String blogId)
       throws ApplicationException {

      try {
        Blog blog = (Blog) session.load(Blog.class, blogId);
        session.delete(bloq);
      } catch (HibernateException e) {
        throw new ApplicationException(e);
      }
    }

    public Collection getTopics(String blogId)
       throws ApplicationException {



      try {
        Blog blog = (Blog) session.load(Blog.class, blogId);
        return blog.getTopics();
      } catch (HibernateException e) {
        throw new ApplicationException(e);
      }
    }

    protected void finalize() throws Throwable {
      session.close();
    }
  }
}
```

Look up Blog and then delete it

Get all Topics belonging to Blog

Close session at garbage-collection time

As a façade class, BlogFacadeHibernate.java exposes some important business functionality while hiding the details of working with Hibernate. Now the web-log application completely relies on Hibernate to perform data persistence.

Although Hibernate is a very good choice for non-EJB data persistence, it's not the only choice. Next we'll look at Sun's Java Data Objects specification and see how XDoclet can help you generate mapping metadata files to be used with JDO.

7.2 Persisting data with JDO

Sun Microsystems answered the call for transparent data persistence by creating the JDO specification. As a specification, JDO defines a standard for Java data persistence to be implemented by a third-party vendor. Even though JDO is a relatively new specification, several implementations already exist, including Sun's reference implementation, Triactive's JDO, LIBeLIS's LiDO, and Solarmetric's Kodo.

JDO takes a slightly different approach to object persistence than Hibernate does. Like Hibernate, JDO uses an XML file to define metadata that maps Java objects and relational tables. But where Hibernate applies the mapping rules at runtime, JDO-persisted classes are *enhanced* post-compile to include persistence logic.

You'll use XDoclet to generate the JDO metadata files for the objects in the web-log application. Then, after they're compiled, you'll enhance them to be persisted by JDO. Let's begin by modifying the build to include the XDoclet task and subtasks that generate JDO metadata files.

7.2.1 Adding JDO generation to the build

The `<jdodoclet>` task is used to generate the metadata files that define the object/database mappings for JDO. Table 7.2 shows the subtasks of `<jdodoclet>`.

Table 7.2 `<jdodoclet>` subtasks and the types of files they generate

Subtask	Description
`<jdometadata>`	Generates object-relational mapping metadata files for JDO persistence
`<kodo>`	Adds Solarmetric Kodo-specific metadata to the JDO mapping file
`<lido>`	Adds LIBeLIS LiDO-specific metadata to the JDO mapping file
`<triactive>`	Adds Triactive JDO-specific metadata to the JDO mapping file

To accommodate JDO mapping generation, create `build-jdo.xml` (listing 7.8), a new sub-build file specific to the JDO portion of the build.

Listing 7.8   build-jdo.xml adds JDO-specific generation to the build.

```xml
<?xml version="1.0" encoding="UTF-8"?>

<project name="Blog" default="generate-jdo" basedir=".">
  <path id="xdoclet.lib.path">
    <fileset dir="${xdoclet.lib.dir}">
      <include name="*.jar"/>
    </fileset>
    <fileset dir="${lib.dir}">
      <include name="*.jar"/>
    </fileset>
```

```
    </path>

    <target name="generate-jdo">
      <taskdef name="jdodoclet"
          classname="xdoclet.modules.jdo.JdoDocletTask"
          classpathref="xdoclet.lib.path" />

      <!-- Generate Hibernate mapping files -->
      <jdodoclet destdir="${jdo.dir}"
          mergeDir="${merge.dir}">
        <fileset dir="${src.dir}">
          <include name="**/*.java" />
        </fileset>

        <jdometadata
            havingClassTag="jdo.persistence-capable"
        />
      </jdodoclet>
    </target>
  </project>
```

Generate
JDO metadata
files

You include the `<jdometadata>` subtask of `<jdodoclet>` in the build to have XDoclet generate a JDO mapping file that meets the minimum JDO specifications and that will work with Sun's reference implementation of JDO. For now, assume that you'll be using the reference implementation. But, as you'll see later, `<jdometadata>` works in concert with other vendor-specific subtasks to include JDO vendor extensions to the generated mapping file.

Notice that you also set the `havingClassTag` attribute of `<jdometadata>` to "jdo.persistence-capable". By default, `<jdometadata>` creates a mapping file for all classes that it finds in the specified `<fileset>`. For your purposes, you want to narrow the focus of `<jdometadata>` to those classes that are tagged with the class-level `@jdo.persistence-capable` tag.

You must also include a call to the `generate-jdo` target of build-jdo.xml in the main build file. The following excerpt from `build.xml` shows how you use the `<ant>` task to add this call:

```
  <target name="generate">
    <ant antfile="build-ejbgen.xml" target="generate-ejb"/>
    <ant antfile="build-webgen.xml" target="generate-web"/>
    <ant antfile="build-hibernate.xml" target="generate-hibernate"/>
    <ant antfile="build-jdo.xml" target="generate-jdo"/>
  </target>
```

The build file is now ready to generate JDO mapping files. Next you must tag your classes with XDoclet tags to declare the mapping metadata.

7.2.2 Tagging classes for JDO persistence

Take a look at how you tag `Blog.java` in listing 7.9. Notice anything unusual?

Listing 7.9 Blog.java tagged for persistence with JDO

```
package com.xdocletbook.blog.pojo;
import java.util.Set;

/**
 * @jdo.persistence-capable          Declare this class as
 *     identity-type="application"   persistence-capable
 */
public class Blog {
  /**
   * @jdo.field                 Declare id property
   *     primary-key="true"     to be primary key
   */
  private String id;

  /**
   * @jdo.field
   *     null-value="exception"
   */
  private String name;

  /**
   * @jdo.field                 These properties are
   *     null-value="exception" JDO persistable
   */
  private String owner;

  /**
   * @jdo.field
   *     null-value="exception"
   */
  private String email;

  public Blog() {
  }

  public String getId() {
    return id;
  }

  public String getEmail() {
    return email;
  }

  public String getName() {
    return name;
  }
```

```
public String getOwner() {
  return owner;
}

public void setEmail(String string) {
  email = string;
}

public void setId(String string) {
  id = string;
}

public void setName(String string) {
  name = string;
}

public void setOwner(String string) {
  owner = string;
}
}
```

You tag `Blog.java` at the class level with `@jdo.persistence-capable`. This tag tells XDoclet that this class should be included in the generated JDO mapping file so that it can be persisted using JDO.

The `identity-type` attribute of `@jdo.persistence-capable` indicates how JDO should identify an object that it persists. You set `identity-type` to "application", indicating that one of `Blog`'s properties will be used as a primary key to uniquely identify a `Blog`. Nothing much seems out of the ordinary with how you used `@jdo.persistence-capable`.

But did you see the `@jdo.field` tag? It's neither a class-level tag nor a method-level tag. Unlike any other tag you've seen up until now, `@jdo.field` is a property-level tag. By applying this tag to all your `Blog` properties, you declare them to be persisted by JDO. In the case of the `id` property, you set the `primary-key` attribute to "true", indicating that `id` is the primary key.

As for the other properties, you set the `null-value` attribute to "exception", telling JDO that if one of these properties is null when a `Blog` is persisted, then a `JDOUserException` should be thrown.

When `<jdometadata>` processes `Blog.java`, the following mapping metadata is written to `Blog.jdo`:

```
<?xml version="1.0" encoding="UTF-8"?>
<!DOCTYPE jdo PUBLIC
  "-//Sun Microsystems, Inc.//DTD Java Data Objects Metadata 1.0//EN"
  "http://java.sun.com/dtd/jdo_1_0.dtd">
```

```
<jdo>
  <package name="com.xdocletbook.blog.pojo">
    <class name="Blog"
          identity-type="application"
      > <!-- end class tag -->
      <field name="id"
            primary-key="true"
      > <!-- end field tag -->
      </field>
      <field name="name"
            null-value="exception"
      > <!-- end field tag -->
      </field>
      <field name="owner"
            null-value="exception"
      > <!-- end field tag -->
      </field>
      <field name="email"
            null-value="exception"
      > <!-- end field tag -->
      </field>
    </class>
  </package>
</jdo>
```

Now that you've defined the metadata for mapping the simple properties of `Blog.java`, you need to declare the relationships that `Blogs` have with `Entrys` and `Topics`.

Tagging JDO relationships

Let's look at the relationship between a `Topic` and its `Entrys` to see how XDoclet can help to define relationships for JDO persistence capable classes. This relationship is one-to-many because a `Topic` can have several `Entrys`, but an `Entry` belongs to exactly one `Topic`. Modify `Topic.java` (as shown in listing 7.10) to define how `Topic` relates to `Entry`.

Listing 7.10 Topic.java tagged to define the relationship between a Topic and its Entrys

```
package com.xdocletbook.blog.pojo;
import java.util.Set;

/**
 * @jdo.persistence-capable
 *     identity-type="application"
 *     objectid-class="java.lang.String"
 */
public class Topic {
...
```

```
/**
 * @jdo.field
 *     collection-type="collection"
 *     element-type="com.xdocletbook.blog.pojo.Entry"
 */
private Set entries;

...

public Set getEntries() {
  return entries;
}

public void setEntries(Set entries) {
  this.entries = entries;
}
}
```

① entries property is a collection of Entry objects

① Just as you did for the other properties, you tag the entries property with the property-level `@jdo.field` tag. This time, however, you use the `collection-type` attribute to indicate that this property is a *collection*. This means the property's type is any subclass of `java.util.Collection` (in this case, `java.util.Set`). If entries were an array, you'd set `collection-type` to "array" instead of "collection". Or, if the property were a `java.util.Map`, you'd set `collection-type` to "map".

You also set the `element-type` attribute to "com.xdocletbook.blog.pojo.Entry", declaring that each element of the collection is an instance of `Entry`.

That's all that's needed to declare the `Topic` side of the relationship. When `<jdometadata>` processes `Topic.java`, the `@jdo.field` tag yields the following mapping written to the generated `Topic.jdo` file:

```
<field name="entries"
> <!-- end field tag -->
  <collection
      element-type="com.xdocletbook.blog.pojo.Entry"
  > <!-- end collection tag -->
  </collection>
</field>
```

Declaring the many side of a one-to-many relationship is even simpler. Because the `Topic` class is persistence-capable, it's equal to `java.lang.String` or any other persistence-capable class as far as JDO is concerned. Therefore, you can declare the `topic` property of `Entry.java` the same way you declared its other properties. Listing 7.11 shows how you tag the `topic` property of `Entry.java` to define this side of the relationship.

Listing 7.11 Entry.java with the topic property tagged for the Topic-Entry relationship

```
package com.xdocletbook.blog.pojo;
import java.util.Date;

/**
 * @jdo.persistence-capable
 *     identity-type="application"
 *     objectid-class="java.lang.String"
 */
public class Entry {
...

  /**
   * @jdo.field                        Persist
   *     null-value="exception"        topic field
   */
  private Topic topic;

...

  public Topic getTopic() {
    return topic;
  }

  public void setTopic(Topic topic) {
    this.topic = topic;
  }
}
```

When the `<jdometadata>` subtask processes `Entry.java`, the following, rather non-exciting, JDO metadata entry is created in `Entry.jdo` for the `topic` field:

```
<field name="topic"
    null-value="exception"
> <!-- end field tag -->
</field>
```

Now that you've generated JDO metadata files for each of your objects, let's see how you can plug them into the web-log application.

7.2.3 *Using the JDO persistence-capable classes*

To demonstrate how to use JDO-persisted classes, let's use these persistence-capable classes in the web-log application in place of entity beans. But, before you can plug the JDO-persisted classes into the web-log application, you must make them persistence-capable with JDO.

Enhancing the compiled classes

Classes that are to be persisted in JDO must implement the `javax.jdo.spi.Per-sistenceCapable` interface. But hold on—your classes don't implement that interface. Do you need to make changes to your code to implement these interfaces? The answer is no.

The JDO specification requires that a JDO implementation provide a *JDO enhancer.* A JDO enhancer is a tool that rips open an existing class and, using a JDO metadata file as its guide, adds code to the class file so that the class implements `PersistenceCapable`. Figure 7.2 shows the process of enhancing a compiled class to make it persistence-capable.

To accommodate JDO enhancement in your build, add the following `enhance-jdo` target to the `build-jdo.xml` file:

```
<target name="enhance-jdo">
  <java fork="yes" failonerror="yes"
      classname="${enhancer.class}"
      classpathref="compile.path">
    <arg line="-f -d ${build.dir}
        ${generated.dir}/jdo/com/xdocletbook/blog/pojo/*.jdo
        ${build.dir}/com/xdocletbook/blog/pojo/*.class"/>
  </java>
</target>
```

The `enhancer.class` Ant property determines which enhancer to use. Setting `enhancer.class` to "com.sun.jdori.enhancer.Main" indicates that you want to enhance your classes for use with Sun's reference implementation of JDO.

Now, when you run the `enhance-jdo` target, your POJOs are enhanced to be JDO persistence-capable. Let's see how you can use these classes instead of entity beans within the web-log application.

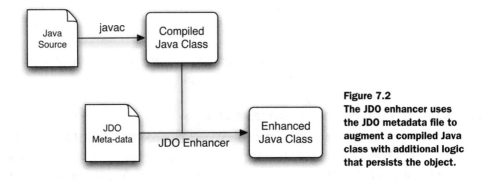

Figure 7.2
The JDO enhancer uses the JDO metadata file to augment a compiled Java class with additional logic that persists the object.

Blogging with the enhanced classes

The EJB version of the web-log application used a stateless session bean called `BlogFacade` that acted as a façade for the entity beans that made up the web-log object model. Because you're interested in replacing the EJB-layer of the web-log application with a persistence layer based on JDO, you need to construct a POJO equivalent of the `BlogFacade` bean.

Create `BlogFacadeJdo.java` (listing 7.12) as a façade for the JDO-persisted POJO classes. `BlogFacadeJdo.java` performs the same business functionality as `BlogFacadeHibernate.java` and `BlogFacadeBean.java`, but it uses JDO-enhanced classes instead of Hibernated POJOs or entity beans.

Listing 7.12   BlogFacadeJdo.java: manipulating JDO-persisted objects

```java
package com.xdocletbook.blog.pojo;

import java.io.IOException;
import java.io.InputStream;
import java.util.Collection;
import java.util.Properties;
import javax.jdo.JDOFatalInternalException;
import javax.jdo.JDOHelper;
import javax.jdo.PersistenceManager;
import javax.jdo.PersistenceManagerFactory;
import javax.jdo.Transaction;
import com.xdocletbook.blog.exception.ApplicationException;

public class BlogFacadeJdo implements BlogFacade {

  private static PersistenceManagerFactory factory = null;
  private PersistenceManager pm = null;

  public static PersistenceManagerFactory
      getPersistenceManagerFactory () {
    if (factory == null) {
      Properties props = new Properties ();
      try {
        InputStream in =
            ClassLoader.getSystemResourceAsStream("jdo.properties");
        props.load (in);
      } catch (IOException ioe) {
        throw new JDOFatalInternalException(
            "Cannot load property file'", ioe);
      }
      factory = JDOHelper.getPersistenceManagerFactory (props);
    }
    return factory;
  }
```

```java
private PersistenceManager getPersistenceManager () {
 if (pm == null) {
   pm = getPersistenceManagerFactory().getPersistenceManager();
 }
 return pm;
}

public Blog createBlog(String name, String owner, String email)
    throws ApplicationException {

  Transaction tx - pm.currentTransaction();
  try {
    Blog blog = new Blog();
    blog.setName(name);
    blog.setOwner(owner);
    blog.setEmail(email);

    getPersistenceManager().makePersistent(blog);
    tx.commit();

    return blog;
  } finally {
    if(tx.isActive()) {
      tx.rollback();
    }
  }
}

public void deleteBlog(String blogId)
    throws ApplicationException {

  Transaction tx = pm.currentTransaction();
  try {
    Blog blog = (Blog)pm.getObjectById(blogId, false);
    pm.deletePersistent(blog);
    tx.commit();
  } finally {
    if(tx.isActive()) {
      tx.rollback();
    }
  }
}

public Collection getTopics(String blogId)
    throws ApplicationException {

  Blog blog =
      (Blog)getPersistenceManager().getObjectById(blogId, false);

  return blog.getTopics();
}
}
```

- **Create and initialize Blog object** (annotation on `Blog blog = new Blog(); blog.setName(name); blog.setOwner(owner); blog.setEmail(email);`)
- ← **Persist Blog object** (annotation on `getPersistenceManager().makePersistent(blog);`)
- ← **Look up Blog by its ID** (annotation on `Blog blog = (Blog)pm.getObjectById(blogId, false);`)
- ← **Delete Blog object** (annotation on `pm.deletePersistent(blog);`)
- **Look up Blog by its ID** (annotation on `(Blog)getPersistenceManager().getObjectById(blogId, false);`)
- ← **Get all topics related to Blog** (annotation on `return blog.getTopics();`)

By changing the web-layer components (servlets, filters, Struts actions, and/or WebWork actions) to use `BlogFacadeJdo` instead of the `BlogFacade` session bean, you make the web-log application rely on JDO as the persistence mechanism instead of entity beans.

You've seen how XDoclet can be used to generate metadata mapping files for basic JDO functionality. But what if you want to take advantage of some of the vendor extensions to JDO that are offered with the JDO implementation you're using? Let's see how XDoclet supports nonstandard JDO features.

7.2.4 *Working with vendor extensions*

Sun's reference implementation of JDO is fine for experimenting with JDO. But because it persists objects to the filesystem instead of to a database, it's not suitable for most production systems. Instead, you're likely to use one of the many other JDO implementations available.

Aside from support for writing the specification's standard JDO metadata files, XDoclet also supports the vendor extensions to JDO for the following JDO implementations:

- Triactive JDO (http://tjdo.sourceforge.net)
- Solarmetric's Kodo (http://www.solarmetric.com)
- LIBeLIS's LiDO (http://www.libelis.com)

Fortunately, the JDO specification has support for vendor extensions built in; therefore additional vendor-specific metadata files are not needed. Instead, vendor extension metadata is injected directly into the same JDO metadata mapping file used by Sun's reference implementation.

JDO vendor extensions take the following form in the metadata file:

```
<extension vendor-name="{vendor name}"
    key="{extension key}"
    value="{extension value}"/>
```

For example, to set the maximum size of a `String` field to 30 characters using Triactive JDO, you include the following `<extension>` declaration in the JDO metadata file:

```
<extension vendor-name="triactive"
    key="length"
    value="max 30"/>
```

There are two ways to include vendor-specific JDO metadata in the generated JDO metadata files:

- Use XDoclet subtasks and tags for the three supported JDO implementations.

- Use the `@jdo.*-vendor-extension` tags.

We'll start by looking at how to use the subtasks and tags for the supported JDO implementations and then see how XDoclet generically supports any vendor extension to JDO.

Adapting the build for supported JDO vendor extensions

XDoclet comes with three vendor-specific subtasks of `<jdodoclet>` to support vendor extensions. Table 7.3 lists the subtasks alongside the JDO implementation they support.

Table 7.3   Vendor-specific subtasks of `<jdodoclet>`

JDO implementation	`<jdodoclet>` subtask
LiDO	`<lido>`
Kodo	`<kodo>`
Triactive JDO	`<triactive>`

What's unusual about these subtasks is that instead of generating a different vendor-specific JDO metadata file, they augment the behavior of the `<jdometadata>` subtask. As a result of using these subtasks, the same JDO file that `<jdometadata>` writes will also include vendor-specific metadata for JDO persistence.

We're using Triactive's JDO implementation for the web-log application, so add the `<triactive>` subtask to the generate-jdo target of `build-jdo.xml`:

```
<target name="generate-jdo">
  <taskdef name="jdodoclet"
    classname="xdoclet.modules.jdo.JdoDocletTask"
    classpathref="xdoclet.lib.path" />

  <jdodoclet destdir="${jdo.dir}"
      mergeDir="${merge.dir}">
    <fileset dir="${src.dir}">
        <include name="**/*.java" />
    </fileset>

    <jdometadata
        havingClassTag="jdo.persistence-capable"
    />

    <triactive/>
  </jdodoclet>
</target>
```

The `<triactive>` subtask processes the POJO source code, looking for `@tjdo` tags that define Triactive JDO-specific metadata to be placed in the mapping file. Let's look at an example of a `@tjdo` tag and see how `<triactive>` processes it.

Tagging classes for XDoclet-supported JDO vendor extensions

Triactive JDO mandates that persistent `String` fields must have a length specified in the JDO metadata file. Almost all the fields of the web-log objects are `String`s, so you need to declare field lengths for them. How can you specify a field length for the `String` fields using XDoclet?

The Triactive JDO module that comes with XDoclet defines a `@tjdo.field` tag to specify Triactive JDO metadata extensions. The `column-length` attribute of `@tjdo.field` is just what you need to specify field lengths. The following excerpt from `Entry.java` shows how you apply the `@tjdo.field` tag to the `String` fields of the Entry POJO:

```
public class Entry {
  /**
   * @jdo.field
   *      primary-key="true"
   *
   * @tjdo.field
   *      column-length="32"
   */

  private String id;
  /**
   * @jdo.field
   *      null-value="exception"
   *
   * @tjdo.field
   *      column-length="unlimited"
   */

  private String text;
  /**
   * @jdo.field
   *      null-value="exception"
   *
   * @tjdo.field
   *      column-length="max 80"
   */

  private String title;
  ...
}
```

The id field will always be exactly 32 characters, so you set the column-length attribute to "32" for that field. However, the other fields are of variable length. The title field, for instance, will vary in length, but will be no longer than 80 characters. So, you set its column-length to "max 80" to indicate a maximum length of 80. The text field, on the other hand, will vary in length and has no maximum length. Therefore, you set its column-length to "unlimited".

As a result of your using the @tjdo.field tag with Entry.java, the generated Entry.jdo file contains the following field definitions:

```
<field name="id"
    primary-key="true"
> <!-- end field tag -->
  <extension vendor-name="triactive" key="length" value="32"/>
</field>
<field name="text"
    null-value="exception"
> <!-- end field tag -->
  <extension vendor-name="triactive" key="length"
      value="unlimited"/>
</field>
<field name="title"
    null-value="exception"
> <!-- end field tag -->
  <extension vendor-name="triactive" key="length"
      value="max 80"/>
</field>
```

This works great if you're using Triactive JDO. But what if you're using a JDO implementation other than the ones directly supported with XDoclet tags? Or, what if you're using a new feature of Triactive that XDoclet doesn't support yet? Let's look at how you can have XDoclet include vendor extension definitions even when there isn't an XDoclet tag for the extension.

Tagging classes for any JDO vendor extensions

Take another look at the field definitions that were generated as a result of the @tjdo.field tag. You may have noticed that the resulting <extension> definition doesn't look all that special. In fact, @tjdo.field is nothing more than a convenient and easily memorable way to create <extension> definitions for Triactive JDO.

But there's a more generic way to define <extension> definitions in XDoclet. Look at the following excerpt from a slightly modified version of Entry.java:

```
public class Entry {
   /**
    * @jdo.field
```

```
 *       primary-key="true"
 *
 * @jdo.field-vendor-extension
 *       vendor-name="triactive"
 *       key="length"
 *       value="32"
 */
private String id;

/**
 * @jdo.field
 *       null-value="exception"
 *
 * @jdo.field-vendor-extension
 *       vendor-name="triactive"
 *       key="length"
 *       value="unlimited"
 */
private String text;

/**
 * @jdo.field
 *       null-value="exception"
 *
 * @jdo.field-vendor-extension
 *       vendor-name="triactive"
 *       key="length"
 *       value="max 80"
 */
private String title;
...
}
```

The `@jdo.field-vendor-extension` tag is a way to generically add vendor extension definitions to fields in the generated JDO metadata file. Using it the way we have here is functionally identical to how you used the `@tjdo.field` tag in the previous excerpt. The same definitions are written to the generated JDO metadata file.

JDO was a long-anticipated specification from Sun. But the developer community grew impatient waiting for the specification to be released and implemented. By the time JDO saw the light of day, other persistence options had been developed. The final persistence framework that we'll look at in this chapter is one of the options that came out of impatience: Castor.

7.3 *Persisting data with Castor*

Another very popular choice for Java data persistence is Exolab's Castor (http://castor.exolab.org). Castor comes in three flavors:

- *Castor JDO*—Used to persist data to and from a relational database
- *Castor XML*—Used to persist data to and from XML
- *Castor DAX*—Used to persist data to and from an LDAP directory

Despite its suspicious name, Castor JDO is not an implementation of Sun's JDO specification. In fact, Castor JDO more closely resembles Hibernate than JDO. Like Hibernate, Castor JDO maps Java objects and object properties to relational tables and columns at runtime using an XML mapping file. In a similar way, Castor XML uses the mapping file to persist Java objects to XML files, and Castor DAX uses the mapping file to persist Java objects to LDAP directories.

XDoclet has a Castor module that comes with support for generating Castor mapping files for Castor JDO and Castor XML. At this time, XDoclet doesn't directly support Castor DAX, so we'll only discuss Castor JDO and Castor XML. Let's look at how you can use XDoclet to generate Castor mapping files.

7.3.1 *Adding Castor generation to the build*

So that XDoclet can generate the Castor mapping file for you, you must add the <castormapping> subtask to your build file. To keep things organized, create build-castor.xml (listing 7.13), a sub-build file containing the Castor portion of the build.

Listing 7.13 build-castor.xml contains the Castor-specific portion of the build.

```
<?xml version="1.0" encoding="UTF-8"?>

<project name="Blog" default="generate-castor" basedir=".">
  <path id="xdoclet.lib.path">
    <fileset dir="${xdoclet.lib.dir}">
      <include name="*.jar"/>
    </fileset>
    <fileset dir="${lib.dir}">
      <include name="*.jar"/>
    </fileset>
  </path>

  <target name="generate-castor">
    <taskdef name="ejbdoclet"
        classname="xdoclet.modules.ejb.EjbDocletTask"
        classpathref="xdoclet.lib.path" />
```

```
      <ejbdoclet destdir="${castor.dir}"        <castormapping> is a
        mergeDir="${merge.dir}">                subtask of <ejbdoclet> task
        <fileset dir="${src.dir}">
          <include name="**/*.java" />
        </fileset>

        <castormapping/>      <─  Generate Castor mapping file
      </ejbdoclet>
    </target>
  </project>
```

Looking at `build-castor.xml`, you may be puzzled that `<castormapping>` is a sub-task of `<ejbdoclet>`. You're not alone—it struck us as a bit odd, too. It seems strange that a subtask having nothing to do with EJBs is used in `<ejbdoclet>`. The likely reason is historical, going back to the roots of XDoclet. Recall that XDoclet evolved out of EJBDoclet. `<castormapping>` may have been created without realizing that it could have been created along with a `<castordoclet>` task.

You must now edit your main build file to call `build-castor.xml`. The following excerpt from `build.xml` shows that you add an additional `<ant>` task to the generate target:

```
<target name="generate">
  <ant antfile="build-ejbgen.xml" target="generate-ejb"/>
  <ant antfile="build-webgen.xml" target="generate-web"/>
  <ant antfile="build-hibernate.xml" target="generate-hibernate"/>
  <ant antfile="build-jdo.xml" target="generate-jdo"/>
  <ant antfile="build-castor.xml" target="generate-castor"/>
</target>
```

Now that your build is prepared for generating Castor mapping files, you must tag the application object classes to provide the meta-information needed for the mapping definitions.

7.3.2 Persisting objects using Castor JDO

Just as you've done before with Hibernate and JDO, you'll start by tagging `Blog.java` with the `@castor` tags as shown in listing 7.14.

Listing 7.14 Blog.java tagged to be mapped in Castor

```
package com.xdocletbook.blog.pojo;

/**                          ❶ This class will be
 * @castor.class              persisted with Castor
 *    id="id"    <─❷ id field is
                    primary key
```

```
 *    table="Blog"
 */
public class Blog {
  private String id;
  private String name;
  private String owner;
  private String email;
  private Set topics;
  private Set entries;

  public Blog() {
  }

  /**
   * @castor.field
   *     set-method="setId"
   *
   * @castor.field-sql
   *     name="id"
   *     type="char"
   */
  public String getId() {
    return id;
  }

  /**
   * @castor.field
   *     set-method="setEmail"
   *
   * @castor.field-sql
   *     name="email"
   *     type="char"
   */
  public String getEmail() {
    return email;
  }

  /**
   * @castor.field
   *     set-method="setName"
   *
   * @castor.field-sql
   *     name="name"
   *     type="char"
   */
  public String getName() {
    return name;
  }

  /**
   * @castor.field
   *     set-method="setOwner"
```

❸ Map this object to Blog table

❺ Map this field to database column

❹ Define this field's setter method

```
 *
 * @castor.field-sql
 *      name="owner"
 *      type="char"
 */
public String getOwner() {
  return owner;
}

public void setEmail(String string) {
  email = string;
}

public void setId(String string) {
  id = string;
}

public void setName(String string) {
  name = string;
}

public void setOwner(String string) {
  owner = string;
}
}
```

❺ Map this field to database column

❶ Use the `@castor.class` tag at the class level to declare that `Blog.java` will be persisted using Castor. This tag is the bare minimum required by XDoclet to include a class in the generated mapping file.

❷ The `id` attribute indicates that the `id` field is the primary key.

❸ Set the `table` attribute of `@castor.class` to indicate that `Blog.java` should be persisted to the `Blog` table.

❹ At the method level, you indicate the properties to be persisted using the `@castor.field` tag on each property's getter method. So that Castor can populate the properties when an object is loaded, the `set-method` attribute defines the setter method for the property. Also at the method level is the `@castor.field-sql` tag, which declares the specifics of how a property is to be persisted.

❺ The `name` attribute indicates the name of the field in the relational table to which the property is to be persisted. The SQL data type is indicated using the `type` attribute.

Why are there two different tags to define how each property is to be persisted? Why couldn't the attributes all belong to the `@castor.field` tag? As you'll see later, you can also use Castor to persist data to XML. The `@castor.field` tag declares metadata generic to either SQL or XML persistence, but the specifics of persisting to SQL and XML are declared using `@castor.field-sql` and `@castor.field-xml` respectively.

When `<castormapping>` processes `Blog.java`, it generates the following `mapping.xml` file:

```
<?xml version="1.0"?>

<!DOCTYPE mapping PUBLIC
    "-//EXOLAB/Castor Mapping DTD Version 1.0//EN"
    "http://castor.exolab.org/mapping.dtd">

<mapping>
  <!-- ===================================================== -->
  <!--   Mapping for class com.xdocletbook.blog.pojo.Blog   -->
  <!-- ===================================================== -->

  <class name="com.xdocletbook.blog.pojo.Blog"
         identity="id"
         access="shared"
         auto-complete="false">
    <map-to table="Blog" />
    <cache-type type="count-limited" />

    <field name="id"
           type="java.lang.String"
           get-method="getId"
           set-method="setId">
      <sql name="id"
           type="char" />
    </field>

    <field name="email"
           type="java.lang.String"
           get-method="getEmail"
           set-method="setEmail">
      <sql name="email"
           type="char" />
    </field>

    <field name="name"
           type="java.lang.String"
           get-method="getName"
           set-method="setName">
      <sql name="name"
           type="char" />
    </field>
```

```
      <field name="owner"
             type="java.lang.String"
             get-method="getOwner"
             set-method="setOwner">
        <sql name="owner"
             type="char" />
      </field>

   </class>

   <!--
      Define your key-generator declaration in a file called
      key-generator.xml and place it in your merge directory.
      -->
</mapping>
```

In addition to Blog.java, you can also tag Entry.java and Topic.java with @castor tags to be persisted by Castor. At this point, you've tagged the classes for simple persistence with Castor. Now let's add the methods and XDoclet tags that define the relationships between the application objects.

Tagging to define relationships

To demonstrate how you can define relationships in Castor using XDoclet, let's examine the relationship between a Blog and its Topics. A Blog can have multiple Topics, but each Topic belongs to exactly one Blog. From the Blog side, this is a one-to-many relationship. To define the Blog side of this relationship, you add a getTopics method and a setTopics method to Blog.java and tag it as shown in listing 7.15.

Listing 7.15 Blog.java changed to add the relationship to Topic

```
package com.xdocletbook.blog.pojo;
import java.util.Set;

/**
 * @castor.class
 *    id="id"
 *    table="Blog"
 */
public class Blog {
...
  private Set topics;

  public Blog() {
  }

...
```

```
/**
 * @castor.field
 *       collection="set"
 *       type="com.xdocletbook.blog.pojo.Topic"
 *       set-method="setTopics"
 *
 * @castor.field-sql
 *       many-key="blog"
 */
public Set getTopics() {
  return topics;
}

public void setTopics(Set set) {
  topics = set;
}
}
```

❶ Define Castor set collection

❷ Topic's blog field is the foreign key

❶ Use the `collection` attribute of the `@castor.field` tag to indicate that the `topics` property is a `java.util.Set`. When used with the `collection` attribute, the `type` attribute indicates the type of object contained in the collection—`com.xdoclet-book.blog.pojo.Topic` in this case.

❷ The `many-key` attribute of `@castor.field-sql` specifies that the `blog` field of `Topic` contains the primary key of the `Blog` to which it's related. In database terms, you can think of this as the foreign key field.

The following excerpt from `mapping.xml` shows how the `<castormapping>` subtask defines the `Blog` side of the `Blog/Topic` relationship:

```
<class name="com.xdocletbook.blog.pojo.Blog"
...

  <field name="topics"
      type="com.xdocletbook.blog.pojo.Topic"
      get-method="getTopics"
      set-method="setTopics"
      collection="set">
    <sql
        many-key="blog" />
  </field>

</class>
```

Defining the `Topic` side of the `Blog/Topic` relationship is fairly straightforward. Listing 7.16 shows how you add `getBlog` and `setBlog` methods and tag them appropriately for the relationship.

Listing 7.16 The relationship between a Topic and a Blog in Topic.java

```
package com.xdocletbook.blog.pojo;

...
public class Topic {
...
  private Blog blog;

  ...

  /**
   * @castor.field
   *     type="com.xdocletbook.blog.pojo.Blog"        blog property is com.
   *     set-method="setBlog"                          xdocletbook.blog.pojo.Blog
   *
   * @castor.field-sql        blog field contains
   *     name="blog"          lookup key
   */
  public Blog getBlog() {
    return blog;
  }

  public void setBlog(Blog blog) {
    this.blog = blog;
  }
}
```

The `@castor` tags you applied to the `getBlog` method do nothing to make it obvious that this is the many side of a one-to-many relationship. The `type` attribute of `@castor.field` simply indicates that the field is a `com.xdocletbook.blog.pojo.Blog` object. Hibernate uses the `blog` field's value as the key to look up the `Blog` that is related to a `Topic`.

In the generated `mapping.xml` file, the `Topic` side of the `Blog/Topic` relationship is represented as follows:

```
<field name="blog"
    type="com.xdocletbook.blog.pojo.Blog"
    get-method="getBlog"
    set-method="setBlog">
  <sql name="blog" />
</field>
```

7.3.3 Using objects persisted with Castor JDO

`BlogFacadeCastor.java` (listing 7.17) is a POJO version of the `BlogFacade-Bean.java` that you wrote in chapter 3. It differs from its EJB counterpart in that instead of using entity beans for persistence, it uses the Castor-persisted classes you wrote in this chapter.

Listing 7.17   BlogFacadeCastor.java

```
package com.xdocletbook.blog.pojo;
import java.util.ArrayList;
import java.util.Collection;
import java.util.List;
import org.exolab.castor.jdo.Database;
import org.exolab.castor.jdo.JDO;
import org.exolab.castor.jdo.OQLQuery;
import org.exolab.castor.jdo.PersistenceException;
import org.exolab.castor.jdo.QueryResults;
import com.xdocletbook.blog.exception.ApplicationException;

public class BlogFacadeCastor implements BlogFacade {
  private static final String DB_NAME = "blog";
  private JDO jdo;
  private Database db;

  public static BlogFacadeCastor getInstance(String configFile)
      throws ApplicationException {
    return new BlogFacadeCastor(configFile);
  }

  private BlogFacadeCastor(String configFile)
      throws ApplicationException {
    jdo = new JDO();
    jdo.setConfiguration(configFile);
    jdo.setClassLoader(getClass().getClassLoader());
    jdo.setDatabaseName(DB_NAME);

    try {
      db = jdo.getDatabase();
    } catch (PersistenceException e) {
      throw new ApplicationException(e);
    }
  }

  public Collection getAllBlogs() throws ApplicationException {
    String select =
        "SELECT b FROM com.xdocletbook.blog.pojo.Blog b";

    try {
      db.begin();

      OQLQuery query = db.getOQLQuery(select);
      QueryResults results = query.execute();
```

❶ Set up Castor JDO database

❷ Look up all Blogs using OQL

```
      List resultsList = new ArrayList();
      while(results.hasMore()) {
        resultsList.add(results.next());
      }

      return resultsList;
    } catch (PersistenceException e) {
      throw new ApplicationException(e);
    } finally {
      try {
        db.rollback();
      } catch (Exception e) {}
    }
  }

  public Blog createBlog(String name, String owner, String email)
        throws ApplicationException {

    Blog blog = new Blog();
    blog.setName(name);
    blog.setOwner(owner);
    blog.setEmail(email);

    try {
      db.begin();
      db.create(blog);
      db.commit();
    } catch(PersistenceException e) {
      throw new ApplicationException(e);
    } finally {
      try {
        db.rollback();
      } catch (Exception e) {
      }
    }

    return blog;
  }

  public void deleteBlog(String blogId)
        throws ApplicationException {

    try {
      db.begin();
      Blog blog = (Blog) db.load(Blog.class, blogId);
      db.remove(blog);
      db.commit();
    } catch (PersistenceException e) {
      try {
        db.rollback();
      } catch (Exception e2) {
```

❸ **Create Blog POJO and then save it**

❹ **Look up Blog and then delete it**

```
        }
            throw new ApplicationException(e);
        }
    }

    public Collection getTopics(String blogId)
        throws ApplicationException {

      try {
        db.begin();
        Blog blog = (Blog) db.load(Blog.class, blogId);
        db.rollback();
        return blog.getTopics();
      } catch (PersistenceException e) {
        throw new ApplicationException(e);
      }
    }

    protected void finalize() throws Throwable {
      db.close();
    }
  }
}
```

❺ Look up Blog and then return its Topics

❶ The constructor of `BlogFacadeCastor.java` sets up a JDO database to be used by the other methods.

❷ You use Castor's Object Query Language (OQL) to look up all Blog objects in the `getAllBlogs` method.

❸ In `createBlog`, you create an instance of a `Blog`, initialize its properties, and then use the `Database` object's `create` method to persist the `Blog`.

❹ The `deleteBlog` method loads a `Blog` by its id and then deletes it.

❺ In a similar way, the `getTopics` method loads a `Blog` by its `id`, and then uses the `Blog`'s `getTopics` method to retrieve the collection of `Topics` belonging to the `Blog`.

Now you've seen how to use XDoclet to generate mapping files for Castor-persisted data objects. Before we wrap up our discussion of using XDoclet with data persistence frameworks, let's look at one more way that Castor can persist data objects.

7.3.4 Working with Castor XML

In recent years, XML has come to be a ubiquitous element of software systems. It's used for everything from configuration files (as you've seen many times in this book) to presentation layer technologies. There are even XML-based databases.

Regardless of how it's used, XML must be parsed. The oldest and most commonly used parsers are SAX (Simple API for XML) and DOM (Document Object Model) parsers. Other popular choices for XML parsing include JDOM (Java DOM) and Apache's Digester. All of these options help read and write XML files, but none of them directly solve the problem of mapping Java objects to XML files.

That's where Castor XML comes in. Castor XML does for XML what Castor JDO does for relational databases. In short, Castor XML binds Java objects to XML structures. It does so by using a slightly modified form of the same mapping file used by Castor JDO.

Tagging a class for XML persistence

To demonstrate using XDoclet with Castor XML, let's tag `Blog.java` for persistence to an XML file. Fortunately, much of the work you did for Castor JDO also applies to Castor XML. There's only one new tag you must learn for Castor XML. Listing 7.18 shows `Blog.java` modified for Castor XML.

Listing 7.18 Blog.java modified to be persisted to XML

```java
package com.xdocletbook.blog.pojo;
import java.util.Set;

/**
 * @castor.class
 *    id="id"
 *    table="Blog"
 *    key-generator="UUID"
 */
public class Blog {
  private String id;
  private String name;
  private String owner;
  private String email;
  private Set topics;
  private Set entries;

  public Blog() {
  }

  /**
   * @castor.field
   *      set-method="setId"
   *
   * @castor.field-sql
   *      name="id"
   *      type="char"
   *
```

```
 * @castor.field-xml          id is an
 *     name="id"              attribute
 *     node="attribute"       node
 */
public String getId() {
  return id;
}


/**
 * @castor.field
 *     set-method="setEmail"
 *
 * @castor.field-sql
 *     name="email"
 *     type="char"
 *
 * @castor.field-xml          These fields are
 *     name="contact"         persisted in XML
 */
public String getEmail() {
  return email;
}


/**
 * @castor.field
 *     set-method="setName"
 *
 * @castor.field-sql
 *     name="name"
 *     type="char"
 */
public String getName() {
  return name;
}


/**
 * @castor.field
 *     set-method="setOwner"
 *
 * @castor.field-sql
 *     name="owner"
 *     type="char"
 *
 * @castor.field-xml          These fields are
 *     name="belongsTo"       persisted in XML
 */
public String getOwner() {
  return owner;
}
```

```
public void setEmail(String string) {
  email = string;
}

public void setId(String string) {
  id = string;
}

public void setName(String string) {
  name = string;
}

public void setOwner(String string) {
  owner = string;
}

/**
 * @castor.field
 *     collection="set"
 *     type="com.xdocletbook.blog.pojo.Entry"
 *     set-method="setEntries"
 *
 * @castor.field-sql
 *     many-key="blog"
 *
 * @castor.field-xml
 *     name="entry"
 */
public Set getEntries() {
  return entries;
}

public void setEntries(Set set) {
  entries = set;
}

/**
 *
 * @castor.field
 *     collection="set"
 *     type="com.xdocletbook.blog.pojo.Topic"
 *     set-method="setTopics"
 *
 * @castor.field-sql
 *     many-key="blog"
 *
 * @castor.field-xml
 *     name="topic"
 */
public Set getTopics() {
  return topics;
}
```

Each Entry in collection is a child of Blog

Each Topic in collection is a child of Blog

```
    public void setTopics(Set set) {
      topics = set;
    }
  }
```

You tag all getter methods (except getName) with @castor.field-xml, setting the
name attribute appropriately. The name attribute specifies the name of the XML
node that is written for a field. By default, Castor XML assumes the node name is
the same as the property name. Therefore, because you don't tag getName, Castor
XML assumes the name of the node is name. For the email and owner properties,
however, you override the default and name the XML nodes contact and
belongsTo, respectively.

In the case of the id property, you also set the node attribute to "attribute",
indicating that this property is an attribute of <blog> when a Blog object is written
to XML.

When <castormapping> processes Blog.java, the following mapping definition
is written to the mapping file:

```
<class name="com.xdocletbook.blog.pojo.Blog"
    identity="id"
    access="shared"
    key-generator="UUID"
    auto-complete="false">
  <map-to table="Blog" />
  <cache-type type="count-limited" />

  <field name="id"
      type="java.lang.String"
      get-method="getId"
      set-method="setId">
    <sql name="id"
        type="char" />
    <bind-xml name="id"
        node="attribute" />
  </field>

  <field name="email"
      type="java.lang.String"
      get-method="getEmail"
      set-method="setEmail">
    <sql name="email"
        type="char" />
    <bind-xml name="contact" />
  </field>
```

```
<field name="name"
    type="java.lang.String"
    get-method="getName"
    set-method="setName">
  <sql name="name"
      type="char" />
</field>

<field name="owner"
    type="java.lang.String"
    get-method="getOwner"
    set-method="setOwner">
  <sql name="belongsTo"
      type="char" />
  <bind-xml name="owner" />
</field>

<field name="entries"
    type="com.xdocletbook.blog.pojo.Entry"
    get-method="getEntries"
    set-method="setEntries"
    collection="set">
  <sql
      many-key="blog" />
  <bind-xml name="entry" />
</field>

<field name="topics"
    type="com.xdocletbook.blog.pojo.Topic"
    get-method="getTopics"
    set-method="setTopics"
    collection="set">
  <sql
      many-key="blog" />
  <bind-xml name="topic" />
</field>
</class>
```

Notice all the <bind-xml> elements in the mapping file. These are the direct result of using the @castor.field-xml tag in Blog.java. Also notice the absence of a <bind-xml> element for the name field. Even though you haven't explicitly defined an XML mapping for the name property of a Blog, Castor XML can still bind the property to an XML node. As you'll see later, Castor XML assumes a default mapping definition for properties that aren't explicitly mapped.

Now let's look at how to use Castor XML to write a Blog object to XML through a process called *marshalling*.

Writing Java objects to XML

Marshalling is the process of translating an object into some other form, usually for data transfer. In the context of Castor XML, marshalling involves translating a Java object into XML. The following four steps can be used to marshal an object to XML:

1   Create an instance of `java.io.Writer` used to write the XML.

2   Create an instance of `org.exolab.castor.mapping.Mapping` and load the mapping file.

3   Create an instance of `org.exolab.castor.xml.Marshaller` and set the mapping.

4   Call the `marshal` method of the `Marshaller`, giving it the `Writer`, to marshal the object.

For example, the following code excerpt uses a `Marshaller` to write XML for a `Blog` object to a file named `SomeBlog.xml`:

```
Blog blog = … ; // Obtain a Blog object somehow
Writer writer = new FileWriter("SomeBlog.xml");
Mapping mapping = new Mapping();
mapping.loadMapping("mapping.xml");
Marshaller marshaller = new Marshaller(writer);
marshaller.setMapping(mapping);
marshaller.marshal(blog);
```

In this example, you construct an instance of `org.exolab.castor.xml.Marshaller`, giving it a `java.io.FileWriter` instance. Then you load the mapping file and feed it to the `Marshaller` to serialize a `Blog` object to an XML file named `SomeBlog.xml`.

Now you know how to marshal an object to XML using Castor XML. But working with XML isn't all output. Quite often, you need to read an XML file into an object. Let's see how you can use Castor XML for *unmarshalling* XML.

Unmarshalling objects from XML

If marshalling in Castor XML is the process of translating Java objects into XML, then *unmarshalling* must be the process of creating Java objects from XML. Unmarshalling XML works similarly to marshalling, only in reverse. There are four steps to unmarshal an XML file:

1   Create an instance of `java.io.Reader` to read the XML.

2   Create an instance of `org.exolab.castor.mapping.Mapping` and load the mapping file.

3 Create an instance of `org.exolab.castor.xml.Unmarshaller` and set the mapping.

4 Call the `unmarshal` method of the `Unmarshaller`, giving it the `Reader` to retrieve the object.

The following code excerpt shows how you might unmarshal the `SomeBlog.xml` file that you marshalled in the previous example:

```
Reader reader = new FileReader("SomeBlog.xml");
Mapping mapping = new Mapping();
mapping.loadMapping("mapping.xml");
Unmarshaller unmarshaller = new Unmarshaller();
unmarshaller.setMapping(mapping);
Blog blog = (Blog)unmarshaller.unmarshal(reader);
```

In this example, you use a `java.io.FileReader` to read the XML file. And, as before, you use the `mapping.xml` file that XDoclet generated for you.

7.4 *Summary*

Seamlessly moving data back and forth between Java objects and persistent storage is quite a challenge. Frameworks such as Hibernate, JDO, and Castor bridge the gap between an application and the database behind it. In this chapter, you've seen how XDoclet can spare you the hassle of keeping application objects synchronized with the metadata that defines the mapping used by these frameworks.

In the next chapter, we'll explain how to use XDoclet to generate deployment descriptor files for Apache SOAP and Axis, two very popular frameworks for publishing web services.

XDoclet and web services

210

I have the world's largest seashell collection. You may have seen it. I keep it spread out on beaches all over the world.

—Steven Wright

In the past few years, the concept of web services has become quite a buzzword in software development. Embedded within the hype, web services bring the promise of seamless integration of disparate systems across the Web. Web services are typically based on XML messages and communicate over firewall-friendly protocols such as HTTP and SMTP. It may be said that web services are web pages for computer programs to read.

The Simple Object Access Protocol (SOAP) has emerged as the de facto standard protocol for the XML messages that are exchanged between systems using web services. The Apache Software Foundation provides two implementations of SOAP for Java. The first, based on code donated to Apache by IBM, is referred to as *Apache SOAP* and supports the SOAP 1.0 specification. The Apache SOAP team saw an opportunity to improve upon its design and to implement the newer SOAP 1.1 and SOAP 1.2 specifications; their efforts resulted in *Axis*, the next generation of Apache SOAP. Although Axis is intended to be a successor to Apache SOAP, Apache SOAP is still widely used.

In this chapter, we'll develop some web services and look at how XDoclet can help you write the deployment descriptors for these web services to be deployed in either Apache SOAP or Axis.

8.1 *Generating deployment descriptors for Apache SOAP*

Apache SOAP was one of the first implementations of the SOAP specification for Java. Even though it's been replaced by Axis as Apache's SOAP implementation, it's still widely used and continues to be maintained by the Apache developers. (For more information about Apache SOAP and to download it, visit http://xml.apache.org/soap.)

Apache SOAP web services are deployed using an XML-based deployment descriptor. Many Apache SOAP users probably use the web-based deployment tool that comes with Apache SOAP and may not even realize that these deployment descriptors exist. In fact, the web-based deployment tool creates a deployment descriptor behind the scenes.

Although the web-based deployment tool is convenient, it makes defining deployment definitions a manual step and leaves you without a reusable deployment descriptor file for deploying the service again. For this reason, it's better to write a deployment descriptor file that can be reused—or better yet, let XDoclet write it for you.

You add the `<apachesoap>` subtask of `<ejbdoclet>` to `build-ejbgen.xml` to generate deployment descriptors for Apache SOAP web services:

```xml
<?xml version="1.0" encoding="UTF-8"?>

<project name="Blog" default="generateEjb" basedir=".">
...
<target name="generate-ejb">
...
  <ejbdoclet destdir="${gen.src.dir}">
...
    <apachesoap destDir="${web.deployment.dir}"/>
  </ejbdoclet>
 </target>
</project>
```

NOTE You may wonder why `<apachesoap>` is a subtask of `<ejbdoclet>` when not all web services are built around EJBs. The reason is that in those cases where a web service is EJB based, `<apachesoap>` can take advantage of certain EJB-level meta-information that would not be readily available if it weren't a subtask of `<ejbdoclet>`.

Now that the build file is ready to generate Apache SOAP deployment descriptors for you, let's write a simple Java web service using XDoclet to generate the deployment descriptor.

8.1.1 Writing simple Java web services for Apache SOAP

With Apache SOAP, any Java class can expose its functionality as a web service. To demonstrate, let's write `PigLatinService.java` (listing 8.1), a simple-minded web service that translates English words into Pig Latin words.

> Listing 8.1 PigLatinService.java defines a simple Pig Latin translation service.

```java
package com.xdocletbook.pig.service;

/**
 * @soap.service                    ❶ Declare
 *     urn="PigLatin"                 PigLatinService to be
 *     scope="Request"                a SOAP web service
 */
public class PigLatinService {
  private final String VOWELS = "AEIOUaeiou";
```

```
/**                        ❷ Declare translate method to
 * @soap.method    ⊲—┘      be exposed as a SOAP method
 */
public String translate(String word) {

  StringBuffer endBuffer = new StringBuffer();
  String start = "";
  for(int i=0; i<word.length(); i++) {
    Character c = new Character(word.charAt(i));
    if(VOWELS.indexOf(c+"") >= 0) {
      start = word.substring(i);
      break;
    }
    endBuffer.append(c.charValue());
  }

  return start + "-" + endBuffer.toString() + "AY";
}
}
```

❶ Use the `@soap.service` class-level tag to declare `PigLatinService` to be an Apache SOAP web service. The `urn` attribute specifies that the name for this service is "Pig-Latin". If `urn` isn't specified, then it defaults to the name of the class. The `scope` attribute specifies the lifetime of this service. By setting it to "Request", you declare that the service is request-oriented.

❷ Tag the `translate` method with `@soap.method` to indicate that this method should be exposed through the web service. This tag takes no attributes.

Generating the Apache SOAP deployment descriptor

When `<apachesoap>` processes `PigLatinService.java`, the following deployment descriptor is generated:

```
<?xml version="1.0" encoding="UTF-8"?>

<isd:service
    xmlns:isd="http://xml.apache.org/xml-soap/deployment"
    id="PigLatin"   >
  <isd:provider
      type="java"
      scope="Request"
      methods="translate ">

    <isd:java
        class="com.xdocletbook.pig.service.PigLatinService"/>
  </isd:provider>

  <!-- Fault Listener -->
```

```
<isd:faultListener>
  org.apache.soap.server.DOMFaultListener
</isd:faultListener>

<!--
  To add SOAP mappings to the deployment descriptor, add a
  file to your XDoclet merge directory called
  soap-mappings-{0}.xml that contains the
  <isd:mappings>...</isd:mappings> markup.
-->
</isd:service>
```

You can see how @soap.service's urn attribute translates to the service's id attribute in the deployment descriptor, and the scope attribute translates to the scope attribute of <isd:provider>. The value of the methods attribute of <isd: provider> is populated based on the methods that are tagged with @soap.method.

Deploying the web service to Apache SOAP

To deploy the PigLatin service to Apache SOAP, make sure that the compiled Pig-LatinService.class file is in Apache SOAP's classpath and that the web container is running. Then use Apache SOAP's command-line deployment tool to parse the deployment descriptor file and deploy the web service:

```
% java org.apache.soap.server.ServiceManagerClient
  http://hostname:port/soap/servlet/rpcrouter deploy
  soap-dds-PigLatinService.xml
```

You can test the Pig Latin translation service using PigLatinSoapClient.java (listing 8.2).

> **Listing 8.2 PigLatinSoapClient.java is a client to the Pig Lating translation web service.**

```
package com.xdocletbook.pig.client;

import java.net.URL;
import java.util.Vector;
import org.apache.soap.Constants;
import org.apache.soap.rpc.Call;
import org.apache.soap.rpc.Parameter;
import org.apache.soap.rpc.Response;

public class PigLatinSoapClient {
  public static void main(String[] args) throws Exception {
    if(args.length < 1) {
      System.err.println("Usage: PigLatinClient word");
      System.exit(-1);
    }
```

```
        Call call = new Call();
    call.setTargetObjectURI("PigLatin");
    call.setMethodName("translate");
    call.setEncodingStyleURI(Constants.NS_URI_SOAP_ENC);
    Vector params = new Vector();
    params.addElement(
        new Parameter("word", String.class, args[0], null));
    call.setParams(params);

    Response response =
        call.invoke(
        new URL("http://localhost/soap/servlet/rpcrouter"), "");

    Parameter result = response.getReturnValue();
    System.out.println("English:   " + args[0]);
    System.out.println("Pig-Speak: " + result.getValue());
    }
}
```

`PigLatinSoapClient` takes a single command-line argument. The argument is assumed to be an English word and is passed in the call to the `translate` method. For example, invoking `PigLatinSoapClient` like this:

```
% java com.xdocletbook.blog.client.PigLatinSoapClient Java
```

yields the following output:

```
English:   Java
Pig-Speak: ava-JAY
```

Now that you've seen how to deploy POJOs (plain old Java objects) in Apache SOAP, let's look at how you can deploy EJBs as web services.

8.1.2 *Exposing EJBs as Apache SOAP web services*

In chapter 3, you developed `BlogFacadeBean.java`, a stateless session EJB that exposes functions to manage a web-log application. Suppose you want to expose some of the methods of `BlogFacadeBean.java` as a web service. How can you expose the functionality of `BlogFacadeBean` through an Apache SOAP interface?

First, you must revisit the build file and add a few attributes to the `<apachesoap>` subtask:

```
<apachesoap
    destDir="${web.deployment.dir}"
    contextProviderUrl="localhost:1099"
    contextFactoryName=
        "org.jnp.interfaces.NamingContextFactory"
/>
```

The contextProviderUrl and contextFactoryName attributes are used to look up a reference to an EJB's home interface in JNDI when that EJB is exposed as a web service. The contextFactoryName is the name of the JNDI context factory. The contextProviderUrl is the URL associated with the JNDI context provider. Here we've used values applicable to a JBoss EJB container; consult your EJB container's documentation for the correct values if you're using a container other than JBoss.

The @soap.service and @soap.method tags work with EJBs in a way that's very similar to how they work with POJOs. Used in their simplest form, they are used exactly the same way with EJBs that they are with POJOs.

For example, consider the getBlogSimple method of BlogFacadeBean.java. This method is used to retrieve a BlogSimpleValue value object given a blog's ID. The following code excerpt shows how you can tag this method to be exposed in a web service:

```
/*
...
 * @soap.service
 *     urn="BlogFacade"
 *     scope="Request"
 */
public abstract class BlogFacadeBean implements SessionBean {
...
  /**
   * @ejb.interface-method
   * @soap.method
   */
  public BlogSimpleValue getBlogSimple(String blogId)
      throws ApplicationException {
...
  }
...
}
```

Processing BlogFacadeBean with <apachesoap> produces the following Apache SOAP deployment descriptor:

```
<?xml version="1.0" encoding="UTF-8"?>

<isd:service
    xmlns:isd="http://xml.apache.org/xml-soap/deployment"
    id="BlogFacade"   >
  <isd:provider
      type="org.apache.soap.providers.StatelessEJBProvider"
      scope="Request"
      methods="create getBlogSimple ">
```

```
    <isd:option key="FullHomeInterfaceName"
        value="com.xdocletbook.blog.interfaces.BlogFacadeHome" />
    <isd:option key="ContextProviderURL" value="localhost:1099" />
    <isd:option key="FullContextFactoryName"
        value="org.jnp.interfaces.NamingContextFactory" />
    <isd:option key="JNDIName" value="BlogFacade"/>

</isd:provider>

<!-- Fault Listener -->
<isd:faultListener>
  org.apache.soap.server.DOMFaultListener
</isd:faultListener>

<!--
  To add SOAP mappings to the deployment descriptor, add a file
  to your XDoclet merge directory called soap-mappings-{0}.xml
  that contains the <isd:mappings>...</isd:mappings> markup.
-->

</isd:service>
```

Although you could use this deployment descriptor as is to deploy the `BlogFacade`
web service into Apache SOAP, the web service won't work—the deployment
descriptor is incomplete. The `getBlogSimple` method returns an instance of
`BlogSimpleValue`, a complex type. Apache SOAP has no problem serializing and
deserializing simple types such as `java.lang.String` when sending SOAP messages, but it has a harder time with complex types. That's where custom serializers
and deserializers come in.

8.1.3 *Mapping custom types*

Custom serializers and deserializers are used to translate between complex data
types (such as `BlogSimpleValue`) and the XML that's part of the SOAP message. In
Apache SOAP, serializers and deserializers are classes that implement
`org.apache.soap.util.xml.Serializer` and `org.apache.soap.util.xml.Deseri-`
`alizer`, respectively. For example, listing 8.3 shows `BlogSimpleValueSerial-`
`izer.java`, a class that is both a serializer and deserializer for instances of
`BlogSimpleValue`.

Listing 8.3   BlogSimpleValueSerializer.java

```
package com.xdocletbook.blog.ejb.soap;

import java.io.IOException;
import java.io.Writer;
import org.apache.soap.encoding.soapenc.SoapEncUtils;
```

```
import org.apache.soap.rpc.Parameter;
import org.apache.soap.rpc.RPCConstants;
import org.apache.soap.rpc.SOAPContext;
import org.apache.soap.util.Bean;
import org.apache.soap.util.StringUtils;
import org.apache.soap.util.xml.DOMUtils;
import org.apache.soap.util.xml.Deserializer;
import org.apache.soap.util.xml.NSStack;
import org.apache.soap.util.xml.QName;
import org.apache.soap.util.xml.Serializer;
import org.apache.soap.util.xml.XMLJavaMappingRegistry;
import org.w3c.dom.Element;
import org.w3c.dom.Node;
import com.xdocletbook.blog.value.BlogSimpleValue;

public class BlogSimpleValueSerializer
    implements Serializer, Deserializer {

  public void marshall(String inScopeEncStyle, Class javaType,
      Object src, Object context, Writer sink, NSStack nsStack,
      XMLJavaMappingRegistry xjmr, SOAPContext ctx)
      throws IllegalArgumentException, IOException {

    nsStack.pushScope();
    SoapEncUtils.generateStructureHeader(inScopeEncStyle, javaType,
        context, sink, nsStack, xjmr);

    sink.write(StringUtils.lineSeparator);

    BlogSimpleValue blogValue = (BlogSimpleValue) src;
    String id = blogValue.getId();
    String name = blogValue.getName();
    String owner = blogValue.getOwner();
    String pk = blogValue.getPrimaryKey();

    if(id != null) {
      xjmr.marshall(inScopeEncStyle, String.class, id, "id",
          sink, nsStack, ctx);
    }

    if(name != null) {
      xjmr.marshall(inScopeEncStyle, String.class, name, "name",
          sink, nsStack, ctx);
    }

    if(owner != null) {
      xjmr.marshall(inScopeEncStyle, String.class, owner, "owner",
          sink, nsStack, ctx);
    }

    if(pk != null) {
```

Marshall all fields as Strings

```
      xjmr.marshall(inScopeEncStyle, String.class, pk, "primaryKey",
          sink, nsStack, ctx);
    }

    sink.write("</"+context+'>');
    nsStack.popScope();
  }

  public Bean unmarshall(String inScopeEncStyle, QName elementType,
      Node src, XMLJavaMappingRegistry xjmr, SOAPContext ctx)
      throws IllegalArgumentException {

    Element blogElement = (Element)src;
    Element tempElement =
        DOMUtils.getFirstChildElement(blogElement);
    BlogSimpleValue blogValue = new BlogSimpleValue();

    while(tempElement != null) {
      String tagName = tempElement.getTagName();

      Bean bean = xjmr.unmarshall(inScopeEncStyle,
          RPCConstants.Q_ELEM_PARAMETER, tempElement, ctx);
      Parameter param = (Parameter)bean.value;

      if(tagName.equals("id")) {
        blogValue.setId((String)param.getValue());
      } else if (tagName.equals("name")) {
        blogValue.setName((String)param.getValue());
      } else if (tagName.equals("owner")) {
        blogValue.setOwner((String)param.getValue());
      } else if (tagName.equals("primaryKey")) {
        blogValue.setPrimaryKey((String)param.getValue());
      }

      tempElement = DOMUtils.getNextSiblingElement(tempElement);
    }

    return new Bean(BlogSimpleValue.class, blogValue);
  }
}
```

Marshall all fields as Strings

Demarshall each field

XDoclet can't help you write serializers and deserializers. There are no XDoclet tags specific to serializers and deserializers. However, there is a merge point in the template for the Apache SOAP deployment descriptor that enables you to merge in a file containing mappings between complex data types and serializers/deserializers.

Declaring custom type mappings using merge files

The merge file for serializer and deserializer declarations is `soap-mappings-{0}.xml`. Notice that the merge file name has a {0} substitution—the {0} is replaced with the name of the class that defines the web service.

For example, you can create `soap-mapping-BlogFacadeBean.xml` (listing 8.4), a merge file that declares `BlogSimpleValueSerializer.java` to be available for the `BlogFacadeBean` web service.

Listing 8.4   soap-mapping-BlogFacadeBean.xml

```
<isd:mappings>
  <isd:map encodingStyle="http://schemas.xmlsoap.org/soap/encoding/"
      xmlns:blog=
          "urn:Blog" qname="blog:BlogSimpleValue"
      javaType="com.xdocletbook.blog.value.BlogSimpleValue"
      xml2JavaClassName=
          "com.xdocletbook.blog.ejb.soap.BlogSimpleValueSerializer"
      java2XMLClassName=
          "com.xdocletbook.blog.ejb.soap.BlogSimpleValueSerializer"
  />
</isd:mappings>
```

Because this merge defines type-mappings on a per-class basis, you need to place it in a directory called com/xdocletbook/blog/ejb/ under the `mergeDir` directory (see figure 8.1).

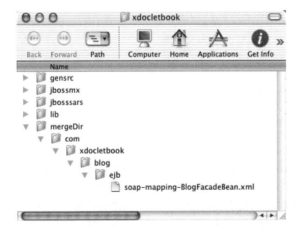

Figure 8.1
Where to place the
soap-mappings-
BlogFacadeBean.xml
merge file

Deploying the web service

Now that you've declared your custom type-mappings in this merge file, the deployment descriptor is complete. You can now deploy the `BlogFacade` web service the same way you deployed the Pig Latin translator service:

```
% java org.apache.soap.server.ServiceManagerClient
    http://hostname:port/soap/servlet/rpcrouter deploy
    soap-dds-BlogFacadeBean.xml
```

Make sure that the classes required by the web service are in SOAP's classpath. These include `BlogSimpleValue` and the home and remote interfaces for `Blog-FacadeBean`. Also be sure that `BlogFacadeBean` is deployed and that the EJB container is started.

`BlogFacadeSoapClient` (listing 8.5) is a test client of the `BlogFacade` web service.

Listing 8.5   BlogFacadeSoapClient.java

```java
package com.xdocletbook.blog.client;

import java.net.URL;
import java.util.Vector;
import org.apache.soap.Constants;
import org.apache.soap.encoding.SOAPMappingRegistry;
import org.apache.soap.rpc.Call;
import org.apache.soap.rpc.Parameter;
import org.apache.soap.rpc.Response;
import org.apache.soap.util.xml.QName;
import com.xdocletbook.blog.ejb.soap.BlogSimpleValueSerializer;
import com.xdocletbook.blog.value.BlogSimpleValue;

public class BlogFacadeSoapClient {
  private static final String ENDPOINT =
      "http://localhost:8008/soap/servlet/rpcrouter";

  public static void main(String[] args) throws Exception {
    if(args.length < 1) {
      System.err.println("Usage: BlogFacadeSoapClient blogId");
      System.exit(-1);
    }

    SOAPMappingRegistry mappings = new SOAPMappingRegistry();
    mappings.mapTypes(Constants.NS_URI_SOAP_ENC,
        new QName("urn:Blog", "BlogSimpleValue"),
        BlogSimpleValue.class,
        new BlogSimpleValueSerializer(),
        new BlogSimpleValueSerializer());

    String blogId = args[0];
```

```
Call call = new Call();
call.setSOAPMappingRegistry(mappings);          Set up
call.setTargetObjectURI("BlogFacade");          remote
call.setMethodName("getBlogSimple");            call
call.setEncodingStyleURI(Constants.NS_URI_SOAP_ENC);
Vector params = new Vector();
params.addElement(
    new Parameter("blogId", String.class, blogId, null));
call.setParams(params);                       Set call
                                              parameters
Response response =                  Call
    call.invoke(new URL(ENDPOINT), "");  service

Parameter result = response.getReturnValue();
BlogSimpleValue blogValue = (BlogSimpleValue) result.getValue();
                                              Get returned
                                                    object
System.out.println("ID:   " + blogValue.getId());
System.out.println("Name:   " + blogValue.getName());
System.out.println("Owner:   " + blogValue.getOwner());
System.out.println("Primary Key:   " +
    blogValue.getPrimaryKey());
  }
}
```

BlogFacadeSoapClient takes a blog ID as its single command-line argument. It uses this blog ID when it calls getBlogSimple on the BlogFacade web service to retrieve a BlogSimpleValue instance.

Working with Apache SOAP has been fun, but Axis is the new way of writing web services in Java. Let's rewind what you've learned so far in this chapter and replace Apache SOAP with Axis, using XDoclet to generate Axis deployment descriptors.

8.2 *Generating deployment descriptors for Axis*

Seeing an opportunity to enhance the code base donated by IBM, the Apache SOAP developers reengineered Apache SOAP; the result was Apache Axis. Apache Axis improves upon Apache SOAP in many ways, including performance and architecture. (For more information about Apache Axis and to download it, visit http://xml.apache.org/axis.)

As with Apache SOAP, web services are deployed to Axis using XML-based deployment descriptor files. You include the <axisdeploy> subtask in build-ejbgen.xml to generate Axis deployment descriptors for your web services:

```
<?xml version="1.0" encoding="UTF-8"?>

<project name="Blog" default="generateEjb" basedir=".">
...
<target name="generate-ejb">
...
    <ejbdoclet destdir="${gen.src.dir}">
...
      <axisdeploy destDir="${web.deployment.dir}"/>
      <axisundeploy destDir="${web.deployment.dir}"/>
    </ejbdoclet>
  </target>
</project>
```

If you no longer want a web service to be published, you need a means to undeploy the web service from Axis. Axis web services can be undeployed using simple
XML-based undeployment descriptors. You use the `<axisundeploy>` subtask to
generate undeployment descriptors for web services.

Now that the build file is prepared to generate Axis deployment and undeployment descriptors, let's see how you should tag the `PigLatinService.java` and
`BlogFacadeBean.java` code to generate these files.

8.2.1 *Writing simple Java web services for Axis*

The Axis meta-information tags mirror the functionality of the Apache SOAP tags.
Listing 8.6 shows `PigLatinService.java` updated with Axis tags.

Listing 8.6   PigLatinService.java updated to use @axis tags

```
package com.xdocletbook.pig.service;

/**
 * @soap.service
 *     urn="PigLatin"
 *     scope="Request"
 *
 * @axis.service            Declare this class
 *     urn="PigLatin"       to be an Axis
 *     scope="request"      SOAP service
 */
public class PigLatinService {
  private String VOWELS = "AEIOUaeiou";

  /**
   * @soap.method
   * @axis.method     <— Expose translate as SOAP method
   */
  public String translate(String word) {
```

```
StringBuffer endBuffer = new StringBuffer();
String start = "";
for(int i=0; i<word.length(); i++) {
  Character c = new Character(word.charAt(i));
  if(VOWELS.indexOf(c+"") >= 0) {
    start = word.substring(i);
    break;
  }
  endBuffer.append(c.charValue());
}

return start + "-" + endBuffer.toString() + "AY";
}
}
```

You use the @axis.service and @axis.method tags exactly the same as you used @soap.service and @soap.method. As an alternative to the @axis.method tag, the @axis.service tag has an include-all attribute. If include-all is set to "true", then all methods of the source class are included in the web service, regardless of whether the methods are tagged with @axis.method. For example, the following includes all methods of PigLatinService.java in the PigLatin web service:

```
package com.xdocletbook.pig.service;

/**
 * @axis.service
 *      urn="PigLatin"
 *      scope="request"
 *      include-all="true"
 */
public class PigLatinService {
...
}
```

Because the translate method is the only method of PigLatinService.java, it's kind of silly to use include-all, but we do so here to demonstrate how it can be used.

Deploying the web service in Axis

When you run your build and PigLatinService.java is processed through the <axisdeploy> subtask, the following deployment descriptor is generated:

```
<?xml version="1.0" encoding="UTF-8"?>

<deployment
    xmlns="http://xml.apache.org/axis/wsdd/"
```

```
        xmlns:java="http://xml.apache.org/axis/wsdd/providers/java"
        xmlns:xsi="http://www.w3.org/2000/10/XMLSchema-instance">

    <service name="PigLatin"
        provider="java:RPC"
    >

        <parameter name="className"
            value="com.xdocletbook.pig.service.PigLatinService" />
        <parameter name="allowedMethods"
            value="translate "
        />
        <parameter name="scope"
            value="request"/>
    </service>
    <!--
        To add type mappings to the deployment descriptor, add a file
        to your XDoclet merge directory called axis-mappings-{0}.xml
        that contains the <beanMapping/> and <typeMapping/> markup.
    -->
</deployment>
```

To deploy the Pig Latin translation web service in Axis, make sure that the compiled `PigLatinService.class` file is in the Axis classpath. Then use the Axis `AdminClient` as follows (assuming the web container in which Axis is deployed is configured to listen for requests on port 80):

```
% java org.apache.axis.client.AdminClient -p80
  deploy-PigLatinService.wsdd
```

The new client program `PigLatinAxisClient.java` (listing 8.7) invokes the Pig Latin web service.

Listing 8.7   PigLatinAxisClient.java

```
package com.xdocletbook.pig.client;

import javax.xml.namespace.QName;

import org.apache.axis.client.Call;
import org.apache.axis.client.Service;

public class PigLatinAxisClient {
  public static void main(String[] args) throws Exception {
    if(args.length < 1) {
      System.err.println("Usage: PigLatinClient word");
      System.exit(-1);
    }

    String endpoint =
        "http://localhost:8008/axis/services/PigLatin";
```

```
    Service service = new Service();
    Call call = (Call)service.createCall();
    call.setTargetEndpointAddress(new java.net.URL(endpoint));
    call.setOperationName(
        new QName("http://soapinterop.org/", "translate"));
    String ret = (String) call.invoke(new Object[] {args[0]});

    System.out.println("English:   " + args[0]);
    System.out.println("Pig-Speak: " + ret);
  }
}
```

Just like `PigLatinSoapClient` earlier in this chapter, `PigLatinAxisClient` takes as a command-line argument a word that is sent to the `PigLatin` web service for translation.

Undeploying Axis web services

When `<axisundeploy>` processes `PigLatinService.java`, it generates `undeploy-PigLatinService.wsdd`, an undeployment descriptor for the `PigLatin` web service:

```
<?xml version="1.0" encoding="UTF-8"?>

<undeployment xmlns="http://xml.apache.org/axis/wsdd/">
  <service name="PigLatin"/>
</undeployment>
```

To undeploy the web service, use the Axis AdminClient with `undeploy-PigLatinService.wsdd`:

```
% java org.apache.axis.client.AdminClient -p80
  undeploy-PigLatinService.wsdd
```

Now let's look at how you can deploy EJBs as web services in Axis.

8.2.2 Exposing EJBs as Axis web services

Like `<apachesoap>`, the `<axisdeploy>` subtask has some attributes that are specific to exposing EJBs as web services:

```
<axisdeploy
    destDir="${web.deployment.dir}"
    contextProviderUrl="localhost:1099"
    contextFactoryName="org.jnp.interfaces.NamingContextFactory"
/>
```

Just as with the `<apachesoap>` subtask, the `contextProviderUrl` and `context-FactoryName` attributes tell Axis where to look up the home interface for EJBs deployed as web services. Axis undeployment descriptor files are so simple, there are no additional EJB-specific attributes for the `<axisundeploy>` subtask.

You also need to tag `BlogFacadeBean.java` with the `@axis.service` tag at the class level and the `@axis.method` tag at the method level. These tags are the Axis equivalents of the `@soap.service` and `@soap.method` tags discussed earlier in this chapter:

```
/*
...
 * @soap.service
 *     urn="BlogFacade"
 *     scope="Request"
 *
 * @axis.service
 *     urn="BlogFacade"
 *     scope="Request"
 */
public abstract class BlogFacadeBean implements SessionBean {
...
  /**
   * @ejb.interface-method
   * @soap.method
   * @axis.method
   */
  public BlogSimpleValue getBlogSimple(String blogId)
      throws ApplicationException {
...
  }
...
}
```

With these changes applied to `BlogFacadeBean.java`, `<axisdeploy>` generates the following deployment descriptor file:

```
<?xml version="1.0" encoding="UTF-8"?>

<deployment
    xmlns="http://xml.apache.org/axis/wsdd/"
    xmlns:java="http://xml.apache.org/axis/wsdd/providers/java"
    xmlns:xsi="http://www.w3.org/2000/10/XMLSchema-instance">

  <service name="BlogFacade"
      provider="java:EJB"
  >

    <parameter name="beanJndiName" value="BlogFacade"/>
    <parameter name="homeInterfaceName"
        value="com.xdocletbook.blog.interfaces.BlogFacadeHome"/>
    <parameter name="jndiURL"
            value="localhost:1099"/>
```

```
    <parameter name="jndiContextClass"
                value="org.jnp.interfaces.NamingContextFactory"/>
    <parameter name="allowedMethods"
                value="getBlogSimple "
    />
    <parameter name="scope"
                value="Request"/>
  </service>
  <!--
    To add type mappings to the deployment descriptor, add a file
    to your XDoclet merge directory called axis-mappings-{0}.xml
    that contains the <beanMapping/> and <typeMapping/> markup.
  -->
</deployment>
```

The comments at the end of the generated deployment descriptor remind you that, just as you did for Apache SOAP, you must merge in deployment information to map complex types to serializers and deserializers.

8.2.3 *Mapping custom types*

Axis serializers and deserializers are slightly more complex than those in Apache SOAP. BlogSimpleValueSerializer.java (listing 8.8) shows a class that acts as a serializer and deserializer for BlogSimpleValue objects and also serves as its own factory class.

Listing 8.8 BlogSimpleValueSerializer.java

```
package com.xdocletbook.blog.ejb.axis;

import java.io.IOException;
import java.util.Iterator;
import java.util.Vector;

import javax.xml.namespace.QName;

import org.apache.axis.Constants;
import org.apache.axis.encoding.DeserializationContext;
import org.apache.axis.encoding.Deserializer;
import org.apache.axis.encoding.DeserializerFactory;
import org.apache.axis.encoding.DeserializerImpl;
import org.apache.axis.encoding.FieldTarget;
import org.apache.axis.encoding.SerializationContext;
import org.apache.axis.encoding.Serializer;
import org.apache.axis.encoding.SerializerFactory;
import org.apache.axis.message.SOAPHandler;
import org.apache.axis.wsdl.fromJava.Types;
import org.w3c.dom.Element;
```

```
import org.xml.sax.Attributes;
import org.xml.sax.SAXException;

import com.xdocletbook.blog.value.BlogSimpleValue;

public class BlogSimpleValueSerializer extends DeserializerImpl
    implements Serializer, SerializerFactory, DeserializerFactory {

  private Vector mechanisms;

  private BlogSimpleValueSerializer() {
    value = new BlogSimpleValue();
  }

  public javax.xml.rpc.encoding.Serializer
      getSerializerAs(String arg0) {
    return new BlogSimpleValueSerializer();
  }

  public javax.xml.rpc.encoding.Deserializer
      getDeserializerAs(String arg0) {
    return new BlogSimpleValueSerializer();
  }

  public Iterator getSupportedMechanismTypes() {
    if(mechanisms == null) {
      mechanisms = new Vector();
      mechanisms.add(Constants.AXIS_SAX);
    }
    return mechanisms.iterator();
  }

  public void serialize(QName name, Attributes attributes,
      Object value, SerializationContext context)
      throws IOException {

    BlogSimpleValue blogValue = (BlogSimpleValue) value;
    context.startElement(name, attributes);
    context.serialize(new QName("", "id"), null, blogValue.getId());
    context.serialize(new QName("", "name"), null,
        blogValue.getName());
    context.serialize(new QName("", "owner"), null,
        blogValue.getOwner());
    context.serialize(new QName("", "primaryKey"), null,    // Serialize
        blogValue.getPrimaryKey());                          // BlogSimpleValue
    context.endElement();                                    // into XML elements
  }

  public String getMechanismType() { return Constants.AXIS_SAX; }

  public Element writeSchema(Class arg0, Types arg1)
```

```
      throws Exception {
    return null;
  }

  public SOAPHandler onStartChild(String namespace,
      String localName, String prefix, Attributes attributes,
      DeserializationContext context) throws SAXException {

    Deserializer dSer =
        context.getDeserializerForType(Constants.XSD_STRING);      ◁─┐

    try {
      dSer.registerValueTarget(new FieldTarget(value, localName));
   .} catch (NoSuchFieldException e) {                          Deserialize all
      throw new SAXException(e);                                fields as Strings
    }

    return (SOAPHandler)dSer;
  }

}
```

To merge deployment information for `BlogSimpleValueSerializer` into the generated deployment descriptor, you write `axis-mappings-BlogFacadeBean.xml` (listing 8.9).

Listing 8.9 axis-mappings-BlogFacadeBean.xml

```
<typeMapping xmlns:blog="urn:Blog" qname="blog:BlogSimpleValue"
  languageSpecificType=
    "java:com.xdocletbook.blog.value.BlogSimpleValue"
  serializer=
    "com.xdocletbook.blog.ejb.axis.BlogSimpleValueSerializer"
  deserializer=
    "com.xdocletbook.blog.ejb.axis.BlogSimpleValueSerializer"
  encodingStyle="http://schemas.xmlsoap.org/soap/encoding/"
/>
```

As you saw earlier with Apache SOAP, the axis-mappings merge file is merged on a per-class basis. Therefore, be sure to place it in the same package path in the `mergeDir` directory where you put `soap-mapping-BlogFacadeBean.xml`.

8.3 *Summary*

Exposing the business functionality of Java classes and EJBs is rather easy with Apache SOAP and Apache Axis. Using XDoclet to generate deployment descriptor files for these web services simplifies the work even more and eliminates the need to manage these artifacts.

In the next chapter, we'll look at how to instrument applications for management using JMX. We'll also discuss using XDoclet to generate the various artifacts associated with JMX-managed beans.

XDoclet and JMX

After one look at this planet any visitor from outer space would say "I want to see the manager."

—William S. Burroughs (1914–1997)

Instrumenting systems for management and reporting is an often-overlooked aspect of software development. For example, suppose that after you deployed the web-log application you started in chapter 3, you decided that you need to be able to expose some simple management functions (such as deleting a blog) as well as some server health functions (such as reporting the amount of available memory).

Developing management interfaces is often a reaction to a problem rather than a proactive movement to prevent (or at least predict) problems. A probable reason for this attitude toward software management is that writing management code typically isn't as much fun as writing the main application code. Furthermore, it's usually hard to write a good software-management solution. When something is difficult and not fun, it tends to not get done.

All that changed with the introduction of Java Management Extensions (JMX). JMX makes it simple to instrument an application for management. But, as with many Java technologies, redundancy exists between the artifacts that make up a JMX management interface. And, as is the theme of this book, redundancy translates into an opportunity for XDoclet to take on some of the development work.

In this chapter, we'll look at some of these redundancies and explain how XDoclet can handle them for you. As we do so, you'll develop a management interface for the web-log application that will enable you to report on how the application is being used.

9.1 A quick JMX overview

JMX is an optional extension to the Java 2 Standard Edition that defines the tools, specifications, services, and APIs necessary for developing management and monitoring solutions in Java. Using JMX, it's possible to instrument applications (both new and legacy systems) for management, monitoring, and configuration. (You can download JMX and read more about it at http://java.sun.com/products/JavaManagement.)

The key component of an application that is instrumented for management using JMX is the MBean (short for Managed Bean). An *MBean* is a JavaBean that exposes certain methods that define the management interface. There are three types of MBeans:

- *Standard MBeans* expose managed operations using a fixed interface. They're good when the management interface is unlikely to change.

- *Dynamic MBeans* are useful when the managed resource's API changes frequently. By exposing the management interface via a metadata class, you shield the MBean's client from the ever-changing management interface.

- *Model MBeans* take the notion of dynamic MBeans a step further. Instead of defining the MBean's management interface using a metadata class, you declare the management interface in an external resource (perhaps an XML file). The MBean server then uses the external resource to create the management interface on the fly at runtime.

We'll focus much of our attention in this chapter on how to use XDoclet to generate MBean interfaces and other artifacts associated with MBean development; we won't dwell on the details of JMX. To learn more about JMX, we recommend that you read *JMX in Action.*[1]

9.2 *Preparing the build for JMX generation*

The `<jmxdoclet>` task is the key to generating artifacts associated with JMX. Like other XDoclet tasks, `<jmxdoclet>` has several subtasks that indicate specific types of artifacts that should be generated. Table 9.1 describes the subtasks of `<jmxdoclet>`.

Table 9.1   Subtasks of `<jmxdoclet>` and the types of files they generate

Subtask	Description
`<mbeaninterface>`	Generates a managed operation interface for standard MBeans
`<mlet>`	Generates an mlet descriptor file
`<jbossxmbean>`	Generates a deployment descriptor for JBossMX model MBeans (XMBeans)
`<jbossxmldoc>`	Generates documentation for an MBean in DocBook format
`<jbossxmlservicetemplate>`	Generates JBossMX service deployment descriptors
`<mx4jdescription>`	Generates an MBean description class for deployment in MX4J

The first thing you need to do is create a new build file specific to JMX generation. Listing 9.1 shows `build-jmxgen.xml`, the build file that uses `<jmxdoclet>` and its subtasks to generate artifacts for MBeans.

---

[1]   Benjamin G. Sullins and Mark B. Whipple, *JMX in Action* (Greenwich, CT: Manning, 2002).

Listing 9.1 The build-jmxgen.xml build file used to generate JMX artifacts

```xml
<?xml version="1.0" encoding="UTF-8"?>

<project name="Blog" default="generate-mock" basedir=".">
  <path id="xdoclet.lib.path">
    <fileset dir="${lib.dir}" includes="*.jar"/>
    <fileset dir="${xdoclet.lib.dir}" includes="*.jar"/>
  </path>

  <target name="generate-jmx">
    <taskdef name="jmxdoclet"
        classname="xdoclet.modules.jmx.JMXDocletTask"
        classpathref="xdoclet.lib.path"/>

    <jmxdoclet destdir="${gen.src.dir}" mergeDir="${merge.dir}">
      <fileset dir="${src.dir}">
        <include name="**/jmx/*.java"/>
      </fileset>
      <mbeaninterface/>      <!-- Generate interfaces for standard MBeans -->
      <mlet/>                <!-- Generate mlet deployment files -->
    </jmxdoclet>
  </target>
</project>
```

Notice that the `<fileset>` you use limits the scope of `<jmxdoclet>` to classes in packages whose name ends with `.jmx`. The build will run faster because `<jmxdoclet>` won't have to process all classes looking for `@jmx.mbean` tags.

Next you must call `build-jmxgen.xml` from your main build file. An `<ant>` task is needed in the `generate` target of `build.xml`:

```xml
<target name="generate">
  <ant antfile="build-ejbgen.xml" target="generate-ejb"/>
  <ant antfile="build-webgen.xml" target="generate-web"/>
  <ant antfile="build-jmxgen.xml" target="generate-jmx"/>
</target>
```

With the build files ready for working with JMX, let's get started by having XDoclet generate interfaces for your MBeans.

9.3 Generating MBean interfaces

Suppose you want to expose some of the management functions of the web-log application as managed operations through JMX. The `BlogFacade` EJB that you wrote in chapter 3 already implements the functions you'd like to expose as managed operations. The quickest way to do this is to write a standard MBean that wraps the BlogFacade EJB. Listing 9.2 shows such an MBean.

Listing 9.2 Standard MBean that wraps BlogFacade to expose management functions

```java
package com.xdocletbook.jmx;

import java.util.List;
import com.xdocletbook.blog.interfaces.BlogFacade;
import com.xdocletbook.blog.interfaces.BlogFacadeHome;
import com.xdocletbook.blog.util.BlogFacadeUtil;

/**
 * @jmx.mbean                          ❶  Declare this as an MBean
 *     name="BlogManager"                 named BlogManager
 */
public class BlogManager implements BlogManagerMBean {
  BlogFacadeHome home;

  public BlogManager() throws Exception {
    home = BlogFacadeUtil.getHome();
  }

  /**
   * @jmx.managed-operation
   */
  public String getBlogName(String blogId) throws Exception {
    BlogFacade facade = home.create();
    return facade.getBlogSimple(blogId).getName();
  }

  /**
   * @jmx.managed-operation
   */
  public void deleteBlog(String blogId) throws Exception {
    home.create().deleteBlog(blogId);
  }

  /**
   * @jmx.managed-operation
   */
  public List getAllBlogs() throws Exception{
    BlogFacade facade = home.create();
    return facade.getAllBlogs();
  }
}
```

❷ Include these methods in the MBean interface

Standard MBeans are composed of two parts:

- An interface that declares methods to be exposed as managed operations
- A class that implements the interface, fleshed out with code that performs the operations

`BlogManager.java` defines the implementation class for the `BlogManager` MBean. Notice that we haven't shown you the interface it implements; that's because you'll let XDoclet generate the interface.

You tag `BlogManager` at the class level with `@jmx.mbean` to identify this class to XDoclet as an MBean named `BlogManager` ❶. Then you tag each method with `@jmx.managed-operation` to tell XDoclet to include these methods in the generated MBean interface ❷.

When you run the build and the `<mbeaninterface>` subtask processes `BlogManager.java`, the following interface is generated:

```
package com.xdocletbook.jmx;

/**
 * MBean interface.
 */
public interface BlogManagerMBean {

  java.lang.String getBlogName(java.lang.String blogId)
     throws java.lang.Exception;

  void deleteBlog(java.lang.String blogId)
     throws java.lang.Exception;

  java.util.List getAllBlogs() throws java.lang.Exception;

}
```

To kick off the `BlogManager` MBean, write `JMXStartupListener.java` (listing 9.3), a context listener that will be deployed with the web-log application and will start up the MBean server and register the `BlogManager` MBean with the MBean server. It also starts the HTML adapter so that you can view and invoke the `BlogManager` MBean through a web browser.

Listing 9.3 JMXStartupListener.java starts JMX services within a web container.

```
package com.xdocletbook.blog.listener;
import javax.management.MBeanServer;
import javax.management.MBeanServerFactory;
import javax.management.ObjectName;
```

```
import javax.servlet.ServletContextEvent;
import javax.servlet.ServletContextListener;
import com.sun.jdmk.comm.HtmlAdaptorServer;
import com.xdocletbook.jmx.BlogManager;

/**
 * @web.listener            Add this class as a
 */                    ⟵── listener in web.xml
public class JMXStartupListener implements ServletContextListener {
  private MBeanServer server;
  private HtmlAdaptorServer htmlAdaptor;

  public void contextDestroyed(ServletContextEvent arg0) {
    System.out.println("STOPPING MBEAN SERVER");
    htmlAdaptor.stop();
  }

  public void contextInitialized(ServletContextEvent arg0) {
    System.out.println("STARTING MBEAN SERVER");

    server = MBeanServerFactory.createMBeanServer("BlogAgent");

    try {
      startBlogManager();
      startHtmlAdaptor();
    } catch (Exception e) {
      System.err.println("Exception:   "+e);
    }
  }

  private void startBlogManager() throws Exception {          Register
    server.registerMBean(new BlogManager(),                  BlogManager
        new ObjectName("BlogAgent:name=blogManager"));       MBean with
  }                                                          MBean server

  private void startHtmlAdaptor() throws Exception {
    htmlAdaptor = new HtmlAdaptorServer();
    htmlAdaptor.setPort(9092);                               Register and
                                                             start HTML
    server.registerMBean(htmlAdaptor,                        Adaptor
        new ObjectName("Server:name=HtmlAdaptor"));
    htmlAdaptor.start();
  }
}
```

With the HTML Adaptor started, you can point your web browser to http://local-host:9092 and see the agent view, as shown in figure 9.1.

Figure 9.1   The agent view shows the list of registered MBeans by domain.

Clicking on the name=blogManager link under the BlogAgent domain, you can access the `BlogManager` MBean through its HTML interface, as shown in figure 9.2.

From the HTML interface, you can interact with the `BlogManager` MBean and manage your application.

9.4 *Generating mlet files*

Suppose that while your application is running, you encounter some performance problems and suspect that there's a memory leak. To keep an eye on the memory consumption, you write a `MemoryMonitor` MBean (listing 9.4).

But suppose you don't want to permanently deploy the `MemoryMonitor` MBean with your application. Furthermore, it'd be great to deploy this bean on the go without having to restart the application. How can you do this?

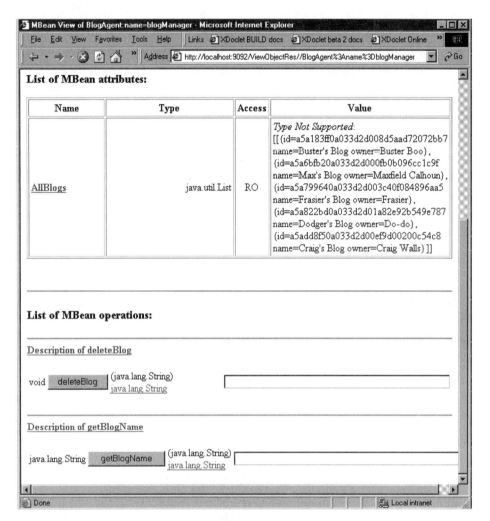

Figure 9.2 The `BlogManager` MBean's HTML interface as presented by the HTML Adaptor

The JMX specification provides a mechanism for hot deployment of MBeans through the mlet (short for management applet) service. The mlet service downloads and installs MBeans from remote locations using an XML-like mlet file that describes the MBean.

Listing 9.4   The MemoryMonitor MBean keeps a watchful eye on available memory.

```
package com.xdocletbook.jmx;

/**
 * @jmx.mbean
 *     name="Memory:name=memoryMonitor"
 *
 * @jmx.mlet-entry                                    Add this MBean
 *     archive="MemoryMonitorMBean.jar"               to the mlet file
 */
public class MemoryMonitor implements MemoryMonitorMBean{
  public MemoryMonitor() {
  }

  /**
   * @jmx.managed-attribute
   */
  public long getAvailableMemory() {
    return Runtime.getRuntime().freeMemory();
  }

  /**
   * @jmx.managed-attribute
   */
  public long getTotalMemory() {
    return Runtime.getRuntime().totalMemory();
  }

  /**
   * @jmx.managed-attribute
   */
  public long getMaxMemory() {
    return Runtime.getRuntime().maxMemory();
  }
}
```

You use the `<mlet>` subtask of `<jmxdoclet>` to have XDoclet generate the mlet deployment file for you:

```
<jmxdoclet destdir="${gen.src.dir}" mergeDir="${merge.dir}">
  <fileset dir="${src.dir}">
    <include name="**/jmx/*.java"/>
  </fileset>

  <mbeaninterface/>
  <mlet/>
</jmxdoclet>
```

When the `<mlet>` subtask processes `MemoryMonitor.java`, the mlet deployment file, named `mbeans.mlet`, is generated:

```
<!--
  Generated file - Do not edit!
-->

                                              | MBean
<MLET NAME="Memory:name=memoryMonitor"  <──   name
    CODE="com.xdocletbook.jmx.MemoryMonitor"  <── MBean implementation class
    ARCHIVE="MemoryMonitorMBean.jar">  <──┐ JAR file containing
</MLET>                                     | the MBean
```

If you've ever written a Java applet, the format of the `mbeans.mlet` file should be familiar. The `<MLET>` tag works for MBeans in a way similar to how the `<APPLET>` tag works for applets.

The `<mlet>` subtask uses meta-information declared with the `@jmx.mbean` and `@jmx.mlet-entry` tags to generate the mlet deployment file. In the case of `Memory-Monitor.java`, the `name` attribute of `@jmx.mbean` maps to the `NAME` attribute of `<MLET>`. And you use the `archive` attribute of `@jmx.mlet-entry` to declare that the agent can download the `MemoryMonitor` MBean as a JAR file called `MemoryMonitor-MBean.jar`.

Optionally, you can instruct the agent to download the MBean one class file at a time by changing the `@jmx.mlet-entry` tag, replacing the `archive` attribute with the `codebase` attribute:

```
/**
 * @jmx.mlet-entry
 *     codebase="mlets/memory"
 */
public class MemoryMonitor implements MemoryMonitorMBean {
...
}
```

This change results in the following `mbeans.mlet` deployment file being generated:

```
<!--
  Generated file - Do not edit!
-->

<MLET NAME="Memory:name=memoryMonitor"
    CODE="com.xdocletbook.jmx.MemoryMonitor"
    CODEBASE="mlets/memory">
</MLET>
```

The `CODEBASE` attribute indicates that the MBean's class files can be downloaded from the `mlet/memory` path relative to the path of the `mbeans.mlet` file.

9.4.1 *Deploying the mlet using the mlet service*

To try out the `MemoryMonitor` MBean, you need to make sure the mlet service is registered in the MBean server. `MletAgent` (listing 9.5) starts the `HtmlAdaptor-Server` and registers the mlet service to enable hot deployment of MBeans.

Listing 9.5   MletAgent.java registers the mlet service.

```java
package com.xdocletbook.jmx;
import javax.management.MBeanServer;
import javax.management.MBeanServerFactory;
import javax.management.ObjectName;
import com.sun.jdmk.comm.HtmlAdaptorServer;

public class MletAgent {
  public static void main(String[] args) throws Exception {
    MBeanServer server =
        MBeanServerFactory.createMBeanServer("MletAgent");
    HtmlAdaptorServer htmlAdaptor = new HtmlAdaptorServer();
    htmlAdaptor.setPort(9092);

    ObjectName htmlName =
        new ObjectName("MletAgent:name=HtmlAdaptor");
    ObjectName mletName = new ObjectName("MletAgent:name=mlet");

    server.registerMBean(htmlAdaptor, htmlName);
    server.createMBean("javax.management.loading.MLet", mletName);

    htmlAdaptor.start();
  }
}
```

Register mlet service MBean

Once `MletAgent` is running, navigate to the mlet service by visiting http://local-host:9092 and then clicking the name=mlet link. If you scroll down the page, you'll see the `getMBeansFromURL` operation. Enter the URL to the `mbeans.mlet` file into the text field, as shown in figure 9.3—in our case, it's in the root of the D: drive.

Finally, click the getMBeansFromURL button to deploy the MBean. If the operation is successful, you should see a page that looks like figure 9.4.

Now let's look at what the `MemoryManager` MBean can tell you. Navigate back to the list of deployed agents by clicking the Back to Agent View link. You should now see a name=memoryMonitor link under the Memory domain. Clicking it yields the screen you see in figure 9.5.

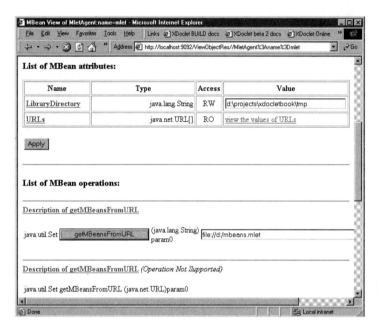

Figure 9.3
Dynamically deploying the `MemoryMonitor` **MBean using the mlet service**

Now you can watch the `AvailableMemory` attribute to gain insight on memory usage. Changing the reload period (near the top) to a nonzero value will

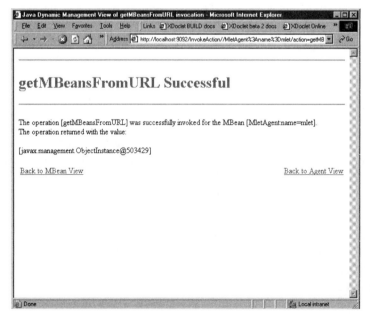

Figure 9.4
The `MemoryMonitor` **MBean is successfully deployed.**

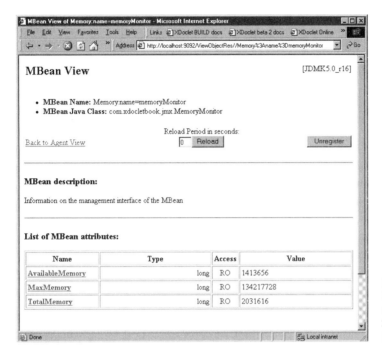

**Figure 9.5
Monitoring memory
usage with the
`MemoryMonitor`
MBean**

cause the screen to be reloaded periodically, making it easier to monitor memory usage.

So far, you've seen how XDoclet can help generate MBean interfaces and mlet deployment files. Now let's look at how XDoclet can help you generate artifacts that support extensions to the JMX specification, starting with JBossMX and a special implementation of a model MBean called an XMBean.

9.5 *Working with MBean services in JBossMX*

Arguably the most well known JMX application is the JBoss application server. At JBoss's core is JBossMX, a JMX server that hosts a collection of MBean services that make up the application server functionality. As a result of this architecture, JBoss is not only a great application server but also instrumented for management through JMX.

To see JBoss's JMX instrumentation in action, make sure JBoss is running and then point your browser to http://{hostname}:8080/jmx-console. Figure 9.6 shows the JBoss JMX console that lists all the MBean services deployed in JBossMX.

Figure 9.6   The JBoss JMX console lets you manage JBoss services through a web interface.

In addition to the MBean services that make up the JBoss application server, you can also deploy your own MBean services in JMX. Let's look at how XDoclet can help you turn the `MemoryMonitor` MBean into an MBean service suitable for deployment in JBossMX.

9.5.1 Creating JBossMX services

JBossMX services are deployed in a service archive (SAR) file. A SAR file is nothing more than a JAR file with an XML service deployment descriptor in the JAR's `META-INF` directory.

The SAR file you'll create, `memory.sar`, needs to include the following files:

- `/com/xdocletbook/jmx/MemoryMonitor.class`—The MBean implementation

- `/com/xdocletbook/jmx/MemoryMonitorMBean.class`—The MBean interface

- `/META-INF/jboss-service.xml`—The service deployment descriptor file

You wrote `MemoryMonitor.java` in the last section, and the `<mbeaninterface>` subtask generates `MemoryMonitorMBean.java` for you. Once compiled, these will give you the two class files that your SAR file needs. But where do you get the service deployment descriptor?

Fortunately, you can add the `<jbossxmlservicetemplate>` subtask to your build to have the deployment descriptor generated:

```
<jmxdoclet destdir="${gen.src.dir}" mergeDir="${merge.dir}">
...
  <jbossxmlservicetemplate destdir="${jboss.service.dir}"
      servicefile="jboss"
  />
</jmxdoclet>
```

You set the `destdir` attribute so that the service descriptor will be generated in a convenient path for later JARing up (or SARing up, to be exact). The value of the `servicefile` attribute is prepended to `-service.xml` to determine the name of the service descriptor file. In this case, the file will be named `jboss-service.xml`. Multiple service descriptor files can be generated by duplicating the `<jbossxmlservicetemplate>` subtask within the build and specifying a different value for the `servicefile` attribute.

The `<jbossxmlservicetemplate>` subtask alone won't generate the service descriptor file. It works in tandem with the `@jboss.service` class-level tag. So, you add this tag to your MBean:

```
/**
 * @jmx.mbean
 *     name="Memory:name=memoryMonitor"
 *     description="Memory Monitor MBean"
...
 * @jboss.service servicefile="jboss"
...
 */
public class MemoryMonitor implements MemoryMonitorMBean {
...
}
```

Pay special attention to the `servicefile` attribute of `@jboss.service`. It's no coincidence that in this example, its value matches that of `<jbossxmlservicetemplate>`'s `servicefile` attribute in the build file. Because it's possible to have multiple service descriptor files generated by XDoclet, there must be a mechanism to indicate which service descriptor file a particular MBean should be part of. This is accomplished by matching `@jboss.service`'s `servicefile` attribute to the `servicefile` attribute of a particular `<jbossxmlservicetemplate>` subtask.

Furthermore, it's also possible for a service to contain multiple MBeans. You can do this by setting the `servicefile` attribute of `@jboss.service` in several MBeans to all match the same `<jbossxmlservicetemplate>` in the build.

When the `<jbossxmlservicetemplate>` subtask processes `MemoryMonitor.java`, the following `jboss-service.xml` file is generated:

```
<?xml version="1.0" encoding="UTF-8"?>

<service>

  <mbean code="com.xdocletbook.jmx.MemoryMonitor"
         name="Memory:name=memoryMonitor"
         >
    <!--Memory Monitor MBean-->
  </mbean>
</service>
```

Clearly, the `name` attribute of `<mbean>` in `jboss-service.xml` is received from the `name` attribute of the `@jmx.mbean` tag in `MemoryMonitor.java`.

Deploying an MBean service to JBossMX

Now that you have your service descriptor file, all that's left to do is to JAR (or SAR) it up along with the MBean's class files. To do this, add the following target to the `build-package.xml` file:

```
<target name="build-sar">
  <mkdir dir="${jboss.sar.dir}"/>

  <jar jarfile="${jboss.sar.dir}/memory.sar">
    <fileset dir="${build.dir}" includes="**/jmx/Memory*.class"/>
    <metainf dir="${jboss.service.dir}"/>
  </jar>
</target>
```

When the build is run, a file named `memory.sar` is created in the directory specified by the `${jboss.sar.dir}` variable. To deploy the memory service, copy this SAR file into the deploy directory for the JBoss server. If you're successful, JBoss should report something like this to its console:

```
[MainDeployer] Starting deployment of package:
    file:/D:/jboss-3.0.4/server/default/deploy/memory.jar
[MainDeployer] Deployed package:
    file:/D:/jboss-3.0.4/server/default/deploy/memory.jar
```

Now, point your web browser to the JBoss management console to see the memory monitor service deployed. It should be visible near the top under the Memory header, as shown in figure 9.7.

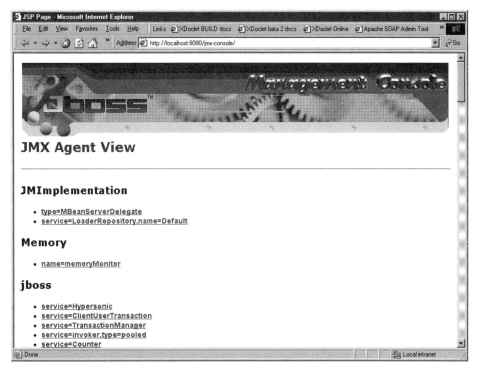

Figure 9.7 The `memoryMonitor` service deployed

To test the memory monitor MBean, click on the name=memoryMonitor link. You should be greeted with a vaguely familiar page showing the current memory levels (figure 9.8).

Now that you've seen how to deploy a standard MBean as a service in JBossMX, let's look at how you can use XDoclet to write model MBean definitions in XML for deployment in JBossMX.

9.5.2 Generating XML for JBossMX model MBeans

What if the management interface for an MBean is likely to change quite often? Using standard MBeans, you'd have to change the MBean interface and then recompile. Model MBeans make it possible to define the MBean's management interface in an external (non-code) entity so that the interface can be changed on the fly. Furthermore, model MBeans can define metadata that describes the MBean and its operations and attributes for improved usability.

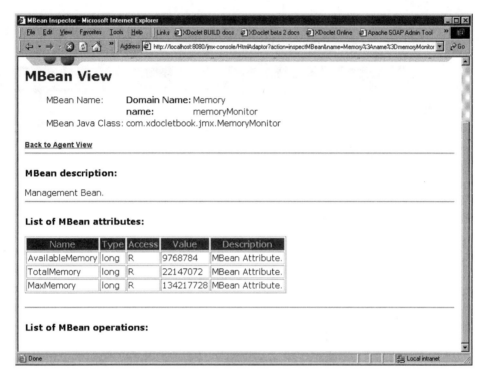

Figure 9.8 Accessing the `memoryMonitor` MBean through the JBoss management console

XMBeans, first made available in JBoss version 3.2.0, are a special type of model MBean whose interface is defined in an XML file. Just as XDoclet generates Java interfaces for standard MBeans, it can also generate XML descriptors that define the management interface of XMBeans.

Let's change the memory monitor MBean to be an XMBean instead of a standard MBean. You start by adding the `<jbossxmbean>` subtask to `<jmxdoclet>` in the build file to have XDoclet generate XMBean interface descriptor files:

```
<jmxdoclet destdir="${gen.src.dir}" mergeDir="${merge.dir}">
...
  <jbossxmbean destdir="${jboss.xmbean.dir}" />
</jmxdoclet>
```

The `<jbossxmbean>` subtask generates a management interface descriptor file for any class that is tagged at the class-level with the `@jboss.xmbean` tag. So, you tag `MemoryMonitor.java` at the class level with `@jboss.xmbean`:

```
/**
 * @jmx.mbean
 *     name="Memory:name=memoryMonitor"
 *     description="Memory Monitor MBean"
 ...
 *
 * @jboss.xmbean
 */
public class MemoryMonitor implements MemoryMonitorMBean {
 ...
}
```

When the build is run and `MemoryMonitor.java` is processed by `<jbossxmbean>`, the following XMBean descriptor, `MemoryMonitor.xml`, is created:

```xml
<?xml version="1.0" encoding="UTF-8"?>
<!DOCTYPE mbean PUBLIC "-//JBoss//DTD JBOSS XMBEAN 1.0//EN"
    "http://www.jboss.org/j2ee/dtd/jboss_xmbean_1_0.dtd">

<mbean>
  <description>Memory Monitor MBean</description>
  <descriptors>
    <persistence/>
  </descriptors>
  <class>com.xdocletbook.jmx.MemoryMonitor</class>

  <!--attributes-->
  <attribute access="read-only" getMethod="getAvailableMemory">

    <description>Amount of free memory available</description>
    <name>AvailableMemory</name>
    <type>long</type>
    <descriptors>
      <persistence/>

    </descriptors>
  </attribute>
  <attribute access="read-only" getMethod="getTotalMemory">

    <description>(no description)</description>
    <name>TotalMemory</name>
    <type>long</type>
    <descriptors>
      <persistence/>

    </descriptors>
  </attribute>
  <attribute access="read-only" getMethod="getMaxMemory">

    <description>(no description)</description>
    <name>MaxMemory</name>
    <type>long</type>
```

```
    <descriptors>
      <persistence/>

    </descriptors>
  </attribute>

<!--artificial attributes-->

<!--operations -->

<!--artificial operations-->

<!--notifications -->

</mbean>
```

Notice that `<jbossxmbean>` pulled together information from other `@jmx.*` tags to help generate the XMBean descriptor file. In this example, `<jbossxmbean>` takes advantage of the `description` and `access` attributes of `@jmx.managed-attribute` when defining the `<attribute>` declarations in `MemoryMonitor.xml`.

Another side effect of tagging `MemoryMonitor.java` with `@jboss.mxbean` is that a reference to `MemoryMonitor.xml` is included in the `jboss-service.xml` service descriptor file:

```
<?xml version="1.0" encoding="UTF-8"?>

<service>

  <mbean code="com.xdocletbook.jmx.MemoryMonitor"
         name="Memory:name=memoryMonitor"
         xmbean-dd="com/xdocletbook/jmx/MemoryMonitor.xml"
         >
    <!--Memory Monitor MBean-->
  </mbean>
</service>
```

To include `MemoryMonitor.xml` in the SAR file, add an additional `<fileset>` that includes the XMBean directory to the `<jar>` task you used before:

```
<target name="build-sar">
  <mkdir dir="${jboss.sar.dir}"/>

  <jar jarfile="${jboss.sar.dir}/memory.sar">
    <fileset dir="${build.dir}" includes="**/jmx/Memory*.class"/>
    <fileset dir="${jboss.xmbean.dir}"
        includes="**/jmx/Memory*.xml"/>
    <metainf dir="${jboss.service.dir}"/>
  </jar>
</target>
```

After you redeploy `memory.sar` to JBoss, look at the JMX Console in JBoss again (figure 9.9). You should see the same MBean as before, except that this time the MBean and its attributes have descriptions other than the default descriptions you saw earlier. Also, you'll notice that the MBean implementation class is now `org.jboss.mx.modelmbean.XMBean`, indicating that this is an XMBean and not a standard MBean.

The nice thing about deploying MBeans as XMBeans is that you can alter the management interface without recompiling. You simply deploy a new XML descriptor file, and when JBossMX picks it up, your MBean service will have a new interface.

Now that you've seen how to use XDoclet to write MBeans for JBossMX, let's look at how XDoclet can help you develop MBeans for MX4J, another implementation of the JMX specification.

Figure 9.9 The `memoryMonitor` MBean deployed as an XMBean

9.6 *Generating MBean description classes for MX4J*

Suppose you're going to deploy your MBeans into MX4J. MX4J is another open-source (Apache-style license) implementation of JMX. Its most notable application is that it serves as the basis for Jakarta Tomcat's management interface. You can download and read more about MX4J at http://mx4j.sourceforge.net.

Your beans will work fine as-is in MX4J. However, with MX4J you also have the option of describing MBeans and their managed operations with MBean description classes.

Using reflection, the JMX agent can retrieve information about managed operations, attributes, constructors, and notifications. However, it can't retrieve information that's important for the user of the managed application, such as operation, attribute, and parameter descriptions; parameter names; and so forth. MBean description classes enable you to customize the descriptions surrounding an MBean's interface for increased usability.

An MBean description class is any class that either implements `mx4j.MBean-Description` or extends `mx4j.MBeanDescriptionAdaptor` and is named with the same fully qualified name of the MBean class ending with `MBeanDescription`.

These are the steps you must take to have XDoclet generate MBean description classes for your MBeans:

1   Add the `<mx4jdescription>` subtask to your build file.

2   Tag your MBean class file with the appropriate `@jmx.*` tags and `description` attributes.

3   Run the build.

4   Deploy the MBean in an MX4J agent.

9.6.1 *Preparing the build for MX4J*

By adding the `<mx4jdescription>` subtask under `<jmxdoclet>` in your build file, you can have XDoclet write MBean description classes for you:

```
<jmxdoclet destdir="${gen.src.dir}" mergeDir="${merge.dir}">
  <fileset dir="${src.dir}">
    <include name="**/jmx/*.java"/>
  </fileset>

  <mbeaninterface/>
  <mlet/>
  <mx4jdescription/>
</jmxdoclet>
```

9.6.2 Tagging MBeans for MX4J

The `<mx4jdescription>` subtask uses the `description` attribute of the following tags to create an MBean descriptor class for each class it processes that's tagged with `@jmx.mbean`:

- `@jmx.mbean`
- `@jmx.managed-constructor`
- `@jmx.managed-constructor-parameter`
- `@jmx.managed-attribute`
- `@jmx.managed-operation`
- `@jmx.managed-operation-parameter`

As you'll see, `<mx4jdescription>` also uses the `name` and `position` attributes of `@jmx.managed-constructor-parameter` and `@jmx.managed-operation-parameter` when describing parameters.

In the event that the MBean (or any of its managed operations and attributes) is not tagged with the description attributes of these tags, then the generated MBean description class will still be generated, but it will give default values for descriptions.

Let's revisit the `BlogManager` MBean. Listing 9.6 shows the new `BlogManager` class, updated with meta-information that `<mx4jdescription>` can use when generating an MBean descriptor class for `BlogManager`.

Listing 9.6   BlogManager.java, updated to be more descriptive for MX4J

```java
package com.xdocletbook.jmx;

import java.util.List;

import com.xdocletbook.blog.interfaces.BlogFacade;
import com.xdocletbook.blog.interfaces.BlogFacadeHome;
import com.xdocletbook.blog.util.BlogFacadeUtil;
/**
 * @jmx.mbean
 *    name="BlogManager"
 *    description="Some basic administrative functions for blogs."    <--|  Describe
 */                                                                      |  MBean
public class BlogManager implements BlogManagerMBean {
  BlogFacadeHome home;

  public BlogManager() throws Exception {
    home = BlogFacadeUtil.getHome();
  }
```

```
/**
 * @jmx.managed-operation
 *     description="Retrieve a blog's name given its ID."   ◁┐  Describe
 *                                                             │  managed
 * @jmx.managed-operation-parameter                            ┘  operations
 *     description="The ID of the blog to be looked up."     ──┐ Describe
 *     name="blogId"                                            │ parameters to
 *     position="1"                                             │ the managed
 */                                                             │ operations
public String getBlogName(String blogId) throws Exception {
  BlogFacade facade = home.create();
  return facade.getBlogSimple(blogId).getName();
}

/**
 * @jmx.managed-operation
 *     description="Delete a blog."    ◁── Describe managed operations
 *
 * @jmx.managed-operation-parameter                         ──┐ Describe
 *     description="The ID of the blog to be deleted."        │ parameters to
 *     name="blogId"                                          │ the managed
 *     position="1"                                           │ operations
 */
public void deleteBlog(String blogId) throws Exception {
  home.create().deleteBlog(blogId);
}

/**
 * @jmx.managed-operation
 *     description="Retrieve a list of all blogs."   ◁─┐ Describe managed
 */                                                    │ operations
public List getAllBlogs() throws Exception{
  BlogFacade facade = home.create();
  return facade.getAllBlogs();
}
}
```

9.6.3 *Running the build*

When `<mx4jdescription>` processes this new `BlogManager.java`, it generates `BlogManagerMBeanDescription.java`:

```
/*
 * Generated file - Do not edit!
 */
package com.xdocletbook.jmx;
import mx4j.MBeanDescriptionAdapter;
import java.lang.reflect.Method;
import java.lang.reflect.Constructor;
```

```java
/**
 * MBean description.
 */
public class BlogManagerMBeanDescription
    extends MbeanDescriptionAdapter {

  public String getMBeanDescription() {
    return "Some basic administrative functions for blogs.";
  }

  public String getConstructorDescription(Constructor ctor) {
    String name = ctor.getName();

    return super.getConstructorDescription(ctor);
  }

  public String getConstructorParameterName(Constructor ctor,
    int index) {

    return super.getConstructorParameterName(ctor, index);
  }

  public String getConstructorParameterDescription(Constructor ctor,
      int index) {

    return super.getConstructorParameterDescription(ctor, index);
  }

  public String getAttributeDescription(String attribute) {

      return super.getAttributeDescription(attribute);
  }

  public String getOperationDescription(Method operation) {
    String name = operation.getName();

    if (name.equals("getBlogName")) {
      return "Retrieve a blog's name given its ID.";
    }
    if (name.equals("deleteBlog")) {
      return "Delete a blog.";
    }
    if (name.equals("getAllBlogs")) {
      return "Retrieve a list of all blogs.";
    }

    return super.getOperationDescription(operation);
  }

  public String getOperationParameterName(Method method,
      int index) {
    String name = method.getName();

    if (name.equals("getBlogName")) {
      switch (index) {
```

```
        case 1:
          return "blogId";
      }
    }
    if (name.equals("deleteBlog")) {
      switch (index) {
        case 1:
          return "blogId";
      }
    }

    return super.getOperationParameterName(method, index);
  }

  public String getOperationParameterDescription(Method method,
      int index) {
    String name = method.getName();

    if (name.equals("getBlogName")) {
      switch (index) {
        case 1:
          return "The ID of the blog to be looked up.";
      }
    }
    if (name.equals("deleteBlog")) {
      switch (index) {
        case 1:
          return "The ID of the blog to be deleted.";
      }
    }

    return super.getOperationParameterDescription(method, index);
  }
}
```

9.6.4 *Deploying the MBean into MX4J*

To take advantage of this MBean descriptor class, you must deploy your MBean (and this class) within an MX4J agent. To do so, change JMXStartupListener.java to include MX4J's HttpAdaptor (MX4J's answer to Sun's HtmlAdaptorServer) among the services it starts (listing 9.7).

> **Listing 9.7 JMXStartupListener.java, modified to also start MX4J's HttpAdaptor**

```
package com.xdocletbook.blog.listener;
import javax.management.MBeanServer;
import javax.management.MBeanServerFactory;
import javax.management.ObjectName;
import javax.servlet.ServletContextEvent;
import javax.servlet.ServletContextListener;
import mx4j.adaptor.http.HttpAdaptor;
```

```java
import com.sun.jdmk.comm.HtmlAdaptorServer;
import com.xdocletbook.jmx.BlogManager;

/**
 * @web.listener
 */
public class JMXStartupListener implements ServletContextListener {
  private MBeanServer server;
  private HttpAdaptor httpAdaptor;
  private HtmlAdaptorServer htmlAdaptor;

  public void contextDestroyed(ServletContextEvent arg0) {
    System.out.println("STOPPING MBEAN SERVER");
    httpAdaptor.stop();
    htmlAdaptor.stop();
  }

  public void contextInitialized(ServletContextEvent arg0) {
    System.out.println("STARTING MBEAN SERVER");

    server = MBeanServerFactory.createMBeanServer("BlogAgent");

    try {
      startBlogManager();
      startHtmlAdaptor();
      startHttpAdaptor();      ◁── Register and start MX4J's HttpAdaptor
    } catch (Exception e) {
      System.err.println("Exception:  "+e);
    }
  }

  private void startBlogManager() throws Exception {
    server.registerMBean(new BlogManager(),
        new ObjectName("BlogAgent:name=blogManager"));
  }

  private void startHtmlAdaptor() throws Exception {
    htmlAdaptor = new HtmlAdaptorServer();
    htmlAdaptor.setPort(9092);

    server.registerMBean(htmlAdaptor,
        new ObjectName("Server:name=HtmlAdaptor"));
    htmlAdaptor.start();
  }

  private void startHttpAdaptor() throws Exception {
    httpAdaptor = new HttpAdaptor();
    httpAdaptor.setPort(9093);

    server.registerMBean(httpAdaptor,
        new ObjectName("Server:name=HttpAdaptor"));
    httpAdaptor.start();
  }
}
```

Register and start MX4J's HttpAdaptor

The HttpAdaptor listens on port 9093 for MX4J commands that come in the form of HTTP requests. For example, to retrieve a list of the MBeans available in the server, point your web browser to http://localhost:9093/server. The result should look something like Figure 9.10.

Notice that the results come back in XML format. Although this may be more difficult for human eyes to read, it makes it much easier to write applications that interface with MBeans through this interface.

Unfortunately, MX4J's server command doesn't tell you much about the Blog-Manager MBean. For example, you can't see any of the managed operations that are exposed via JMX. The mbean command allows you to drill down and see more details about a specific MBean. Point your browser to http://localhost:9093/mbean?objectname=BlogAgent:name=blogManager to see the MBean detail for the BlogManager MBean (figure 9.11).

From the MBean detail screen, you can see the purpose of the MBean description class. Notice that all the descriptions with which you tagged your MBean class are visible in the XML returned from the mbean command.

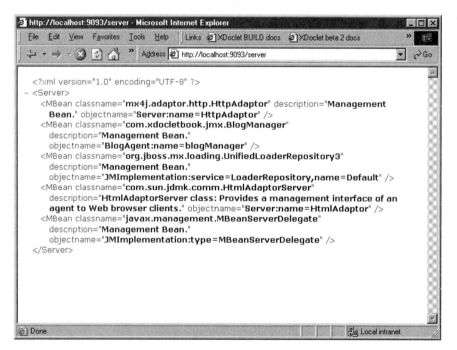

Figure 9.10 All the deployed MBeans as reported by MX4J's `server` command

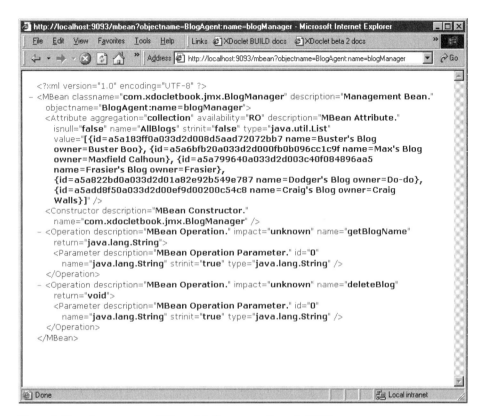

Figure 9.11 **BlogManager** MBean details as seen through MX4J

9.7 *Summary*

You've seen how JMX can make it easy to instrument an application for management. You've also seen how MBean development can be further simplified using XDoclet to generate MBean interfaces, mlet deployment files, and other artifacts associated with extensions to the JMX specification.

In the next chapter, we'll wrap up our discussion of the code generation modules that come with XDoclet by looking at how XDoclet can generate mock object classes that can be used to perform unit testing from the inside out.

XDoclet and mock objects

You're mocking me, aren't you?

—Buzz Lightyear, *Toy Story* (Disney/Pixar)

In recent years, a revolution of sorts has been taking place in the world of software development. More and more developers are abandoning traditional software development methodologies in favor of extreme programming, Scrum, and others collectively known as the *agile methodologies*.

Among the tenets of the agile methodologies is the concept of test-driven development. *Test-driven development* advocates that every unit of developed code is accompanied (or preceded) by code that tests that unit. These unit tests are typically implemented within the JUnit testing framework (http://www.junit.org).

Unfortunately, some units of code are hard to unit-test. Sometimes, setting up the preconditions for a test is very elaborate. For example, testing a servlet requires that `HttpServletRequest` and `HttpServletResponse` objects be set up prior to the test. Or, you may need to test how a certain object is used by another set of code. For instance, you may have a class with several callback methods that should be called, and you need to test that those methods are called as expected.

In this chapter, we'll look at how to use XDoclet to generate mock objects—stub classes that make it easier to unit-test code that would be difficult to test otherwise.

10.1 What are mock objects?

In a paper entitled "Endo-Testing: Unit Testing with Mock Objects" (http://www.connextra.com/aboutUs/mockobjects.pdf), three agile methodologists, Tim Mackinnon, Steve Freeman, and Philip Craig, present the technique of writing mock objects to assist in unit testing. Most simple test cases invoke a method on the object being tested and verify that the value returned is as expected. This approach is fine for testing simple objects. But the funny thing about simple objects is that they're rarely found in real-world code. Often, the object being tested is more complex, and you're interested in more than just the end result. That's where mock objects come in.

Put simply, mock objects are stand-ins for actual objects that participate in a test case. They're injected into the code being tested so they can test it from the *inside*. Rather than treat an object as a black box, verifying only the end results, a test case can send in undercover mock objects to test target to verify that the tested object acts on the mock objects as expected.

To visualize how mock objects work, imagine that a restaurant critic wants to write a review of a newly opened restaurant. If this critic uses a simple approach to reviewing (testing) the restaurant, he'll stand outside of the restaurant, poll the patrons as they leave, and summarize their answers to write his review. But that approach will give only a limited second-hand report of the restaurant. Instead, any respectable critic will visit the restaurant (as a mock customer) and witness for himself the quality of the food and service.

The restaurant analogy exposes an important concept to understand about mock objects: Mock objects aren't the objects being tested. They're merely mock implementations of classes that the tested object collaborates with in the course of performing its functionality. In our example, the restaurant is the object being tested, whereas the critic is the mock object.

A wonderful thing about testing with mock objects is that you can test an object in isolation, without the test being tainted by side effects from the collaborator objects. If you use real objects and a test fails, you can never be sure that it wasn't a bug in the collaborator object that caused the failure. Likewise, a test may have succeeded only because a bug in the collaborator balanced out a bug in the tested object.

10.1.1 *Knowing when to mock*

When should you use a mock object and when should you rely on a plain-vanilla JUnit test case? The mock objects Wiki (http://c2.com/cgi/wiki?MockObject) lists the following seven reasons for mocking an object:

- *The real object has non-deterministic behavior.* Perhaps the real object generates random results, but your test case tests a specific result.

- *The real object is difficult to set up.* As we mentioned before, setting up an Http-ServletRequest object to test a servlet's service method can be quite a chore. Mocking HttpServletRequest with the preconditions necessary for a test case is often easier than setting up a full-blown instance of HttpServletRequest.

- *The real object has behavior that's hard to cause.* Perhaps your test case tests what would happen in the event of a network error. A mock implementation can pretend that there is a network problem.

- *The real object is slow.* Maybe the collaborator object performs a complicated operation that is slow. There's no sense in unnecessarily slowing down the test case to wait on a collaborator that isn't the target of the test. Instead, you can create a mock implementation that gives a much quicker response.

- *The real object has (or is) a user interface.* Testing user interfaces is notoriously tricky. If you're testing a class that interacts with a user interface, mocking the UI objects can make testing easier.

- *The test needs to query the object, but the queries aren't available in the real object.* What if your test needs to gather statistics about how a collaborator is used by the object being tested? Maybe the test needs to verify that a certain collaborator method is called a specific number of times. The real object wouldn't have methods that return this type of information, but a mock implementation can have such methods.

- *The real object does not yet exist.* You may have written only part of a system, and other team members are implementing the collaborators. Rather than wait on them to finish, you can create mock implementations of collaborator objects to test your piece.

10.1.2 *Testing from the inside out*

The sequence diagram in figure 10.1 shows generically how a test case can use a mock implementation of a collaborator object to test another class.

The test case sets up preconditions in the mock object and sets its expectations of how the target class should use the mock object. Then it makes a method call on the target class, passing the mock collaborator as a parameter. In the course of performing its functionality, the target method makes calls on the collaborator's

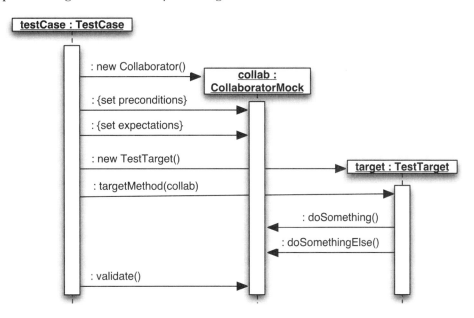

Figure 10.1   A test case uses a mock collaborator to test a target class from the inside.

methods. If any of the test case expectations are violated, the test case fails immediately. Finally, after the target method returns, the mock collaborator's `validate` method is called to verify that the expectations of the test were met.

Now that you know what mock objects are, let's see how you can harness the power of XDoclet to generate mock object classes.

10.2 *Generating mock objects with XDoclet*

Mock objects are probably the simplest thing you can generate with XDoclet. Mock object generation is supported in XDoclet by only one task, only one subtask, and only one class-level tag. Making things even simpler, the task, subtask, and tag each have no required attributes.

As an example of how you can use XDoclet to generate mock objects, consider the following scenario: Imagine you're the owner of a full-service gas station. (If you don't know what a full-service gas station is, ask someone older or move to Oregon, where state law requires that an attendant pump gasoline.) You've been receiving complaints that the service isn't as "full" as it should be, so you'd like to test your service station to see how well your employees treat the customers. You decide to send a "mock" customer to the service station to have their automobile serviced and to identify any problems with the level of service provided.

Let's construct this test in software using mock objects. First, you need to add the proper XDoclet tasks and subtasks to your build to support mock-object generation.

10.2.1 *Adding mock-object generation to the build*

For the service station example, create a new `build.xml` file (listing 10.1). When running the `main` target, this build file performs the following three steps:

1. Generates mock implementations for your interfaces
2. Compiles all source code, including mock implementations
3. Runs all JUnit test classes

> **Listing 10.1 build.xml includes tasks for generating mock objects and running JUnit tests.**

```
<?xml version="1.0" encoding="UTF-8"?>

<project name="XDoclet Mockery" default="main" basedir=".">
  <description>XDoclet example for MockObjects</description>

  <property name="src.dir" location="src"/>
  <property name="build.dir" location="build"/>
  <property name="lib.dir" location="lib"/>
```

```
<property name="web.dir" location="web"/>
<property name="merge.dir" location="mergeDir"/>
<property name="test.results.dir" location="testresults"/>

<path id="compile.path">
  <fileset dir="${lib.dir}" includes="*.jar"/>
</path>

<path id="xdoclet.lib.path">
  <fileset dir="${lib.dir}" includes="*.jar"/>
  <fileset dir="${xdoclet.lib.dir}" includes="*.jar"/>
</path>

<path id="test.classpath">
  <path refid="xdoclet.lib.path" />
  <pathelement location="${build.dir}" />
</path>

<target name="generate">
  <taskdef name="mockobjectdoclet"
    classname="xdoclet.modules.mockobjects.MockObjectDocletTask"
    classpathref="xdoclet.lib.path"/>

  <mockobjectdoclet destdir="${gen.src.dir}">
    <fileset dir="${src.dir}">
      <include name="**/*.java" />
    </fileset>

    <mockobjects/>
  </mockobjectdoclet>
</target>

<target name="compile" depends="generate">
  <mkdir dir="${build.dir}"/>
  <javac destdir="${build.dir}"
      classpathref="xdoclet.lib.path">
    <src path="${gen.src.dir};${src.dir}"/>
  </javac>
</target>

<target name="junit-test" depends="compile">
  <junit printsummary="withOutAndErr"
      haltonfailure="yes">
    <classpath refid="test.classpath" />

    <formatter type="plain" usefile="no" />

    <batchtest fork="no" >
      <fileset dir="${build.dir}">
        <include name="**/*Test.class" />
      </fileset>
    </batchtest>
```

Load
<mockobjectdoclet>
task

<── **Generate mock implementations**

Run
JUnit
tests

```
        </junit>
    </target>

    <target name="main" depends="junit-test"/>
</project>
```

In the generate task, you use the <mockobjectdoclet> task and its <mockobjects> subtask to generate mock implementations of your interfaces. After the classes are compiled, the junit-test target runs all JUnit test cases (*Test.class) through JUnit to test the code.

Now that the build is ready to generate mock objects, you can begin tagging interfaces to be implemented by mock objects.

10.2.2 *Tagging interfaces to generate mock implementations*

In the tradition of test-first programming (writing test cases *before* writing application code), you'll write the Automobile interface (listing 10.2) first. You'll have XDoclet generate the mock implementation of Automobile without your having written the code for the service station.

Listing 10.2 Automobile.java declares the basic functions of an automobile.

```
package com.xdocletbook.mock;

/**
 * @mock.generate      <— Generate mock object
 */
public interface Automobile {
  public int getTankCapacity();
  public int getCurrentTankLevel();
  public void addOneGallon();

  public boolean isWindshieldClean();
  public void cleanWindshield();

  public void inflateFrontLeftTire();
  public void inflateFrontRightTire();
  public void inflateRearLeftTire();
  public void inflateRearRightTire();
  public boolean isFrontLeftTireInflated();
  public boolean isFrontRightTireInflated();
  public boolean isRearLeftTireInflated();
  public boolean isRearRightTireInflated();

  public float getRadioStation();
  public void setRadioStation(float station);
}
```

By applying the class-level (or is it interface-level?) `@mock.generate` tag to `Auto-mobile.java`, you tell the `<mockobjects>` subtask to generate a mock implementation of this interface. When `<mockobjects>` processes `Automobile.java`, it generates `AutomobileMock.java`, a class that implements the `Automobile` interface and provides methods for setting preconditions and expectations for testing a full-service station.

The generated `AutomobileMock` class is too lengthy (over 700 lines of code) to reproduce here, but the following list should give you some idea of the types of methods it includes:

- `addActualGetTankCapacityReturnValue`—Sets the value that `getTankCapacity` should return

- `setExpectedAddOneGallonCalls`—Sets the number of times that `addOneGallon` should be called

- `setExpectedCleanWindshieldCalls`—Sets the number of times that `cleanWindshield` should be called

And this is only a small fraction of the methods that `AutomobileMock` contains for setting preconditions and expectations. Now you'll write a JUnit test case that uses many of these methods to set up a mock implementation of `Automobile` so you can test the `FullServiceStation` test.

10.2.3 *Testing FullServiceStation.java with mock objects*

`FullServiceStationTest.java` (listing 10.3) is a JUnit test case that you can use to test the implementation of `FullServiceStation.java`. You'll use the `testService-Automobile` method to test the `serviceAutomobile` method of `FullService-Station.java`.

Listing 10.3   Testing FullServiceStation.java with AutomobileMock

```
package com.xdocletbook.mock;
import junit.framework.TestCase;
import junit.framework.TestSuite;
import junit.textui.TestRunner;

public class FullServiceStationTest extends TestCase {

  public FullServiceStationTest(String name) {
    super(name);
  }
```

```
public void testServiceAutomobile() {
    AutomobileMock auto = new AutomobileMock();

    auto.clear();
    auto.addActualGetTankCapacityReturnValue(17);
    auto.addActualGetCurrentTankLevelReturnValue(3);

    auto.addActualIsFrontLeftTireInflatedReturnValue(false);
    auto.addActualIsFrontRightTireInflatedReturnValue(true);
    auto.addActualIsRearRightTireInflatedReturnValue(true);
    auto.addActualIsRearLeftTireInflatedReturnValue(true);

    // SET EXPECTATIONS
    auto.setExpectedGetTankCapacityCalls(1);
    auto.setExpectedGetCurrentTankLevelCalls(1);
    auto.setExpectedAddOneGallonCalls(14);

    auto.setExpectedIsFrontLeftTireInflatedCalls(1);
    auto.setExpectedIsFrontRightTireInflatedCalls(1);
    auto.setExpectedIsRearLeftTireInflatedCalls(1);
    auto.setExpectedIsRearRightTireInflatedCalls(1);
    auto.setExpectedInflateFrontLeftTireCalls(1);
    auto.setExpectedInflateFrontRightTireCalls(0);
    auto.setExpectedInflateRearLeftTireCalls(0);
    auto.setExpectedInflateRearRightTireCalls(0);

    auto.setExpectedCleanWindshieldCalls(1);

    auto.setExpectedSetRadioStationFloatCalls(0);

    FullServiceStation station = new FullServiceStation();
    station.serviceAutomobile(auto);

    auto.verify();
    }
}
```

❶❷ Set preconditions for test

❸ Set preconditions for test

❹❺ Set expectations
❻❼
❽
❾

Send mock Automobile to be serviced

Verify expectations

Before sending the mock customer through, you set up a few preconditions for the test:

❶ The car's fuel tank has a maximum capacity of 17 gallons.

❷ The fuel tank currently contains only three gallons of fuel.

❸ The front-left tire is slightly under-inflated. The other tires are fully inflated.

You also make a list of expectations for the service to be applied to the vehicle:

❹ The car's fuel level should be checked once, before pumping.

❺ Exactly 14 gallons of fuel should be added to the car's fuel tank.

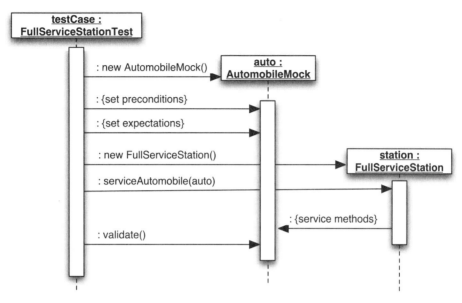

Figure 10.2 **You test `FullServiceStation`'s `serviceAutomobile` method by sending a mock `Automobile` for service.**

❻ All four tires should be checked for proper inflation.

❼ If under-inflated, a tire should be aired up.

❽ The windshield should be cleaned even if it isn't dirty.

❾ The radio should not be changed.

The sequence diagram in figure 10.2 shows how `FullServiceStationTest` uses the generated `AutomobileMock` class to test the `serviceAutomobile` method of `FullServiceStation`.

You can run the test by running your build file. When the test is run, it fails. Why? Oh yeah—you haven't developed a `FullServiceStation` class yet. Let's do that now.

Satisfying the test

`FullServiceStation.java` (listing 10.4) gives the first try at implementing a full-service gas station.

Listing 10.4   FullServiceStation.java implements a full-service gas station. Or does it?

```java
package com.xdocletbook.mock;

public class FullServiceStation {
  public FullServiceStation() {
  }

  public void serviceAutomobile(Automobile auto) {
    int gallonsToPump = auto.getTankCapacity();

    for(int i=0; i<gallonsToPump; i++) {
      auto.addOneGallon();
    }

    if(!auto.isFrontLeftTireInflated()) {
      auto.inflateFrontLeftTire();
    }

    if(!auto.isFrontRightTireInflated()) {
      auto.inflateFrontRightTire();
    }

    if(!auto.isRearLeftTireInflated()) {
      auto.inflateRearLeftTire();
    }

    if(!auto.isRearRightTireInflated()) {
      auto.inflateRearRightTire();
    }

    auto.setRadioStation(99.5F);
  }
}
```

Now that you've written the FullServiceStation class, run your test again. This time it fails, reporting that *Automobile.addOneGallon() should not be called more than 14 times*. It seems that the service station employees are overfilling gas tanks and spilling fuel on the ground.

Looking at FullServiceStation.java, you see that the gallonsToPump variable in serviceAutomobile is being incorrectly calculated. Make the following change to correct this problem:

```java
int gallonsToPump = auto.getTankCapacity() -
    auto.getCurrentTankLevel();
```

Now that gas isn't spilling on the ground, will the `FullServiceStation` class pass the test? Not yet. When you run the test this time, it fails, telling you that *Automobile.set-RadioStation() should not be called more than 0 times.* The service-station attendants are being rude and changing the radio station from the customer's favorite jazz station to a country music station! This behavior should certainly be corrected.

The offending line of code is at the very end of the `serviceAutomobile` method:

```
auto.setRadioStation(99.5F);
```

To remedy this problem, remove that line from the method and try the test again.

The radio station is being left alone, so surely the test will run this time, right? But when you run it again, it fails again. This time, the error says that *Automobile.cleanWindshield() did not receive the expected Count. Expected: 1. Received: 0.* You expect everyone's windshield to be cleaned, regardless of whether it's dirty, but the mock automobile went away without having its windshield washed.

Taking another look at `FullServiceStation.java`, you find that you forgot to include a call to the `cleanWindshield` method. Add the following line to the `service-Automobile` method:

```
auto.cleanWindshield();
```

This time, when you run the test, it completes successfully. The `FullService-Station` class now meets the expectations of a full-service gas station.

10.3 *Summary*

Unit-testing code helps to ensure that business requirements are met and serves as a form of documentation for the intent of a unit of software. JUnit is a great framework for unit-testing Java code.

But some units of code are hard to test using JUnit alone. Sometimes, setting up preconditions and expectations can be difficult. Mock objects enable you to test code from the inside by injecting mock implementations of collaborator classes into the code being tested.

You've seen how XDoclet can be used to generate mock implementation classes of your application interfaces. Using these mock classes, you can set up preconditions and expectations of tests and properly test code from the inside.[1]

---

[1] To learn more about unit-testing with mock objects and JUnit, see *JUnit in Action* by Vincent Massol and Ted Husted (Greenwich, CT: Manning, 2003).

In the next chapter, we'll look at an exciting new Java specification, the portlet API. You'll not only learn how to write a simple portlet application, but also learn how to employ XDoclet to generate a `portlet.xml` deployment descriptor file so that you can deploy your portlets in a compliant portlet container.

XDoclet and portlets

The only really good place to buy lumber is at a store where the lumber has already been cut and attached together in the form of furniture, finished, and put inside boxes.

—Dave Barry, *The Taming of the Screw*

The Web has come along way from the days when a web page consisted of a plain white background, unformatted text, and maybe some poorly placed images. Modern web sites consist of complex pages designed with aesthetics and usability in mind (although this is debatable about some sites). Moreover, a typical web page may pull its data from a variety of sources, aggregating information in a format that makes it possible for the user to quickly digest multiple tidbits of information.

Web portals are a technology concept that, among other things, makes it simple to aggregate data and content from multiple sources in a single web page. Arguably the best known portal application on the Internet is Yahoo's My Yahoo (http://my.yahoo.com). My Yahoo enables a web visitor to create a personalized web site by picking and choosing the content that appears on their personal home page, including news, sports scores, and stock prices.

Although it may seem less obvious, even Amazon.com is made up of portal pages. Amazon takes a different twist on portals, however, aggregating content whose purpose is to cross-sell and up-sell products to a customer based on that customer's previous activity and interests.

Portlets are the building blocks used to construct a portal page. Each individual piece of content or functionality that is exposed to the user on a portal page is exposed by way of a portlet. You can usually recognize portlets because they're typically drawn with a box or some other graphical element that sets them apart from each other on a page.

In this chapter, we'll look at how to write a simple portlet application, using XDoclet to generate the deployment descriptor for the portlet.

11.1 *Introducing JSR-168 (the portlet API)*

On October 6, 2003, the Java community process voted almost unanimously to finalize JSR-168, the portlet API. JSR-168 is significant to portlet developers because it standardizes the contract between a portlet and a portlet container (or a portal server). Prior to JSR-168, each portal server provided its own API and deployment mechanism. This hindered the notion of "write once, run anywhere" with regard to portlets, because once a portlet had been written for one portal server, it had to be rewritten if it was to be deployed in a different vendor's server.

To put this in perspective, imagine what it would be like if the servlet specification didn't exist (if you've been working with server-side Java long enough, you may remember when it didn't exist). Without the servlet specification, writing a web application would mean making a commitment to a specific server. Without the servlet specification, a web application deployed on Jakarta Tomcat wouldn't work on WebLogic or WebSphere. Likewise, a perfectly functional WebSphere web application wouldn't deploy in Jetty or WebLogic.

JSR-168 does for portlets what the servlet specification does for Java-based web applications. It sets a standard API and deployment mechanism for portlets, enabling a portlet to be deployed successfully on any JSR-168–compliant portal server.

As you explore JSR-168 further, you'll discover that it resembles the servlet specification in many ways. This similarity is intentional, so the learning curve for portlets isn't steep for someone who already knows servlets.

Let's start by looking at what is required at the class level to write a simple portlet.

11.1.1 Writing a simple portlet

Listing 11.1 shows a very simple "Hello World" portlet that highlights the basics of portlet development.

Listing 11.1   HelloWorldPortlet.java: a simple portlet

```
package com.xdocletbook.portlets;

import java.io.IOException;
import javax.portlet.GenericPortlet;
import javax.portlet.PortletException;
import javax.portlet.RenderRequest;
import javax.portlet.RenderResponse;

public class HelloWorldPortlet extends GenericPortlet {
  public void doView(RenderRequest request, RenderResponse response)
      throws PortletException, IOException {

    response.getWriter().write("Hello World!");         Process a
  }                                                     View mode
                                                         request

  public void doEdit(RenderRequest request, RenderResponse response)
      throws PortletException, IOException {

    response.getWriter().write("Hello World: Edit Mode");   Process an
  }                                                          Edit mode
                                                              request
```

```
    public void doHelp(RenderRequest request, RenderResponse response)
        throws PortletException, IOException {

        response.getWriter().write("Hello World: Help Mode");
    }
}
```

**Process a
Help mode
request**

If you're already familiar with servlets, then you probably feel right at home with the code in listing 11.1. The doView, doEdit, and doHelp methods are roughly analogous to an HttpServlet's doGet and doPost methods. But instead of responding to an HTTP request method, these methods respond to a request to render a portlet in a specific mode.

Portlets can present different sides of themselves, depending on how the user wants to interact with them. The most common mode is the View mode, which is the mode that typically displays the portlet's main interface (for example, a list of stock prices). To configure a portlet (perhaps to choose a set of stocks to display), the user can request to see the portlet's Edit mode. And, if the user is confused and needs assistance, he can request to see the portlet's Help mode.

These methods each take a RenderRequest and RenderResponse as parameters, which are roughly analogous to HttpServletRequest and HttpServletResponse. In the previous example, each mode retrieves a Writer object from the RenderResponse object and uses it to render content to be displayed by the portlet. The portlet could've just as easily used a separate JSP to render its content:

```
    public void doView(RenderRequest request, RenderResponse response)
        throws PortletException, IOException {

        PortletRequestDispatcher dispatcher =
            getPortletContext().getRequestDispatcher("hello.jsp");
        dispatcher.include(request, response);
    }
```

11.1.2 Deploying a portlet

Portlet applications are deployed to a portal server using an XML deployment descriptor called portlet.xml. The portlet.xml file is strikingly similar to the web.xml file used to deploy servlets, as seen in listing 11.2.

Listing 11.2 HelloWorldPortlet is deployed by `portlet.xml`.

```
<?xml version="1.0" encoding="UTF-8"?>

<portlet-app>
  <portlet>
```

```
      <description>Hello World Portlet</description>
      <portlet-name>HelloPortlet</portlet-name>
      <display-name>Hello World</display-name>
      <portlet-class>
        com.xdocletbook.portlets.HelloWorldPortlet
      </portlet-class>

      <portlet-info>
        <title>Hello World!</title>
      </portlet-info>
    </portlet>
</portlet-app>
```

Notice that information is duplicated between `portlet.xml` and the `HelloWorld-Portlet.java` class. Furthermore, there's no longer a single authoritative representation of the Hello World portlet, because it's fully defined by two files. This presents an opportunity for XDoclet to remove the duplication and handle some of the work for you.

11.2 Adding portlet.xml generation to the build file

The `<portletdoclet>` task is the Ant task responsible for generation of portlet files. More specifically, the `<portletxml>` subtask is responsible for generating deployment descriptors for JSR-168–compliant portlets. Listing 11.3 shows the `build.xml` file used to generate `portlet.xml`.

Listing 11.3 The portlet application build file

```
<?xml version="1.0" encoding="UTF-8"?>

<project name="WeatherPortlet"
    default="generate" basedir=".">
  <description>XDoclet example for Portlets</description>

  <property name="app.name" value="mikportlets"/>

  <property name="src.dir" location="src"/>
  <property name="lib.dir" location="lib"/>
  <property name="merge.dir" location="mergeDir"/>
  <property name="generated.dir" location="generated"/>
  <property name="xdoclet.lib.dir" location="xdocletlib"/>

  <path id="xdoclet.lib.path">
    <fileset dir="${lib.dir}" includes="*.jar"/>
    <fileset dir="${xdoclet.lib.dir}" includes="*.jar"/>
  </path>
```

```
<target name="clean">
  <delete dir="${generated.dir}"/>
</target>

<target name="generate">
  <taskdef name="portletdoclet"
      classname="xdoclet.modules.portlet.PortletDocletTask"
      classpathref="xdoclet.lib.path"/>

  <portletdoclet destdir="${generated.dir}"
      mergedir="${merge.dir}">
    <fileset dir="${src.dir}">
      <include name="**/*Portlet.java" />
    </fileset>

    <portletxml/>
  </portletdoclet>
</target>
</project>
```

Draw metadata from classes ending in Portlet

Generate portlet.xml deployment descriptor

As you can see, the `<portletxml>` subtask is fairly straightforward, requiring no attributes.

Now let's look at how to write a portlet class that's tagged for inclusion in the generated `portlet.xml` file.

11.3 *Writing a portlet*

Weather information is a common type of data presented in a portlet. To demonstrate how to write a portlet application with XDoclet, you're going to write a portlet that displays the current weather conditions for a specified city and state.

Listing 11.4 shows such a portlet. Notice that it's already tagged with some of the basic XDoclet tags for portlets.

Listing 11.4   WeatherPortlet.java displays weather conditions.

```
package com.xdocletbook.portlets;

import java.io.IOException;
import java.io.PrintWriter;
import javax.portlet.GenericPortlet;
import javax.portlet.PortletContext;
import javax.portlet.PortletException;
import javax.portlet.PortletPreferences;
import javax.portlet.PortletRequestDispatcher;
import javax.portlet.RenderRequest;
import javax.portlet.RenderResponse;
```

```
/**
 * @portlet.portlet
 *     name="WeatherPortlet"
 *     description="Weather Forecast Portlet"
 *     display-name="Weather Forecast"
 *     expiration-cache="3600"
 *
 * @portlet.portlet-info
 *     title="Current Weather"
 *
 * @portlet.portlet-init-param
 *     name="BaseUrl"
 *     value="http://banners.wunderground.com/banner/infobox/US/"
 */
public class WeatherPortlet extends GenericPortlet {

  public void doView(RenderRequest request, RenderResponse response)
      throws PortletException, IOException {

    PortletPreferences prefs = request.getPreferences();
    String city = prefs.getValue("city", "Dallas");
    String state = prefs.getValue("state", "TX");

    String weatherUrl = getInitParameter("BaseUrl") +
        state + "/" + city + ".gif";

    PrintWriter writer = response.getWriter();
    writer.write("<img src='"+weatherUrl+"'>");
  }

  public void doEdit(RenderRequest request, RenderResponse response)
      throws PortletException, IOException {

    PortletContext context = getPortletContext();
    PortletRequestDispatcher dispatch =
        context.getRequestDispatcher(
        "/WEB-INF/jsp/html/WeatherEdit.jsp");

    dispatch.include(request, response);
  }
}
```

Define basic portlet information

Expire portlet in cache after one hour

Give portlet a title

Define base URL of weather data

Let's see how the tags in WeatherPortlet.java affect the generated portlet. xml file.

11.3.1 *Defining portlet basics*

Just as with servlets, portlets have some basic information that can be defined at the class level. You can define this information using the `@portlet.portlet` tag:

```
/**
 * @portlet.portlet
 *     name="WeatherPortlet"
 *     description="Weather Forecast Portlet"
 *     display-name="Weather Forecast"
 *     expiration-cache="3600"
 */
public class WeatherPortlet extends GenericPortlet {
 ...
}
```

The `name` attribute—the only required attribute of `@portlet.portlet`—gives the portlet a unique name within the portlet container. The `description` and `display-name` attributes are informational only and may be displayed in the portlet container's administrative tools.

By default, a portlet's content is generated anew each time the portlet is accessed. But if the portlet container implements caching, setting `expiration-cache` instructs the container to use cached content to conserve system resources. The value of `expiration-cache` is in seconds; so, as defined previously, the content of `WeatherPortlet` is cached for one full hour.

Within the generated `portlet.xml` file, the values set with `@portlet.portlet` are reflected as follows:

```
<portlet-app>
  <portlet>
    <description>Weather Forecast Portlet</description>
    <portlet-name>WeatherPortlet</portlet-name>
    <display-name>Weather Forecast</display-name>
    <portlet-class>
        com.xdocletbook.portlets.WeatherPortlet
    </portlet-class>
 ...
    <expiration-cache>3600</expiration-cache>
 ...
  </portlet>
</portlet-app>
```

In addition to basic portlet information, you can set user-oriented information, such as a user-friendly title for the portlet, using the `@portlet.portlet-info` tag:

```
/**
 * ...
 *
```

```
 * @portlet.portlet-info
 *     title="Current Weather"
 */
public class WeatherPortlet extends GenericPortlet {
...
}
```

As a result of the `@portlet.portlet-info` tag, the following deployment information is included in the generated `portlet.xml` file:

```
<portlet-info>
  <title>Weather Portlet</title>
</portlet-info>
```

Now let's see how to set initial portlet configuration values.

11.3.2 *Initializing portlets*

As with servlets, portlets can be configured with some initial configuration parameters. These parameters are set at deploy time and are global to all users—unlike preferences, which, as you'll see later, can be configured individually on a per-user basis.

`WeatherPortlet.java` retrieves its data from a web-based weather service called Weather Underground. For convenience, the base URL of the weather service is configured in a portlet initialization parameter called `BaseUrl`:

```
/**
 * @portlet.portlet-init-param
 *     name="BaseUrl"
 *     value="http://banners.wunderground.com/banner/infobox/US/"
 */
public class WeatherPortlet extends GenericPortlet {
...
}
```

In the generated `portlet.xml` file, this `@portlet.portlet-init-param` is rendered as follows:

```
<init-param>
  <name>BaseUrl</name>
  <value>http://banners.wunderground.com/banner/infobox/US/</value>
</init-param>
```

At runtime, `WeatherPortlet` retrieves the value of `BaseUrl` using the following excerpt of code:

```
getInitParameter("BaseUrl")
```

You may be wondering what good it does to set a portlet initialization parameter in XDoclet tags. What's the difference between hard-coding it in XDoclet tags and hard-coding it directly in code? The quick answer is that there isn't much difference. The previous `@portlet.portlet-init-param` is meant only as an example. A more typical use of `@portlet.portlet-init-param` wouldn't set the `value` attribute to a static value, but would instead use an Ant property. For example:

```
/**
 * @portlet.portlet-init-param
 *     name="BaseUrl"
 *     value="${weather.url}"
 */
public class WeatherPortlet extends GenericPortlet {
...
}
```

Used this way, the weather service URL can be set in an Ant build properties file:

```
weather.url=http://banners.wunderground.com/banner/infobox/US/
```

Or it can be set at build time using the `-D` option to set properties:

```
% ant -Dweather.url=
weather.url=http://banners.wunderground.com/banner/infobox/US/
```

Either way, it's probably best not to hard-code values for `@portlet.portlet-init-param`.

11.3.3 *Supporting multiple display options*

Although a web browser is the likely client for most portlet applications, other clients may also be used to access your portal. How can you ensure that your portlet application will look its best on all clients (or not be available on clients you don't want it to be used on)?

The answer is found in the `@portlet.supports` tag:

```
/**
 ...
 * @portlet.supports
 *     mime-type="text/html"
 *     modes="EDIT,HELP"
 */
public class WeatherPortlet extends GenericPortlet {
...
}
```

In this case, the `mime-type` attribute specifies that `WeatherPortlet` is supported only on devices that can display the "text/html" MIME type (such as web browsers). Furthermore, the `modes` attribute specifies that in addition to the "VIEW" mode (which is required for all portlets), both the "EDIT" and "HELP" modes are available.

When `portlet.xml` is generated, this `@portlet.supports` tag results in the following declaration:

```
<supports>
  <mime-type>text/html</mime-type>
  <portlet-mode>EDIT</portlet-mode>
  <portlet-mode>HELP</portlet-mode>
</supports>
```

Suppose, however, that you want your portlet to be used on WAP-enabled cellular phones. For this to happen, your portlet must support the "text/vnd.wap.wml" MIME type. All you need to do is add an additional `@portlet.supports` tag to the `WeatherPortlet` class, and you're set:

```
/**
 ...
 * @portlet.supports
 *     mime-type="text/html"
 *     modes="EDIT,HELP"
 *
 * @portlet.supports
 *     mime-type="text/vnd.wap.wml"
 *     modes="HELP "
 */
public class WeatherPortlet extends GenericPortlet {
 ...
}
```

In this case, only the "VIEW" and "HELP" modes are supported for WAP-enabled devices.

11.3.4 *Defining preferences*

Using portlet initialization parameters, you were able to set up global parameters for your portlet at deployment time. For the `WeatherPortlet` to be useful, however, the user must be able to configure the portlet to display weather data personalized for their location. This is where preferences come into play.

A *preference* is a configuration parameter that's defined on a per-instance basis for a portlet. That is, if three users are using a portlet, each of them may have different settings for their preferences. This makes it possible for people in Dallas, New York, and Santa Fe to each see weather data pertinent to their location.

Preferences are defined for a portlet using the `@portlet.preferences` tag at the class level of the portlet. For example:

```
/**
 ...
 * @portlet.preferences
```

```
*       name="city"
*       value="Dallas"
*
* @portlet.preferences
*       name="state"
*       value="TX"
*/
public class WeatherPortlet extends GenericPortlet {
...
}
```

Here, you defined two preferences, city and state, to be configured by each user viewing the portlet. The value attribute defines a default to be used if the user hasn't configured their portlet.

In the generated portlet.xml, these preferences will be reflected as follows:

```
<portlet-preferences>
  <preference>
    <name>city</name>
    <value>Dallas</value>
  </preference>
  <preference>
    <name>state</name>
    <value>TX</value>
  </preference>
</portlet-preferences>
```

To enable users to configure these preferences, your portlet must support the "EDIT" mode and display a form with fields for overriding the default values.

11.3.5 *Validating preferences*

Ideally, the user of your portlet will always enter valid information for their preferences. But how can you guarantee that what they enter is valid? What if they enter *XY* for the state?

JSR-168 defines the notion of preference *validators*. Writing a preference validator is fairly straightforward, as shown in listing 11.5.

Listing 11.5 A preferences validator for WeatherPortlet

```
package com.xdocletbook.portlets;

import java.util.Arrays;
import java.util.HashSet;
import java.util.Set;
import javax.portlet.PortletPreferences;
import javax.portlet.PreferencesValidator;
import javax.portlet.ValidatorException;
```

```
public class WeatherPreferenceValidator
    implements PreferencesValidator{

  private static String[] states = {
      "AK", "AL", "AR", "AZ", "CA", "CO", "CT", "DC", "DE",
      "FL", "GA", "HI", "IA", "ID", "IL", "IN", "KS", "KY",
      "LA", "MA", "MD", "ME", "MI", "MN", "MO", "MS", "MT",
      "NC", "ND", "NE", "NH", "NJ", "NM", "NV", "NY", "OH",
      "OK", "OR", "PA", "RI", "SC", "SD", "TN", "TX", "UT",
      "VA", "VT", "WA", "WI", "WV", "WY"
      };
  private static Set stateSet = new HashSet();

  static {
    stateSet.addAll(Arrays.asList(states));
  }

  public void validate(PortletPreferences prefs)
      throws ValidatorException {

    String state = prefs.getValue("state", "TX");

    if(!stateSet.contains(state)) {     <─── Check that state is valid
      throw new ValidatorException(
          state + " is not a state.", null);
    }
  }
}
```

Writing a preferences validator is a simple matter of implementing `javax.port-let.PreferenceValidator` and its `validate` method. When a preferences form is submitted, the portlet container calls the `validate` method, passing in the preferences. If the preferences prove to be valid, then `validate` does nothing. But if the preferences are invalid, it should throw a `ValidatorException`.

Unfortunately, no XDoclet task exists for writing a preferences validator. However, using the `@portlet.preferences-validator` tag, you can declare which validator will be used in conjunction with your portlet. For example, to use `WeatherPreferenceValidator` with `WeatherPortlet`:

```
/**
...
 * @portlet.preferences-validator
 *      class="com.xdocletbook.portlets.WeatherPreferenceValidator"
 */
public class WeatherPortlet extends GenericPortlet {
...
}
```

As a result of `@portlet.preferences-validator`, the following declaration is written to the generated `portlet.xml` file:

```
<portlet-preferences>
  <preference>
    <name>city</name>
    <value>Dallas</value>
  </preference>
  <preference>
    <name>state</name>
    <value>TX</value>
  </preference>

  <preferences-validator>
    com.xdocletbook.portlets.WeatherPreferenceValidator
  </preferences-validator>
</portlet-preferences>
```

11.4 *Running the build*

Now that the `WeatherPortlet` is completely tagged, run the Ant build using the generate target, as follows:

```
% ant generate
```

Once the build is finished, the following newly generated `portlet.xml` file will be waiting for you in the generated directory:

```
<?xml version="1.0" encoding="UTF-8"?>

<portlet-app>
  <portlet>
    <description>Weather Forecast Portlet</description>
    <portlet-name>WeatherPortlet</portlet-name>
    <display-name>Weather Forecast</display-name>
    <portlet-class>
      com.xdocletbook.portlets.WeatherPortlet
    </portlet-class>

    <init-param>
      <name>BaseUrl</name>
      <value>
        http://banners.wunderground.com/banner/infobox/US/
      </value>
    </init-param>

    <expiration-cache>3600</expiration-cache>
    <supports>
      <mime-type>text/html</mime-type>
      <portlet-mode>EDIT</portlet-mode>
    </supports>
```

```
    <portlet-info>
      <title>Weather Portlet</title>
    </portlet-info>
    <portlet-preferences>
      <preference>
        <name>city</name>
        <value>Dallas</value>
      </preference>
      <preference>
        <name>state</name>
        <value>TX</value>
      </preference>
      <preference-validator>
        com.xdocletbook.portlets.WeatherPreferenceValidator
      </preference-validator>
    </portlet-preferences>
  </portlet>
</portlet-app>
```

Now you're ready to package your portlet classes and `portlet.xml` file in a WAR file and deploy it to a portlet container. The following Ant target produces a WAR file containing the portlet application source code, deployment descriptors, and JSPs used when displaying the content for the portlet's modes:

```
<target name="makeWar" depends="compile">
  <mkdir dir="${deploy.dir}"/>

  <war destfile="${deploy.dir}/${ant.project.name}.war"
      webxml="./web.xml">
    <classes dir="${build.dir}"/>

    <webinf dir="${generated.dir}" includes="*.xml"/>
    <webinf dir="${jsp.dir}" includes="**/*.jsp"/>
  </war>
</target>
```

Once the WAR file is generated, you can deploy it in your servlet container. To deploy it in Pluto (the JSR-168 reference implementation), use the portlet deployment script in Pluto's `build` directory:

```
C:/> deployPortlet.bat weather.war (Windows)
```

or

```
% deployPortlet.sh weather.war (UNIX)
```

Figure 11.1 shows how the weather portlet appears when deployed in Pluto.

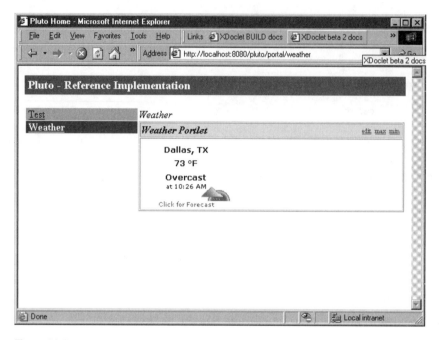

Figure 11.1 `WeatherPortlet` as it appears when deployed in Jakarta Pluto

11.5 *Summary*

The amount of information we consume on the Internet is staggering. Web portals enable you to aggregate multiple sources of content into an easily digestible format for more efficient web surfing. The portlet specification brings the Java promise of "write once, run anywhere" to portlets, removing the need for you to learn vendor-specific APIs when developing portlets.

You've seen how XDoclet can eliminate redundancy when working with JSR-168 portlets. Once again, XDoclet manages duplicate information among Java source code and deployment descriptors, making the portlet source code the authoritative and unambiguous definition of a portlet.

This chapter concludes the discussion of the modules that come with XDoclet. In the next chapter, we'll look at how you can extend XDoclet by writing your own modules for custom code generation. We'll move beyond the standard uses of XDoclet into ways to use XDoclet to generate files specific to individual projects.

Part 4

Extending XDoclet

In parts 2 and 3, you learned about the core XDoclet code generation tasks. In part 4, you'll see how to go beyond these standard tasks and use XDoclet as a code generation platform for your own custom code generation tasks. We'll also look at IDEs and other code generation tools you can use to further leverage the power of XDoclet.

Chapter 12, "Custom code generation with XDoclet," jumps straight into the heart of XDoclet code generation and explains how XDoclet generates code using templates, tags, and tasks. You'll learn how to use XDoclet to perform code generation magic in your own in-house projects. From simple one-shot code generation to complex tasks intended to be used over multiple projects, this chapter shows you how to write and package code generation routines.

Chapter 13, "XDoclet extensions and tools," explains how to apply external tools to make working with XDoclet even easier. You'll see how to configure Eclipse and IntelliJ IDEA, two popular IDEs for Java development, so they understand the XDoclet tags in your source files. This chapter also introduces two tools that sit on top of XDoclet and allow you to generate XDoclet-aware code from external data: AndroMDA, which generates XDoclet code from a UML model; and Middlegen, which generates XDoclet code from relational database schema.

Custom code generation
with XDoclet

12

This chapter covers

- Writing custom XDoclet templates
- Using and creating XDoclet tags
- Creating custom XDoclet tasks

The greatness of art is not to find what is common but what is unique.

—Isaac Singer (1904–1991); Polish-U.S. novelist, short-story writer

XDoclet's built-in tasks are quite powerful and simplify many common day-to-day development tasks. However, real-world applications usually extend beyond these bounds. When faced with these less standardized tasks, we don't have to leave the simplicity and elegance of code generation behind. Although it's possible to create a powerful code generation system entirely from scratch, we believe it's better to avoid reinventing the wheel when you have alternatives. XDoclet brings a stable, mature code generation framework to the table for these custom tasks. XDoclet provides many benefits that make it an attractive platform for in-house code generation tasks:

- Full integration into an Ant-based build system (including dependency analysis)
- Easy access to custom XDoclet attributes in Java source files
- A powerful templating language with a large number of built-in constructs for generating Java code
- The ability to introduce tasks and tags that are as powerful as the native XDoclet tags
- A standard way to package and distribute code generation tasks

12.1 When should you bother with custom code generation?

It's easy to see when code generation can be applied in environments such as EJB, but it can sometimes be a bit more difficult to determine when code generation can be applied to your own in-house projects. However, there are a few common smells that signal when code generation might be useful:

- *Information is duplicated in multiple files.* Whenever information is duplicated in multiple files, developers are faced with the challenge of how to keep the information in sync. If a piece of information needs to change, it can be quite a burden to change all the versions of that information. In some cases, it's possible to refactor the code base to eliminate the redundant information. In other cases, it might be time to consider whether those independent sources of information can be generated from a common source, eliminating the hassle of keeping them in sync.

- *One class is a simple transform of another.* Whenever one class is a simple transformation of another, code generation might be applicable. Consider the case of an interface and an implementation class. It may be possible to generate the interface directly from the implementation class. Adapters are another case where one class is directly derived from another class.

- *Classes look like cookie-cutter versions of each other.* Do many of your classes follow the same basic pattern? Do they contain common database access patterns or standard utility or helper code that varies only slightly in each instance? Code generation is a good tool to use in these cases.

12.1.1 The risks of custom generation

Code generation is a wonderful tool, but you need to weigh some associated risks:

- *Developing code generation requires a lot of up-front work.* Developing custom code generation takes a lot of time up front with very little visible reward until the code generation system is completed. It can often be difficult to gain and maintain approval for an investment in tool creation.

- *Maybe tasks aren't as similar as you thought.* Sometimes the tasks to which you want to apply code generation aren't as similar as you thought. As a result, your code generation may end up being applicable to only a small subset of the tasks you originally intended it for. In these cases, the investment in code generation may not pay the huge rewards you initially anticipated.

- *Code generation may become a series of special cases.* Another risk is that the code generation system becomes nothing more than a series of special cases. The more special cases are required, the less of a payoff code generation provides.

- *Future developers might abandon the generation phases.* One of the worst fates a code generation system can suffer is abandonment. As projects evolve and team members move on, new members may not feel as comfortable with the code generation system as the original designers. They might decide to use the generated code as a base for development instead of maintaining the generation engine. Worse yet, they could decide to rewrite the generated code by hand, throwing out all the benefits of code generation.

12.1.2 The rewards of custom generation

Despite the risks involved, the potential rewards of custom code generation are quite compelling:

- *Development is rapid.* Once the initial development costs are paid, code generation systems allow for very rapid development. The development time for producing the input for a generated class is normally a tiny fraction of the cost of writing the class by hand.

- *Information has a single source.* In a code generation system, there tends to be one source for pieces of information. This greatly reduces the chance of having inconsistencies in the system. It also means that a change needs to be made in only one place, making maintenance easier.

- *Testing is simpler.* Once the code generation has been tested and debugged, every generated class derived from it benefits. If a bug is found, it can be fixed once in the generator, and the fix will be applied to each instance.

- *Design and architecture are consistent.* In a system that relies on code generation, the design and architecture imposed by the generator permeate throughout the system. A code base that has a consistent design is easier to analyze and understand.

12.1.3 *Making the leap*

If you've decided that code generation makes sense for your project, XDoclet provides several levels of commitment depending on the complexity of your task and the amount of development effort you're willing to devote to developing your code generation:

- *Custom templates*—At the simplest level, XDoclet provides the ability to invoke custom templates to generate code. The effort is comparable to writing XSLT to transform an XML document. In both cases, a single template or transform file needs to be written and manually passed to an engine for evaluation.

- *Custom tags*—Custom templates are adequate for simple tasks, but when more complex processing is required, you'll need to write custom tags. This task is comparable to but, as you'll see, significantly simpler than writing a JSP tag library. Java code needs to be written and exposed to XDoclet for use in your templates.

- *Custom tasks*—At the highest level, you'll want to make your task more generic and configurable to allow it to be applied to multiple projects. This involves writing a custom task handler and providing a deployment descriptor to describe the task to the XDoclet engine. This approach requires the maximum investment of development time but provides maximum returns in terms of functionality and reusability.

12.2 Using XDoclet templates

When you're working with built-in tasks such as <ejbdoclet>, you probably won't even realize that XDoclet code generation revolves around templates. As a developer, you specify only the input and output files; the task selects the template(s) to be run to generate the code. In chapter 2, we looked at XDoclet templates from a high level and saw that XDoclet offers two styles of code generation: aggregate generation and transform generation. Now let's work through examples of both styles of generation to see how to use templates to generate custom code.

12.2.1 Using aggregate generation

In aggregate generation, a task aggregates data from the entire input set to generate a single output file. Deployment descriptors are a good example: They aggregate information concerning many sources into a single target. Figure 12.1 shows aggregate generation in use in generating a web.xml deployment descriptor. In this case, two servlets and a filter provide information that is used by a template to generate a single aggregate view in the web.xml file. Documentation often follows this pattern, too, because a single piece of documentation (a javadoc-generated page, for example) can span multiple source files.

To demonstrate custom aggregation, we'll consider the task of generating a summary listing of the classes in a project. This is an easy task for XDoclet. We'll break it into two steps. First we'll look at how to register and invoke a template task in Ant, and then we'll see exactly how to create a template file.

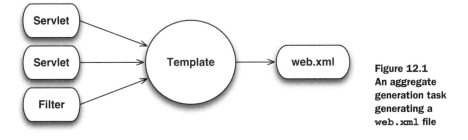

Figure 12.1
An aggregate
generation task
generating a
web.xml file

Registering and invoking the XDoclet task

The process starts with the <xdoclet> Ant task. Before you can invoke your own generation task, you need to register the base <xdoclet> task with Ant:

```
<taskdef name="xdoclet"
         classname="xdoclet.DocletTask"
         classpathref="xdoclet.lib.path" />
```

Once the base <xdoclet> task is registered, you can use the generic <template> subtask to perform simple code generation tasks. Here, you generate a text summary page listing all the classes in your system:

```
<target name="summary" depends="init">
    <xdoclet destdir="${gen.src.dir}">
        <fileset dir="${src.dir}" includes="**/*.java" />
        <template templateFile="summary.xdt"
                  destinationfile="summary.txt" />
    </xdoclet>
</target>
```

You must specify three pieces of information: the input file set, the template file, and the output file. The input file set is specified in the <fileset> element. This is a standard Ant <fileset> datatype. In this case, you include all Java files in the src.dir (source) directory.

The <template> subtask tells the <xdoclet> task to process a template. The templateFile and destinationFile attributes indicate the template file to be processed and where to store the results. You could set several other attributes, but before you get overwhelmed with the options, let's look at a template file.

Creating the template file for aggregation

If you're familiar with JavaServer Pages (JSP) tag libraries, then you'll feel right at home with XDoclet templates. But even if you're not experienced with JSPs, using templates isn't difficult. An XDoclet template (.xdt) file contains a number of XML tags that are evaluated. The output after all the tags have been evaluated is placed directly in an output document:

```
<XDtPackage:forAllPackages>
Package: <XDtPackage:packageName/>
<XDtClass:forAllClasses>
  -- Class: <XDtClass:className
      /> // <XDtClass:classCommentText no-comment-signs="true"/>
</XDtClass:forAllClasses>
</XDtPackage:forAllPackages>
```

The first tag in this template, <XDtPackage:forAllpackages>, evaluates its body once for each Java package in the source tree. When the body is evaluated, it knows that it's being evaluated in the context of that package. The template outputs the text *Package:* and then invokes the `<XDtPackage:packageName>` tag, which outputs the fully qualified package name of the current package into the document.

Next, the embedded `<XDtClass:forAllClasses>` tag is evaluated. It iterates across all the classes in the context of the current package only. If you were not in the context of a package, then `<XDtClass:forAllClasses>` would iterate over all the classes in the entire source tree.

In the context of each class, you output the current class name and the text of the javadoc class comments associated with this class. This is accomplished by the `<XDtClass:className>` and `<XDtClass:classCommentText>` tags. We'll look more at these and other XDoclet tags in a moment.

Reviewing the output

The result of executing the template is a new text file. In your Ant file, where you specify the template to be evaluated, you also specify that the output document should be placed in a file named `summary.txt`. Here's the output of the template run against the source tree for the blog manager application:

```
Summary:
Package: com.xdocletbook.blog.ejb
-- Class: BlogBean // An entity bean representing a blog (weblog).
-- Class: BlogFacadeBean // A session facade for managing a blog
-- Class: EntryBean // Entity bean representing a blog entry.
-- Class: TopicBean // An entity bean representing a blog topic.
Package: com.xdocletbook.blog.exception
-- Class: ApplicationException //
```

Now let's look at how to apply XDoclet to a task that's a bit larger and more interesting.

12.2.2 Using transformation generation

Unlike aggregate generation, where the template is evaluated only once, in transformation generation the template is evaluated multiple times, once for each of the input source files. Each time the template is evaluated, it has a different source context, which gives the template a base to produce unique output files.

Transformation generation is useful for generating source files that have a one-to-one mapping with other source files. The relationship between an EJB and its home interface is a good example. Think back to how you generated interfaces for EJBs. Figure 12.2 shows how transform generation worked in that case.

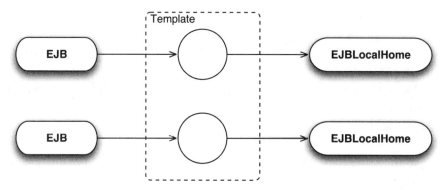

Figure 12.2   Transformation generation of an EJB into a local home interface

Although you didn't see the template at that time, the local home template was evaluated once for each bean, each time producing a local home interface unique to the source EJB.

In addition to simple class transformations, this type of generation might also be used for deployment or documentation files when you need to generate one file for each input file. However, this type of generation is relatively rare.

As an example, you'll use transformation generation to apply the Factory design pattern and generate factories for some of your classes. The approach you'll take is to model the output you hope to create and work that into a generic template. Once you have your template, you'll need to tell XDoclet how to evaluate the template.

Modeling the output

When you're working with a code generation task, it's usually best to begin with a concrete input example and a hand-coded version of the output you want to generate. The following listing shows a Widget class:

```
package com.xdocletbook.ch12;
/**
 * This is a widget class
 * @author Norman Richards
 */
public class Widget
{
    Widget() {
    }
    // ... widget methods ...
}
```

And here is the type of WidgetFactory class that you would like to generate for it:

```
package com.xdocletbook.ch12;

/**
 *  A factory for generating Widgets
 *  @author Norman Richards
 */
public class WidgetFactory
{
    /**
     *  create a new Widget instance
     */
    public Widget new Widget() {
        return new Widget();
    }
}
```

This isn't a very complicated application of the Factory pattern, but there's plenty for you to get your feet wet generating some Java code. But before we jump into the code, let's take a quick high-level look at where we're going with this example.

You want to develop a code generator that will generate the `WidgetFactory` from the `Widget` class. However, once you have abstracted the concept of generating the `WidgetFactory` from a `Widget`, you can apply that same knowledge to other classes. Figure 12.3 shows that once you have a factory template, you can also use that template to generate a `FrobFactory` for your `Frob` objects. That is the power of code generation.

Creating the template file for transformation

To create a template from a hand-coded file, you need to consider which parts of the generated file will be common to all generated classes. Think about the `Widget` and `Frob` example. What portions of the code would be common to both a

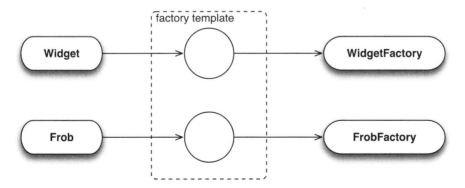

Figure 12.3   The factory template as a transformation generation task

`WidgetFactory` and a `FrobFactory`? If this were a more complicated example, then you might want to generate both of these targets and discover the commonalities that way. However, in such a small example, it's relatively easy to imagine the common points. These are the static portions of the template. Everything else is dynamic.

For these dynamic portions, you need to consider where in the source file you'll get this information. If the information isn't available, you should define XDoclet attributes to provide the additional information needed.

In this example, all the information you need is readily available in the input source file. You need the package name and name of the class for which you're generating the factory. You saw the XDoclet tags you can use to get these pieces of information in the aggregation generation example. Keep in mind that unlike in the aggregation case, where you iterated over a set of packages and classes to get a package and class context to work with, in the transformation case the template is invoked with that context.

The usage of `<XDtPackage:packageName>` and `<XDtClass:className>` is relatively straightforward. You can use these tags wherever you'd like to place the package or class name in the output document. Note that to generate the name of your `Factory` classes, you append *Factory* to the name of the base class:

```
/*
 * <XDtI18n:getString resource="do_not_edit"/>
 */
package <XDtPackage:packageName/>;
/**
 * A factory for generating <XDtClass:className />s
<XDtClass:classCommentTags indent="0" /> */
public class <XDtClass:className />Factory {
    /**
     *  create a new <XDtClass:className /> instance
     */
    public <XDtClass:className /> new<XDtClass:className />() {
        return new <XDtClass:className />();
    }
}
```

We've also introduced a couple of new XDoclet tags. `<XDtI18n:getString>` is used to pull a string out of a resource bundle. If the idea of internationalizing generated code seems odd, think of this as a simple way to ensure that textual portions of the code can be customized at a later date. The `"do_not_edit"` resource is provided by XDoclet; it outputs a warning message informing the reader that this code is automatically generated and should not be edited by hand.

In the javadoc comment section of the class, you use `<XDtClass:classComment-Tags>`. This tag copies the javadoc tags from the transformed input source into the output source. In this case, you want tags such as `@author` to be copied over from the source file. XDoclet gives you the ability to be more selective about what is copied and even allows you to specify new tags to be inserted at generation time.

Invoking the template subtask for transformation

Now that you have the template defined, you need to pass it to XDoclet for evaluation. You use the same Ant task that you used in the aggregate example, but you make use of some of the more advanced features:

```
<target name="factory" depends="init">
    <xdoclet addedTags="@xdoclet-generated">
        <fileset dir="${src.dir}" includes="**/*.java" />
        <template destdir="${gen.src.dir}"
                  acceptInterfaces="false"
                  acceptAbstractClasses="false"
                  templateFile="factory.xdt"
                  destinationFile="{0}Factory.java" />
    </xdoclet>
</target>
```

The new features here require a bit of explanation. The `addedTags` attribute tells XDoclet to add additional class-level attributes to the generated file. You'll see later how this is reflected in the template. The important detail is that you're requesting the output file to include the `@xdoclet-generated` tag, which tells XDoclet to ignore this source file if it should be seen on a future run. This ensures that generated files are not themselves used as the source for code generation. In the case of the `Factory` class, this means `Widget` can generate `WidgetFactory`, but `WidgetFactory` won't be used to generate `WidgetFactoryFactory` even if the generated `WidgetFactory` ends up in the input fileset.

Next, you specify an explicit destination directory with the `destdir` attribute on the `<template>` subtask. XDoclet users prefer to place source code in a separate tree so that revision-controlled source files and generated source files aren't mixed. The `<fileset>` controls the scope of the set of files that will be used as part of the input set. However, at this level you can only select by class and package name. XDoclet also offers the ability to narrow the input set based on class type, XDoclet class attributes, or even (as you're doing now) whether the class is a concrete class, an abstract class, or an interface. The attributes `acceptInterfaces="false"` and `acceptAbstractClasses="false"` tell XDoclet not to consider any classes that are interfaces or that are abstract. This makes sense for the factory example, because you wouldn't be able to instantiate an interface or an abstract class.

The most important attribute change is in `destinationFile`. You add a `{0}` marker at the beginning of the destination file. The `{0}` substitution marker is the only indication to XDoclet that you want transformation generation instead of aggregate generation. This marker represents the base class name of the input file being considered and allows you to create an output file with a name that is a variation of the input filename. In this case, you want to append `Factory.java` to the base class name. Notice that you don't specify the directory structure. In the transformation case, XDoclet assumes a directory structure that corresponds to the package structure of the input class. If the input class is in the `com.xdocletbook` package, then the output file will also be in that package. This behavior can be overridden by the `prefixWithPackageStructure` and `packageSubstitutions` attributes, but you don't want to do that here.

Reviewing the output

When you invoke the template against the `Widget` class, the template produces the following output:

```
/*
 * Generated file - Do not edit!
 */
package com.xdocletbook.ch12;

/**
 * @author Norman Richards
 * @xdoclet-generated
 */
public class WidgetFactory {
    /**
     *   returns a new Widget instance
     */
    public Widget newWidget() {
        return new Widget();
    }
}
```

With the exception of the additional comment text, this is exactly the output you hoped to see.

12.3 *Exploring design alternatives*

There are many ways to approach every code generation task. Template design decisions impact how the template should be written and invoked. They also impact the configurability and extensibility of the system. In this section, you'll

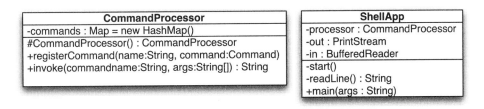

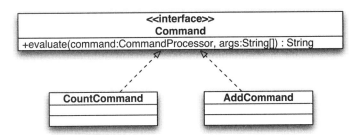

Figure 12.4   UML for `CommandProcessor`

apply two different techniques for generating code for a command registry and see how your decisions impact the overall system. We'll also introduce some new tags and explain a bit more about the capabilities of XDoclet in the process.

You'll be working with the command processor system shown in figure 12.4. This particular system is part of a command-line interpreter. The Command interface encapsulates commands that can be invoked by the user. The commands are registered with the CommandProcessor, which is responsible for invoking the commands on behalf of an application. The sample application is the ShellApp, which provide a standard read-eval-print loop: The application reads an expression from the user, evaluates the expression, and prints out the results.

12.3.1 *Registering commands*

The missing element is how Command objects are registered with the Command-Processor. The method you'll use here is for the application to provide a CommandProcessor subclass that's responsible for registering the commands that are of interest to the application. Because the Command list is initially static, you could take the approach of hard-coding this information in the ShellAppCommand-Processor, as in the following example:

```
package com.xdocletbook.command;

import com.xdocletbook.command.CommandProcessor;
```

```
public class ShellAppCommandProcessor
    extends CommandProcessor
{
    public ShellAppCommandProcessor() {
        registerCommand("add",
            new com.xdocletbook.command.AddCommand());
        registerCommand("count",
            new com.xdocletbook.command.CountCommand());
        // more commands...
    }
}
```

This class has two smells that call out for XDoclet generation. First, the name of
the command is stored separately from the implementation of the command.
This goes against the XDoclet single-source philosophy, which suggests that all the
information about an object should be stored in one place. The second issue is
that if a new command is added or removed, this class needs to be updated by
hand. Both of these are problems that XDoclet is well suited to fix.

12.3.2 Generating the command processor

If you want to generate the CommandProcessor subclass, the first decision is
whether this is an aggregate or transformation generation task. Although you're
generating a single output file, aggregate generation might not be the best solution. In the aggregate case, no context is available to tell you what package to
place the new command in. One solution would be to hard-code the package in
the template. Doing so would limit the reusability of the template and would
require duplicating the package name in the build file and in the template. You
could also pass in the package name as a configuration parameter to the template. (You haven't seen configuration parameters yet, but they provide a way to
pass extra information to a template from a the build file.) However, configuration parameters are intended to provide overrides to default values and shouldn't
be used for required input data.

To escape these issues, you'll use transform generation. You'll generate Shell-
AppCommandProcessor from ShellApp. The choice of what class to use as the basis
for the transform can be tricky, but this choice makes sense because the application command processor is tightly coupled to the application class.

Creating the command processor template

Let's jump straight into the template (listing 12.1).

Listing 12.1 command.xdt

```
/*
 * <XDtI18n:getString resource="do_not_edit"/>
 */

package <XDtPackage:packageName/>;

import com.xdocletbook.command.CommandProcessor;

/**
<XDtClass:classCommentTags indent="0" /> */
public class <XDtClass:className />CommandProcessor
    extends CommandProcessor                              Class name is a
{                                                         transformation
    public <XDtClass:className />CommandProcessor() {     of source class

        <XDtClass:forAllClasses                          Iterate
            type="com.xdocletbook.command.Command"       through input
            abstract="false">                            classes looking
        <XDtClass:ifHasClassTag                          for ones you
            tagName="cmd.command" paramName="name">      want

        registerCommand("<XDtClass:classTagValue         Register each
                    tagName="cmd.command"                command using
                    paramName="name" />",                metadata in the
                new <XDtClass:fullClassName />());        class

        </XDtClass:ifHasClassTag>
        </XDtClass:forAllClasses>
}
```

This template bears a striking resemblance to the factory template we looked at earlier. The difference is that in the body of the constructor, you now iterate through all the non-abstract implementations of the Command interface using the `<XDtClass:forAllClasses>` iterator. You take the selection one step further by using the `<XDtClass:ifHasClassTag>` conditional to test whether the @cmd.command tag has a name attribute. If it does, you generate a registerCommand call that extracts the value of the name attribute and uses it as the name of the command. This means the Command classes need to contain a @cmd.command tag in the class comments. Here's one of the commands:

```
/**
 * Command to add integer values
 * @cmd.command name="add"
 */
```

```
public class AddCommand
    implements Command
{
    public String evaluate(CommandProcessor command,
                           String[] args)
        throws CommandException
    {
        int total = 0;

        for (int i=0; i<args.length; i++) {
            total += Integer.parseInt(args[i]);
        }

        return String.valueOf(total);
    }
}
```

The AddCommand class implements the Command interface and provides the functionality of the add command, which is to add the numeric arguments passed to it, in the evaluate method. The @cmd.command tag marks the class as a command and provides the name of the command.

Selecting the source classes

The last step is to invoke the XDoclet template. The only real question is how you should tell XDoclet which classes to run the template against. It might be tempting to limit the <fileset> that you specify in the Ant task to only include the ShellApp, but doing so would be a mistake. This would cause XDoclet to parse only that one class. When the template called the <XDtClass:forAllClasses> iterator, it would fail to find the commands you want it to find.

A better way to approach the task is to add a tag to the classes for which you want to generate code. Suppose you add a @cmd.processor tag to the ShellApp:

```
/**
 *  A shell-like application to test the command processor
 *  @cmd.processor
 *
 */
public class ShellApp
{
        // ...
}
```

The @cmd.processor tag acts as a marker. This is the XDoclet equivalent of a marker interface such as java.io.Serializable. The Serializable interface provides no methods and merely serves to indicate the intent of the class at runtime. In the same way, the @cmd.processor tag indicates the intent of the class without providing any additional metadata to the code generation engine.

Invoking the template

It then becomes easy to select only the `ShellApp` to run the template against. You do so using the `havingClassTag` attribute to the `<template>` subtask:

```
<target name="command" depends="init">
    <xdoclet destdir="${src.dir}" force="true"
            addedTags="@xdoclet-generated">
        <fileset dir="${src.dir}" includes="**/*.java" />

        <template destdir="${gen.src.dir}"
                havingClassTag="cmd.processor"
                templateFile="xdt/command.xdt"
                destinationFile="{0}CommandProcessor.java" />
</target>
```

The `havingClassTag` attribute selects only those classes that have the specified tag at the class level, but that's all you need here. You simply want to locate any classes that have the `@cmd.processor` marker tag.

The end result

For completeness, the final generated code follows:

```
/*
 * Generated file - Do not edit!
 */

package com.xdocletbook.command;

import com.xdocletbook.command.CommandProcessor;

/**
 * @xdoclet-generated
 */
public class ShellAppCommandProcessor
    extends CommandProcessor
{
    public ShellAppCommandProcessor() {
        registerCommand("add",
            new com.xdocletbook.command.AddCommand());
        registerCommand("count",
            new com.xdocletbook.command.CountCommand());
    }
}
```

There is usually more than one way to approach a code generation task. Let's look at another way you could have approached this task.

12.3.3 *Generating a configuration file*

Instead of statically binding the list of commands at compile time, you might instead prefer to read the command list from a configuration file at runtime. Then you would be able to change the command set at runtime just by changing a configuration file. This is a common practice in Java systems, regardless of whether code generation is employed. There are advantages and disadvantages to both approaches, but under most circumstances the configuration file is the more natural choice. In light of that, let's consider an alternative version of the `Shel-lApp`, the `DynamicShellApp`, which uses `DynamicShellAppCommandProcessor` to read configuration items from a property file (see listing 12.2).

Listing 12.2   DynamicShellAppCommandProcessor

```java
package com.xdocletbook.command;

import java.io.*;
import java.util.Properties;
import java.util.StringTokenizer;

public class DynamicShellAppCommandProcessor
    extends CommandProcessor
{
    public static final String COMMAND_RESOURCE =
        "/com/xdoclet/command/command.properties";

    public static final String COMMAND_LIST   = "commands";
    public static final String COMMAND_PREFIX = "command.";

    public DynamicShellAppCommandProcessor() {
        registerCommands();        ◁── Commands are registered
    }                                   at object creation time

    public void registerCommands() {
        InputStream in =                          Configuration file is
            DynamicShellAppCommandProcessor.class  read as a resource
            .getResourceAsStream(COMMAND_RESOURCE); of the classpath

        if (in == null) {
            throw new RuntimeException(
                "Can't locate command file " +
                COMMAND_RESOURCE);
        }

        Properties props = new Properties();
        try {
            props.load(in);          ◁── Configuration is a
        } catch (IOException e) {         simple properties file
```

```
        throw new RuntimeException(
            "problem reading properties file", e);
    }

    String commands = props.getProperty(COMMAND_LIST);    ◁─┐
                                                  Read property
    if (commands == null) {                       item containing
        return;                                   list of commands
    }                                                          ─┘

    StringTokenizer toks =
        new StringTokenizer(commands);
    while (toks.hasMoreTokens()) {
        String name      = toks.nextToken();
        String classname = props.getProperty(
            COMMAND_PREFIX + name);

        try {
            Class   c   = Class.forName(classname);
            Command cmd = (Command) c.newInstance();

            registerCommand(name, cmd);   ◁── Register configured command
        } catch (Exception e) {
            System.out.println("#Error: " +
                e.getMessage());
        }
    }
  }
}
```

This is a straightforward, dynamically configured class. Have you eliminated the need for XDoclet by making the application more dynamic? Not at all. You now have a properties file that duplicates information in the Command classes with no easy way to keep the configuration file in sync with your code (at least with the straight Java version, you could count on the compiler to help you a bit). XDoclet makes even more sense now.

Let's use an XDoclet template to generate the properties file. The portions of the template that output code have been highlighted (the remaining tags are for control flow):

```
# <XDtI18n:getString resource="do_not_edit"/>
commands=<XDtClass:forAllClasses
  type="com.xdocletbook.command.Command"
  abstract="false"><XDtClass:ifHasClassTag
  tagName="cmd.command"
  paramName="name"> <XDtClass:classTagValue
```

```
      tagName="cmd.command" paramName="name"
      /></XDtClass:ifHasClassTag></XDtClass:forAllClasses>

  <XDtClass:forAllClasses
      type="com.xdocletbook.command.Command"
      abstract="false">
  <XDtClass:ifHasClassTag tagName="cmd.command"
      paramName="name">command.<XDtClass:classTagValue
      tagName="cmd.command" paramName="name"
      />=<XDtClass:fullClassName />
  </XDtClass:ifHasClassTag>
  </XDtClass:forAllClasses>
```

One big change here is that you have switched to aggregate generation because you no longer need the package context to generate a package statement like you did for the source code. You simply need to be able to iterate through all the classes. Another change is that you need to be more careful about whitespace. In Java source code, extra spaces and newlines are not normally meaningful. However, in a Java properties file, spacing is a big deal. That's why in this case, the template file is a little messier than in earlier examples.

In the aggregate case, the template invocation is much simpler. The only trick is that you want to generate the properties file into the build output directory so that the properties file will show up on the classpath and be loadable as a system resource:

```
<template destdir="${build.dir} "
          templateFile="xdt/dynamiccommand.xdt"
          destinationFile="com/xdoclet/command/command.properties" />
```

The final property file you generate follows:

```
# Generated file - Do not edit!
commands= count add
command.count=com.xdocletbook.command.CountCommand
command.add=com.xdocletbook.command.AddCommand
```

Of course, if you were to add more commands (tagged appropriately with @cmd.command), the properties file would be updated automatically. XDoclet has allowed you to create an application that is dynamic yet has eliminated the need for you to manually keep the configuration in sync with your code base.

12.3.4 *Choosing a generation method*

This decision between generating static Java code and generating deployment or configuration files for a more dynamic system is very common. On one hand, you have the option of generating Java code for your tasks. This code is static, but it will be regenerated whenever you recompile. Static code enjoys the benefit of better runtime performance, and the compilation step adds a layer of sanity checking early in the development cycle. Incorrectly generated code can often be detected at compile time as opposed to at runtime for dynamic information.

On the other hand, runtime extensibility is very valuable. If you wanted to be able to reconfigure the system at deployment time, static generation wouldn't be sufficient. When runtime performance isn't critical, the dynamic approach is usually best. XDoclet performs both types of code generation with few problems, but as we've seen, templates that perform aggregation tasks can be significantly easier to code and work with.

12.4 *Template tag concepts*

A template's most basic need is to extract and use the input classes' metadata. A template makes use of this information by using the XDoclet tag libraries. In the examples so far, you have seen tags that iterate packages and classes, and tags that extract core data from classes. Now it's time to dig deeper and see the full range of tags that XDoclet provides.

12.4.1 *Block and content tags*

Block tags are similar to body tags in a JSP tag library. A block tag's body contains text that it can choose to evaluate. Block tags are often used to implement conditionals and iterators.

The following template contains three body tags:

```
<XDtClass:forAllClasses>
    <XDtClass:ifIsClassAbstract>
        class <XDtClass:className /> is abstract
        <XDtComment:comment>
            this text isn't copied
            to the output document
        </XDtComment:comment>
    <XDtClass:ifIsClassAbstract>
</XDtClass:forAllClasses>
```

`<XDtClass:forAllClasses>` is an example of an iterating block tag. The body of the tag, which is all the text between the opening and closing tags, is evaluated once for each Java class that XDoclet processes.

The body of the class iterator contains a conditional block tag `<XDtClass:ifIsClassAbstract>`. This block tag evaluates its body only if the current class being examined (in this case, by the surrounding iterator) is abstract. If the class isn't abstract, the tag produces no output.

XDoclet doesn't have any way to directly test the negation of a conditional tag. For this reason, XDoclet conditional tags always come in pairs. One tag tests if the condition is true, and the other tag tests if the condition is false. The companion tag for `<XDtClass:ifIsClassAbstract>` is `XDtClass:ifIsClassNotAbstract`.

The third block tag in the template is `<XDtComment:comment>`. The comment tag is used to place a comment in a template that won't be placed into the output document. You can think of the comment tag as a type of conditional tag that always tests false and never evaluates its body.

Content tags, on the other hand, have no body to evaluate. They produce content to be placed in the output stream. In this example, `<XDtClass:className>` is a content tag. When it's evaluated, XDoclet examines the current class context and places the name of the class into the output document.

12.4.2 *Tag namespaces*

You have probably noticed a pattern in XDoclet tag names. XDoclet tags are organized into logical namespaces. The structure is `XDt<Namespace>:<tagName>`. Figure 12.5 shows how a template tag is decomposed. The namespace name is capitalized using the UpperCamelCase convention (where each word is capitalized), whereas the tag name is capitalized according to the lowerCamelCase convention (where the first word is in lowercase, but each remaining word is capitalized). The namespace and tag capitalization conventions correspond to the normal Java naming conventions for class names and method names, respectively.

Namespaces provide groupings of logically related tags. You'll see later that namespaces correspond to tag-handler implementation classes. The tags provided by a tag handler form the natural namespace boundaries.

XDoclet provides more than 50 namespaces; however, most of them provide very specialized functionality that is only relevant to a single XDoclet task. For

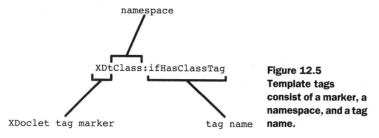

**Figure 12.5
Template tags
consist of a marker, a
namespace, and a tag
name.**

example, almost 20 namespaces are devoted to providing functionality to the various `<ejbdoclet>` subtasks. Unless you're writing templates for EJB merge points, you're unlikely to use any of them. Table 12.1 summarizes the common tag namespaces that you'll probably need to use in creating templates. We'll explore the basic uses of these tags in the rest of this chapter, but for more complete documentation of all the XDoclet template tags, see appendix D.

Table 12.1 Common tag namespaces for creating templates for custom code generation. These are a subset of the more than 50 XDoclet namespaces.

Namespace	Purpose of tags in namespace
`Package`	Working with packages
`Class`	Working with classes
`Method`	Working with class methods
`Constructor`	Working with class constructors
`Parameter`	Working with method parameters
`Field`	Working with method fields
`Type`	Working with Java types
`Comment`	Embedding comments in templates
`Config`	Working with configuration parameters
`Merge`	Including custom template extensions
`TagDef`	Providing the ability to declare new tag handlers

12.4.3 Types of tags

Most of the core namespaces (`Package`, `Class`, `Method`, and so on) provide tags that reflect on the classes that XDoclet parses into its internal model. These namespaces tend to provide a few basic types of tags that operate on the model element to which the namespace corresponds: iteration tags, attribute tags, naming tags, and property tags. These divisions are somewhat arbitrary but still useful.

Iteration tags

We've already looked at `<XDtClass:forAllClasses>` and have seen how it iterates over all the classes in the system (or all the classes in a given package, if you have an explicit package context). Each type of model component has at least one iterator tag. For example, methods in class scope can be iterated with `<XDt-Method:forAllMethods>`, and parameters on a method can be iterated with `<XDt-Parameter:forAllMethodParameters>`.

Attribute tags

Any component that can accept javadoc comments can contain XDoclet attributes. XDoclet attributes can be queried with content tags or tested using conditional block tags. Consider the following template fragment, which assigns a log level based on the presence or absence of tag on the source class. Keep in mind that each component type defines its own tags, but they all follow the same basic naming conventions:

```
public static final int LOG_LEVEL =
<XDtClass:ifHasClassTag tagName="example.debug">
DEBUG;
</XDtClass:ifHasClassTag>
<XDtClass:ifDoesntHaveClassTag tagName="example.debug">
NONE;
</XDtClass:ifDoesntHaveClassTag>
```

The `<XDtClass:ifHasClassTag>` block is evaluated if the `@example.debug` tag is found in the class comment; the `<XDtClass:ifDoesntHaveclassTag>` block is evaluated otherwise. It's important to realize that you're asking only about XDoclet attributes on the class. Attributes on specific fields or methods are not considered. This would look like the following:

```
/**
 * This is a great class, but it still needs debugging
 * @example.debug
 */
public class GreatClass {
    // ...
}
```

Let's suppose you want to define an attribute called `active` that should determine whether logging is enabled as opposed to the mere presence of any `@example.debug` tag. Your source class might look like the following:

```
/**
 * This is a great class, but it still needs debugging
 * @example.debug active="true"
 */
public class GreatClass {
    // ...
}
```

The `<XDtClass:ifClassTagValueEquals>` and `<XDtClass:ifClassTagValueNotEquals>` block tags can be used to differentiate these two cases. You can use the `paramName` and `value` attributes to specify the XDoclet attribute parameter you want to test and the value to compare to. Of course, if the entire XDoclet attribute is missing, the comparison will return false:

```
public static final int LOG_LEVEL =
<XDtClass:ifClassTagValueEquals tagName="example.debug"
                                paramName="active"
                                value="true">
    DEBUG;
</XDtClass:ifClassTagValueEquals>
<XDtClass:ifClassTagValueNotEquals tagName="example.debug"
                                   paramName="active"
                                   value="true">
 NONE;
</XDtClass:ifClassTagValueNotEquals>
```

As a final example, let's examine how you might change the following example to allow the log level to be specified as an attribute to the XDoclet tag:

```
/**
 * This is a great class, but it still needs debugging
 * @example.debug active="true" level="WARNING"
 */
public class GreatClass {
    // ...
}
```

If debugging is active, then you want to extract the value of the level attribute, if one exists. To do so, you use the <XDtClass:classTagValue> template tag. You can specify the name of the tag and the name of the parameter as well as a default value to use if the parameter isn't defined on the class:

```
public static final int LOG_LEVEL =
<XDtClass:ifClassTagValueEquals tagName="example.debug"
                                paramName="active"
                                value="true">
    <XDtClass:classTagValue tagName="example.debug" paramName="level"
                            default="DEBUG" />;
</XDtClass:ifClassTagValueEquals>
<XDtClass:ifClassTagValueNotEquals tagName="example.debug"
                                   paramName="active"
                                   value="true">
 NONE;
</XDtClass:ifClassTagValueNotEquals>
```

Naming tags

All components have names. Packages have names, classes have names, methods have names, and so on. Some components have more than one way to represent the name. A class name, for example, might be fully qualified (java.lang.Object) or unqualified (ArrayList). Another example is package names. Package names need to be dot-separated in the Java package statement but might be slash (/) separated when used to specify resource names.

Each component follows vastly different naming:

```
<XDtPackage:forAllPackages>
Examining package <XDtPackage:packageName />
path form is <XDtPackage:packageNameAsPath />
</XDtPackage:forAllPackages>
```

Evaluating this template produces output of the following form:

```
Examining package com.xdocletbook.ch11
path form is com/xdocletbook/ch11

Examining package com.xdocletbook.ch11.test
path form is com/xdocletbook/ch11/test
```

Property tags

Every component type has certain properties that may need to be queried or tested. One example you've seen so far is `<XDtClass:ifIsClassAbstract>`, which tests whether a class is abstract. Properties can be much more advanced. The following template iterates through the methods of each class and considers whether each method is a getter or setter method:

```
ArrayList readProperties  = new ArrayList();
ArrayList writeProperties = new ArrayList();

<XDtMethod:forAllMethods superclasses="true">
<XDtMethod:ifIsGetter>
    // <XDtMethod:methodName />
    readProperties.add("<XDtMethod:propertyName/>");
</XDtMethod:ifIsGetter>
<XDtMethod:ifIsSetter>
    // <XDtMethod:methodName />
    writeProperties.add("<XDtMethod:methodName/>");
</XDtMethod:ifIsSetter>
</XDtMethod:forAllMethods>
```

This code sample creates a list of read property names and a list of write property names. Iterating through each method in the current class, you use the `<XDt-Method:ifIsGetter>` and `<XDtMethod:ifIsSetter>` tags to test if the current method follows the JavaBeans get or set method conventions. If it does, the body is evaluated and the property name, which you query using the `<XDtMethod:propertyName>` tag, is added to the appropriate array. We've also added the associated method name in a comment to show how to access the method name.

12.4.4 *Using some basic template tags*

To wrap up our coverage of the core tags, let's look at a few examples of tag usage. These examples are intended to give you insight into the type of functions available in the tags as well as show basic usage idioms for some of the tags in table 12.1 that we haven't touched on yet. Specifically, we'll look at method parameters, fields, types, comments, and configuration parameters.

Working with method parameters

You may have noticed that the `Method` and `Constructor` namespaces seem to have omitted tags for working with parameters. That's because the parameter tags have been placed in their own namespace. Let's first look at the parameter iterators: `<XDtParameter:forAllConstructorParams>` and `<XDtParameter:forAllMethodParams>`. Inside the parameter context are three content tags that return information about the current parameter.

When you're generating code, it's generally more useful to use the `<XDtParameter:parameterList>` content tag. It returns a comma-separated list of the parameters suitable for inclusion in Java code:

```
<XDtMethod:forAllMethods>
<XDtMethod:methodType/>

<XDtMethod:methodName/> (<XDtParameter:parameterList />){
    // ...
}
</XDtMethod:forAllMethods>
```

When used in a constructor context, the `forConstructor` attribute should be set to true. Additionally, the `includeDefinition` attribute specifies whether the parameter type definitions should be output in the list. The default is true, which is suitable for method definitions. When set to false, the list is suitable for method calls:

```
<XDtConstructor:forAllConstructors>
<XDtConstructor:constructorName/>
    (<XDtParameter:parameterList forConstructor="true"/>) {
    super(<XDtParameter:parameterList forConstructor="true"
        includeDefinition="false"/>);
    // ...
}
</XDtConstructor:forAllConstructors>
```

Applying the previous template to the following class:

```
public class SimpleTest
{
    public SimpleTest(String name) {
      // ...
    }

    public SimpleTest(String name, String title) {
```

```
        // ...
    }
}
```

produces the following output:

```
SimpleTest(java.lang.String name) {
    super(name);
    // ...
}

SimpleTest(java.lang.String name,java.lang.String title) {
    super(name,title);
    // ...
}
```

Working with fields

The `Field` namespace provides basic access to fields defined in a class. The iterator for fields in a class is the `<XDtField:forAllFields>` tag. The block tag for testing XDoclet tags on the field is `<XDtField:ifHasFieldTagValueEquals>`. There is no corresponding `<XDtField:ifHasFieldTagValueNotEquals>` block tag.

Inside a field context, the basic content tags are similar in form to those you've already seen. The name and type of the field are accessible, as are the comments and XDoclet tags associates with the field.

The following template fragment creates a debug method that dumps the state of each field:

```
public void dumpState() {
<XDtField:forAllFields>
    System.out.print("<XDtField:fieldName
        /> (type is <XDtField:fieldType />)");
    System.out.println(" has value " + <XDtField:fieldName />);
</XDtField:forAllFields>
}
```

The template outputs text that looks like the following:

```
public void dumpState() {

    System.out.print("name (type is java.lang.String)");
    System.out.println(" has value " + name);

    System.out.print("title (type is java.lang.String)");
    System.out.println(" has value " + title);

}
```

It's important to remember, however, that the fields being iterated are on the source class. The class in which this method is being generated might not have the same fields available. Even if the class is a subclass of the source class, access permissions might prohibit access.

Working with types

When you're working with fields, methods, and constructors, type information comes into play. Although the type is accessible on each case, you may want to ask questions about a type and generate your code based on those types. XDoclet provides the following conditional block tags that test properties of a type and evaluate their bodies accordingly. In each case, the type in question is placed in the value attribute. For the type comparison tags, the type you're comparing against is given in the type attribute:

```
public Object getSomeValue() {
    return
<XDtType:ifIsNotPrimitive value="<XDtField:fieldType />">
<XDtField:fieldName />
</XDtType:ifIsNotPrimitive>
<XDtType:ifIsPrimitive value="<XDtField:fieldType />">
new <XDtType:ifIsOfType value="<XDtField:fieldType />"
    type="int">Integer</XDtType:ifIsOfType>
<XDtType:ifIsOfType value="<XDtField:fieldType />"
    type="float">Float</XDtType:ifIsOfType>
<XDtType:ifIsOfType value="<XDtField:fieldType />"
    type="double">Double</XDtType:ifIsOfType>
<XDtType:ifIsOfType value="<XDtField:fieldType />"
    type="boolean">Boolean</XDtType:ifIsOfType>
<XDtType:ifIsOfType value="<XDtField:fieldType />"
    type="char">Character</XDtType:ifIsOfType>
(<XDtField:fieldName/>)
</XDtType:ifIsPrimitive>;
}
```

This template operates in a field context and generates a method that returns the field value as an object. If the field is a primitive type, it creates an object version (converting an int to a java.lang.Integer, for example). Here are two examples of the output that could be generated by this template fragment. The first is an int field named counter, and the second is a String field named name:

```
public Object getSomeValue() {
    return new Integer(counter);
}

public Object getSomeValue() {
    return name;
}
```

The `Field` namespace also provides a content tag `<XDtType:typeWithoutDimensions>` that takes an array type and returns the base type of the array:

```
<XDtType:typeWithoutDimensions type="<XDtField:fieldType />" />
```

Placing comments in templates

The `Comment` namespace provides the `comment` tag, which lets you embed comments into template files. Any text inside the comment tag won't be evaluated when processing the template:

```
<XDtComment:comment>
    Comment text here is not placed in the output file.
    XDoclet tags such as <XDtClass:className /> are not evaluated.
</XDtComment:comment>
```

Using configuration parameters

Templates are normally driven by XDoclet attributes embedded in source files. However, XDoclet also includes a mechanism to provide attributes at runtime in the form of configuration parameters. *Configuration parameters* are name/value pairs that are specified using the `<configParam>` subelement of the `<template>` subtask:

```
<template templateFile="..." destinationfile="...">
    <configParam name="arraysize" value="110" />
</template>
```

Configuration parameters can be queried with the `<XDtConfig:configParameterValue>` tag:

```
ArrayList list = new ArrayList(<XDtConfig:configParameterValue
                  paramName="arraysize" />);
```

XDoclet provides several conditional block tags to test the presence and values of configuration parameters. The parameter name to be tested is given in the `paramName` attribute. If a value is needed for comparison, it can be passed in the value attribute.

12.5 Creating custom template tags

The template tags we have examined so far provide enough functionality to tackle a wide range of code generation tasks. However, many tasks simply can't be done using XDoclet tags. Consider the earlier template, where you created an `ArrayList` of all the properties that had a getter method on the class:

```
ArrayList readProperties  = new ArrayList();

<XDtMethod:forAllMethods superclasses="true">
```

```
<XDtMethod:ifIsGetter>
    readProperties.add("<XDtMethod:propertyName/>");
</XDtMethod:ifIsGetter>
```

Suppose instead that you wanted to create a `String` array of the names. You'd like to generate the following:

```
String[] readProperties = {
    "propertyOne",
    "proprtyTwo",
    "propertyThree"
};
```

How could this be coded in XDoclet?

```
String[] readProperties = {
<XDtMethod:forAllMethods superclasses="true">
<XDtMethod:ifIsGetter>
    "<XDtMethod:propertyName/>",
</XDtMethod:ifIsGetter>
}
```

This approach doesn't work, because there will always be a comma after the last property. XDoclet doesn't provide any tag support for this code generation task. It's possible to accomplish this task in XDoclet, but the template quickly becomes unmanageable:

```
<XDtCollection:create name="marker" />
String[] readProperties = {
<XDtMethod:forAllMethods superclasses="true">
<XDtMethod:ifIsGetter>
<XDtCollection:ifContains name="marker" value="1">     ❶
,
</XDtCollection:ifContains>
<XDtCollection:ifDoesntContain name="marker" value="1">   ❷
<XDtCollection:put name="marker" value="1" />
</XDtCollection:ifDoesntContain>
    "<XDtMethod:propertyName />"
</XDtMethod:ifIsGetter>
</XDtMethod:forAllMethods>
};
<XDtCollection:destroy name="marker" />   ◁─❸
```

❶ If you see the marker, this isn't the first time through the loop. You want a comma.

❷ Set the marker on the first iteration.

❸ Tidy up, and delete the collection resource you used.

This solution uses the `Collection` namespace to store a marker that tells you you're not on the first element and should prepend a comma to the list. It's clear now why tags like `<XDtClass:importedList>` and `<XDtMethod:exceptionList>` are needed. It would be difficult to generate these comma-separated lists using the iterators you have seen thus far.

Although XDoclet could do a better job of providing more comprehensive tags, it has instead taken the view that some complex coding is better done in Java. XDoclet provides the ability to define custom tags, written in Java, to provided higher-level functionality. To create custom tags, you need to provide a tag handler that exposes the tags.

12.5.1 *Creating a content tag*

In an earlier example, you needed to convert a primitive value to an object value. This is a case where you had to write a large amount of template text for a very small piece of functionality. The template became cluttered, keeping you from being able to clearly see what it was doing. This is a perfect place to add a template tag.

Adding a tag handler

Let's jump into a template handler that provides a useful tag (listing 12.3).

Listing 12.3   PrimitiveTagsHandler

```
package com.xdocletbook.ch11;

import xdoclet.XDocletTagSupport;
import xdoclet.XDocletException;
import java.util.Properties;

public class PrimitiveTagsHandler
    extends XDocletTagSupport
{
    public String objectType(Properties attributes) {
        String type = attributes.getProperty("type");
        return objectType(type);
    }

    private static String objectType(String type) {
        if (type.equals("int")) {
            return "java.lang.Integer";
        }

        if (type.equals("short")) {
            return "java.lang.Short";
        }
```

- Tag handlers should extend **XDocletTagSupport**
- This method signature is all that's necessary to expose content tag
- **String value returned is output of content tag**
- Separating tag logic from tag interface is good style

```
        if (type.equals("float")) {
            return "java.lang.Float";
        }

        if (type.equals("double")) {
            return "java.lang.Double";
        }

        if (type.equals("long")) {
            return "java.lang.Long";
        }

        if (type.equals("boolean")) {
            return "java.lang.Boolean";
        }

        if (type.equals("character")) {
            return "java.lang.Character";
        }

        if (type.equals("byte")) {
            return "java.lang.byte";
        }

        return type;
    }
}
```

A tag handler provides tags by providing methods with well-known signatures. Any methods with an appropriate signature will be accessible as a tag in a template. A content tag has the form `String` *tagName*`(Properties attributes)`. The content to be placed in the template is returned from the tag method. The attributes on the tag in the XML document are passed in using a `java.util. Properties` object.

The tag is named `objectType`. It takes a single attribute, `type`, which contains any Java type and returns the type of the `Object` form. As you saw earlier, `int` maps to `java.lang.Integer`, and `boolean` maps to `java.lang.Boolean`. Notice that the logic is separated out from the method that provides that tag. Although there isn't any requirement to do this, having the logic separated out makes it easier to understand the code and introduce related tags later. As a matter of style, a tag method should not invoke any other tag methods; it should only invoke the internal methods.

Using the tag handler

Now that you have a tag handler defined, how can you use it? The first step is to make sure the class is visible to XDoclet. We'll explore packaging custom XDoclet components later. For now, compile the tag handler and place the class in a JAR file visible to xdoclet.lib.path in your local tree.

That's all you need to do to allow XDoclet to find your new tag handler. However, to make use of a new tag handler, you need to use the <XDtTagDef:tagDef> tag:

```
<XDtTagDef:tagDef namespace="Primitive"
    handler="com.xdocletbook.ch12.PrimitiveTagsHandler" />
```

This tells XDoclet to make the PrimitiveTagsHandler visible under the Primitive namespace. The objectType tag can now be referenced as <XDtPrimitive:object-Type>, and the code from 12.4.4 can be greatly simplified:

```
public Object getSomeValue() {
    return
<XDtType:ifIsNotPrimitive value="<XDtField:fieldType />">
    <XDtField:fieldName />
</XDtType:ifIsNotPrimitive>
<XDtType:ifIsPrimitive value="<XDtField:fieldType />">
    new <XDtPrimitive:objectType
            type="<XDtField:fieldType />" />(<XDtField:fieldName/>)
</XDtType:ifIsPrimitive>;
}
```

12.5.2 Creating a body tag

You're using the conditional <XDtType:ifIsPrimitive> and <XDtType:ifIs-NotPrimitive> body tags from the Type namespace. They work fine here, but let's look at how you could implement these tags locally. In the process, you'll change the input attribute name from value to type, to more accurately reflect the nature of value input value:

```
public void ifIsPrimitive(String template,          Declare body tag for
                      Properties attributes)         positive condition
    throws XDocletException
{
    String type = attributes.getProperty("type");

    if (isPrimitiveType(type)) {
        generate(template);      ◁── Evaluate body only
    }                                if type is primitive
}

public void ifIsNotPrimitive(String template,       Declare body tag for
                      Properties attributes)          negative condition
```

```
    throws XDocletException
{
    String type = attributes.getProperty("type");

    if (!isPrimitiveType(type)) {
        generate(template);        ◁─┐ Evaluate body only if
    }                                 │ type isn't primitive
}

private static boolean isPrimitiveType(String name)   ◁─┐ Separating
{                                                        │ out logic lets
    return name.equals("int")      ||                    │ you reuse
           name.equals("long")     ||                    │ code in both
           name.equals("float")    ||                    │ tags
           name.equals("double")   ||
           name.equals("boolean")  ||
           name.equals("byte")     ||
           name.equals("short")    ||
           name.equals("char");
}
```

Body tags are simple to work with. A body tag method takes a String input parameter, which is the text of the tag body, and a Properties parameter that contains the XML attributes of the tag. A body tag doesn't return text like a content tag does. Instead, it uses the generate method to evaluate template fragments into the output stream.

Using the body tags

Let's look at how the template is written using the new tags:

```
public Object getSomeValue() {
    return
<XDtPrimitive:ifIsNotPrimitive           ─┐ For objects (non-
    type="<XDtField:fieldType />">         │ primitive types),
<XDtField:fieldName />                     │ output field name
</XDtPrimitive:ifIsNotPrimitive>   ◁──────┘
<XDtPrimitive:ifIsPrimitive
    type="<XDtField:fieldType />">
    new <XDtPrimitive:objectType          ─┐ Wrap primitives
            type="<XDtField:fieldType /"    │ in corresponding
                />(<XDtField:fieldName/>)   │ object type
</XDtPrimitive:ifIsPrimitive>;
}
```

When the <XDtPrimitive:ifIsNotPrimitive> tag is invoked, the corresponding tag method is called. The Properties object contains a single property whose name is type and whose value is the result of evaluating <XDtField:fieldType />. This tag is evaluated by the template engine, and only the results of the evaluation are passed on to the tag handler. The template text, on the other hand, is the text `<XDtField:fieldname />`. The template engine doesn't attempt to evaluate the body. It's the job of the body tag method to determine when and where to evaluate the template fragment. In this example, the template should be evaluated only if the type passed in isn't primitive.

The `generate` method, provided by the `XDocletTagSupport` superclass, handles the template evaluation. Here you pass the template to the `generate` method if the condition is true.

This approach does improve the readability of the template, but if you find yourself doing a large number of conversions to `Object` values, even this could get unwieldy. In that case, you might want to move even more of the generation into a tag.

12.5.3 *Refactoring common functionality into a tag*

If you find yourself writing the same long template fragments over and over, you should consider refactoring the template and pushing the duplicate code into a custom tag. Doing so makes the template more readable and more maintainable. When you push functionality into a tag, you need to first consider whether you're creating a content tag or a body tag. In some cases, the choice is obvious (an iterator or conditional, for example, which can only be implemented as a body tag). In other cases (like the current object conversion example) either method would work. Let's look at both options:

```
public String convertToObjectValue(Properties attributes)        ◁──
    throws XDocletException                              Content tag
{                                                          version
    String type  = attributes.getProperty("type");
    String value = attributes.getProperty("value");

    if (isPrimitiveType(type)) {
        return "new " + objectType(type) +
                "(" + value + ")";
    } else {
        return value;
    }
}


public void convertToObjectValue(String template,        │ Body tag
                            Properties attributes)        │ version
    throws XDocletException
{
    String type  = attributes.getProperty("type");
```

```
        if (isPrimitiveType(type)) {
            generate("new ");
            generate(objectType(type));
            generate("(");
            generate(template);
            generate(")");
        } else {
            generate(template);
        }
    }
```

Here you have both a body tag and a content tag implementation of convert-
ToObjectValue. An interesting aspect of XDoclet is that a single tag handler can
contain both a body tag and a content tag of the same name without being confused. XDoclet determines the correct tag to call based on whether the XML tag
has a body.

Both of these approaches provide simple usages. The difference is that in one
case you pass the value to be converted to object form in an attribute, and in the
other case you pass it in the tag body:

```
public Object getSomeValue() {
    return <XDtPrimitive:convertToObjectValue
            type="<XDtField:fieldType />"
            value="<XDtField:fieldName />" />;
}

public Object getSomeValue() {
    return <XDtPrimitive:convertToObjectValue
            type="<XDtField:fieldType
            />"><XDtField:fieldname
            /></XDtPrimitive:convertToObjectValue>;
}
```

The content tag is easier to write in Java, and the template is slightly cleaner. In
such a case, the only compelling reason to choose a body tag would be if the value
expression were complicated enough that expressing it in an attribute value
would be unwieldy. As a general rule, you should use a body tag only if the body
content may be optionally evaluated (a conditional) or evaluates an arbitrary
number of times (an iterator). In this case, the body is evaluated exactly one time,
making the content tag the better choice.

12.6 Creating custom tasks

Templates and custom tags represent the back end of a custom generation task.
You've seen how to invoke an individual template from within Ant, but these are

low-level XDoclet components. In cases where the template is needed in only one place, the <template> subtask is more than sufficient. However, if the template needs to be reused between projects or modules, you should consider packaging the task.

Packaging an XDoclet generation task makes the custom task look and behave as if it were a built-in task. As with the built-in tasks, two levels are important: the Ant task and the XDoclet subtask. The Ant task corresponds to a top-level XDoclet task, such as <ejbdoclet> or <webdoclet>, which is a container for generation subtasks. The subtask does the actual generation. You can think of it as a custom implementation of the <template> subtask that provides default values for template parameters like the name of the template file and the destination file. You can also add in custom parameters on either the task or the subtask if your generation task calls for additional information.

In this section, you'll bundle the factory task to make it simpler to use. Using the <template> subtask, the Ant target is rather large:

```
<target name="factories">
    <xdoclet destdir="${gen.src.dir}">
        <fileset dir="${src.dir}" includes="**/*.java" />

        <template acceptInterfaces="false"
                  acceptAbstractClasses="false"
                  havingClassTag="example.factory"
                  templateFile="factory.xdt"
                  destinationFile="{0}Factory.java" />
    </xdoclet>
</target>
```

This is manageable for a single-use generation task, but if you were to reuse the factory template, you might want something a little simpler. Consider the following Ant target:

```
<target name="factories">
    <factories>
        <fileset dir="${src.dir}" includes="**/*.java" />
        <factory />
    </factories>
</target>
```

A lot less could go wrong here. But before you can get to this point, you need to create the Ant task and subtask you'll use and then bundle up the task for easy distribution.

12.6.1 *Creating the Ant task*

The first step is to create the top-level Ant task that corresponds to the `<factories>` task. This turns out to be a matter of creating a subclass of `xdoclet.DocletTask`:

```
package com.xdocletbook.ch12;

import xdoclet.DocletTask;

public class FactoryTask
    extends DocletTask
{
    public FactoryTask() {
        super();
    }
}
```

You aren't adding any additional parameters here, so this is all that's necessary. This task is a proper Ant task, so you could add parameters and sub-elements using Ant's task mechanisms. However, it's rare to need to add additional attributes to the task. For more information on creating custom Ant tasks, see *Java Development with Ant.*[1]

In fact, the task itself isn't necessary. It's possible to attach your subtasks directly to `DocletTask` so that they can be used from any XDoclet task. However, as a matter of style, it's better not to expose a subtask at higher level than is necessary. Making a subtask global in scope risks name collisions and general confusion just to save you from creating a single class.

12.6.2 *Creating the subtask*

Next, you need to implement the `<factory>` subtask to perform the generation. Subtasks should extend `xdoclet.TemplateSubTask`. The code is incredibly simple. In your subclass, you specify the default code generation values in the constructor and let the magic of inheritance take over:

```
package com.xdocletbook.ch11;

import xdoclet.TemplateSubTask;
import xdoclet.XDocletException;

public class FactorySubTask
    extends TemplateSubTask
{
    private static String XDT_RESOURCE =
        "/com/xdocletbook/ch11/factory.xdt";
```

---

[1] Erik Hatcher and Steve Loughran, *Java Development with Ant* (Greenwich, CT: Manning, 2003).

```
        public FactorySubTask()
        {
            setTemplateURL(FactorySubTask.class
                        .getResource(XDT_RESOURCE));
            setAcceptInterfaces(false);
            setAcceptAbstractClasses(false);
                setDestinationFile("{0}Factory.java");
                setHavingClassTag("example.factory");
        }

        public void validateOptions()
          throws XDocletException
        {
            // validation logic, if any
        }

    }
```

If the subtask were a little more complex, you might need to provide attributes or even sub-elements for configuration. Simple attributes would take the form of getter and setter methods on the class and would be exposed as attributes on the factory subtask in the Ant file. If you need to do sanity checking on the options, validation logic can be set in the validateOptions method.

One key difference in using this approach is that the template file needs to be available as a system resource. You'll see exactly where to place the template file when we look at bundling the task. For now, here's a reminder what the template looks like:

```
/*
 * <XDtI18n:getString resource="do_not_edit"/>
 */

package <XDtPackage:packageName/>;

/**
<XDtClass:classCommentTags indent="0" /> */
public class <XDtClass:className />Factory
    {
    /**
     * returns a new <XDtClass:className /> instance
     */
    public <XDtClass:className
                /> new<XDtClass:className />()
    {
        return new <XDtClass:className />();
    }
}
```

Follow the convention of naming XDoclet template files with the .xdt extension and call this template `factory.xdt`.

12.6.3 *Distributing custom tasks*

Before you can bundle the code generation task, you need to create an `xdoclet.xml` deployment descriptor. This deployment descriptor tells XDoclet how the tasks and subtasks relate. Here's the deployment descriptor for the task:

```
<xdoclet-module>
    <subtask name="factory"
            implementation-class=
                    "com.xdocletbook.ch12.FactorySubTask"
            parent-task-class=
                    "com.xdocletbook.ch12.FactoryTask" />
</xdoclet-module>
```

This code says that `FactoryTask` has a subtask named `factory`, which is implemented by `FactorySubTask`. You aren't providing any tag libraries, but if you were, you could declare them using a `<taghandler>` element. For example, to bundle `PrimitiveTagsHandler`, you could add the following.

```
<taghandler namespace="Primitive"
            class="com.xdocletbook.ch11.PrimitiveTagsHandler" />
```

Once you have the deployment descriptor, you need to place it in a JAR along with the task and subtask classes and the template file. The `xdoclet.xml` file goes in the META-INF directory. All the other files should be placed in the JAR according to their package structure (see figure 12.6).

Once the task is bundled in a JAR, the only thing left to do is to use it.

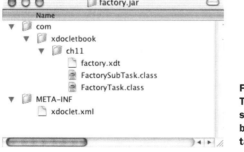

**Figure 12.6
The directory
structure of a
bundled XDoclet
task**

12.6.4 *Registering custom tasks in Ant*

Now that the custom task is packaged, you need to make the JAR visible to XDoclet in xdoclet.lib.path and declare the task. Assuming that factory.jar is available in the local libs directory, the following is all that's necessary to allow XDoclet to see your tasks and to make your task visible to Ant:

```
<taskdef name="factories"
         classname="com.xdocletbook.ch12.FactoryTask"
         classpathref="xdoclet.lib.path" />
```

Now the <factories> tag you saw at the beginning of this section is available in your Ant build file.

12.7 *Summary*

Real-world code generation tasks can easily extend beyond the scope of the built-in XDoclet tasks. In this chapter, you've seen how to customize XDoclet using templates. Templates can be used by merge points to customize existing tasks or can be used as the basis for entirely new tasks.

You write templates using tags defined in tag handlers. XDoclet provides a large library of tags, but sometimes it's necessary to write custom tag handlers for special-purpose tasks. We've also explained how custom generation tasks can be bundled for easy re-use between projects.

13

XDoclet extensions and tools

> *Give us the tools, and we will finish the job.*
>
> —Winston Churchill (1874–1965), English statesman, author

XDoclet doesn't force you to bring much baggage into your development process. The only required tool is Apache Ant, but Ant is so ubiquitous that this is more of an affirmation of a normal Java build process than a requirement to bring a new tool into the mix. But just because XDoclet doesn't require any outside support doesn't mean it can't greatly benefit from outside tools. Several external tools that work with XDoclet can further simplify the development process:

- *IntelliJ IDEA*—A commercial Java integrated development environment (IDE)
- *Eclipse*—An open-source Java IDE
- *AndroMDA*—A tool that generates XDoclet-enhanced classes from a UML model file
- *Middlegen*—A tool that generates XDoclet-enhanced classes from database schema

Before we discuss each tool, let's start with an overview of how tools like this can help you with XDoclet development.

13.1 The role of tools in XDoclet

XDoclet tags are much simpler and easier to maintain than the generated deployment descriptors and classes. But there's still a lot of work to be done creating and maintaining the tags. Keeping track of the various options and validating that you haven't made any mistakes is not trivial. In the best case, mistakes will show up as build errors. Detecting more subtle mistakes might require unit testing or functional testing. This is no worse than many other types of development errors, but with the right tools you can lessen the impact of errors or avoid them all together.

The tools we'll look at can perform a number of functions:

- *Generate XDoclet tags*—It may seem redundant at first to use a tool to generate the input for a code generator, but as you'll see later, this is a great way to separate concerns. A tool that needs to generate EJBs, for example, can generate XDoclet metadata for the beans it generates. The generator can focus on creating the correct metadata, which is really the core of the application, leaving the non-domain-specific details to the lower level generator, XDoclet.

- *Validate XDoclet tags*—XDoclet can be picky about tags and parameters. It's easy to misname a tag or to omit a required parameter. Even if you're lucky enough that a mistake results in a build-time error, the problem isn't always obvious from the error message. Fortunately, tools exist to validate XDoclet tags, checking that the XDoclet tags specified are correct. The sooner mistakes are detected, the less costly they are.

- *Maintain XDoclet tags*—As your code base changes, the metadata associated with it needs to change too. An IDE or editor with XDoclet support can help you write XDoclet tags, for example, by providing context-sensitive help and syntax highlighting. An XDoclet-aware tool can save you from needing to constantly refer to the documentation, help you avoid simple mistakes, and make your XDoclet-based work much quicker.

13.2 IntelliJ IDEA

IntelliJ IDEA (http://www.intellij.com/) is a popular commercial Java IDE from JetBrains. IDEA is known as a no-fluff IDE, and true to that image, it doesn't provide any direct support for XDoclet outside of the normal Javadoc and Ant support. IDEA is worth mentioning in the context of XDoclet because the XDoclet project also offers an XDoclet template file you can use in IDEA to generate XDoclet tags in your classes.

Figure 13.1 shows the blog application loaded into an IDEA project. The error bar on the right side of the window is littered with bright red marks, which is IDEA's way of informing you that it doesn't like the code you're looking at.

IDEA will have two problems in working with a project using XDoclet: IDEA doesn't know anything about the classes generated by XDoclet, and it doesn't know anything about the XDoclet tags. Fortunately, you can give IDEA a few hints to make it happy with your project.

13.2.1 Helping IDEA find your generated classes

Because you're following the practice of keeping your generated source files outside the main source tree, you need to tell IDEA where to find them so it can resolve references to those classes. In this project, the generated source files go into the `gensrc` directory, so you need to add that directory to the project properties. Figure 13.2 shows the Project Properties window with a reference to the `gensrc` directory.

There is one small catch: If you haven't generated the files yet or have cleaned your build tree, the generated classes won't be there for IDEA to use. You can still

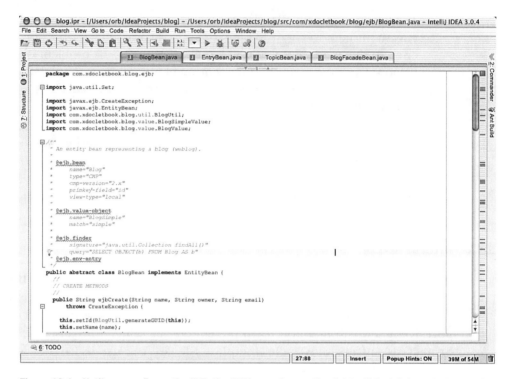

Figure 13.1   Until you configure the IDE, the IDEA error bar on the right will be bright red when you're working with XDoclet.

compile your project, but the red bars won't go away until you do a build. Yes, it's a minor annoyance, but there's no way for IDEA to figure out what classes XDoclet will generate until they are generated.

13.2.2   *Configuring IDEA to accept XDoclet tags*

The other problem IDEA has with the classes is the use of XDoclet tags. IDEA only knows about javadoc tags, and it's smart enough to give you an error if you use an invalid tag. Unfortunately, XDoclet tags aren't proper javadoc tags and get flagged.

You can't teach IDEA the specifics of your tags, but you can let it know that it's OK if you use javadoc tags it doesn't recognize. This functionality can be configured in the Errors tab of the IDE Settings control panel. The Unknown Javadoc Tags setting controls how IDEA responds to unknown tags. In figure 13.3, it's set to green, which means IDEA will ignore unknown tags. This setting causes you to give up IDEA's ability to detect unknown tags. If you want to leave the option enabled

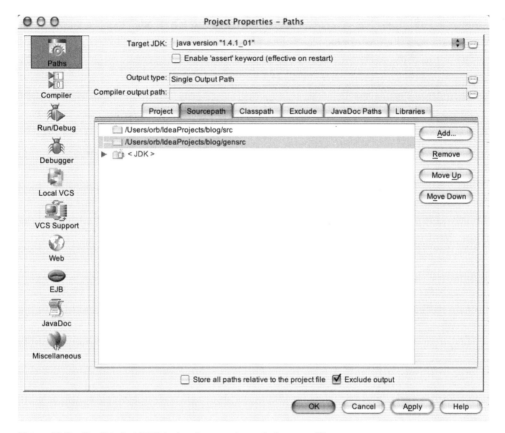

Figure 13.2   Configuring IDEA to locate your generated source files

(as a red error or yellow warning), then you need to explicitly list each XDoclet tag you'll be using in the Additional Javadoc Tags field. This is a bit of a hassle, so we prefer to turn off the check for unknown tags.

At this point, you can work with your XDoclet project and take advantage of all of IDEA's normal features. The IDEA error bar should be solid green, as shown in figure 13.4.

IDEA doesn't directly provide any special support for XDoclet, but many of IDEA's built-in features are useful with XDoclet. One powerful feature is IDEA's live templates.

Figure 13.3   Configuring IDEA to ignore the unknown javadoc tags used in XDoclet

13.2.3 *Using IDEA's live templates to generate XDoclet tags*

Live templates are tiny, passive code generation templates that you can invoke with only a few keystrokes. The XDoclet web site provides a set of live templates for IDEA that can generate XDoclet tags. These templates don't come with XDoclet, so you'll have to manually download the template definition file from the XDoclet web site (http://www.xdoclet.org/ide/) and place it in the config/templates directory of your IDEA install.

There are live templates for generating persistent fields, including the getter and setter methods, tagging methods as interface methods, setting transaction

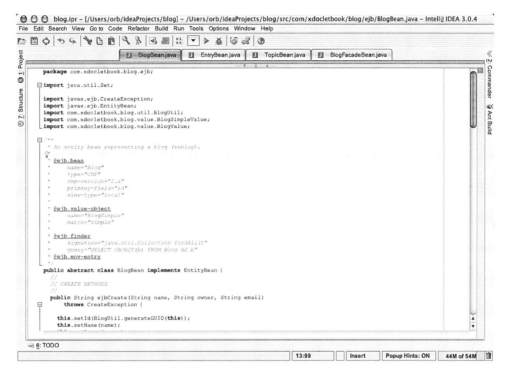

Figure 13.4 A green error bar means that IDEA is happy with the XDoclet project.

properties, and so on. This may not seem like much, but unless you have all the XDoclet tags memorized, such templates can save you a lot of debugging time.

Figure 13.5 shows the IDEA Live Templates window after the templates have been imported. There are 18 XDoclet live templates at your disposal. You can trigger a live template in the coding window by typing the live template abbreviation followed by a tab.

We've shown the `ejb.cmp` live template. If you're working on a new BMP entity bean, you can now go to the javadoc statements for the class, type **ejb.bmp**, and press Tab. IDEA will create an `@ejb.bean` tag that's ready to go with values based on the class name. If the new bean is `TestBean`, IDEA will generate the following XDoclet tag:

```
/**
 *   @ejb.bean type="BMP"
 *            name="TestBean"
 *            jndi-name="ejb/TestBean"
 */
```

Figure 13.5   IDEA live templates for working with XDoclet

Although IDEA doesn't provide any out-of-the-box features directly targeted at XDoclet, with a little configuration, it can serve as a powerful and productive IDE for XDoclet development.

13.3 *Eclipse*

Eclipse (http://www.eclipse.org/) is a very popular open source Java IDE. Like IDEA, Eclipse has no direct support for XDoclet. However, one of Eclipse's key attractions is its open plugin architecture and a vast library of freely available plug-ins that provide higher-level functionality.

13.3.1 Using JBoss IDE

Several Eclipse plugins interact with XDoclet on some level, but one of the more interesting ones is JBoss IDE. The JBoss IDE plugin for Eclipse is available directly from the JBoss project. JBoss IDE provides some basic JBoss management functions, but it also provides an interesting XDoclet module for managing XDoclet tags.

We'll skip over the general project configuration, because the defaults in Eclipse are compatible with XDoclet. Remember to add the generated source directory (`gensrc` for the web-log application) to the project; otherwise you'll encounter a red status bar complaining about the missing files.

There isn't much you can do beyond editing the XDoclet tags by hand until you install JBoss IDE. You can download it from the JBoss web site (http://www.jboss.org/). Copy the JBoss IDE plugins and features from the JBoss IDE distribution directory into the Eclipse `plugins` and `features` directories to get started.

Once JBoss IDE is installed, you need to instruct it to examine the XDoclet modules and look for information about the supported tags. The JBoss IDE preferences are available using the Window ▶ Preferences menu item. Figure 13.6

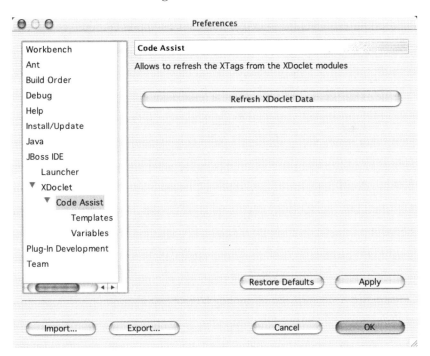

Figure 13.6   Loading the XDoclet modules in JBoss IDE

shows the JBoss IDE preferences options. To load the XDoclet data, click the Refresh XDoclet Data button. After the XDoclet data is loaded, you can make sure of the JBoss IDE's smart completion.

Once JBoss IDE understands all the XDoclet tags, you can use auto-completion when you create and edit XDoclet tags. Auto-completion can be used for creating XDoclet tags, creating parameters for tags, and even inserting default values for parameters. In addition to completing tags, JBoss IDE also provides limited documentation for each tag. To trigger XDoclet auto-completion, press Ctrl-spacebar inside any javadoc comment block. Figure 13.7 shows auto-completion in action.

13.3.2 Generating an XDoclet build file

Eclipse uses standard Ant build files for building. If you're importing an XDoclet project, you'll probably want to continue using your existing Ant build files. If

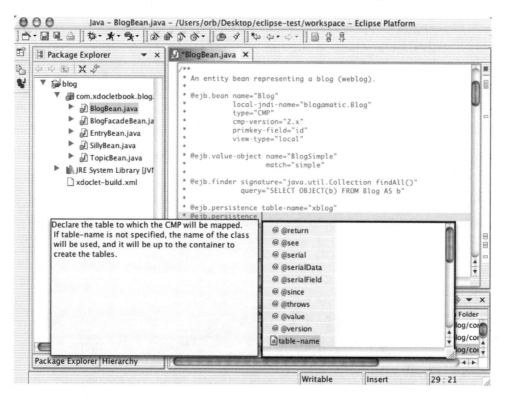

Figure 13.7   JBoss IDE gives smart completion and documentation for the `ejb.persistence` tag.

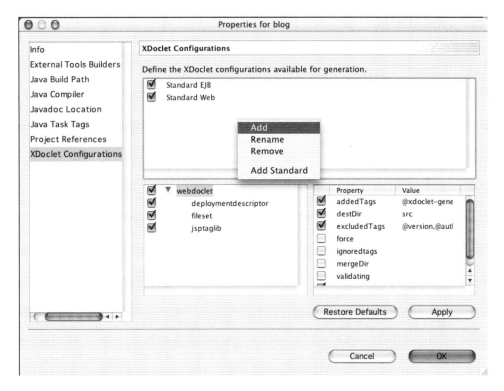

Figure 13.8   Configuring XDoclet build parameters

you're starting from scratch, JBoss IDE can generate the XDoclet portion of your build file.

XDoclet configuration options are available under the Project ▶ Properties menu option. Figure 13.8 shows the XDoclet configurations options. Initially the screen will be blank. The upper-right box lists the XDoclet tasks that are configured. You can add a new task by right-clicking and selecting Add in the pop-up menu. Below the task selection box are two additional boxes. The box on the left selects subtasks for the currently chosen task, and the box on the right sets attributes on the currently selected subtask.

With the XDoclet build file generated, you can run XDoclet code generation by right-clicking in the current project and selecting Run XDoclet from the pop-up menu. The build file generated can be used both inside and outside Eclipse.[1]

---

[1]   For more information on using Eclipse, see *Eclipse in Action* by David Gallardo, Ed Burnette, and Robert McGovern (Greenwich, CT: Manning, 2003).

13.4 *AndroMDA*

Model-driven architecture (MDA) is a design technique that is growing in popularity. The idea is to start with a generic UML model of a domain and add in the specific details necessary for implementing the model on a given platform. For our purposes, you can think in the context of generating code from a UML model.

AndroMDA (http://www.andromda.org/) is an XDoclet front-end tool that generates code with XDoclet tags directly from an XMI (XML Meta-Data Interchange) file that can be produced by UML modeling tools such as Poseidon for UML (http://www.gentleware.com/), Borland Together (http://www.borland.com/together/), and IBM Rational Rose (http://www.rational.com/). In an EJB application, AndroMDA allows you to take a step back and model the desired beans using expressive UML models rather than express the design in code.

Figure 13.9 shows a UML class diagram with stereotypes that provide some basic information to guide code generation. From a model like this, AndroMDA can generate a stateless session bean and an entity bean complete with XDoclet tags. XDoclet can then process these generated beans to generate the interfaces, utility classes, and deployment descriptors you've seen XDoclet generate so easily.

In addition to EJB generation, AndroMDA can generate Jakarta Struts and Hibernate code. AndroMDA has a flexible extension mechanism similar to XDoclet, which allows for arbitrary code generation modules to be developed and plugged into the base framework.

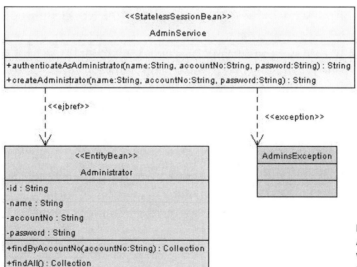

Figure 13.9
A simple UML diagram with stereotypes used to guide code generation

AndroMDA enhances the benefit of XDoclet code generation by letting you do more high-level design work before you have to consider the more mundane details necessary to express your design in Java code. If your development process includes UML models, then AndroMDA could be a perfect fit for your project. If you don't yet use UML because of the difficulty involved in keeping your model and your code base in sync, AndroMDA might be the missing link that lets you move to UML.

13.5 *Middlegen*

Not all application development is model driven. For enterprise applications, it's common for development to be database driven. Many enterprise applications revolve around a relational database with schemas created by database experts. The application developer is responsible for creating applications around the existing schema.

Writing an entity bean to map to an existing database schema is a time-consuming and error-prone task. Middlegen (http://boss.bekk.no/boss/middlegen/) can take a lot of the pain out of this process by reading database schema from a database and generating XDoclet-enhanced Java classes directly from that schema.

As you can imagine, an automatic mapping from a relational database table to an entity bean might be a bit rougher around the edges than a hand-coded solution. If you need to guide the mapping process, then Middlegen provides a nice GUI that visually shows the tables in the database and their relationships. The GUI lets you edit table and field mappings, relation mappings, primary keys, and so on.

Figure 13.10 shows Middlegen at work mapping the schema for a flight reservation system. Here you're editing a field name and can select the name, type, and visibility of the property on the Java class to map to. The column shown would map to the following methods on the ReservationBean generated by Middlegen:

```
/**
 * Returns the registrationUtc
 * @todo support OracleClob,OracleBlob on WLS
 *
 * @return the registrationUtc
 *
 * @ejb.interface-method view-type="local"
 * @ejb.persistence column-name="registration_utc"
 */

public abstract java.sql.Timestamp getRegistrationUtc();
```

```
/**
 * Sets the registrationUtc
 *
 * @param java.sql.Timestamp the new registrationUtc value
 * @ejb.interface-method view-type="local"
 */

public abstract void
    setRegistrationUtc(java.sql.Timestamp registrationUtc);
```

Middlegen can also generate a finder method for this field:

```
/**
 * @ejb.finder
 *     signature="java.util.Collection
 *         findByRegistrationUtc(java.sql.Timestamp registrationUtc)"
 *     result-type-mapping="Local"
 *     method-intf="LocalHome"
 *     query="SELECT DISTINCT OBJECT(o) FROM Reservation o
 *         WHERE o.registrationUtc = ?1"
 *     description="registration_utc is indexed."
 */
```

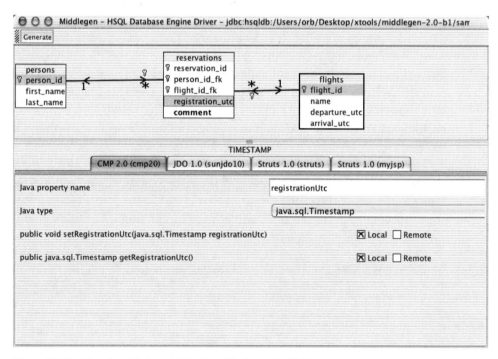

Figure 13.10   Mapping database tables to entity beans in Middlegen

Middlegen can't generate the business methods or business logic in your application, but as a tool for quickly mapping database schema to J2EE components, it does a good job. The time it takes to map relational tables using Middlegen is a tiny fraction of what it would take to do the task by hand.

13.6 *Summary*

XDoclet is an extremely powerful code generation engine that can significantly reduce application development time. However, that doesn't mean XDoclet is the be-all and end-all of application development. XDoclet's productivity can be further enhanced by close cooperation with other tools.

IDEs can provide support for generating and editing XDoclet tags. Code assistance like this is no substitute for understanding XDoclet, but these tools can help a skilled XDoclet developer code more quickly and avoid some of the dumb mistakes we all make.

Tools such as AndroMDA and Middlegen support the generation of XDoclet-enhanced classes from outside input sources. This can not only save you time, but also simplify development by allowing you to make design decisions at a level appropriate to your development process. If your process is model-centric or database-centric, then these tools are great front-ends to XDoclet that can leverage the strengths of your process while retaining the power of code generation.

Installing XDoclet

A

Before you begin

Both Ant and XDoclet depend on a suitable Java 2 runtime environment being available in your development environment. This shouldn't be an issue, because this book is targeted at Java developers who probably already have Java installed. If you need to install Java on your system, visit http://java.sun.com/j2se and follow the download links.

Setting up Ant

XDoclet is implemented as a collection of Ant tasks and subtasks. Therefore, you must have Ant installed to use XDoclet. Follow these steps to set up Ant in your development environment:

1. **Download the Ant binaries.** You can download the Ant binaries from http://ant.apache.org. Follow the Download/Binary Distributions link and choose an appropriate distribution archive for your environment (.zip for Windows, .tar.gz or .tar.bz2 for UNIX). Be sure to download the latest version of Ant (XDoclet depends on version 1.5 or higher).

2. **Unpack the binaries.** Choose an appropriate path for Ant and unpack the distribution archive to that path.

3. **Set the JAVA_HOME environment variable.** Set the JAVA_HOME environment variable to the path of Java's base directory.

4. **Add the bin directory to the path.** Ant comes with some convenient batch files to make it easy to invoke Ant. To make these batch files readily available, add them to your environment path as follows:

   - *For Windows*—SET PATH=%PATH%;%ANT_HOME%\bin
   - *For UNIX (bash)*—export PATH=${PATH}:${ANT_HOME}/bin
   - *For UNIX (csh)*—set path=($path $ANT_HOME/bin)

IMPORTANT The Windows 9x family of operating systems (Windows 95, Windows 98, and Windows ME) has trouble working with long filenames in batch files. Therefore, if you're working on one of these operating systems, you need to rename Ant's home directory so that it has a short (8.3) filename such as ant153 or simply ant. Remember to set your ANT_HOME environment variable to use the short name.

Installing XDoclet

Installing XDoclet follows a four-step process:

1. **Download the XDoclet binaries.** To download XDoclet, visit http://xdoclet. sourceforge.net and follow the Download/Installation link. You have three distributions to choose from:

   - xdoclet-lib-1.2[1]—Includes only the XDoclet JAR files. This distribution contains all of the required libraries and is convenient if you only

---

[1] At the time of this writing, the most current version of XDoclet was 1.2, but we're anticipating that version 1.2 will be released by the time you read this. If we're wrong, then you may have to substitute 1.2b3 for 1.2.

want to download the latest compiled binaries and don't need the documentation or sample code.

- xdoclet-bin-1.2—Includes the JAR files, documentation, and examples. We recommend that you download this archive to receive all documentation and example code.

- xdoclet-src-1.2—Includes scripts and sources needed to build XDoclet. This distribution is recommended only if you are truly adventurous and want to look under the hood at how XDoclet works.

2 **Unpack the binaries.** Choose an appropriate path for XDoclet and unpack the downloaded archive in that path.

3 **Add the XDoclet path to your build file.** Using Ant's `<path>` type, add the XDoclet path to your build file. Be sure to include any external libraries your source code will rely on (such as `j2ee.jar`) in this path. For example:

```
<property name="lib.dir" location="lib"/>
<property name="xdoclet.lib.dir" location="xdocletlib"/>
<path id="xdoclet.lib.path">
  <fileset dir="${lib.dir}" includes="*.jar"/>
  <fileset dir="${xdoclet.lib.dir}" includes="*.jar"/>
</path>
```

4 **Add XDoclet to your build file.** Add appropriate `<taskdef>` entries to your Ant build scripts to include the XDoclet modules you want to use. For example, the following adds support for `<ejbdoclet>` to your build file:

```
<taskdef name="ejbdoclet"
    classname="xdoclet.modules.ejb.EjbDocletTask"
    classpathref="xdoclet.lib.path"/>
```

Gotchas

Although the XDoclet installation is fairly straightforward, you may encounter some trouble along the way. Here are a few gotchas to watch for and how to deal with them.

Task not found

You may get a build-time error that says something like *taskdef class xdoclet.modules. ejb.EjbDocletTask cannot be found.*

What it means

Ant was unable to locate the task in the classpath specified in `<taskdef>`. It may also mean that the task was found in the classpath, but some other class the task depends on was not found.

How to fix it

Be sure that the required XDoclet's JAR files are in the `<taskdef>` classpath.

Missing libraries

When doing a build, you may get an error that resembles the following: *Make sure the jar file containing the [some class] class is in the classpath specified in the `<taskdef>` that defined XDoclet. These classes are needed in order to generate correct output.*

What it means

Your application code depends on certain third-party libraries that can't be found in XDoclet's classpath. For example, you may have developed some EJBs that depend on `javax.ejb.EntityBean` or `javax.ejb.SessionBean`. XDoclet needs these files in order to process your code.

How to fix it

Be sure the appropriate third-party libraries are available in the classpath specified in the `<taskdef>` that defined the XDoclet task you're trying to use. For example, if you're using XDoclet to generate artifacts for EJBs, then you need to be sure `j2ee.jar` (or equivalent) is in XDoclet's classpath.

Deprecated tasks

The xdoclet.ejb.EjbDocletTask is deprecated and will be removed in a future version of XDoclet. Please update your taskdef to use xdoclet.modules.ejb.EjbDocletTask instead.

What it means

In versions of XDoclet prior to 1.2.0, XDoclet tasks weren't packaged under the `xdoclet.modules` package structure. If you've been using an older version of XDoclet or reading documentation that covers older versions of XDoclet, you may encounter this error.

How to fix it

Change the `classname` of the task in question to reflect the new packaging of XDoclet tasks.

XDoclet task/subtask quick reference

XDoclet does all its work through a collection of Ant tasks and subtasks. These tasks and subtasks collect metadata from XDoclet tags placed in Java source code and use that metadata to generate deployment descriptors, additional Java source code, and other files.

Sometimes, however, you may want to include extra information (additional deployment data, Java method definitions, and so on) that's beyond XDoclet's responsibility in one of the generated files. For those cases, many of the subtasks are equipped with associated merge points. By placing an appropriate merge file that contains the extra information in the subtask's merge directory, you can have the subtask include your extra code in the generated artifact.

This appendix is a reference to all the XDoclet tasks, subtasks, and merge files as of XDoclet version 1.2.0.

Common task attributes

All XDoclet tasks have these common attributes:

- destdir—The destination directory for generated files.

- excludedtags—Specifies tags that shouldn't be automatically written to output files. The normal behavior is to include all @ tags from the source file to the output files. This may cause trouble if you use CVS-like tags, such as $Revision: 1.5 $, which will be overwritten at each build and cause a difference for CVS even if the code isn't changed. Example: excluded-tags="@version".

- force—Specifies whether file-generation should be forced. In normal cases, the timestamp of a generated file is checked against the timestamp of the class (and its superclasses) it was generated from. When this timestamp checking should be bypassed (for example, after the installation of a new XDoclet version), then you should force the regeneration. The easiest way is to run the Ant build file with a parameter -Dxdoclet.force=true and add the option force=${xdoclet.force} to the task call.[1]

- mergedir—Directory where subtasks look for files to be merged with generated files.

- verbose—Sets the Verbose attribute of the DocletTask object.

Template subtask attributes

All subtasks have these common attributes:

- havingclasstag—Sets the HavingClassTag attribute of the TemplateSubTask object. HavingClassTag is used to select which classes are to be processed by a subtask based on whether a class has a particular class-level tag.

- oftype—Sets the OfType attribute of the TemplateSubTask object. OfType is used to select which classes are to be processed by a subtask based on the class's type.

- prefixwithpackagestructure—Indicates whether to prefix with the package structure.

- subtaskclassname—Sets a different name for the subtask, which will be seen in the log messages.

---

[1] Although the force attribute will help to ensure that new code is always generated, we recommend that you have a clean target in your Ant build file that resets the build state so that XDoclet is forced to generate all code anew.

- subtaskname—Sets an optional name for the subtask, which will be seen in XDoclet's debug messages.

XML subtask attributes

All subtasks that are used to generate XML artifacts have these common attributes in addition to those specified earlier:

- schema—Sets the Schema attribute of the XmlSubTask object.
- subtaskname—Sets an optional name for the subtask that will be seen in XDoclet's debug messages.
- useids—If true, XDoclet generates id attributes in the XML document. Note that this is only available in some subtasks.
- validatexml—If true, the generated XML is validated against its DTD or XML schema.
- xmlencoding—The encoding of the produced XML file. If your XML file uses international characters, you might want to set this to ISO-8859-1.

The \<documentdoclet> task

This task is used for general-purpose document generation.

Table B.1 \<documentdoclet> subtasks

Subtask/Attributes	Description
\<documenttags>	Extracts @doc.* tags from xdoclet.* sources and generates an HTML file describing the tags and their parameters. Used internally by XDoclet to generate documentation for XDt tag handlers.
\<info>	Extracts tag values from classes and method docs and generates an HTML report that summarizes all occurrences of this tag in a source tree. This task can be used to generate todo lists or any list with metrics about the occurrence of a certain tag.
header	Sets the Header attribute of the InfoSubTask object.
tag	Sets the Tag attribute of the InfoSubTask object.
projectname	Sets the Projectname attribute of the InfoSubTask object.

The *<ejbdoclet>* task

This task executes various EJB-specific subtasks. Be sure you include the JAR file containing Sun's `javax.ejb.*` classes on the taskdef's classpath.

In addition to the attributes common to all tasks, the `<ejbdoclet>` task has the following EJB-specific attributes:

- `ejbSpec`—The version of the EJB specification that `<ejbdoclet>` should adhere to. Valid values are "1.1" and "2.0". The default is "2.0".

- `ejbClassNameSuffix`—A comma-separated list of endings which should be removed from the bean class name to generate a bean's name if the `name` attribute of `@ejb.bean` is not specified. Defaults to "Bean,EJB,Ejb".

Table B.2 `<ejbdoclet>` subtasks

Subtask/Attributes	Description
`<apachesoap>`	Generates deployment descriptor files for Apache SOAP that expose EJBs as web services.
`contextFactoryName`	Sets the name of the JNDI context factory used when looking up an EJB's home interface.
`contextProviderUrl`	Sets the URL associated with the JNDI context provider used when looking up an EJB's home interface.
`entityEjbProvider`	Specifies the provider class to use for entity EJBs that are exposed as web services.
`providerclasspath`	Sets the classpath for the provider class.
`statefulSessionEjbProvider`	Specifies the provider class to use for stateful session EJBs that are exposed as web services.
`statelessSessionEjbProvider`	Specifies the provider class to use for stateless session EJBs that are exposed as web services.
`<axisdeploy>`	Generates deployment descriptor files for Apache Axis that expose EJBs as web services.
`contextFactoryName`	Sets the name of the JNDI context factory used when looking up an EJB's home interface.
`contextProviderUrl`	Sets the URL associated with the JNDI context provider used when looking up an EJB's home interface.
`<axisundeploy>`	Generates undeployment descriptor files for Apache Axis for the same web services that were deployed using the deployment descriptor files generated by `<axisdeploy>`.

Table B.2 `<ejbdoclet>` subtasks *(continued)*

Subtask/Attributes	Description
`<borland>`	Generates an EJB deployment descriptor file for EJBs that are to be deployed in Borland's Enterprise Server application server.
`datasource`	Specifies the JNDI-name used to look up the datasource.
`<castormapping>`	Generates a `mapping.xml` deployment descriptor.
`<dao>`	Generates Data Access Object classes for use with BMP entity beans.
`pattern`	Sets the pattern to use when naming the generated DAO classes. Defaults to {0}DAO.
`<dataobject>`	Creates data objects for entity EJBs. This task is currently being deprecated in favor of Value Object, which is more powerful in terms of relationships (1-1, 1-n, and n-m).
`pattern`	The pattern by which the data object classes are named. {0} designates the EJB name.
`<deploymentdescriptor>`	Creates an `ejb-jar.xml` deployment descriptor file for EJBs.
`clientjar`	Specifies a JAR file that contains the class files necessary for a client program to access the EJB.
`description`	Sets the description of the EJB.
`displayname`	Sets the display name for the EJB.
`largeicon`	Sets the large icon to be displayed for the EJB.
`smallicon`	Sets the small icon to be displayed for the EJB.
`<easerver>`	Generates configuration files for EJB jars in EAServer 4.1+.
`packageDescription`	Set the Jaguar package description.
`packageName`	[Required] Sets the Jaguar package name.
`version`	Sets the Jaguar version.
`<entitybmp>`	Creates entity bean classes for BMP entity EJBs. The classes are derived from the abstract entity bean class.
`pattern`	The pattern by which the BMP implementation classes are named. Defaults to {0}BMP.

Table B.2 `<ejbdoclet>` subtasks *(continued)*

Subtask/Attributes	Description
`<entitycmp>`	Creates entity bean classes for CMP entity EJBs. The classes are derived from the abstract entity bean class.
`cmpSpec`	Sets the version of the CMP specification to use when generating CMP implementation classes. Valid values: 1.x, 2.x. Defaults to 2.x.
`pattern`	The pattern by which the CMP implementation classes are named. Defaults to {0}CMP.
`<entityfacade>`	Generates session façade EJB classes for entity EJBs. The session EJBs generated by `<entityfacade>` depend on data objects generated by the `<dataobject>` subtask, which is being deprecated. Therefore, use of this subtask isn't recommended.
`ejbNamePattern`	The naming pattern to use for naming the generated façade bean. This is the name of the bean implemented by the generated class, not the name of the class itself. Defaults to {0}Facade.
`pattern`	The naming pattern to use for naming the generated class. Defaults to {0}FacadeEJB.
`<entitypk>`	Generates primary key classes for entity EJBs.
`pattern`	The pattern by which the primary key classes are named. {0} designates the EJB name.
`<homeinterface>`	Generates remote home interfaces for EJBs.
`pattern`	The pattern by which the home interfaces are named. {0} designates the EJB name.
`<hpas>`	Creates an `hp-ejb-jar.xml` deployment descriptor for HPAS.
`persistenceClass`	Specifies the class that implements the persistence manager interface. Applies only when using CMP.
`persistenceProduct`	Specifies the name of a third-party persistence manager product. Applies only when using CMP.
`persistenceSuffix`	Specifies a suffix to be appended to the abstract bean class name to obtain the generated bean class name. Applies only when using CMP.
`persistenceVersion`	Specifies the version of the third-party product. Applies only when using CMP.

Table B.2   `<ejbdoclet>` subtasks *(continued)*

Subtask/Attributes	Description
sfsbPassivationRoot	The path to a local directory indicating where the container should passivate stateful session bean instances.
<jboss>	Creates `jboss-xml` and `jaws.xml` deployment descriptors for JBoss.
createTable	Specifies whether JBoss is allowed to create new tables for entity EJBs if the tables don't already exist.
datasource	Specifies the JNDI name used to look up the data-source.
datasourceMapping	Specifies the name of the type mapping to be used for the datasource.
debug	Debug flag for `jaws.xml`.
jawsTemplateFile	Sets the name of the `jaws.xml` template file.
jbosscmpTemplateFile	Sets the name of the `jbosscmp-jdbc.xml` template file.
jbossTemplateFile	Sets the name of the `jboss.xml` template file.
preferredRelationMapping	Specifies the preferred mapping style for relation-ships. Valid values are foreign-key and relation-table.
removeTable	Specifies whether JBoss is allowed to drop entity EJB tables during shutdown.
securityDomain	The security domain to use.
typemapping	Specifies to JAWS which set of mappings from Java types to JDBC and SQL types to use for CMP entity beans.
unauthenticatedPrincipal	The principal to use when a user isn't authenticated.
version	The version of JBoss to target. Valid values: 2.4, 3.0, 3.1.
<jonas>	Generates the deployment descriptor for JOnAS.
version	The version of JOnAS to target. Valid values: 2.3, 2.4, 2.5, 2.6, 3.0.
<jrun>	Generates a deployment descriptor specific to Macromedia's JRun application server.
createtables	Specifies whether JRun is allowed to create tables for entity EJBs.

Table B.2 `<ejbdoclet>` **subtasks** *(continued)*

Subtask/Attributes	Description
`source`	Specifies the JNDI name of the datasource to be used to deploy the EJB.
`version`	Sets the version of JRun to be deployed to.
`<localhomeinterface>`	Generates local home interfaces for EJBs.
`pattern`	The pattern by which the local home interfaces are named. {0} designates the EJB name.
`<localinterface>`	Generates local interfaces for EJBs.
`pattern`	The pattern by which the interfaces are named. {0} designates the EJB name.
`<mvcsoft>`	Generates MVCSoft's XML.
`connectionjndiname`	Specifies the JNDI name of a transactional database connection.
`deploymentVersion`	Sets the MVCSoft version number to target. Valid values are 1.0.0 and 1.1. Default: 1.0.
`lightweightfactoryname`	Specifies a lightweight factory used to create home interfaces.
`loggingtype`	Sets the logging type. Defaults to no logging.
`<orion>`	Generates Orion's `orion-ejb-jar.xml`.
`version`	Specifies the version of Orion that the generated files will target (for example, "1.6.0").
`<pramati>`	Generates Pramati deployment files.
`datasource`	Specifies the JNDI name used to look up the datasource.
`jarName`	Sets the name of the EJB JAR file.
`version`	Specifies the version of Pramati being targeted. Defaults to 3.0.
`<remotefacade>`	Stage 2 of remote facade generation.
`pattern`	The pattern by which remote façade classes are named. Default: {0}Remote.
`<remoteinterface>`	Generates remote interfaces for EJBs.
`pattern`	The pattern by which the interfaces are named. {0} designates the EJB name.

Table B.2 `<ejbdoclet>` subtasks *(continued)*

Subtask/Attributes	Description
`<resin-ejb-xml>`	Subtask for generation of Resin EJB deployment descriptors.
cacheSize	Specifies the size of the entity EJB cache. If not specified, Resin defaults to 8192.
cacheTimeout	Specifies how long a loaded EJB will remain loaded without having to requery the database.
generateSourceComments	Specifies whether the generated file should contain comments.
`<session>`	Creates session bean classes for session EJBs. The classes are derived from the abstract session bean class.
pattern	Sets the `Pattern` attribute of the `SessionSubTask` object.
`<strutsform>`	Generates a Struts `ActionForm`, based on an entity EJB.
pattern	The pattern by which a generated `ActionForm` class is named. Default: {0}{1}Form.
`<sunone>`	Generates configuration files for EJB jars in iPlanet/SunONE.
cmpDestinationFile	Sets the destination filename of the CMP mappings file.
cmpResourceJndiName	Specifies the absolute `jndi-name` of the database to be used for storing CMP beans in the EJB JAR file.
cmpResourcePrincipalName	Specifies the default sign-on name to the resource manager.
cmpResourcePrincipalPassword	Specifies the default password to the resource manager.
cmpSchema	Specifies the database schema filename (minus the .dbschema extension), as captured using Sun's utilities.
transactionManagerType	Optional default transaction manager type for all components. Allowed values: local and global.
version	The SunONE/iPlanet version. Supported versions are 6.0, 6.5, and 7.0.

Table B.2 `<ejbdoclet>` **subtasks** *(continued)*

Subtask/Attributes	Description
`<utilobject>`	Generates utility classes for EJBs, including methods for looking up an EJB's home interface and for generating globally unique IDs.
cacheHomes	Specifies whether home interfaces should be cached.
includeGUID	Specifies whether a performant GUID generator method should be included in the utility object.
kind	Specifies the method used to look up home interfaces from JNDI. Valid values: Logical, Physical. Default: Logical.
pattern	The pattern by which a generated utility object is named. Defaults to {0}Util.
`<valueobject>`	Creates value objects for entity EJBs. This task replaces the `<dataobject>` subtask.
pattern	The pattern by which the value object classes are named. {0} designates the EJB name.
`<weblogic>`	Generates a vendor specific EJB deployment descriptor file for BEA's WebLogic.
createtables	Specifies whether WebLogic should create tables for entity beans. Defaults to false.
datasource	Specifies the JNDI name used to look up the datasource.
persistence	Sets the persistence type to use. Useful if you're using a different persistence manager like MVC-Soft.
poolname	Specifies the default WebLogic connection pool to be used for all EJBs that don't specify a different connection pool using the `@weblogic.pool-name` tag.
validateDbSchemaWith	Specifies how the container verifies whether the database table contains all the columns the bean's deployment descriptor contains. Using TableQuery, the container queries the table using column names to ensure that the database doesn't return an error. Using MetaData, the container gets metadata about the table from the database and uses it to verify that all the columns exist in the table. Defaults to TableQuery.
version	Sets the version of WebLogic to be deployed to.

Table B.2 `<ejbdoclet>` subtasks *(continued)*

Subtask/Attributes	Description
`<websphere>`	Generates a vendor specific EJB deployment descriptor file for IBM's WebSphere.

Table B.3 `<ejbdoclet>` merge files

Subtask/Merge files	Description
`<apachesoap>`	
`soap-mappings-{0}.xml`	Used to merge SOAP type mapping definitions (`<isd:mappings>`) into the generated SOAP deployment descriptor.
`<axisdeploy>`	
`axis-mappings-{0}.xml`	Used to merge Axis type mapping definitions (`<beanMapping/>` and `<typeMapping/>`) into the generated Axis deployment descriptor.
`<borland>`	
`ejb-borland-authorization-domain.xml`	An XML document containing the optional `authorization-domain` element.
`ejb-borland-datasources.xml`	An XML unparsed entity containing the `datasource` elements.
`ejb-borland-ejb-local-refs-{0}.xml`	An XML unparsed entity containing the `ejb-local-ref` elements for a bean, to be used instead of generating from `@bes.ejb-local-ref` tags.
`ejb-borland-ejb-refs-{0}.xml`	An XML unparsed entity containing the `ejb-ref` elements for a bean, to be used instead of generating from `@bes.ejb-ref` tags.
`ejb-borland-properties-{0}.xml`	An XML unparsed entity containing the `property` elements for a bean, to be used instead of generating from `@bes.property` tags.
`ejb-borland-resource-env-refs-{0}.xml`	An XML unparsed entity containing the `resource-env-ref` elements for a bean, to be used instead of generating from `@bes.resource-env-ref` tags.

Table B.3 `<ejbdoclet>` merge files *(continued)*

Subtask/Merge files	Description
`ejb-borland-resource-refs-{0}.xml`	An XML unparsed entity containing the `resource-ref` elements for a bean, to be used instead of generating from `@bes.resource-ref` tags.
`<castormapping>`	
`key-generator.xml`	An XML unparsed entity containing the `key-generator` element(s) for the mapping file.
`<dataobject>`	
`dao-custom.xdt`	A text file containing custom template and/or Java code to include in the data access object interface.
`<deploymentdescriptor>`	
`assembly-descriptor.xml`	An XML unparsed entity containing additional assembly descriptor information.
`ejb-finders-{0}.xml`	An XML unparsed entity containing query elements for a bean, for additional finder and select methods not defined in the bean class or its tags.
`ejb-ejbrefs-{0}.xml`	An XML unparsed entity containing (`ejb-ref*`, `ejb-local-ref*`) elements for a bean, to use instead of generating them from `@ejb.ejb-ref` and `@ejb.ejb-external-ref` tags.
`ejb-env-entries-{0}.xml`	An XML unparsed entity containing `env-entry` elements for a bean, to use instead of generating them from `@ejb.env-entry` tags.
`ejb-resource-env-refs-{0}.xml`	An XML unparsed entity containing `resource-env-ref` elements for a bean, to use instead of generating them `from @ejb.resource-env-ref` tags.
`ejb-resourcerefs-{0}.xml`	An XML unparsed entity containing `resource-ref` elements for a bean, to use instead of generating them from `@ejb.resource-ref` tags.
`ejb-sec-rolerefs-{0}.xml`	An XML unparsed entity containing `security-role-ref` elements for a bean, to use instead of generating them from `@ejb.security-role-ref` tags.
`ejb-security-roles.xml`	An XML unparsed entity containing `security-role` elements, to use instead of generating them from `role-name` parameters on `@ejb.permission`, `@ejb.finder`, and `@ejb.pk` tags.

Table B.3 `<ejbdoclet>` merge files *(continued)*

Subtask/Merge files	Description
`entity-beans.xml`	An XML unparsed entity containing entity elements for beans you wish to include that aren't processed by XDoclet.
`message-driven-beans.xml`	An XML unparsed entity containing message-driven elements for beans you wish to include that aren't processed by XDoclet.
`session-beans.xml`	An XML unparsed entity containing session elements for beans you wish to include that aren't processed by XDoclet.
`<entitybmp>`	
`entitybmp-custom.xdt`	A text file containing custom template and/or Java code to include in the EJB BMP class.
`<entitycmp>`	
`entitycmp-custom.xdt`	A text file containing custom template and/or Java code to include in the EJB CMP class.
`<entitypk>`	
`entitypk-custom.xdt`	A text file containing custom template and/or Java code to include in the primary key class.
`<homeinterface>`	
`home-custom.xdt`	A text file containing custom template and/or Java code to include in the home interface.
`<jboss>`	
`jaws-{0}.xml`	An XML unparsed entity containing (`cmp-field*`, `finder*`) elements for a bean.
`jaws-db-settings-{0}.xml`	An XML unparsed entity containing various database settings for a bean. The contents should consist of (`read-only?`, `table-name?`, `tuned-updates?`, `create-table?`, `remove-table?`, `row-locking?`, `time-out?`, `pk-constraint?`) elements.
`jboss-{0}.xml`	An XML document containing the `session`, `entity`, or `message-driven` element for a bean, to be used instead of generating it from the bean's tags.

Table B.3 `<ejbdoclet>` merge files *(continued)*

Subtask/Merge files	Description
`jboss-beans.xml`	An XML unparsed entity containing the `session`, `entity`, and `message-driven` elements for beans you wish to include that aren't processed by XDoclet.
`jboss-container.xml`	An XML document containing the optional `container-configurations` element for `jboss.xml`.
`jboss-resource-managers.xml`	An XML document containing the `resource-managers` element, to use instead of generating it from `jboss.resource-manager` tags.
`jboss-security.xml`	An XML unparsed entity containing the optional `enforce-ejb-restrictions`, `security-domain`, and/or `unauthenticated-principal` elements for `jboss.xml`.
`jbosscmp-jdbc-{0}.xml`	An XML unparsed entity containing various other settings for a bean. Should consist of the (`cmp-field*`, `load-groups?`, `eager-load-group?`, `lazy-load-groups?`, `query*`) elements.
`jbosscmp-jdbc-beans.xml`	An XML unparsed entity containing `entity` elements for any beans you wish to include that aren't processed by XDoclet.
`jbosscmp-jdbc-db-settings-{0}.xml`	An XML unparsed entity containing various database settings for a bean. The contents should consist of (`ejb-name`, (`datasource`, `datasource-mapping`)?, `create-table?`, `remove-table?`, `read-only?`, `read-time-out?`, `row-locking?`, `pk-constraint?`, `read-ahead?`, `list-cache-max?`, `fetch-size?`, `table-name?`) elements.
`jbosscmp-jdbc-defaults.xml`	An XML document containing the `defaults` element for `jbosscmp-jdbc.xml`.
`jbosscmp-jdbc-dvc.xml`	An XML unparsed entity containing any additional `dependent-value-class` elements not generated from `jboss.dvc` tags.
`jbosscmp-jdbc-entity-commands.xml`	An XML document containing the optional `entity-commands` element.
`jbosscmp-jdbc-typemappings.xml`	An XML document containing the optional `type-mappings` element.

Table B.3 `<ejbdoclet>` merge files *(continued)*

Subtask/Merge files	Description
`<jonas>`	
`jonas-{0}.xml`	An XML document containing the `jonas-session`, `jonas-entity`, or `jonas-message-driven` element for a bean, according to its type.
`<jrun>`	
`ejb-container.xml`	An XML unparsed entity containing the contents of the `ejb-container` element (`entity-default-store-type?`, `session-default-store-type?`, `file-store-directory?`, `cmp20-store-manager?`).
`<localhomeinterface>`	
`local-home-custom.xdt`	A text file containing custom template and/or Java code to include in the local home interface.
`<localinterface>`	
`local-custom.xdt`	A text file containing custom template and/or Java code to include in the local interface.
`<orion>`	
`orion-{0}.xml`	An XML document containing the `session-deployment`, `entity-deployment`, or `message-driven-deployment` element for a bean, instead of generating it from tags.
`orion-{0}-attributes.xml`	A text file containing the attributes for a bean's `session-deployment`, `entity-deployment`, or `message-driven-deployment` element, instead of specifying it with `orion.bean` tag parameters.
`orion-{0}-settings.xml`	An XML unparsed entity containing the (`env-entry-mapping*`, `ejb-ref-mapping*`) elements for a bean.
`orion-assembly-descriptor.xml`	An XML document containing the assembly-descriptor element for `orion-ejb-jar.xml`.
`<remoteinterface>`	
`remote-custom.xdt`	A text file containing custom template and/or Java code to include in the remote interface.

Table B.3 `<ejbdoclet>` merge files *(continued)*

Subtask/Merge files	Description
`<resin-ejb-xml>`	
`resin-query-functions.xml`	An XML document containing optional `<query-function>` declarations.
`<session>`	
`session-custom.xdt`	A text file containing custom template and/or Java code to include in the EJB session class.
`<sunone>`	
`sunone-ior-security-config-{0}.xml`	An XML document containing the `<ior-security-config>` element for a bean.
`sunone-pm-descriptors.xml`	An XML document containing the `<pm-descriptors>` element.
`sunone-role-mappings.ent`	An unparsed XML entity file that contains the `<role-mapping>` elements.
`<utilobject>`	
`lookup-custom.xdt`	A text file containing custom template and/or Java code to include in the utility class.
`util-custom.xdt`	A text file containing custom template and/or Java code to include in the utility class.
`<valueobject>`	
`valueobject-custom.xdt`	A text file containing custom template and/or Java code to include in the value object class.
`<weblogic>`	
`weblogic-enterprise-beans.xml`	An XML unparsed entity containing `weblogic-enterprise-bean` elements for any beans not processed by XDoclet.
`weblogic-security-role-assignment.xml`	An XML unparsed entity containing `security-role-assignment` elements.

The *<hibernatedoclet>* task

This Ant task is responsible for generating artifacts associated with the Hibernate object-persistence framework.

Table B.4 `<hibernatedoclet>` subtasks

Subtask/Attributes	Description
`<factoryclass>`	Generates a SessionFactory facade that is capable of configuring Hibernate inline, as well as provide a convenient method of switching later to other SessionFactory implementations.
`dataSource`	The data source name.
`dialect`	The Hibernate DB dialect.
`driver`	The JDBC driver class name.
`factoryClass`	The fully qualified class name of the generated factory.
`password`	The password used when connecting to the data source.
`username`	The username used when connecting to the data source.
`<hibernate>`	Generates Hibernate object-relational mapping files.
`version`	Sets the Hibernate version to use. Legal values are 1.1 and 2.0.
`<jbossservice>`	Generates JBoss MBean descriptors for Hibernated classes.
`dataSource`	[Required] JNDI name of the datasource to use in the session factory.
`dialect`	[Required] SQL dialect of the database.
`jndiName`	[Required] JNDI name to bind to the SessionFactory.
`password`	Password to use to log in to the database.
`serviceName`	[Required] Specifies the JBoss MBean name for a Hibernated class.
`showSql`	Logs SQL statements.
`transactionManagerStrategy`	The fully qualified class name of the Hibernate TransactionFactory implementation.
`transactionStrategy`	[Required] Strategy for obtaining the JTA TransactionManager.
`useOuterJoin`	Specifies whether to use an outer join.
`userName`	User name to use to log in to the database.
`userTransactionName`	JNDI name of the JTA UserTransaction object.

Table B.5 `<hibernatedoclet>` merge files

Subtask/Merge files	Description
`<hibernate>`	
`hibernate-properties.xml`	An XML unparsed entity containing additional property mappings for all classes.
`hibernate-properties-{0}.xml`	An XML unparsed entity containing additional property mappings for a class.

The *<jdodoclet>* task

This task executes various JDO-specific subtasks for generating JDO metadata mapping files.In addition to the attributes common to all tasks, the `<jdodoclet>` task has the following JDO-specific attribute:

- `jdoSpec`—The version of the JDO specification that `<jdodoclet>` should adhere to. Currently the only valid value is "1.0", which is also the default.

Table B.6 `<jdodoclet>` subtasks

Subtask/Attributes	Description
`<jdometadata>`	Generates the XML metadata for the JDO classes.
`generation`	Specifies the level at which a JDO metadata file should be generated. Valid values are class, package, and project. Defaults to class, meaning that a metadata file will be generated for each class processed.
`jdospec`	Sets the version of the JDO specification to adhere to. Defaults to 1.0.
`project`	Specifies the project name if `generation` is set to project. Defaults to metadata.
`<kodo>`	Adds JDO vendor extension metadata for Solarmetric's Kodo to the JDO metadata file generated by `<jdometadata>`.
`version`	The version of Kodo. Supported version is 2.3.
`<lido>`	Adds JDO vendor extension metadata for Libelis's LiDO to the JDO metadata file generated by `<jdometadata>`.
`version`	The version of Lido. Supported version is 1.3.

Table B.6 `<jdodoclet>` subtasks *(continued)*

Subtask/Attributes	Description
`<triactive>`	Adds JDO vendor extension metadata for Triactive JDO to the JDO metadata file generated by `<jdometadata>`.
version	The version of TJDO. Supported version is 2.0.

Table B.7 `<jdodoclet>` merge file

Subtask/Merge files	Description
`<jdometadata>`	
`vendor-extensions.xml`	An XML unparsed entity containing any additional vendor extensions (such as top-level extension elements).

The *<jmxdoclet>* task

This task is responsible for generating artifacts associated with deploying JMX MBeans.

Table B.8 `<jmxdoclet>` subtasks

Subtask/Attributes	Description
`<jbossxmbean>`	Generates XML deployment files for JBossMX.
`<jbossxmldoc>`	Generates documentation for an MBean in DocBook format.
`<jbossxmlservicetemplate>`	Generates a skeleton `{0}-service.xml` file for JBoss MBean configuration. This can help you see what you can set in an MBean; you can fill in your values and deploy. Currently only managed attributes with getters show up in the results; however, there is a comment for those with only a setter. It treats read-only managed attributes as if they can be written.
servicefile	Sets the `Servicefile` value.
`<mbeaninterface>`	Generates MBean interfaces for JMX MBeans.
`<mlet>`	Generates mlet descriptions for JMX MBeans.
`<mx4jdescription>`	Generates the `MbeanDescriptionAdaptor` subclass for MX4J.
pattern	Sets the pattern by which a description class is named. Defaults to {0}MBeanDescription.

Table B.9 `<jmxdoclet>` merge files

Subtask/Merge files	Description
`<jbossxmlservicetemplate>`	
`jboss-service.ent`	An XML unparsed entity containing JBoss deployment descriptors for MBeans you wish to include in the `{servicefile}-service.xml` that aren't processed by XDoclet. It can also include `classpath` and global `depends` elements. `servicefile` is specified in the `ant` subtask.
`<mlet>`	
`mlet-entry-{0}.mlet`	An XML document containing the `MLET` entry for a class, instead of generating it from a `jmx.mlet-entry` tag.

The *<mockobjectdoclet>* task

This task is responsible for generating mock object implementation classes.

Table B.10 `<mockobjectdoclet>` subtask

Subtask/Attributes	Description
`<mockobjects>`	Generates mock implementations of collaborator interfaces used to test an object from the inside using the MockObjects testing framework.
`mockClassPattern`	The pattern by which the mock class is named.

The *<portletdoclet>* task

This task is responsible for generating portlet deployment descriptors.

Table B.11 `<portletdoclet>` subtask

Subtask/Attributes	Description
`<portletxml>`	Generates the `portlet.xml` deployment descriptor for deploying portlets in a JSR-168 compliant portlet container.

Table B.12 `<portletdoclet>` merge files

Subtask/Merge files	Description
`<portletxml>`	
`custom-portlet-modes.xml`	An XML unparsed entity containing `<custom-portlet-mode>` entities for a portlet application.
`portlet-custom-window-states.xml`	An XML unparsed entity containing `<custom-window-state>` entities for a portlet application.
`portlet-user-attributes.xml`	An XML unparsed entity containing `<user-attribute>` entities for a portlet application.
`portlet-security.xml`	An XML unparsed entity containing `<security-constraint>` entities for a portlet application.

The `<webdoclet>` task

This task is responsible for generating artifacts associated with web-layer technologies such as servlets and JSP tag libraries.

Table B.13 `<webdoclet>` subtasks

Subtask/Attributes	Description
`<deploymentdescriptor>`	Generates a `web.xml` file for deployment of servlets, filters, listeners, and JSP tag libraries.
`contextParams`	A comma-separated list of context parameter settings.
`description`	Sets the servlet description.
`displayname`	Sets the display name of the servlet.
`distributable`	Specifies whether a servlet is distributable. Defaults to true.
`largeicon`	Sets the large icon for the servlet.
`servletspec`	Sets the version of the servlet specification to target. Defaults to 2.3.
`sessiontimeout`	Sets the session timeout.
`smallicon`	Sets the small icon for the servlet.
`tagLibs`	A comma-separated list of tag library declarations.
`welcomefiles`	A comma-separated list of welcome files.

Table B.13   `<webdoclet>` subtasks *(continued)*

Subtask/Attributes	Description
`<jbosswebxml>`	Generates the `jboss-web.xml` deployment descriptor.
contextroot	Sets the context root.
securitydomain	Sets the security domain.
version	Sets the target JBoss version.
virtualhost	Sets the virtual host.
`<jonaswebxml>`	Generates the web application deployment descriptor for JOnAS.
contextroot	Specifies the context root for the web application.
host	Specifies the name of host used to deploy the web application.
version	Sets the version of JOnAS. Supported version: 2.6.
`<jrunwebxml>`	Generates the `jrun-web.xml` deployment descriptor for the JRun application server.
compile	Sets the `Compile` setting to true or false.
contextRoot	Sets the context root.
loadSystemClassesFirst	Sets the `LoadSystemClassesFirst` setting to true or false.
reload	Sets the `Reload` setting to true or false.
`<jsptaglib>`	Generates JSP tag library descriptor (TLD) files.
description	Sets the description of the JSP tag library.
displayname	Sets the display name of the JSP tag library.
filename	Sets the name to be given to the generated TLD file. Defaults to `tablib.tld`.
jspversion	Sets the target JSP version.
largeicon	Sets the large icon to use when displaying the JSP tag library.
shortname	Sets the short name of the JSP tag library.
smallicon	Sets the small icon to use when displaying the JSP tag library.
taglibversion	Sets the target JSP tag library version.
uri	Sets the URI of the JSP tag library.

Table B.13 `<webdoclet>` subtasks *(continued)*

Subtask/Attributes	Description
`<resin-web-xml>`	Generates `web.xml` with Caucho Resin extensions.
appDir	Specifies the application's directory. By default, the application has the same path as the application ID.
charEncoding	Specifies the default character encoding for form parameters.
classUpdateInterval	How often (in seconds) the container checks for class updates.
configUpdateInterval	How often (in seconds) the container checks for configuration updates.
directoryServlet	Specifies the servlet used to display directories. Set to none to disable directory listing.
generateSourceComments	Tells XDoclet whether comments should be included in the generated files.
lazyInit	Specifies whether the web app is lazily initialized. Setting this to any non-empty value sets the app to be lazily initialized. If it isn't set, the web app is initialized at server startup.
searchForConfigElements	If true, then Resin-specific configuration elements are included in the generated deployment descriptor. Valid values: true, false.
secure	Specifies that the web application should be accessed only from a secure connection.
tempDir	Sets the application's temporary working directory.
urlRegexp	Specifies a regular expression used to match the application to a URL pattern.
useStandardMergeFiles	If true, standard Resin merge files are merged into the generated `resin-web.xml` file.
workDir	Specifies the web application's working directory. This is the directory Resin uses for generated files such as JSP, XSL, and EJBs.
`<strutsconfigxml>`	Generates `struts-config.xml` deployment descriptors for Struts applications.
controller	Sets the Struts version to use. Legal values: 1.0 and 1.1.
version	Sets the fully qualified class to use when instantiating `ActionMapping` objects.

Table B.13 **<webdoclet> subtasks** *(continued)*

Subtask/Attributes	Description
<strutsvalidationxml>	Generates the Struts Validator `validation.xml` file.
<weblogicwebxml>	Generates `weblogic.xml` deployment descriptors for WebLogic web applications.
`contextRoot`	Set the context root.
`description`	Set the web application's description.
`securityDomain`	Set the security domain.
`version`	Sets the version of WebLogic to be deployed to.
<webspherewebxml>	Generates WebSphere-specific deployment descriptors (`ibm-web-bnd.xmi` and `ibm-web-ext.xmi`) for web applications. The `ibm-web-bnd.xmi` file is used to bind EJB and resource references in `web.xml` to a JNDI name in the local namespace. The `ibm-web-ext.xmi` file is used to specify IBM-specific deployment information for a web application.
`additionalClassPath`	Specifies a path to resources outside of those in the application archive.
`defaultErrorPage`	The URI of a page to be displayed in the event of an error.
`directoryBrowsingEnabled`	Specifies whether the application is able to browse disk directories. Defaults to true.
`fileServingEnabled`	Specifies whether the server is enabled to serve static files (such as HTML or GIF files). Defaults to true.
`reloadingEnabled`	An implementation of this method is needed, or the framework doesn't see `reloadingEnabled` as a Java bean property (that is, read-only properties don't work).
`reloadInterval`	Specifies how often (in seconds) a web application's files should be checked and reloaded if they're found to be newer than what is currently deployed.
`serveServletsByClassnameEnabled`	Specifies whether servlets can be accessed by their class name. Defaults to true.
`virtualHostName`	Sets the virtual host name configuration parameter.
<webworkactiondocs>	Generates an HTML file containing a description of defined WebWork actions.
`javadocDir`	Specifies the javadoc directory where the WebWork action documents should be generated.

Table B.13 `<webdoclet>` subtasks *(continued)*

Subtask/Attributes	Description
`<webworkactionsxml>`	Generates an `actions.xml` deployment descriptor file for WebWork actions.
`<webworkconfigproperties>`	Generates a `views.properties` deployment descriptor file for WebWork actions.

Table B.14 `<webdoclet>` merge files

Subtask/Merge files	Description
`<deploymentdescriptor>`	
`ejb-resourcerefs.xml`	An XML unparsed entity containing `resource-ref` entities for any resources not specified in `web.resource-ref` tags.
`ejb-resourcerefs-{0}.xml`	An XML unparsed entity containing `resource-ref` entities for any resources for a class not specified in `web.resource-ref` tags.
`error-pages.xml`	An XML unparsed entity containing the `error-page` elements for the web application.
`filters.xml`	An XML unparsed entity containing the `filter` elements for any additional filters not processed by XDoclet.
`filter-mappings.xml`	An XML unparsed entity containing the `filter-mapping` elements for any additional filters not processed by XDoclet.
`listeners.xml`	An XML unparsed entity containing the `listener` elements for any additional listeners not processed by XDoclet.
`mime-mappings.xml`	An XML unparsed entity containing the `mime-mapping` elements for the web application.
`servlet-mappings.xml`	An XML unparsed entity containing the `servlet-mapping` elements for any additional servlets not processed by XDoclet.
`servlets.xml`	An XML unparsed entity containing the `servlet` elements for any additional servlets not processed by XDoclet.
`taglibs.xml`	An XML unparsed entity containing `taglib` elements for tag libraries not defined in `tagLibs` parameter of the web `<deployment-descriptor>` subtask.

Table B.14 **<webdoclet> merge files** *(continued)*

Subtask/Merge files	Description
web-ejbrefs.xml	An XML unparsed entity containing `ejb-ref` entities for any EJB references not specified in `web.ejb-ref` tags.
web-ejbrefs-{0}.xml	An XML unparsed entity containing `ejb-ref` entities for any EJB references for a class not specified in `web.ejb-ref` tags.
web-ejbrefs-local.xml	An XML unparsed entity containing `ejb-local-ref` entities for any EJB local references not specified in `web.ejb-local-ref` tags.
web-ejbrefs-local-{0}.xml	An XML unparsed entity containing `ejb-local-ref` entities for any EJB local references for a class not specified in `web.ejb-local-ref` tags.
web-env-entries.xml	An XML unparsed entity containing `env-entry` entities for any entries not specified in `web.env-entry` tags.
web-env-entries-{0}.xml	An XML unparsed entity containing `env-entry` entities for any entries for a class not specified in `web.env-entry` tags.
web-resource-env-refs.xml	An XML unparsed entity containing `resource-env-ref` elements for any resources not specified by `web.resource-env-ref` tags.
web-sec-roles.xml	An XML unparsed entity containing `security-role` entities for any roles not specified in `web.security-role` tags.
web-sec-rolerefs-{0}.xml	An XML unparsed entity containing any `security-role-ref` elements for a servlet, to be used instead of generating from `web.security-role-ref` tags.
web-security.xml	An XML unparsed entity containing the (`security-constraint*`, `login-config?`) elements for the web application.
web-settings.xml	An XML unparsed entity containing (`icon?`, `display-name?`, `description?`, `distributable?`, `context-param*`) elements, to be used instead of generating them from `config` parameters.
welcomefiles.xml	An XML document containing a `welcome-file-list` element, used instead of `welcomeFiles` config parameters.

Table B.14 `<webdoclet>` merge files *(continued)*

Subtask/Merge files	Description
`<jrunwebxml>`	
`session-config.xml`	An XML document containing the optional `session-config` element.
`virtual-mapping.xml`	An XML unparsed entity containing the `virtual-mapping` elements.
`<jsptaglib>`	
`taglib-listener.xml`	An unparsed XML entity containing additional `listener` elements, for including listeners not processed by XDoclet.
`taglib-settings.xml`	An unparsed XML entity containing (`tlib-version`, `jsp-version`, `short-name`, `uri?`, `display-name?`, `small-icon?`, `large-icon?`, `description?`) elements.
`taglib-tag.xml`	An unparsed XML entity containing additional `tag` elements, for including tags not processed by XDoclet.
`taglib-validator.xml`	An XML document containing the `validator` element, used to include a validator that isn't processed by XDoclet.
`<resin-web-xml>`	
`resin-jndi-link-{0}.xml`	An XML unparsed entity containing `jndi-link` elements for a bean, to be used instead of generating from `resin.jndi-link` tags.
`resinweb-custom.xml`	Adds optional `Resin-web` custom configuration.
`<strutsconfigxml>`	
`global-exceptions.xml`	An XML document containing the optional `global-exceptions` element.
`global-forwards.xml`	An XML document containing the optional `global-forwards` element.
`struts-actions.xml`	An XML unparsed entity containing `action` elements, for additional non-XDoclet actions.
`struts-controller.xml`	An XML document containing the optional `controller` element.
`struts-data-sources.xml`	An XML document containing the optional `data-sources` element.

Table B.14 `<webdoclet>` **merge files** *(continued)*

Subtask/Merge files	Description
`struts-forms.xml`	An XML unparsed entity containing `form-bean` elements, for additional non-XDoclet forms.
`struts-message-resources.xml`	An XML unparsed entity containing any `message-resources` elements.
`struts-plugins.xml`	An XML unparsed entity containing any `plug-in` elements.
`<strutsvalidationxml>`	
`validation-global.xml`	An XML unparsed entity containing the global elements for the validation descriptor.
`<webworkactionsxml>`	
`Action.xml`	An XML file containing WebWork action definitions that aren't managed by XDoclet.
`<webworkconfigproperties>`	
`views.properties`	A properties file containing WebWork action definitions that aren't managed by XDoclet.

XDoclet tag quick reference

In the course of generating files, XDoclet relies on doclet tags placed in Java source code to give it the specifics of what goes into a generated file. These tags and their attributes provide XDoclet with the metadata it needs to fill in the blanks in the files it generates.

This appendix documents all the tags and attributes that come with XDoclet, as of XDoclet version 1.2.0.

Apache Axis tags

Table C.1 Class-level Axis tags

Class-level tag/Attributes	Description
`@axis.service`	Declares the class to be an Axis SOAP service.
include-all	If true, all methods are exposed through the web service, without regard to whether they're tagged with `@axis.method`.
provider	Service provider for the web service. Default: java:EJB for EJB web services and java:RPC for non-EJB web services.
scope	Service scope. Valid values: Request, Session, Application. Default: Request.
urn	[Required] URN for the web service.

Table C.2 Method-level Axis tag

Method-level tag/Attributes	Description
`@axis.method`	Declares a method as a SOAP service method. Has no parameters. Note: When used with EJBs, if no methods are tagged with `@axis.method`, EJB `create` methods are exposed as web service methods by default.

Apache SOAP tags

Table C.3 Class-level Apache SOAP tags

Class-level tag/Attributes	Description
`@soap.service`	Declares the class to be an Apache SOAP service.
checkMustUnderstands	Declares whether the server is to throw a `Fault` if there are SOAP headers in the request that are marked as MustUnderstand.
provider	Provider class name. There's special support for EJB beans, so if you don't specify the provider parameter, Apache SOAP tries to assign the correct provider name to the service based on the type of the EJB bean. The provider name for the EJB is taken from statelessSessionEjbProvider, statefulSessionEjbProvider, or entityEjbProvider configuration parameters based on the EJB type.

Table C.3   Class-level Apache SOAP tags *(continued)*

Class-level tag/Attributes	Description
scope	Service scope. Valid values: Request, Session, Application. Default: Request.
type	Service type. Valid value: message.
urn	URN for the web service.

Table C.4   Method-level Apache SOAP tag

Method-level tag/Attributes	Description
@soap.method	Declares a method to be a SOAP service method. Has no parameters. For EJB web services, the EJB create method(s) are automatically exposed as SOAP service methods.

Borland Enterprise Server (BES) EJB tags

Table C.5   Class-level BES tags

Class-level tag/Attributes	Description
@bes.bean	Defines an EJB for deployment in Borland's Enterprise Server.
connection-factory-name	JNDI name of the connection factory used to establish a connection to the message broker. For message-driven beans.
message-driven-destination-name	Queue or topic to which the MDB listens and from which it consumes messages. For message-driven beans.
pool-init-size	Initial size of the database connection pool.
pool-max-size	Maximum size of the database connection pool.
pool-wait-timeout	Specifies how long a thread should wait for a database connection from the pool before timing out.
timeout	Transaction timeout for session beans.
@bes.datasource	Defines a database datasource for entity EJBs. Requires @ejb.bean.
jndi-name	JNDI name of the entity datasource. Default: DefaultDataSource.

Table C.5   Class-level BES tags *(continued)*

Class-level tag/Attributes	Description
`res-ref-name`	Reference to entity datasource. Default: jdbc/${jndi-name}.
`@bes.ejb-local-ref`	Defines a reference to a local EJB. There must be a matching `@ejb.ejb-local-ref`.
`jndi-name`	JNDI name of the referenced bean.
`ref-name`	[Required] Local reference name of the EJB.
`@bes.ejb-ref`	Defines a reference to an EJB outside of the EJB package. There must be a matching `@ejb.ejb-ref`.
`jndi-name`	JNDI name of the referenced bean.
`ref-name`	[Required] Local reference name of the EJB.
`@bes.property`	Sets a property.
`prop-name`	Name of the property.
`prop-type`	Type of the property.
`prop-value`	Value of the property.
`@bes.resource-env-ref`	Sets a reference to a resource.
`jndi-name`	JNDI name of the referenced resource.
`name`	[Required] Reference name of the resource.
`@bes.resource-ref`	Reference to a resource. There must be a matching `@ejb.resource-ref`.
`cmp-resource`	Specifies whether this resource is a CMP resource. Valid values: true, false.
`jndi-name`	JNDI name of the referenced resource.
`res-name`	Local resource name.
`res-ref-name`	Resource ref name.

Table C.6   Method-level BES tag

Method-level tag/Attributes	Description
`@bes.relation`	Defines the database configuration for persistent relations. Requires `@ejb.relation`.
`left-column-name`	Name of the column used for the left side of the relation.

Table C.6   Method-level BES tag *(continued)*

Method-level tag/Attributes	Description
left-table-name	Database table name for the left side of the relation.
right-column-name	Name of the column used for the right side of the relation.
right-table-name	Database table name for the right side of the relation.

Castor tags

Table C.7   Class-level Castor tags

Class-level tag/Attributes	Description
@castor.class	Defines the Castor-persisted class and its attributes. For full coverage of the mapping options, refer to Castor's mapping documentation.
access	[Required] Defines the access to the class. Valid values: read-only, shared, exclusive, db-locked. Default: shared.
auto-complete	If true, the class is introspected to determine its field, and the fields specified in the mapping file are used to override the field found during the introspection.
cache-capacity	Maximum number of objects to be kept in cache.
cache-type	Type of object cache to use. Valid values: none, count-limited, time-limited, unlimited. none indicates no caching. count-limited limits the cache to a specific number of objects specified by cache-capacity. time-limited allows an object to reside in cache only for a specific time period. unlimited places no limit on the cache. Default: count-limited.
depends	Name of the class this class depends on.
extends	Should be used only if this class extends another class for which mapping information is provided. Should not be used if the extended class isn't used in the mapping file.
id	[Required] Fields that form the class's primary key.
key-generator	Key-generator strategy to be used by Castor.

Table C.7   Class-level Castor tags *(continued)*

Class-level tag/Attributes	Description
ns-prefix	Namespace prefix to be used for the class.
ns-uri	Namespace URI to be used for the class.
table	[Required] Name of the table in the database to which the class is mapped.
xml	XML element to which this class will be persisted if you're using Castor XML.

Table C.8   Method-level Castor tags

Class-level tag/Attributes	Description
@castor.field	Defines the Castor-persisted field and its attributes. Applies to the field's setter method.
collection	If the field represents the many side of a relationship, specifies the type of collection used to hold the related objects. Valid values: array, arraylist, vector, hashtable, collection, set, map. Default: vector.
create-method	Factory method for instantiation of FieldHandler.
direct	Flag that indicates whether the field should be accessed directly rather than using getter/setter methods.
handler	Implementation of FieldHandler used to handle the tagged field.
lazy	Flag that indicates whether the field loaded lazily.
required	Flag that indicates whether the field is compulsory.
set-method	Method used to set the property value.
transient	Flag that indicates whether the field should be ignored during marshalling. Useful when used with the auto-complete attribute of @castor.class.
type	Java type of the field. Used to access the field. Castor uses this information to cast the XML information (like string into integer). Also used to define the signature of the accessors method. If a collection is specified, this is used to specify the type of the object inside the collection. If type isn't specified, it defaults to the return type of the method.

Table C.8 Method-level Castor tags *(continued)*

Class-level tag/Attributes	Description
@castor.field-sql	Defines SQL-specific persistence metadata for Castor persistent fields.
dirty	Flag that indicates whether the field is checked for dirty status.
many-key	[Required] Many key of the field.
many-table	[Required] Many table of the field.
name	[Required] Column name the field is mapped to.
type	[Required] SQL type of the field.
@castor.field-xml	Defines XML-specific persistence metadata for Castor persistent fields.
dirty	Flag that indicates whether the field is checked for dirty status.
matches	Allows overriding the matches rules for the name of the element. A standard regular expression used instead of the name field.
name	[Required] Name of the element or attribute.
node	Indicates whether the name corresponds to an attribute, an element, or text content. By default, primitive types are assumed to be an attribute; otherwise the node is assumed to be an element. Valid values: element, attribute, text. Default: text.
Qname-prefix	Default prefix used when marshalling a value of type Qname.
reference	Indicates whether this field must be treated as a reference by the unmarshaller. In order for it to work properly, you must specify the node type as attribute for both the id and the reference fields.
type	XML schema type (of the value of this field) that requires specific handling in the Castor Marshalling Framework (such as Qname).

Template documentation tags

Table C.9   Method-level template tags

Method-level tag/Attributes	Description
`@doc.param`	Describes a parameter of the template tag.
description	[Required] Description of the parameter.
name	Name of the parameter.
optional	Specifies whether the parameter is optional. Default: true.
values	Comma-separated list of possible values the parameter can take.
`@doc.tag`	Indicates that the method implements a template tag.
type	[Required] Specifies whether it's a content or block type tag. Valid values: block, content.

EJB tags

Table C.10   Class-level EJB tags

Class-level tag/Attributes	Description
`@ejb.bean`	Provides information about the EJB. It's the one compulsory tag for all EJBs. However, not all parameters are applicable for all types of EJBs, and some parameters apply differently for different types of EJBs.
acknowledge-mode	Acknowledge mode for MDB. Valid values: Auto-acknowledge, Dups-ok-acknowledge. Default: Auto-acknowledge.
cmp-version	Version of the CMP specification the bean adheres to. Valid values: 1.x, 2.x. Default: 1.x.
description	Description of the bean. Default: the first sentence of the class-level javadoc comment of the bean class.
destination-type	Type of destination for MDB. Valid values: javax.jms.Queue, javax.jms.Topic. Default: javax.jms.Queue.
display-name	Display name of the bean.

Table C.10 Class-level EJB tags *(continued)*

Class-level tag/Attributes	Description
generate	If false, excludes the class from the list of EJBs. This is useful for abstract EJBs that other EJBs are to derive from (obviously, you don't want the abstract EJB wrongly specified in deployment descriptors as a concrete EJB). Default: true.
jndi-name	Provides the JNDI name of the bean to be used in the vendor-specific deployment descriptors.
large-icon	Large icon for the bean.
local-business-interface	Local business interface for the bean. Similar to `remote-business-interface`, but the interface doesn't need to declare `RemoteException` in the `throws` clause.
local-jndi-name	JNDI name of the bean to be used in the vendor-specific deployment descriptors. It's the JNDI name for the local EJB.
message-selector	Optional message selector for MDB.
name	[Required] Name of the bean to be used in the `ejb-jar.xml` deployment descriptor.
primkey-field	Primary key field for the bean as per the spec.
reentrant	Defines the entity bean's reentrancy.
remote-business-interface	Remote business interface for the bean. If present, `@ejb.interface-method` tags aren't required; instead the remote interface extends the business interface. The business interface must declare all methods as throwing `RemoteException` as per the business interface pattern.
schema	Abstract schema name for the bean.
small-icon	Small icon for the bean.
subscription-durability	Defines the durability of messages for MDB as per the EJB 2.0 spec. Valid values: Durable, NonDurable. Default: Durable.
transaction-type	Bean's transaction type. Valid values: Container, Bean. Default: Container.
type	[Required] Bean's type. Valid values: CMP, BMP, Stateless, Stateful. Default: CMP.

Table C.10 Class-level EJB tags *(continued)*

Class-level tag/Attributes	Description
use-soft-locking	If true, generates a `public int` version attribute in the auto-generated concrete class, to form an optimistic locking mechanism. The value of `version` attribute is incremented in `ejbStore`. Note: It's applicable to both CMP and BMP; but many containers have optimistic locking capability built in, so you don't need to worry about locking issues. Valid values: true, false. Default: false.
view-type	Indicates what view-type(s) is(are) supported by the bean. Valid values: local, remote, both. Default: remote.
@ejb.dao	Data Access Object of an entity bean. If the `<dao/>` subtask is included, then DAO interfaces will be generated for any entity beans containing this tag, unless the `generate` attribute of `@ejb.dao` is present and set to false.
class	Fully qualified name of the DAO interface. If absent, the interface name is determined using the pattern and package parameters.
create-methods	Indicates whether `create` methods should be automatically included in the DAO interface. Default: true.
finder-methods	Indicates whether `finder` methods should be automatically included in the DAO interface. Default: true.
generate	Indicates whether the DAO interface should be generated. Default: true.
impl-class	Fully qualified name of a class that implements the DAO interface. If present, then generated code for obtaining a DAO creates a new instance of this class.
impl-jndi	Indicates a JNDI environment reference containing a `String` that is the fully qualified name of a class implementing the DAO interface. If present, generated code for obtaining a DAO will look up this reference and then create a new instance of the class whose name is found there. This allows the actual implementation class to be determined at runtime.
package	Package the DAO interface is in (generated or not). Use `<packageSubstitution/>` to configure which package the interface should end up in.

Table C.10   Class-level EJB tags *(continued)*

Class-level tag/Attributes	Description
`pattern`	Pattern (using {0} for the EJB name) to be used for constructing the unqualified (package-specific) name of the DAO interface. Default: {0}DAO.
`@ejb.data-object`	Defines configuration attributes used for generation of data object classes. Applicable only to entity EJBs.
`extends`	Declares which class the generated bulk data class should extend. Default: java.lang.Object. The class must be `java.io.Serializable`. This is useful if you want to add methods that should always be available in bulk data objects.
`implements`	Comma-separated list of which interface(s) the generated bulk data class should implement.
`user-super-equals`	Specifies whether the superclass's `equals` method should play a part in the implementation of the data object's `equals` method. If true, then `super.equals` will be called at the beginning of the data object's `equals` method. Valid values: true, false. Default: false.
`@ejb.ejb-external-ref`	Defines an EJB reference to an EJB that will be packaged in a different EJB JAR file. Applicable to all types of EJBs.
`business`	[Required] Fully qualified class name of the business interface (local or remote interface) of the referenced bean.
`ejb-name`	*Deprecated.* Use `ref-name` instead. Name used to refer to the referenced bean. For example, to refer to the bean `Customer` as `java:comp/env/ejb/Customer`, ejb-name should be ejb/Customer. Default: ejb/[*ejb-name*], where [*ejb-name*] is the name of the referenced bean (`Customer`) prefixed by ejb/.
`home`	[Required] Fully qualified class name of the home interface of the referenced bean.

Table C.10   Class-level EJB tags *(continued)*

Class-level tag/Attributes	Description
link	Defines an `<ejb-link>` to the referenced EJB. The value of the `<ejb-link>` element is the name of the target enterprise bean. (It's the name defined in the `<ejb-name>` element of the target enterprise bean.) The target enterprise bean can be in any ejb-jar file in the same J2EE application as the referencing application component.
ref-name	[Required] Name used to refer to the referenced bean. For example, to refer to the bean `Customer` as `java:comp/env/ejb/Customer`, name should be ejb/Customer. Default: ejb/[ejb-name], where [ejb-name] is the named of the referenced bean (`Customer`).
remote	***Deprecated.*** Synonym for the `business` parameter. Works only if the `view-type` is remote.
type	[Required] Type of EJB being referenced. Valid values: Entity, Session. Default: Entity.
view-type	[Required] View type of the referenced bean. Valid values: local, remote.
@ejb.ejb-ref	Defines an EJB reference. Applicable to all EJB types.
ejb-name	[Required] Name of the EJB being referenced.
ref-name	Name used to refer to the referenced bean. For example, to refer to the bean `Customer` as `java:comp/env/ejb/Customer`, name should be ejb/Customer. Default: ejb/[ejb-name], where [ejb-name] is the named of the referenced bean (`Customer`).
view-type	[Required] View type the reference uses. Valid values: local, remote. Default: remote.
@ejb.env-entry	Defines an environment entry for an EJB.
description	Optional description of the environment entry.
name	[Required] Name of the environment entry.

Table C.10   Class-level EJB tags *(continued)*

Class-level tag/Attributes	Description
type	Type of the environment entry, such as `java.lang.String`. Supported types are outlined in the EJB spec. Valid values: java.lang.Boolean, java.lang.Byte, java.lang.Character, java.lang.String, java.lang.Short, java.lang.Integer, java.lang.Long, java.lang.Float, java.lang.Double. Default: java.lang.String.
value	Value of the environment entry.
@ejb.facade	[Optional] Allows generation of session façade EJBs for entity EJBs. The façade EJB provides all finder and creation methods to the outside and also all data-setting methods for data and value objects. Finder methods return collections of data or value objects instead of remote interfaces. The façade bean connects to the EJB using local (if generated) or remote interfaces. The resulting bean needs processing by XDoclet together with all EJB classes.
description	Description of the bean. Default: the first sentence of the class-level javadoc comment of the bean class.
display-name	Display name of the bean.
jndi-name	Provides the JNDI name of the bean to be used in the vendor-specific deployment descriptors.
large-icon	Large icon for the bean.
local-jndi-name	Provides the JNDI name of the bean to be used in the vendor-specific deployment descriptors. It's the JNDI name for the local EJB.
name	Name of generated façade EJB. Default: {0}Façade.
small-icon	Small icon for the bean.
transaction-type	Bean's transaction type. Valid values: Container, Bean. Default: Container.
type	[Required] EJB's type. Valid values: Stateless, Stateful. Default: Stateless.
view-type	View-type(s) is (are) supported by the EJB. Valid values: local, remote, both. Default: remote.
@ejb.finder	Defines a finder method for the home interface. Multiple finder methods may be defined by using multiple @ejb.finder tags.
description	Description of the finder method.

Table C.10 Class-level EJB tags *(continued)*

Class-level tag/Attributes	Description
method-intf	Interface (Home or LocalHome) for which the finder permissions should be set. If the permissions should apply to both the Home and LocalHome interfaces, this parameter shouldn't be specified. Valid values: Home, LocalHome. Default: Home.
oc4j-query	Definition of a CMP finder method. Defines the selection criteria in a findByXXX method in the bean's home interface. Applicable only to Oracle application server.
oc4j-query-is-partial	Indicates whether the query specified by oc4j-query is a partial query. Valid values: true, false. Applicable only to Oracle application server.
pramati-query-name	Name of a query method. Applicable only to Pramati Server.
query	EJB-QL query for the finder method.
result-type-mapping	Result type mapping (indicates the return type) for the finder method. Valid values: none, Local, Remote. Default: none.
role-name	Comma-separated list of roles that can invoke this finder method.
signature	[Required] Signature of the method, such as java.util.Collection findAll. The return type in the signature must be fully qualified.
transaction-type	Sets the transaction type of the EJB.
unchecked	Flags the finder method as having unchecked permission. If present, the role-name attribute must be omitted.
view-type	Restricts the home interface in which the finder method is defined. Valid values: local, remote, both. Default: both.
@ejb.home	Provides information about an entity or session EJB's home interface. All parameters are applicable to both entity and session EJBs.
extends	Declares which interface the generated home interface should extend. Default: javax.ejb.EJBHome.
generate	Indicates which home interfaces should be generated. Valid values: true, false. Default: true.
local-class	Fully qualified name of the local home interface.

Table C.10   Class-level EJB tags *(continued)*

Class-level tag/Attributes	Description
local-extends	Declares which interface the generated local home interface should extend. Default: javax.ejb.EJBLocalHome.
local-package	Package the local home interface should be in. Used only where local-class isn't present. Use `<packageSubstitution/>` to configure which package the interface should end up in.
local-pattern	Pattern to be used in determining the unqualified name of the local home interface. Used only if local-class isn't present.
package	Package the home interfaces should be placed in. Used only where *-class or *-package isn't present. Use `<packageSubstitution/>` to configure which package the interface should end up in.
pattern	Pattern to be used in determining the unqualified name of either the local or remote home interface. Used where *-class and *-pattern tags are absent for the bean.
remote-class	Fully qualified name of the remote home interface.
remote-package	Package the remote home interface should be in. Used only where remote-class isn't present. Use `<packageSubstitution/>` to configure which package the interface should end up in.
remote-pattern	Pattern to be used in determining the unqualified name of the remote home interface. Used only if remote-class isn't present.
@ejb.interface	Provides information about an entity or session bean's component interfaces (remote and/or local). Not applicable to message-driven beans. All parameters are applicable to both entity and session beans.
extends	Declares which interface the generated remote interface should extend. Default: javax.ejb.EJBObject.
generate	Declares which interfaces should be generated. Default: true. Valid values: true, false. Default: true.
local-class	Fully qualified name of the local interface.

Table C.10   Class-level EJB tags *(continued)*

Class-level tag/Attributes	Description
local-extends	Declares which interface the generated local interface should extend. Default: javax.ejb.EJBLocalObject.
local-package	Package the local interface should be in. Used only where local-class isn't present. Use <packageSubstitution/> to configure which package the interface should end up in.
local-pattern	Pattern to be used in determining the unqualified name of the local interface. Used only if local-class isn't present.
package	Package the interfaces should be placed in. Used only where *-class and *-package aren't present. Use <packageSubstitution/> to configure which package the interface should end up in.
pattern	Pattern to be used in determining the unqualified name of either the local or remote interface. Used where *-class and *-pattern tags are absent for the bean.
remote-class	Fully qualified name of the remote interface.
remote-package	Package the remote interface should be in. Used only where remote-class isn't present. Use <packageSubstitution/> to configure which package the interface should end up in.
remote-pattern	Pattern to be used in determining the unqualified name of the remote interface. Used only if remote-class isn't present.
@ejb.permission	Defines the transactional behavior for this method. Applicable to methods with @ejb.create-method and @ejb.interface-method tags. When used on the class level, applies to all interface methods cumulatively.
role-name	Comma-separated list of roles allowed to call this method.
unchecked	Flags the method as having unchecked permission. If present, role-name must be omitted.

Table C.10   Class-level EJB tags *(continued)*

Class-level tag/Attributes	Description
`@ejb.persistence`	Provides information about the persistence of a CMP entity bean.
table-name	Declares the table to which the CMP will be mapped. If `table-name` isn't specified, the name of the class will be used, and it will be up to the container to create the tables.
`@ejb.pk`	Defines the primary key of an entity bean. If the `<entitypk/>` subtask is included, then primary key classes are generated for all entity beans unless the `generate` attribute is set to false or the primary class is in the `java.lang` package.
class	Fully qualified name of the primary key class. If absent, the primary key class name is determined using the `pattern` and `package` attributes.
extends	Defines which class the generated primary key class must extend.
generate	Indicates whether the primary key class should be generated. Default: true.
implements	Defines which interface the generated primary key class must implement.
method-intf	Indicates the interface (`Home` or `LocalHome`) for which the `findByPrimaryKey` permissions should be set. Applies only if `role-name` or `unchecked` is specified. If the permissions should apply to both `Home` and `LocalHome` interfaces, this attribute shouldn't be specified. Valid values: Home, LocalHome. Default: Home.
package	Package the primary key class is in (generated or not). Use `<packageSubstitution/>` to configure which package the primary key class should end up in.
pattern	Pattern (using {0} for the EJB name) to be used for constructing the unqualified (package-specific) name of the primary key class.
role-name	Comma-separated list of roles that can execute `findByPrimaryKey`.
unchecked	Flags the `findByPrimaryKey` method as having unchecked permission. If present, `role-name` must be omitted.

Table C.10 Class-level EJB tags *(continued)*

Class-level tag/Attributes	Description
`@ejb.remote-facade`	Generates a remote façade class for entity beans. This class provides a convenient view on session beans and performs all the necessary lookups. Session bean methods marked with `@ejb.facade-method` are included and transparently proxied. The generated class name follows the pattern {0}Remote.
`@ejb.resource-env-ref`	Defines a resource environment reference with the name `name` to a resource of type `type`.
description	Resource description.
name	[Required] Name of the resource.
type	[Required] Type of the resource.
`@ejb.resource-ref`	Defines a resource reference with the name specified by the `res-ref-name` attribute to a resource of type specified by `res-type`. The authentication is done by either the container or by the application, as specified in `res-auth`.
jndi-name	Physical JNDI name of the resource.
res-auth	[Required] Resource authentication type. Valid values: Container, Application. Default: Container.
res-ref-name	[Required] Name of the environment entry used in the enterprise bean's code.
res-sharing-scope	Resource sharing scope Valid values: Shareable, Unshareable. Default: Shareable.
res-type	[Required] Resource type.
`@ejb.security-identity`	Specifies whether the caller's security identity is to be used for the execution of the methods of the enterprise bean or whether a specific `run-as` identity is to be used. It contains an optional description and a specification of the security identity to be used.
description	Description of the security identity.
run-as	`run-as` identity to be used for the execution of the methods of an enterprise bean.
sunone-principal	Real username on the server to which this identity is to be mapped. Applicable only to SunONE.

Table C.10 Class-level EJB tags *(continued)*

Class-level tag/Attributes	Description
`use-caller-identity`	Specifies that the caller's security identity should be used as the security identity for the execution of the enterprise bean's methods.
`@ejb.security-role-ref`	Defines a security role reference with the name specified by `role-name` to a security role link named `role-link`.
`role-link`	[Required] Name of the role link.
`role-name`	[Required] Name of the role reference
`@ejb.transaction`	Defines the transactional behavior for this method. Applicable to methods with `@ejb.create-method` and `@ejb.interface-method` tags. If used on the class level, applies to all interface methods unless overridden.
`type`	[Required] Type of transactional behavior. Valid values: NotSupported, Supports, Required, RequiresNew, Mandatory, Never. Default: Supports.
`@ejb.util`	[Optional] Lets you define whether an EJB utility class should be generated and whether to use the logical component name (`java:comp/env`) or the physical JNDI name to do the lookup. If this tag isn't specified, the `util` class is generated using logical lookups (provided the `<utilobject/>` subtask is used).
`generate`	[Required] Valid values: false, no, logical, physical. false or no omits the generation of the utility class. logical generates a utility class that uses the component name for lookup. physical generates a class that uses the JNDI name for lookups. Default: logical.
`@ejb.value-object`	Definition for value objects that follow the `TransferObject` pattern from http://java.sun.com/blueprints/corej2eepatterns/Patterns/TransferObject.html. Value objects can link to other objects (of a relation) in two ways: aggregation and composition. Aggregation means the other object is loosely coupled; in composition, the other object is embedded. Note that aggregation and composition are mutually exclusive.
`abstract`	Indicates that this value object is intended to be an abstract object that other value objects extend.
`extends`	Name of the class the generated value object class should extend, if any.

Table C.10 Class-level EJB tags *(continued)*

Class-level tag/Attributes	Description
`implements`	Comma-separated list of interfaces the generated value object should implement, if any. Note that XDoclet won't generated methods to implement these interfaces, so use this only if the interface doesn't contains any methods or if the value object superclass (indicated in the `extends` attribute) already implements all interface methods.
`match`	Identifier that can be used to select groups of attributes to be included in this value object. You can repeat this identifier in the method-level `@ejb.value-object` tag to add a property to a value object. You can use * as a special value, indicating that all entity properties will be included in this value object.
`name`	Name for this value object. The name is used to form the generated class name. Using the default pattern, for example, if `name` is User, a `UserValue` class will be generated.

Table C.11 Method-level EJB tags

Method-level tag/Attributes	Description
@dao.call	Defines this method as a call to a Data Access Object. The method will be included in the DAO interface, and the EJB's generated subclass will contain a call to the DAO's method.
`name`	[Optional] Method's name in the DAO (it need not be the same as the calling method in the EJB). If not specified, the default is the usual interface equivalent of the method's name (generally the same, but `ejbFindByX` becomes `findByX`, and so on).
@ejb.aggregate	Marks a persistent field containing a reference to another entity bean as being aggregated in this bean. The data object contains accessor methods for the aggregated entity's data object instead of a reference to the entity itself. The aggregated entity is also removed when this entity is removed. For example, aggregates are useful for sending graphs of data to the client. This is applicable only to entity beans and has no parameters.

Table C.11   Method-level EJB tags *(continued)*

Method-level tag/Attributes	Description
`@ejb.create-method`	Defines this method as an `ejbCreate` method that will be included in the home interface. It's applicable to session and entity beans. In stateless session beans, `ejbCreate` is created if it isn't in the code.
`view-type`	[Optional] Specifies which view type the method will be exposed in. Valid values: local, remote. Default: remote.
`@ejb.facade-method`	Marks session bean methods for inclusion in remote façades.
`cache`	Sets up result caching for this method result. Has no effect on `void` methods.
`immutable`	If value is immutable, it's never invalidated. Has no effect on `void` methods.
`invalidate`	Marks this method as invalidating. Remote façades will fire callbacks and zap caches. Use this on methods that change EJBs or create/remove entities. Note that setting this to true has no effect on façade methods that cache their result.
`@ejb.home-method`	Defines this method as a home method (its name is `ejbHomefoo`, and the corresponding home method should be defined in the home interface).
`view-type`	[Optional] Specifies which view type the method will be exposed in. Valid values: local, remote. Default: local.
`@ejb.interface-method`	Declares the interface (local/remote) in which this method must appear. If the `view-type` attribute is absent, then the method will be added to whatever component interfaces are defined in `@ejb.bean`.
`view-type`	[Optional] Specifies which view type the method will be exposed in. The value local or both is applicable only to EJB 2.0 beans. Valid values: local, remote, both. Default: remote.
`@ejb.permission`	Defines the transactional behavior for this method. Applicable to methods with `@ejb.create-method` and `@ejb.interface-method` tags. When used on the class level, applies to all interface methods cumulatively.
`role-name`	Comma-separated list of roles allowed to call this method.

Table C.11 Method-level EJB tags *(continued)*

Method-level tag/Attributes	Description
unchecked	Flags the method as having unchecked permission. If present, `role-name` must be omitted.
`@ejb.persistence`	Provides information about the persistence of a CMP entity bean's fields. Use this on property getter and setter methods (including `isXXX` methods for `boolean` properties). This creates the CMP field in the generated CMP layer and concrete implementations of the getter and setter methods. For BMP, it generates getter and setter methods that keep track of a dirty flag so `ejbStore` is called only if necessary. If you don't define the setter method, no setter method is generated for the concrete BMP/CMP class (a concrete CMP class is generated only if you're EJB 1.1 or EJB 2.0 but using CMP 1.x). This is useful for cases where, for example, nothing is set programmatically but instead via external sources such as a stored procedure. Applicable for entity beans.
column-name	Declares the column name to which the CMP field will be mapped.
jdbc-type	Declares the JDBC type. Its value must be one of the fields of `java.sql.Types` (BIT, CHAR, and so on). This JDBC type is used by the CMP provider to determine which method to call on `PreparedStatement` and `ResultSet` for INSERT / UPDATE / SELECT queries. Valid values: ARRAY, BIGINT, BINARY, BIT, BLOB, BOOLEAN, CHAR, CLOB, DATALINK, DATE, DECIMAL, DISTINCT, DOUBLE, FLOAT, INTEGER, JAVA_OBJECT, LONGVARBINARY, LONGVARCHAR, NULL, NUMERIC, OTHER, REAL, REF, SMALLINT, STRUCT, TIME, TIMESTAMP, TINYINT, VARBINARY, VARCHAR. Default: VARCHAR.
read-only	Indicates that a field is read-only.
sql-type	Declares the actual type of the field in the database. This value is used only when the CMP container creates your table (if possible).
`@ejb.persistent-field`	***Deprecated***. Use the `@ejb.persistence` tag instead.

Table C.11   Method-level EJB tags *(continued)*

Method-level tag/Attributes	Description
`@ejb.pk-field`	Denotes the persistent field as a primary key field, which will be included in the generated primary key class. Use this for getter methods. Must be used with the `@persistent-field` tag. This tag is only valid for entity beans.
`@ejb.relation`	Defines a container-managed relationship between entity beans.
`cascade-delete`	Indicates whether the EJB container should perform cascade deletes.
`name`	[Required] Name of the relationship. For bidirectional relationships, specify the same name on both sides.
`role-name`	[Required] Name of the relationship role.
`target-cascade-delete`	Indicates whether the EJB container should perform cascade deletes for the other side of the relation. Should occur only if the relationship is unidirectional.
`target-ejb`	Name of the EJB on the other side of the relation. Should occur only if the relationship is unidirectional.
`target-multiple`	If yes, this EJB represents a many side of the other side of the relation. Should occur only if the relationship is unidirectional.
`target-role-name`	Name of the relationship role on the other side of the relation. Should occur only if the relation is unidirectional.
`@ejb.relationship`	Defines how a bean-managed relationship method is implemented in the concrete implementation class generated by the `<entitybmp>` subtask.
`home`	Related class's home interface.
`method`	Method on the home interface used to retrieve a collection of related entity EJBs.
`params`	Comma-separated list of parameters to be passed to the method specified by the `method` attribute.
`@ejb.select`	Defines a select method. This tag is placed on the `ejbSelect` methods.
`query`	[Required] EJB-QL query for the select method.

Table C.11 Method-level EJB tags *(continued)*

Method-level tag/Attributes	Description
`result-type-mapping`	Result type mapping for the select method. Valid values: none, Local, Remote. Default: none.
`@ejb.transaction`	Defines the transactional behavior for this method. Applicable to methods with `@ejb.create-method` and `@ejb.interface-method` tags. If used on the class level, applies to all interface methods unless overridden.
`method-intf`	Indicates the interface (`Home` or `LocalHome`) for which the transaction type should be set. Valid values: Home, Remote, LocalHome, Local.
`type`	[Required] Type of transactional behavior. Valid values: NotSupported, Supports, Required, RequiresNew, Mandatory, Never. Default: Supports.
`@ejb.value-object`	Defines an EJB property to be included in a generated value object class.
`aggregate`	Type of the items contained in the multivalued property. This should be a fully qualified class name.
`aggregate-name`	Specifies how the accessor methods to this property in the value object should be called. The value of this attribute should be the method name, sans `get` or `set`.
`compose`	Type of items contained in the multivalued property. This should be a fully qualified class name.
`compose-name`	Specifies how the accessor methods to this property in the value object should be called. The value of this attribute should be the method name, sans `get` or `set`.
`match`	Repeat here the match attribute declared in a class-level `@ejb.value-object` tag to link this property to the declared value object. If not specified, include the property in the default value object.
`members`	Class of the local or remote interface of the associated or composed bean.
`members-name`	Bean name of the associated or composed bean.
`relation`	Specifies that this property can be updated outside the scope of this value object, so the generated method should always retrieve the property value. For relationships, always set `relation` to external.

Table C.11 Method-level EJB tags *(continued)*

Method-level tag/Attributes	Description
`type`	On a multivalued property, indicates the type of the collection returned by the EJB property accessor. This should be set to Collection or Set in all multi-valued properties. Valid values: Collection, Set.

Hibernate tags

Table C.12 Class-level Hibernate tags

Class-level tag/Attributes	Description
`@hibernate.cache`	Configures a SessionFactory-level cache on a class.
`usage`	The type of caching. Valid values: read-only, read-write, nonstrict-read-write.
`@hibernate.class`	Indicates that a class is to be persisted using Hibernate.
`discriminator-value`	Value that distinguishes individual subclasses. Used for polymorphic behavior.
`dynamic-insert`	Specifies that `INSERT` SQL should be generated at runtime and contain only those columns whose values have changed. Valid values: true, false. Default: false.
`dynamic-update`	Specifies that `UPDATE` SQL should be generated at runtime and contain only those columns whose values aren't null. Valid values: true, false. Default: false.
`mutable`	Specifies that instances of the class are (not) mutable. Valid values: true, false.
`polymorphism`	Determines whether implicit or explicit query polymorphism is used. Valid values: explicit, implicit.
`proxy`	Interface to use for proxies (JDK 1.3+ only) and lazy loading.
`schema`	Overrides the schema name specified by the root `<hibernate-mapping>` element.
`table`	[Required] Name of the database table this class will be persisted to.
`where`	Specifies an arbitrary SQL WHERE condition to be used when retrieving objects of this class.

Table C.12 **Class-level Hibernate tags** *(continued)*

Class-level tag/Attributes	Description
`@hibernate.discriminator`	Defines a discriminator.
column	Default: the property name. The name of the mapped database table column.
length	Length of the mapped database table column.
type	Name that indicates the Hibernate type. Defaults to string.
`@hibernate.jcs-cache`	Configures a SessionFactory-level cache on a class using Apache Turbine's JCS. (Deprecated in favor of `@hibernate.cache`.)
usage	The type of caching. Valid values: read-only, read-write, nonstrict-read-write.
`@hibernate.joined-subclass`	Marks a subclass as being persisted to its own table (table-per-subclass mapping strategy).
dynamic-insert	Specifies that `INSERT` SQL should be generated at runtime and contain only those columns whose values have changed. Valid values: true, false. Default: false.
dynamic-update	Specifies that `UPDATE` SQL should be generated at runtime and contain only those columns whose values aren't null. Valid values: true, false. Default: false.
proxy	Interface to use for proxies (JDK 1.3+ only) and lazy loading.
schema	Overrides the schema name specified by the root `<hibernate-mapping>` element.
table	Table to persist to. Default: the unqualified class name.
`@hibernate.joined-subclass-key`	Declares the key property for a joined subclass.
column	Property that is the key.
`@hibernate.query`	Declares a named query for the class.
name	[Required] Name of this query.
query	[Required] Name of this query.
`@hibernate.subclass`	Declares the current class as a subclass.
discriminator-value	Value that distinguishes individual subclasses. Used for polymorphic behavior.

Table C.12 Class-level Hibernate tags *(continued)*

Class-level tag/Attributes	Description
dynamic-insert	Specifies that INSERT SQL should be generated at runtime and contain only those columns whose values have changed. Valid values: true, false. Default: false.
dynamic-update	Specifies that UPDATE SQL should be generated at runtime and contain only those columns whose values aren't null. Valid values: true, false. Default: false.
proxy	Interface to use for proxies (JDK 1.3+ only) and lazy loading.

Table C.13 Method-level Hibernate tags

Method-level tag/Attributes	Description
@hibernate.array	Defines an array field.
cascade	Specifies which operations should be cascaded from the parent object to the associated object. Valid values: all, none, save/update, delete.
element-class	Fully qualified class name of the elements that make up the array.
inverse	Marks this collection as the inverse end of a bidirectional relationship.
schema	Name of a table schema to override the schema declared.
table	Name of the collection table (not used for one-to-many associations). Default: role name.
where	Specifies an arbitrary SQL WHERE condition to be used when retrieving or removing the collection. Useful if the collection should contain only a subset of the available data.
@hibernate.bag	Defines a bag collection field.
cascade	Specifies which operations should be cascaded from the parent object to the associated object. Valid values: all, none, save/update, delete.
inverse	Inverse relation collection. Equivalent to readonly. Valid values: true, false. Default: false.
lazy	Enables lazy initialization. Default: false.
order-by	Table columns that define the iteration order.

Table C.13   Method-level Hibernate tags *(continued)*

Method-level tag/Attributes	Description
readonly	Specifies that this is a read-only collection.
schema	Name of a table schema to override the schema declared.
table	Name of the collection table (not used for one-to-many associations). Default: role name.
where	Specifies an arbitrary SQL WHERE condition to be used when retrieving or removing the collection. Useful if the collection should contain only a subset of the available data.
`@hibernate.colletion-cache`	Configures a SessionFactory-level cache on a collection property.
usage	The type of caching. Valid values: read-only, read-write, nonstrict-read-write.
`@hibernate.collection-composite-element`	Type of elements in a collection.
class	Fully qualified class name of the elements that make up a collection.
`@hibernate.collection-element`	Declares a collection element.
column	Name of the mapped database table column.
length	Length of the mapped database table column.
not-null	Specifies a column as non-nullable. Default: false.
type	Name that indicates the Hibernate type.
unique	Specifies that the column must have a unique value.
`@hibernate.collection-index`	Declares a collection index.
column	Name of the mapped database table column. Default: the property name.
length	Length of the mapped database table column.
type	Name that indicates the Hibernate type.
`@hibernate.collection-jcs-cache`	Defines the caching strategy of an entity class.
usage	Specifies how caching is applied. Valid values: read-only, read-write.
`@hibernate.collection-key`	Declares a collection key.
column	Name of the mapped database table column. Default: the property name.

Table C.13 Method-level Hibernate tags *(continued)*

Method-level tag/Attributes	Description
`length`	Length of the mapped database table column.
`@hibernate.collection-many-to-many`	Declares a many-to-many relationship.
`class`	Fully qualified class name.
`column`	Name of the mapped database table column.
`outer-join`	Enables outer-join fetching for this relationship.
`@hibernate.collection-one-to-many`	Declares a one-to-many relationship.
`class`	Fully qualified class name for the collection contents.
`@hibernate.column`	Enables customization of the DDL type where a property is persisted.
`index`	Name of a multicolumn index.
`length`	Column length.
`name`	Name of the column.
`not-null`	Specifies that the column should be non-nullable. Valid values: true, false. Default: false.
`sql-type`	Overrides the default column type.
`unique`	Specifies that the column should have a unique constraint. Valid values: true, false. Default: false.
`unique-key`	Name of a multicolumn unique constraint.
`@hibernate.component`	Declares a component.
`class`	Fully qualified class name.
`@hibernate.composite-element`	Declares a composite collection element.
`class`	[Required] Name of the element class.
`@hibernate.generator-param`	Sets parameters to the identifier's generator class. This tag can be used multiple times to set multiple parameters.
`name`	Name of the parameter to be set.
`value`	Value to which the parameter should be set.
`@hibernate.id`	Declares an identifier property.
`class`	If a composite ID, specifies the class that embodies the ID.

Table C.13 Method-level Hibernate tags *(continued)*

Method-level tag/Attributes	Description
`column`	Name of the mapped database table column. Default: the property name.
`generator-class`	[Required] Key generator class. Valid values: uuid.hex, uuid.string, vm.long, vm.hex, assigned, native, sequence, hilo.long, hilo.hex, seqhilo.long.
`generator-parameter-1`	Parameter for key generator class.
`generator-parameter-2`	Parameter for key generator class.
`generator-parameter-3`	Parameter for key generator class.
`length`	Length of the mapped database table column.
`type`	Name that indicates the Hibernate type.
`unsaved-value`	[Required] Value that distinguishes transient instances with existing persistent state from new transient instances. Valid values: any, none, null.
`@hibernate.jcs-cache`	Configures a SessionFactory-level cache on a collection property using Apache Turbine's JCS. (Deprecated in favor of `@hibernate.collection-cache`.)
`usage`	The type of caching. Valid values: read-only, read-write, nonstrict-read-write.
`@hibernate.list`	Defines a list field.
`cascade`	Specifies which operations should be cascaded from the parent object to the associated object. Valid values: all, none, save-update, delete.
`inverse`	Marks this collection as the inverse end of a bidirectional relationship.
`lazy`	Enable lazy initialization. Default: false.
`schema`	Name of a table schema to override the schema declared.
`table`	Default: role name. The name of the collection table (not used for one-to-many associations)
`where`	Specifies an arbitrary SQL WHERE condition to be used when retrieving or removing the collection. Useful if the collection should contain only a subset of the available data.

Table C.13   Method-level Hibernate tags *(continued)*

Method-level tag/Attributes	Description
`@hibernate.many-to-one`	Declares a many-to-one association.
cascade	Specifies which operations should be cascaded from the parent object to the associated object. Valid values: all, none, save-update, delete.
class	Name of the associated class. Default: the property type determined by reflection.
column	Name of the mapped database table column. Default: the property name.
insert	Specifies whether the mapped columns are included in SQL `INSERT` statements. Valid values: true, false. Default: true.
not-null	Specifies that the column isn't nullable.
outer-join	Enables outer-join fetching for this association when `@hibernate.use_outer_join` is set. Valid values: true, false, auto. Default: auto.
unique	Specifies that a unique constraint should be imposed on the column.
update	Specifies whether the mapped columns are included in SQL `UPDATE` statements. Valid values: true, false. Default: true.
`@hibernate.map`	Defines a map field.
cascade	Specifies which operations should be cascaded from the parent object to the associated object. Valid values: all, save/update, delete, none.
inverse	Marks this map as the inverse end of a bidirectional relationship.
lazy	Enables lazy initialization. Default: false.
order-by	Specifies table columns that define the iteration order.
schema	Name of a table schema to override the schema declared.
sort	Specifies a sorted collection with natural sort order, or a given comparator class.
table	Name of the collection table (not used for one-to-many associations). Default: role name.

Table C.13 Method-level Hibernate tags *(continued)*

Method-level tag/Attributes	Description
where	Specifies an arbitrary SQL WHERE condition to be used when retrieving or removing the collection. Useful if the collection should contain only a subset of the available data.
@hibernate.one-to-one	Defines a one-to-one association.
cascade	Specifies which operations should be cascaded from the parent object to the associated object. Valid values: all, none, save-update, delete.
class	Name of the associated class. Default: the property type determined by reflection.
constrained	Specifies whether a foreign key constraint on the primary key of this class's table references the table of the related class. Valid values: true, false. Default: false.
outer-join	Enables outer-join fetching for this association when @hibernate.use_outer_join is set. Default: true.
@hibernate.primitive-array	Defines a primitive array field.
schema	Name of a table schema to override the schema declared.
table	Name of the collection table (not used for one-to-many associations). Default: role name.
where	Specifies an arbitrary SQL WHERE condition to be used when retrieving or removing the collection. Useful if the collection should contain only a subset of the available data.
@hibernate.property	Defines a Hibernate property field.
column	Name of the mapped database table column. Default: the property name.
insert	Specifies whether the property is included in SQL INSERT statements. Valid values: true, false. Default: true.
length	Length of the mapped database table column.
not-null	Specifies that the column isn't nullable.
type	Name that indicates the Hibernate type.
unique	Specifies that a unique constraint should be imposed on the column.

Table C.13 Method-level Hibernate tags *(continued)*

Method-level tag/Attributes	Description
`update`	Specifies whether the property is included in SQL UPDATE statements. Valid values: true, false. Default: true.
`@hibernate.set`	Defines a set field.
`cascade`	Specifies which operations should be cascaded from the parent object to the associated object. Valid values: all, none, save/update, delete.
`inverse`	Marks this collection as the inverse end of a bidirectional relationship.
`lazy`	Enables lazy initialization. Default: false.
`order-by`	Specifies table columns that define the iteration order.
`readonly`	Specifies a read-only collection.
`schema`	Name of a table schema to override the schema declared.
`sort`	Specifies a sorted collection with natural sort order, or a given comparator class.
`table`	Name of the collection table (not used for one-to-many associations). Default: role name.
`where`	Specifies an arbitrary SQL WHERE condition to be used when retrieving or removing the collection. Useful if the collection should contain only a subset of the available data.
`@hibernate.timestamp`	Declares a timestamp property.
`column`	Name of a column holding the timestamp.
`@hibernate.version`	Indicates that the table contains versioned data.
`column`	Name of a column holding the version number.
`type`	Type of the version number.

HP Application Server EJB tags

Table C.14   Class-level HPAS tags

Class-level tag/Attributes	Description
`@hpas.bean`	Most of the class-level HPAS options are specified in attributes of this tag.
`concurrent-message-processing`	Specifies whether concurrent message processing is enabled.
`connection-retry`	Specifies whether an exception listener is registered for the connection. If no exception listener is established, there will be no connection failover.
`jndi-destination`	[Required] Lookup string for the destination topic or queue for which the bean is registered as a listener.
`jndi-factory`	[Required] Lookup string used to obtain the factory to be used to create the connection used by the MDB.
`max-messages`	Maximum number of messages assigned to a single session. This value is passed to the JMS server.
`max-message-threads`	Maximum number of separate server sessions (threads) that will be created to handle messages.
`message-thread-timeout`	Amount of time after which an idle server session will be available to be removed from the pool.
`passivate-threshold`	Number of beans for a deployed EJB above which the container will attempt to passivate instances. Applicable to stateful session beans only, when the `passivation` parameter is used.
`passivation`	Determines whether the container can manage the passivation behavior of beans; indicates whether passivation is enabled for the bean.
`read-only`	Specifies whether the bean is marked as read-only.
`session-timeout`	Timeout for the session.
`@hpas.ejb-ref`	Mapping of EJB references to deployed EJBs.
`application`	Name of the application in which the EJB component is deployed.
`host`	Host name for the name server.
`jndi-name`	[Required] Actual name under which the bean is registered in the name service.
`port`	Port number for the name server.

Table C.14   Class-level HPAS tags *(continued)*

Class-level tag/Attributes	Description
ref-name	[Required] Mapping into the `<ejb-ref>` entry in the standard deployment descriptor.
type	[Required] Valid values: co-located, distributed. Use co-located for references to EJBs in the same application. Use distributed for references to EJBs in other applications. Default: co-located.
@hpas.pool	Contains the information required to set up an object pool.
cache-limit	Maximum size of the pool. When the cache limit is reached, pooled entries that are returned to the pool are discarded; if the cache limit is reached, new objects may still be created.
idle-timeout	Idle timeout for the pool.
initial-size	Initial size of the pool.
reap-asynch	Specifies whether pool reaping should occur asynchronously with respect to inserting or removing objects from the pool. Setting this to true makes pool accesses faster but consumes more system resources.
use-reaper	Specifies whether the pool should enforce the cache-limit. The reaper can be disabled to optimize pool performance.

JavaBean tags

Table C.15   Class-level JavaBean tags

Class-level tag/Attributes	Description
@javabean.attribute	Defines the attributes of the JavaBean (`propertyorder` and so on).
name	[Required] Name of the attribute
rtexpr	Specifies whether the value is a Java expression. Valid values: true, false. Default: false.
value	[Required] Value of the attribute.
@javabean.class	Specifies class-related information of JavaBean `BeanInfo`.
class	Class name of the real bean.

Table C.15   Class-level JavaBean tags *(continued)*

Class-level tag/Attributes	Description
`customizer`	Fully qualified class name of the JavaBean customizer.
`defaultProperty`	Default property of the JavaBean.
`displayName`	Name displayed for the JavaBean.
`expert`	Specifies whether the JavaBean is used in expert mode. Valid values: true, false. Default: false.
`hidden`	Specifies whether the JavaBean is hidden. Valid values: true, false. Default: false.
`name`	[Required] Name of the JavaBean (typically the unqualified class name).
`preferred`	Specifies whether the JavaBean is preferred. Valid values: true, false. Default: false.
`shortDescription`	Short description of the JavaBean.
`stopClass`	Fully qualified class name of the JavaBean ancestor used to stop introspection for additional information.
`@javabean.icons`	Defines the icons used for the visual aspect of the JavaBean.
`color16`	Absolute or relative resource name for the color icon of 16x16 pixels.
`color32`	Absolute or relative resource name for the color icon of 32x32 pixels.
`mono16`	Absolute or relative resource name for the monochrome icon of 16x16 pixels.
`mono32`	Absolute or relative resource name for the monochrome icon of 32x32 pixels.

Table C.16   Method-level JavaBean tags

Method-level tag/Attributes	Description
`@javabean.method`	Defines the JavaBean method found by introspection.
`displayName`	Name displayed for the method.
`expert`	Specifies whether the method is used in expert mode. Valid values: true, false. Default: false.

Table C.16   Method-level JavaBean tags *(continued)*

Method-level tag/Attributes	Description
hidden	Specifies whether the method is hidden. Valid values: true, false. Default: false.
name	[Required] Name of the method.
preferred	Specifies whether the method is preferred. Valid values: true, false. Default: false.
shortDescription	Short description of the method.
@javabean.param	Defines parameters for a JavaBean method.
displayName	Name displayed for the parameter.
name	[Required] Name of the parameter.
propertyEditor	Fully qualified class name of the PropertyEditor used to edit the parameter.
shortDescription	Short description of the parameter.
@javabean.property	Defines the JavaBean property found by introspection.
bound	Specifies whether the property is bound. Valid values: true, false. Default: false.
constrained	Specifies whether the property is constrained. Valid values: true, false. Default: false.
displayName	Name displayed for the property.
expert	Specifies whether the property is used in expert mode. Valid values: true, false. Default: false.
hidden	Specifies whether the property is hidden. Valid values: true, false. Default: false.
preferred	Specifies whether the property is preferred. Valid values: true, false. Default: false.
propertyEditor	Fully qualified class name of the PropertyEditor used to edit the property.
readOnly	Specifies whether the JavaBean property is read-only. Valid values: true, false. Default: false.
shortDescription	Short description of the property.

JBoss tags

Table C.17   Class-level JBoss tags

Class-level tag/Attributes	Description
`@jboss.audit`	Indicates that a default JBoss audit trail should be created.
`@jboss.audit-created-by`	Defines a `created-by` audit field in a CMP entity EJB.
`column-name`	Name of the column to contain the created-by data.
`field-name`	Name of the field to contain the created-by data.
`jdbc-type`	JDBC type of the column that contains the created-by data.
`sql-type`	SQL type of the column that contains the created-by data.
`@jboss.audit-created-time`	Defines a created-time audit field in a CMP entity EJB.
`column-name`	Name of the column to contain the creation time data.
`field-name`	Name of the field to contain the creation time data.
`jdbc-type`	JDBC type of the column that contains the creation time data.
`sql-type`	SQL type of the column that contains the creation time data.
`@jboss.audit-updated-by`	Defines an `updated-by` audit field in a CMP entity EJB.
`column-name`	Name of the column to contain the updated by data.
`field-name`	Name of the field to contain the updated by data.
`jdbc-type`	JDBC type of the column that contains the updated by data.
`sql-type`	SQL type of the column that contains the updated by data.
`@jboss.audit-updated-time`	Defines an `updated-time` audit field in a CMP entity EJB.
`column-name`	Name of the column to contain the update time data.
`field-name`	Name of the field to contain the update time data.

Table C.17   Class-level JBoss tags *(continued)*

Class-level tag/Attributes	Description
`jdbc-type`	JDBC type of the column that contains the update time data.
`sql-type`	SQL type of the column that contains the update time data.
`@jboss.cache-invalidation`	Tells the container to emit cache invalidation messages when these entities are changed.
`value`	Indicates whether this EJB should listen to cache invalidation events and clear its cache accordingly as well as send cache invalidation messages. Used on entity beans (only commit-options A and D will invalidate their cache). Valid values: True, False. Default: True.
`@jboss.cache-invalidation-config`	Configures the behavior of JBoss cache invalidation.
`invalidation-group-name`	Name of an invalidation group to which this entity belongs.
`invalidation-manager-name`	JMX `ObjectName` of the `InvalidationManager` to use.
`@jboss.cluster-config`	Sets JBoss clustering configuration, overriding the default container on a per-EJB basis. The defaults mentioned here aren't actual XDoclet behavior but rather JBoss defaults cited for convenience.
`bean-policy`	Sets the algorithm used for bean load-balancing policy, such as `<bean-load-balance-policy>` in `jboss.xml`.
`home-policy`	Sets the algorithm used for home load-balancing policy, such as `<home-load-balance-policy>` in `jboss.xml`.
`partition-name`	Sets the name of the JBoss cluster partition in which this EJB is to be deployed.
`state-manager`	Sets the JNDI name used for looking up the clustered session state manager, such as `<session-state-manager-jndi-name>` in `jboss.xml`.
`@jboss.clustered`	Marks the EJB as clustered in the `jboss.xml` deployment descriptor.
`cluster`	Turns clustering on/off.

Table C.17   Class-level JBoss tags *(continued)*

Class-level tag/Attributes	Description
`@jboss.cmp-field`	Defines a `<cmp-field>` element for a CMP field of `ejb-jar.xml`. This is used for dependant objects field mapping. See `@jboss.not-persisted-field`.
`column-name`	[Required] Name of the column.
`field-name`	[Required] Name of the field.
`@jboss.container-configuration`	Name of the container configuration to use for the bean. Applicable to all types of EJBs.
`name`	[Required] Container configuration for the bean.
`@jboss.datasource`	Specifies a JBoss datasource.
`name`	JNDI name of the datasource.
`mapping`	Type mapping to be used for the datasource.
`@jboss.declared-sql`	Configures a custom query (defined by `@ejb.finder`) by defining explicitly declared SQL fragments to be added to the SQL generated by the JBossCMP engine (requires JBoss 3+).
`alias`	Alias to be used for the main select table. Default: ejb-name.
`description`	Description of this custom query.
`distinct`	If true, JBossCMP adds the `DISTINCT` keyword to the generated `select` clause. Default: to use `DISTINCT` if the method returns a `java.util.Set`.
`eager-load-group`	Contains the name of the load group that will be eager-loaded for this entity.
`ejb-name`	`ejb-name` of the entity to be selected. Required if `ejbSelect` method.
`field-name`	Name of the CMP field to be selected from the specified entity. Default: selects the entire entity.
`from`	Declares additional SQL to append to the generated `from` clause. Example: `<from>FullAddressEJB as a</from>`.
`order`	Declares the `order` clause for the query. Example: `<order>TITLE</order>`.

Table C.17   Class-level JBoss tags *(continued)*

Class-level tag/Attributes	Description
`other`	Declares the other SQL that is appended to the end of a query. Example: `<other>LIMIT 100 OFFSET 200</other>`.
`page-size`	Number of entities to be read in a single read-ahead load query.
`signature`	[Required] Signature of the method. Example: `java.util.Collection findAll`. The return type in the signature must be fully qualified.
`strategy`	Strategy used to read-ahead data in queries. Valid values: none, on-load, on-find.
`where`	`where` clause for the query. Example: `<where>TITLE={0} OR ARTIST={0} OR TYPE={0} OR NOTES={0}</where>`.
@jboss.depends	Declares an MBean dependency.
`object-name`	Name of the object the MBean depends on.
@jboss.destination-jndi-name	Defines the JNDI name of the queue/topic used by the message-driven bean.
`name`	[Required] Name of the destination.
@jboss.ejb-ref-jndi	Sets the JNDI name of a referenced bean. There must be an `@ejb.ejb-ref` tag that points to the referenced bean.
`jndi-name`	[Required] JNDI name of the bean.
`ref-name`	[Required] Name of the bean reference.
@jboss.entity-command	Supplies information about an entity command used to create the entity EJB.
`class`	Command class.
`name`	[Required] Command name.
@jboss.entity-command-attribute	Supplies information about an entity command used to create the entity EJB.
`name`	[Required] Attribute name.
`value`	[Required] Attribute value.
@jboss.finder-query	Assigns a custom query to a finder method. An `@ejb.finder` tag for the named finder must also be present.
`name`	[Required] Name of the finder.

Table C.17   Class-level JBoss tags *(continued)*

Class-level tag/Attributes	Description
order	Order for the finder results.
query	[Required] Query for the finder. See the JAWS documentation for the finder query syntax.
read-ahead	Indicates whether the query should have read-ahead.
@jboss.lazy-load-group	Defines a named group of fields that will be lazily loaded together.
name	Group name.
@jboss.load-group	Defines a named group of fields that will be loaded together.
description	Group description.
name	Group name.
@jboss.method-attributes	Allows for the specification of nonstandard attributes for the named method(s).
pattern	[Required] A complete method name or a pattern consisting of an initial match followed by *.
read-only	Flags method(s) as read-only. The named method(s) never trigger a store.
@jboss.optimistic-locking	Specifies an optimistic locking configuration.
column-name	Name of the column used for optimistic locking.
field-name	Name of the field used for optimistic locking.
field-type	Type of the field used for optimistic locking.
group-name	The optimistic locking field group name. Must match one of the entity's load group names.
jdbc-type	JDBC type of the column used for optimistic locking.
key-generator-factory	JNDI name of a key generator factory used to obtain a key generator for the locking column.
modified-strategy	If set, specifies that the fields that were modified during the transaction will be used for optimistic locking.
read-strategy	If set, specifies that the fields that were read/changed during the transaction will be used for optimistic locking.
sql-type	SQL type of the column used for optimistic locking.

Table C.17   Class-level JBoss tags *(continued)*

Class-level tag/Attributes	Description
`timestamp-column`	If set, an additional field of type `java.util.Date` is added to the entity EJB and used as a timestamp for optimistic locking.
`version-column`	If set, an additional version field of type `java.lang.Long` is added to the entity EJB and used for optimistic locking.
`@jboss.persistence`	Provides information about how a CMP entity EJB should be persisted.
`create-table`	Specifies whether the persistence manager should attempt to create tables if they're not present.
`datasource`	JNDI name used to look up the datasource.
`datasource-mapping`	Name of the type mapping to be used for this datasource.
`fetch-size`	Number of entities to read in one round-trip to the underlying datastore.
`list-cache-max`	Number of simultaneous queries that can be tracked by the cache for an entity.
`pk-constraint`	Specifies whether a primary key constraint is added when creating tables.
`read-only`	Specifies whether the entity is read-only.
`read-time-out`	Amount of time a read-only entity is considered valid (milliseconds).
`remove-table`	Specifies whether the persistence manager attempts to remove tables during shutdown.
`row-locking`	Specifies that select statements should use the `SELECT...FOR UPDATE` syntax.
`table-name`	Name of the table to which this entity should be persisted.
`@jboss.query`	Configures a custom query (defined by `@ejb.finder`) for the JBossCMP engine (requires JBoss 3+).
`description`	Description of this custom query.
`dynamic`	Dynamic JBossQL query. The JBossQL is passed to the query and compiled on the fly.
`eager-load-group`	Contains the name of the load group that will be eager-loaded for this entity.

Table C.17   Class-level JBoss tags *(continued)*

Class-level tag/Attributes	Description
`page-size`	Number of entities to be read in a single read-ahead load query.
`query`	JBossQL query that overrides the EJB-QL specified in the EJB deployment descriptor. JBossQL is a superset of EJB-QL.
`signature`	[Required] Signature of the method. Example: `java.util.Collection findAll`. The return type in the signature must be fully qualified.
`strategy`	Strategy used to read-ahead data in queries. Valid values: none, on-load, on-find.
`@jboss.read-ahead`	Specifies the read-ahead strategy for this entity bean. Applicable to entity beans using the JBossCMP persistence engine.
`eager-load-group`	Contains the name of the load group that will be eager-loaded for this entity.
`page-size`	Number of entities to be read in a single read-ahead load query.
`strategy`	[Required] Strategy used to read-ahead data in queries. Valid values: none, on-load, on-find.
`@jboss.read-only`	Marks a bean as read-only. This avoids `ejbStore` calls.
`read-only`	[Required] Declares the bean as read-only.
`@jboss.resource-env-ref`	Maps a code name of an environment resource (`<res-ref-name>`, provided by the Bean Developer) to its deployed JNDI name.
`jndi-name`	[Required] JNDI name to which the reference should link.
`resource-env-ref-name`	[Required] Code name of a resource provided by the bean developer.
`@jboss.resource-manager`	Maps a logical resource name to its runtime JNDI name.
`res-man-jndi-name`	[Required] JNDI name of the resource.
`res-man-name`	[Required] Name of the resource.

Table C.17   Class-level JBoss tags *(continued)*

Class-level tag/Attributes	Description
`@jboss.resource-ref`	Maps a code name of a resource (`<res-ref-name>`, provided by the bean developer) and its xml name (`<resource-name>`, provided by the application assembler). If no `@jboss.resource-ref` is provided, JBoss assumes that `xml-name = code name`.
`jndi-name`	JNDI name to which the reference should link.
`resource-name`	Gives the XML name of the resource provided by the application assembler.
`res-ref-name`	[Required] Code name of a resource as provided by the bean developer.
`res-url`	The runtime JNDI name as a URL of the resource, provided by the deployer.
`@jboss.security-proxy`	Class name of the security proxy implementation. This may be an instance of `org.jboss.security.SecurityProxy` or an object that implements methods in the home or remote interface of an EJB without implementing any common interface.
`name`	[Required] Name of the security proxy for the bean.
`@jboss.select-for-update`	Configures an entity bean as select for update.
`select-for-update`	Specifies whether a `SELECT...FOR UPDATE` query is used when loading the entity EJB. Valid values: true, false. Default: false.
`@jboss.service`	Configures the generation of `*-service.xml` files for JBoss
`archives`	Individual filenames that should be used to construct the service classpath. This parameter should never come alone in a `@jboss.service` tag, but should always appear together with the `classpath` attribute.
`classpath`	Directory to use as codebase for this service classpath. This parameter may be used in conjunction with the `archives` attribute to form the service classpath.

Table C.17 Class-level JBoss tags *(continued)*

Class-level tag/Attributes	Description
servicefile	Prefix to be prepended to the generated `*-service.xml` file name. For example, if `servicefile=test`, the generated file is called `test-service.xml`. Note that you must include at least one `@jboss.service servicefile` tag in your MBean, or generation will fail.
@jboss.tuned-updates	Configures an entity bean for tuned updates.
tune	Specifies that JBoss should only include changed columns when performing updates. Valid values: true, false.
@jboss.unknown-pk	Supplies information about the unknown primary key (a primary key provided or generated outside the application). At least the class should be supplied, with optional column name, JDBC, and SQL types.
auto-increment	Set if the primary key field is auto-incremented by the database.
class	[Required] Unknown primary key class.
column-name	Name of the primary key column in the database table.
field-name	Name of the field that contains the primary key.
jdbc-type	JDBC type for the primary key column. Should be specified together with `sql-type`.
readonly	Hint to treat the primary key as read-only.
read-time-out	Read timeout value for the primary key field.
sql-type	SQL type for the primary key column. Should be specified together with `jdbc-type`.

Table C.18 Method-level JBoss tags

Method-level tag/Attributes	Description
@jboss.column-name	Declares the column name to which the CMP field will be mapped.
name	[Required] Column name.
@jboss.dvc-property	Defines a dependent value class property.
column-name	Column name of the property.

Table C.18 Method-level JBoss tags *(continued)*

Method-level tag/Attributes	Description
jdbc-type	JDBC type of the property.
name	Name of the property.
not-null	Specifies that the field is non-nullable.
sql-type	SQL type of the property.
@jboss.jdbc-type	Declares the JDBC type. Its value must be one of the fields of java.sql.Types (BIT, CHAR, and so on). This JDBC type is used by the CMP provider to determine which method to call on PreparedStatement and ResultSet for INSERT/UPDATE/SELECT queries.
type	[Required] Valid JDBC type. Valid values: ARRAY, BIGINT, BINARY, BIT, BLOB, BOOLEAN, CHAR, CLOB, DATALINK, DATE, DECIMAL, DISTINCT, DOUBLE, FLOAT, INTEGER, JAVA_OBJECT, LONGVARBINARY, LONGVARCHAR, NULL, NUMERIC, OTHER, REAL, REF, SMALLINT, STRUCT, TIME, TIMESTAMP, TINYINT, VARBINARY, VARCHAR. Default: VARCHAR.
@jboss.method-attributes	Allows for the specification of nonstandard attributes for the method.
read-only	Flags the method as read-only. Such a method never triggers a store.
@jboss.not-persisted-field	Specifies that a field shouldn't be persisted. Applicable to entity EJBs using JAWS CMP on the method level.
@jboss.persistence	Provides information about the persistence of a CMP field.
auto-increment	Specifies whether the field should be auto-incremented by the database.
dbindex	If set (to anything), indicates that an index named <field name>_index should be created on the database column.
not-null	Specifies whether null values should be allowed.
read-only	Specifies whether the field is read-only.
read-time-out	Amount of time a read-only field is considered valid (milliseconds).

Table C.18 Method-level JBoss tags *(continued)*

Method-level tag/Attributes	Description
@jboss.relation	Used to customize the relationships via `jbosscmp-jdbc.xml` for JBoss 3.0.
fk-column	[Required] Name of the column that should be used for foreign key mapping. (Corresponds to `<column-name>` in `jbosscmp-jdbc.xml`.)
fk-constraint	Indicates whether a foreign key constraint should be placed on the relation column.
related-pk-field	[Required] Name of the primary key field of the 1-end of the relationship that this foreign key constraint applies to. Required for support of complex primary keys in the 1- end of the relation. (Corresponds to `<field-name>` in `jbosscmp-jdbc.xml`.)
@jboss.relation-mapping	Forces the use of a relation table mapping in a relationship even when the relation isn't M-N.
style	Valid value: relation-table.
@jboss.relation-read-ahead	Customizes the read-ahead component of relationships via `jbosscmp-jdbc.xml` for JBoss 3.0.
eager-load-group	Contains the name of the load group that will be eager-loaded for this entity.
page-size	Number of entities to be read in a single read-ahead load query.
strategy	[Required] Strategy used to read-ahead data in queries. Valid values: none, on-load, on-find.
@jboss.relation-table	Tells the JBoss persistence manager to use a relation table for managing entity relationships.
create-table	Specifies whether the persistence manager should attempt to create tables if they're not present.
datasource	Datasource to place the relation table in.
datasource-mapping	Name of the type mapping to be used for this datasource.
pk-constraint	Specifies whether a primary key constraint is added when creating tables.
remove-table	Specifies whether the persistence manager should attempt to remove tables during shutdown.
row-locking	Specifies whether select statements should use the `SELECT...FOR UPDATE` syntax.

Table C.18 **Method-level JBoss tags** *(continued)*

Method-level tag/Attributes	Description
`table-name`	Name of the relation table.
`@jboss.sql-type`	Declares the type of the field in the database. This value is only used when the CMP container creates your table (if possible).
`type`	[Required] Database-specific SQL type.
`@jboss.subscriber`	Defines a message-driven bean subscription.
`client-id`	Subscription client ID.
`name`	Subscription username.
`password`	Subscription password.
`subscription-id`	Subscription ID.
`@jboss.target-relation`	Customizes the relationships via `jbosscmp-jdbc.xml` for JBoss 3.0. This tag should be used to modify the blind side of the relation in a unidirectional relationship. Aside from this, it's exactly the same as `@jboss.relation`.
`fk-column`	[Required] Name of the column that should be used for foreign key mapping. (Corresponds to `<column-name>` in `jbosscmp-jdbc.xml`.)
`fk-constraint`	Indicates whether a foreign key constraint should be placed on the relation column.
`related-pk-field`	[Required] Name of the primary key field of the 1-end of the relationship that this foreign key constraint applies to. Required for support of complex primary keys in the 1- end of the relation. (Corresponds to `<field-name>` in `jbosscmp-jdbc.xml`.)

JDO tags

Table C.19 **Class-level JDO tags**

Class-level tag/Attributes	Description
`@jdo.class-vendor-extension`	Declares vendor-extension metadata for an entire class.
`content`	Content of an `<extension>` block.
`key`	Name of the vendor extension property.
`value`	Value of the vendor extension property.

Table C.19 **Class-level JDO tags** *(continued)*

Class-level tag/Attributes	Description
vendor-name	Name of the vendor to whom this extension applies.
@jdo.package-vendor-extension	Declares vendor-extension metadata for an entire package.
content	Content of an <extension> block.
key	Name of the vendor extension property.
value	Value of the vendor extension property.
vendor-name	Name of the vendor to whom this extension applies.
@jdo.persistence-capable	Provides information about the JDO persistent bean. Its presence determines if your class will be included in the generated JDO metadata.
identity-type	[Required] Specifies whether objects are uniquely identified by a JDO implementation–provided abstract identifier (datastore identity), accessible fields in the object (application identity), or at all (nondurable identity). Valid values: application, datastore, nondurable. Default: datastore.
objectid-class	Fully qualified class name for the application identity object ID. Use only with application identity.
persistence-capable-superclass	Fully qualified class name of the PersistenceCapable superclass, if any.
requires-extent	Specifies whether the JDO implementation must provide an extent for this class.
@sql.table	Defines the mapping to a relational database. Used if the JDO bean is to be persisted on a relational database. Currently this tag is useful only when targeting Solarmetric's Kodo or LIBeLIS's LiDO implementation of JDO.
table-name	Name of the table to map to.

Table C.20 **Property-level JDO tags**

Property-level tag/Attributes	Description
@jdo.array-vendor-extension	Declares vendor-extension metadata for an array field.
content	Content of an <extension> block.

Table C.20   Property-level JDO tags *(continued)*

Property-level tag/Attributes	Description
key	Name of the vendor extension property.
value	Value of the vendor extension property.
vendor-name	Name of the vendor to whom this extension applies.
@jdo.collection-vendor-extension	Declares vendor-extension metadata for a collection field.
content	Content of an `<extension>` block.
key	Name of the vendor extension property.
value	Value of the vendor extension property.
vendor-name	Name of the vendor to whom this extension applies.
@jdo.field	Defines a class property as being JDO-persistent.
collection-type	For collection fields, specifies the collection type. Valid values: collection, map, array.
default-fetch-group	Specifies whether the field is part of the default fetch group. Fields that are part of the default fetch group are eagerly loaded. Valid values: true, false. Default: true.
element-type	For collection fields, specifies the type of objects stored in the collection.
embedded	Gives a hint to the JDO implementation to store the field as part of the class instance in the datastore, rather than as a separate entity. Valid values: true, false. Default: true.
embedded-element	Gives a hint to the JDO implementation to store elements of a collection as part of the class instance in the datastore, rather than as separate entities. Valid values: true, false.
embedded-key	For collection fields of type map, gives a hint to the JDO implementation to store the map keys as part of the class instance in the datastore, rather than as separate entities. Valid values: true, false.
embedded-value	For collection fields of type map, gives a hint to the JDO implementation to store the map values as part of the class instance in the datastore, rather than as separate entities. Valid values: true, false.

Table C.20   Property-level JDO tags *(continued)*

Property-level tag/Attributes	Description
key-type	For collection fields of type map, specifies the type of the objects used as keys.
null-value	Behavior when a field containing a null value is written to the datastore. Valid values: none, default, exception. If none, then the datastore should hold a null value for the field. If default, then a default value should be written. If exception then the JDO implementation should throw an exception. Default: none.
persistence-modifier	Specifies how JDO should manage the field. Valid values: persistent for persistent fields, transactional for nonpersistent fields that can be rolled back when a transaction is rolled back, and none. Default: persistent.
primary-key	Specifies a field as a primary key field. Valid values: true, false. Default: false.
value-type	For collection fields of type map, specifies the type of the objects stored in the map values.
@jdo.field-vendor-extension	Declares vendor-extension metadata for a noncollection field.
content	Content of an <extension> block.
key	Name of the vendor extension property.
value	Value of the vendor extension property.
vendor-name	Name of the vendor to whom this extension applies.
@jdo.map-vendor-extension	Declares vendor-extension metadata for a map field.
content	Content of an <extension> block.
key	Name of the vendor extension property.
value	Value of the vendor extension property.
vendor-name	Name of the vendor to whom this extension applies.
@sql.field	Defines vendor-specific metadata specific to mapping a field to a relational database table. Currently this tag is useful only when targeting Solarmetric's Kodo or LIBeLIS's LiDO implementation of JDO.
column-name	Database column name to which this field should be mapped.

Table C.20   Property-level JDO tags *(continued)*

Property-level tag/Attributes	Description
`related-field`	Field name on the other side of a relationship that is the link back to this object.
`table-name`	Table to which this field is persisted.
@sql.relation	Used in place of `@sql.field` to define a relationship field. Currently this tag is only useful when targeting Solarmetric's Kodo or LIBeLIS's LiDO implementation of JDO.
`related-field`	Field name of the other side of a relationship between two objects.
`style`	[Required] Relationship style. Valid values: foreign-key, relation-table.
`table-name`	Name of the relationship table when `style=relation-table`.

JMX tags

Table C.21   Class-level JMX tags

Class-level tag/Attributes	Description
@jmx.descriptor	Defines a descriptor for a JBoss XMBean.
`name`	Name of the descriptor.
`value`	Descriptor value.
@jmx.mbean	Identifies the class as an MBean. It can be used to generate the interface for a standard MBean and the JBoss-specific XMBean XML descriptor and `service.xml` file format.
`currencyTimeLimit`	Specifies how long the MBean's state may be considered valid.
`description`	Description for the MBean that can be used in MBean documentation.

`descriptor`	Additional custom descriptor for the MBean that can be used in MBean documentation. To make this work as an XDoclet parameter, you need to escape the double quotes:
	`descriptor="name=\"name\"`
	`value=\"value\"".`

Table C.21   Class-level JMX tags *(continued)*

Class-level tag/Attributes	Description
display-name	MBean's display name.
extends	Superclass for the standard MBean interface.
name	Object name for an mlet or can be used as a default in an extension template.
persistence-manager	Fully qualified class name of a persistence manager for this MBean. (JBoss specific.)
persistLocation	Location where the MBean's state should be saved.
persistName	Name to identify the MBean's saved state.
persistPeriod	Specifies when the MBean state will be saved.
persistPolicy	Persistence policy for this MBean, Valid values: OnUpdate, NoMoreOftenThan, Never, OnTimer.
state-action-on-update	Specifies what the JBoss state management should do when an attribute is updated on a started MBean. (JBoss specific.)
@jmx.mlet-entry	Allows you to specify entries for a generated mlet.
archive	ARCHIVE property for an mlet configuration.
codebase	Path to the package for the MBean class.
@jmx.notification	Defines a JMX notification.
currencyTimeLimit	Specifies how long the MBean's state may be considered valid.
description	Description of the notification.
descriptor	Additional custom descriptor for the MBean that can be used in MBean infos. This should be of the form *name="name" value="value"*. To make this work as an XDoclet parameter, you need to escape the double quotes: `descriptor="name=\"name\" value=\"value\"".`
name	[Required] Name for the notification.
notificationType	Notification type for the MBean. Used in the JBoss XMBean descriptor file.
persistLocation	Location where the MBean's state should be saved.
persistName	Name to identify the MBean's saved state with.
persistPeriod	Specifies when the MBean state will be saved.

Table C.21   Class-level JMX tags *(continued)*

Class-level tag/Attributes	Description
persistPolicy	Persistence policy for this MBean. Valid values: OnUpdate, NoMoreOftenThan, Never, OnTimer.

Table C.22   Method-level JMX tags

Method-level tag/Attributes	Description
@jmx.descriptor	Defines a descriptor for a JBoss XMBean method.
name	Name of the descriptor.
value	The descriptor value.
@jmx.managed-attribute	Defines a JMX-managed attribute. This method is included in a standard MBean interface and an attribute based on its name is included as a managed attribute in XMBean metadata. This must be included on any getter or setter you want exposed in a standard MBean. For XMBeans, the methods with these tags are identified as the getMethod and setMethod for the attribute.
access	Specifies the access to the managed-attribute. Valid values: read-only, write-only, read-write. Default: read-write.
currencyTimeLimit	Specifies how long the MBean state may be considered valid.
description	Description of the managed attribute that can be used in MBean documentation.
descriptor	Additional custom descriptor for the MBean that can be used in MBean documentation. This should be of the form *name="name" value="value"*. To make this work as an XDoclet parameter, you need to escape the double quotes: descriptor="name=\"name\" value=\"value\"".
display-name	Display name of the managed attribute.
interceptor-classes	Defines a descriptor named interceptor-classes for a JBoss XMBean.
name	Name of the managed attribute.
persistLocation	Location where the MBean's state should be saved.
persistName	Name to identify the MBean's saved state with.

Table C.22   Method-level JMX tags *(continued)*

Method-level tag/Attributes	Description
`persistPeriod`	Specifies when the MBean state will be saved.
`persistPolicy`	Persistence policy for this MBean. Valid values: OnUpdate, NoMoreOftenThan, Never, OnTimer.
`state-action-on-update`	Specifies what the JBoss state management should do when an attribute is updated on a started MBean. (JBoss specific.)
`value`	(Initial) value for the managed attribute. This is used in the JBoss `*-service.xml` file and the XMBean descriptor. In both cases, the result is that the value is set as the initial value of the newly deployed MBean.
`@jmx.managed-constructor`	Defines a managed constructor.
`description`	Description of the managed constructor.
`servicefile`	Service file to match the `servicefile` attribute of `<jbossxmlservicetemplate>`. If it matches, the managed constructor is included in the generated service file descriptor.
`@jmx.managed-constructor-parameter`	Defines a parameter to a managed constructor. Used only for generation of MX4J MBean description classes.
`description`	Description of the managed constructor parameter.
`name`	Name of the managed constructor parameter.
`position`	Index position of the managed constructor parameter.
`@jmx.managed-operation`	Defines a JMX managed operation. This method is included in a standard MBean interface and marked as a managed operation in XMBean metadata. `@jmx.managed-parameter` tags must be used to describe the parameters.
`description`	Specifies a description for the managed operation that can be used in MBean documentation.
`impact`	Impact of the operation. Valid values: ACTION, INFO, ACTION_INFO. Default: ACTION_INFO.
`interceptor-classes`	Descriptor named `interceptor-classes` for a JBoss XMBean.
`name`	Name of the managed operation.
`return-type`	Return type of the managed operation.

Table C.22   Method-level JMX tags *(continued)*

Method-level tag/Attributes	Description
`@jmx.managed-operation-parameter`	Defines an MBean managed operation parameter. Used only for generation of MX4J MBean description classes.
`description`	Description of the managed operation parameter description.
`name`	Name of the managed operation parameter.
`position`	Index position of the managed operation parameter.
`@jmx.managed-parameter`	Defines a parameter to a managed operation or managed constructor.
`description`	Description of the managed parameter.
`managed-operation`	Managed operation to which this parameter applies.
`name`	Name of the managed parameter.
`type`	Type of the managed parameter.
`value`	Value of the managed parameter.

JOnAS tags

Table C.23   Class-level JOnAS tags

Class-level tag/Attributes	Description
`@jonas.bean`	Declares the JOnAS-specific information for an enterprise bean.
`ejb-name`	[Required] Enterprise bean's name specified in the standard EJB deployment descriptor.
`jndi-name`	JNDI name of the enterprise bean's home. Concerns only the entity and session beans. Mandatory for versions prior to 2.5, but optional for session beans for 2.5 and up.
`@jonas.ejb-ref`	Declares the JOnAS-specific information for a reference to another enterprise bean's home.
`ejb-ref-name`	[Required] Name of the EJB reference specified in the standard EJB deployment descriptor.
`jndi-name`	[Required] JNDI name of the EJB.

Table C.23   Class-level JOnAS tags *(continued)*

Class-level tag/Attributes	Description
`@jonas.finder-method-jdbc-mapping`	Declares the SQL WHERE clause associated with a finder method of a container-managed persistence entity.
`jdbc-where-clause`	[Required] SQL WHERE clause.
`method-name`	[Required] Method's name.
`method-params`	Single method among multiple methods with an overloaded method name.
`@jonas.is-modified-method-name`	Name of an entity's `is-modified` method.
`is-modified-method-name`	[Required] Name of an entity's `is-modified` method.
`@jonas.jdbc-mapping`	Declares the mapping of an entity with container-managed persistence to the underlying database.
`automatic-pk`	If true, auto-generates the primary key.
`jdbc-table-name`	[Required] Name of the relational table.
`jndi-name`	[Required] JNDI name of the datasource.
`@jonas.max-cache-size`	Defines the maximum number of instances that can be held in memory. The default value is infinite. This tag has only been present since version 2.4.
`max-cache-size`	[Required] Maximum number of instances that can be hold in memory. The default value is infinite.
`@jonas.message-driven-destination`	Declares the JOnAS-specific information for a message-driven bean destination.
`jndi-name`	[Required] JNDI name of the message-driven destination.
`@jonas.min-pool-size`	Number of instances to be created to populate the pool when the bean is loaded for the first time. The default value is 0. This tag has only been present since version 2.4.
`min-pool-size`	[Required] Number of instances to be created to populate the pool when the bean is loaded for the first time. The default value is 0.
`@jonas.passivation-timeout`	Specifies the value of the timeout in seconds for passivation of entity instances when no transactions are used.
`passivation-timeout`	[Required] Value of the timeout in seconds for passivation of entity instances when no transaction is used.

Table C.23 Class-level JOnAS tags *(continued)*

Class-level tag/Attributes	Description
`@jonas.resource`	Declares the JOnAS-specific information for an external resource referenced by a bean.
`jndi-name`	[Required] JNDI name of the resource.
`res-ref-name`	[Required] Name of the resource reference specified in the standard EJB deployment descriptor.
`@jonas.resource-env`	Declares the JOnAS-specific information for an external resource environment referenced by a bean.
`jndi-name`	[Required] JNDI name of the resource environment.
`resource-env-ref-name`	[Required] Name of the resource environment reference specified in the standard EJB deployment descriptor.
`@jonas.session-timeout`	Specifies the value of timeout in seconds for expiration of session instances.
`session-timeout`	[Required] Value of the timeout in seconds for expiration of session instances.
`@jonas.shared`	Specifies if the bean state can be accessed outside JOnAS. This tag has only been present since version 2.4.
`shared`	[Required] True if the bean state can be accessed outside JOnAS. Default: False.

Table C.24 Method-level JOnAS tags

Method-level tag/Attributes	Description
`@jonas.cmp-field-jdbc-mapping`	Declares the mapping of a container-managed field of an entity to a column of a relational table.
`field-name`	[Required] Field's name.
`jdbc-field-name`	[Required] Column name of the relational table.

Macromedia JRun tags

Table C.25   Class-level JRun tags

Class-level tag/Attributes	Description
`@jrun.always-dirty`	Forces synchronization with the datasource at the ends of transactions even when there has been no change to the entity bean's fields. This tag has no attributes. Specify the value on the tag itself.
`@jrun.cluster-home`	Denotes whether the `EJBHome` should be clustered for this bean. If clustering is enabled in `jrun.xml`, this value is True by default. You can use this element to override this behavior on a bean-by-bean basis. This tag has no attributes. Specify the value on the tag itself.
`@jrun.cluster-object`	Denotes whether the `EJBObject` should be clustered for this bean. If clustering is enabled in `jrun.xml`, this value is True by default. You can use this element to override this behavior on a bean-by-bean basis. This tag has no attributes. Specify the value on the tag itself.
`@jrun.commit-option`	Specifies the commit option from Sections 10.5.9 and 12.1.9 of the EJB 2.0 specification. This tag has no attributes. Specify the value on the tag itself.
`@jrun.ejb-local-ref`	Describes a mapping between the `ejb-ref-name` the bean developer provides and its JNDI name. The deployer provides the actual JNDI name.
`ejb-ref-name`	[Required] Name of an EJB from the `ejb-jar.xml` file specified by the bean developer.
`jndi-name`	[Required] JNDI name where the bean or resource will be bound.
`@jrun.ejb-ref`	Describes a mapping between the `ejb-ref-name` the bean developer provides and its JNDI name. The deployer provides the actual JNDI name.
`ejb-ref-name`	[Required] Name of an EJB from the `ejb-jar.xml` file specified by the bean developer.
`jndi-name`	[Required] JNDI name where the bean or resource will be bound.
`@jrun.instance-pool`	Sets the maximum and minimum size parameters for `StatelessSessionBean` instance pools.
`maximum-size`	[Required] Maximum size for `StatelessSessionBean` instance pools.

Table C.25 Class-level JRun tags *(continued)*

Class-level tag/Attributes	Description
`minimum-size`	[Required] Minimum size for `StatelessSessionBean` instance pools.
`@jrun.jdbc-mappings`	Holds information specific to JRun and not declared in the `ejb-jar.xml` file about the CMP mappings for an entity bean. `@jrun.jdbc-mappings` are used to specify the SQL used to create, load, store, find, and remove entity beans.
`create-table`	[Required] Specifies whether JRun will attempt to create database tables.
`delete-table`	[Required] Specifies whether JRun will attempt to delete database tables.
`@jrun.jndi-name`	Sets the JNDI name where the bean or resource will be bound.
`jndi-name`	[Required] JNDI name for the EJB.
`@jrun.message-driven-destination`	Provides the destination the message-driven container uses.
`name`	[Required] Parameter name.
`jndi-name`	JNDI name used to look up the MDB destination.
`@jrun.message-driven-subscription`	Provides the destination the message-driven container uses.
`client-id`	[Required] Client ID for `DurableSubscription` setup and sign-on.
`@jrun.resource-env-ref`	Describes a mapping between the `resource-env-name` the bean developer provides and its JNDI name. The deployer provides the actual JNDI name.
`jndi-name`	[Required] JNDI name where the bean or resource will be bound.
`mdb-destination`	[Required] Message-driven bean destination.
`resource-env-ref-name`	[Required] Resource `env` from EJB view provided by the bean developer.
`@jrun.resource-ref`	Describes a mapping between the resource name the bean developer provides and its JNDI name. The deployer provides the actual JNDI name.
`jndi-name`	[Required] JNDI name where the bean or resource will be bound.

Table C.25   **Class-level JRun tags** *(continued)*

Class-level tag/Attributes	Description
password	[Required] User credentials to be used with the `user` element to identify and authenticate a specified resource.
resource-ref-name	[Required] Name of a resource from EJB view provided by the bean developer.
user	[Required] User identity to be used with a specified resource.
@jrun.server-session-pool	Describes a JMS server session pool of the message-driven bean containers.
max-lap-size	Maximum overlap size for server session pools in the MDB container.
maximum-size	Maximum size of the server session pool.
minimum-size	Minimum size of the server session pool.
@jrun.timeout	Specifies the timeout value, in seconds, of a stateful session bean. The bean will be passivated if left idle for this duration. This tag has no attributes. Specify the value on the tag itself.
@jrun.tx-domain	Gives the transaction domain name in which the bean's transactions will take place. This tag has no attributes. Specify the value on the tag itself.

Table C.26   **Method-level JRun tags**

Method-level tag/Attributes	Description
@jrun.jdbc-mapping	Defines the SQL used to create, load, store, find, and remove CMP entity beans.
action	SQL used in the JDBC `mapping` statement.
name	Name of the JDBC `mapping` statement.
source	JNDI name of the datasource to be used to execute this JDBC mapping statement.
@jrun.jdbc-mapping-field	Name of a JDBC mapping field. This tag has no attributes—the value is placed on the tag itself.
@jrun.jdbc-mapping-param	Defines a JDBC mapping parameter.
name	Name of the JDBC mapping parameter.
type	Type of the JDBC mapping parameter.

Solarmetric's Kodo tags

Table C.27   Class-level Kodo tags

Class-level tag/Attributes	Description
`@kodo.table`	Gives access to the Kodo extensions at the class level to be included in the generated JDO metadata file.
class-column	Class name of the object represented by each table row. The column must be a string type and must be large enough to hold the full class name of any persistent class mapped to the table. It must not be mapped to any fields of the class. If the extension isn't present, Kodo JDO adds its own class column, usually named JDOCLASSX. If the table's corresponding persistent class has no persistent subclasses and you don't want a column to be generated, specify a value of none.
lock-column	Column used to record the version number of objects. Versioning is used to detect concurrent modification of objects during optimistic transactions. The given column must be of a numeric type and must not be mapped to any fields of the class. If the extension isn't present, Kodo JDO adds its own lock column, usually named JDOLOCKX. You can prevent the creation of a lock column by specifying a value of none. In this case, concurrent modification violations will not be detected.
pk-column	Primary key column for the table in which the class is held. Only for classes using datastore identity. This column must be of a numeric type and must not be mapped to any fields of the class. If the pk-column extension isn't specified, Kodo adds its own primary key column, usually named JDOIDX.

Table C.28   Method-level Kodo tags

Method-level tag/Attributes	Description
`@kodo.field`	Specifies JDO metadata specific to Solarmetric's Kodo implementation of JDO.
blob	Specifies that a field is to be persisted as a blob type. Valid values: true, false.
column-index	Specifies whether the database column for this field should be indexed. Valid values: true, false.

Table C.28   Method-level Kodo tags *(continued)*

Method-level tag/Attributes	Description
column-length	For `String` fields, specifies the maximum length of the `String` that will be stored in the database. The default maximum is 255 characters. A value of -1 indicates that there should be no limit on a `String` field's length.
ordered	For collection and array fields, specifies whether the ordering of elements of the array or collection should be preserved. Can't be used for one-to-many relations or shared many-to-many relations. Valid values: true, false.
order-column	For collection fields that also have the `ordered` attribute set to true, specifies the column of the secondary table used to hold ordering information. The ordering column must be of a numeric type. If `ordered` is true, but `order-column` isn't set, then Kodo will create its own order column.
read-only	For one-to-one relationships, marks which class doesn't own the field in its table and thus has a read-only view of the data. For collection fields that represent a many-to-many relationship, this attribute marks one side of the relationship as read-only to avoid duplicate inserts into the shared table. Valid values: true, false.

MockObject tags

Table C.29   Class-level MockObject tags

Class-level tag/Attributes	Description
@mock.generate	Specifies that the class should have a mock class created for it.
className	Name of the class to create.

i18n message bundle tags

Table C.30   Class-level i18n tag

Class-level tag/Attributes	Description
@msg.bundle	Used on the class level to customize generation of message bundles and translator classes.

MVCSoft Persistence Manager tags

Table C.31 Class-level MVCSoft tags

Class-level tag/Attributes	Description
`@mvcsoft.entity`	Sets various configuration options that apply to the entity as a whole.
`cache`	[Required] Sets how entity data is synchronized with the database. Valid choices: CommitOptionA and CommitOptionBC.
`data-expires`	[Required] Time-out value for `CommitOptionA` and read-only caches. Default: no expiration.
`delete`	[Required] Determines when an entity is deleted from the database. Valid choices: AtRemove and AtTransactionCompletion.
`insert`	[Required] Determines when a new entity is inserted into the database. Valid choices: AfterCreate, AfterPostCreate, and AtTransactionCompletion.
`lock-col-name`	[Required] Database column name for the implementation of the Counter and Timestamp locking strategies.
`lock-col-sql-type`	[Required] Database column type for the implementation of the Counter and Timestamp locking strategies.
`locking-strategy`	[Required] Locking strategy for concurrent entity access. Valid choices: None, Pessimistic, Counter, Timestamp, and FieldComparison.
`table`	[Required] Name of the table to which the entity is persisted.
`@mvcsoft.fault-group`	Configures *fault groups*, which are named groups of fields that are loaded as a unit for an EJB-QL query or on demand.
`fields`	[Required] Comma-separated list of fields in the entity that are members of the named fault group.
`name`	[Required] Name of the fault group.
`nested`	[Required] A semicolon-separated list of related fields in the form `cmr1.cmr2.cmr3:field1,field2,field3`.

Table C.31   Class-level MVCSoft tags *(continued)*

Class-level tag/Attributes	Description
`@mvcsoft.high-low-key`	Configures the MVCSoft Persistence Manager to automatically and efficiently provide a sequence value for a specified primary key field. (This strategy is also known as *sequence blocks*.) This strategy requires a database table to hold the value for the next block of sequence numbers.
`chunk-size`	[Required] Number of sequences retrieved in a single database access. Setting this to a high value reduces database I/O (at the negligible cost of potentially wasted sequence numbers).
`key-field`	[Required] Name of the primary key field that should be configured with a sequence value when the entity is created, or the special string *Unknown Key* for the case of an unknown primary key.
`non-transactional-pool-name`	[Required] JNDI name of a datasource that will provide a `Connection` that doesn't participate in the current transaction.
`retry-count`	[Required] Determines the number of retries in case of an optimistic rollback (sequence numbers are retrieved using optimistic concurrency).
`sequence-name`	[Required] Name that identifies a particular sequence. (Sequences may be reused across entity bean types if desired.)
`sequence-name-column`	[Required] Name of the column that holds the sequence name information.
`sequence-name-sql-type`	[Required] SQL type for the column that holds the sequence name information.
`table-name`	[Required] Name of the database table in which sequence values are stored.
`value-column`	[Required] Name of the column that holds the last-used sequence number.
`value-sql-type`	[Required] SQL type for the column that holds the last-used sequence number.
`@mvcsoft.query`	Configures finder and `ejbSelect` methods for the fields that should be eagerly loaded within the transaction, whether the transaction data should be flushed before executing, and the sort order of the returned results.
`fault-group`	[Required] Name of the fault group that indicates which fields should be loaded when the query is executed.

Table C.31 Class-level MVCSoft tags *(continued)*

Class-level tag/Attributes	Description
lightweight	Specifies whether the returned interfaces from an ejbSelect query are lightweight interfaces that bypass the J2EE stack. Note that finder methods can't be configured to return lightweight values.
name	[Required] Name of the finder or ejbSelect method.
should-flush	[Required] The EJB 2.0 specification mandates that changes within a transaction be visible to queries issued within that transaction. The MVC-Soft Persistence Manager meets this requirement by flushing all pending changes to the database before issuing the query. It may be that the results of a particular query will never depend on these changes, in which case you can set should-flush to false.
sort-order	[Required] Comma-separated list of fields in the entity by which to sort the query. Optionally, asc or desc may be specified after the field name to indicate the direction of the sort. There can't be any spaces between fields on which to sort. In other words, *sort-order=id, value desc* will not work, but *sort-order=id,value desc* will.
@mvcsoft.unknown-key	Configures the MVCSoft Persistence Manager for the case of an unknown primary key. You must also specify a UUID key configuration or a high-low-key configuration to provide a value for the unknown primary key at runtime.
col-name	[Required] Column name of the key in the entity database table.
java-type	[Required] Java class to be used to represent the unknown primary key at runtime. This should be compatible with the UUID or high-low strategy you choose for generating the value of this key.
jdbc-type	[Required] JDBC type of the unknown key. This should be a constant from the java.sql.Types class.
sql-type	[Required] SQL type for the column of the key in the entity database table.

Table C.31 Class-level MVCSoft tags *(continued)*

Class-level tag/Attributes	Description
`@mvcsoft.uuid-key`	Configures the MVCSoft Persistence Manager to provide a universally unique identifier value (of type `String` or `BigInteger`) for a specified primary key field. The components of this UUID are specified by indicating the source of a value (such as counter, IP address, or class hash code) and the number of bytes for that value.
`classhash`	[Required] Number of bytes from a hash of the container class that should be included in the UUID.
`classstarttime`	[Required] Number of bytes from the container start time that should be included in the UUID.
`counter`	[Required] Number of bytes from a counter that should be included in the UUID.
`field-type`	[Required] Type of UUID created. Valid values: String and BigInteger.
`ipaddress`	[Required] Number of bytes from the IP address that should be included in the UUID.
`key-field`	[Required] Name of the primary key field that should be configured with a UUID value when the entity is created, or the special string Unknown Key for the case of an unknown primary key.
`timestamp`	[Required] Number of bytes from a timestamp that should be included in the UUID.

Table C.32 Method-level MVCSoft tags

Method-level tag/Attributes	Description
`@mvcsoft.col-name`	Column name for the field in the table where this bean will be persisted.
`type`	[Required] Name of the column for the field.
`@mvcsoft.custom-conversion-object`	Defines a custom conversion object.
`bean-to-db-method`	Name of the method used to convert a bean into a database row.
`class`	Class used to convert beans to and from the database.
`db-to-bean-method`	Name of the method used to convert a database row into a bean.

Table C.32 Method-level MVCSoft tags *(continued)*

Method-level tag/Attributes	Description
`@mvcsoft.exclude-from-optimistic-lock`	Indicates that the field shouldn't be used in field-based comparisons for optimistic locking. This tag has no attributes—its presence indicates that the field should be excluded from optimistic locking.
`@mvcsoft.jdbc-type`	JDBC type for the column where this field will be persisted. See the javadoc for `java.sql.Types` for a list of valid types.
type	[Required] JDBC type of the field. Example: VARCHAR.
`@mvcsoft.lightweight`	Indicates that a CMR field should return lightweight local interfaces. This tag has no attributes—its presence indicates that the field should return lightweight local interfaces.
`@mvcsoft.relation`	Defines MVCSoft-specific relationship attributes.
key-aliases	[Required] Names of the database columns that persistently store a relationship. These names are mapped to entity primary key fields by a simple comma-separated list in the format key=alias,key=alias. For a table-mapped relationship, both participants can have aliases, so the format is role1:key=alias,key=alias;role2:key=alias,key=alias.
map-style	[Required] Valid values: foreign-key and table.
relationship-in-pk	[Required] Indicates that the foreign keys for the relationship are also components of the primary key for the entity. (For foreign-key mapped relationships only.)
role-with-key	[Required] Indicates the side of the relationship where the foreign keys are located. (For foreign-key mapped relationships only.) The source entity of that role has those keys in its table. (In a one-one relationship, either role can be chosen. In a one-many relationship, the entity in the many role must have the keys.)
table-name	Name of the relationship table.
`@mvcsoft.sql-type`	SQL type for the column where this field will be persisted.
type	[Required] Name of the SQL type for the field.

Table C.32   Method-level MVCSoft tags *(continued)*

Method-level tag/Attributes	Description
`@mvcsoft.wrap`	Indicates that the method is a wrapper for a query. (Wrapper methods allow the bean developer to efficiently retrieve subsets of query results.)
query-name	[Required] Name of the associated finder or `ejbSelect` query.

MX4J tags

Table C.33   Class-level MX4J tags

Class-level tag/Attributes	Description
`@mx4j.description`	Specifies a superclass for the MBean descriptor class generated by the `<mx4jdescription>` subtask.
extends	Superclass for the MBean descriptor class. Default: mx4j.MbeanDescriptionAdapter.

Oracle Application Server tags

Table C.34   Class-level Oracle AS tags

Class-level tag/Attributes	Description
`@oc4j.bean`	All parameters of `<session-deployment/>`, `<entity-deployment/>` and `<message-driven-deployment/>` are placed under this class-level tag.
cache-timeout	Number of seconds before a cached instance can be timed out. Can be set to never to never time out or to 0 (zero) to never cache. Default: 60. Applicable to message-driven beans.
call-timeout	Time (`long` milliseconds in hex) to wait for an EJB if it's busy (before throwing a `RemoteException`, treating it as a deadlock). 0 equals forever and is the default. Applicable to session and entity beans.
clustering-schema	[Required] Name of the datasource used if you're using container-managed persistence. Applicable to entity beans.
connection-factory-location	[Required] JNDI location of the connection factory to use. Applicable to message-driven beans.

Table C.34   Class-level Oracle AS tags *(continued)*

Class-level tag/Attributes	Description
`copy-by-value`	Specifies whether to copy (clone) all the incoming/ outgoing parameters in EJB calls. Set this to false if you're certain your application doesn't assume copy-by-value semantics for a speed-up. Default: true. Applicable to session and entity beans.
`data-source`	[Required] Name of the datasource used if you're using container-managed persistence. Applicable to entity beans.
`delay-updates-until-commit`	Specifies that all updates should be delayed until commit. Valid values: true, false. Default: true.
`destination-location`	[Required] JNDI location of the destination (queue/ topic) to use. Applicable to message-driven beans.
`disable-wrapper-cache`	Specifies whether the wrapper cache should be disabled. Valid values: true, false. Default: false.
`do-select-before-insert`	Specifies that a select should be performed prior to insert to ensure that the insert will be unique.
`exclusive-write-access`	Specifies whether the EJB-server has exclusive write (update) access to the database backend. If it does, it will speed up common bean operations and enable better caching. Default: true. Applicable to entity beans.
`instance-cache-timeout`	Amount of time in seconds that an entity is to be kept in the instance (assigned to an identity) state. Specifying never retains the entities forever. Default: 60. Applicable to entity beans.
`isolation`	Isolation level for database actions. Applicable to entity beans. Valid values: serializable, uncommitted, committed, repeatable_read. Default: serializable.
`jndi-name`	JNDI name of the bean.
`listener-threads`	Listener threads for a message-driven bean.
`locking-mode`	Locking mode used when updating an entity bean's persistence. Valid values: pessimistic, optimistic, read-only, old_pessimistic.
`max-instances`	Number of maximum instances to be kept instantiated or pooled. Default: infinite. Applicable to entity beans.
`max-instances-per-pk`	Maximum number of entity bean wrapper instances allowed in its pool for a given primary key.

Table C.34 Class-level Oracle AS tags *(continued)*

Class-level tag/Attributes	Description
`max-tx-retries`	Number of times to retry a transaction that was rolled back due to system-level failures. Default: 0 (no retries). Applicable to session and entity beans.
`min-instances`	Minimum number of bean instances to instantiate. The set amount will be instantiated at startup, and there will always be at least the set amount of instances active. Default: 0 (none). Applicable to message-driven beans.
`min-instances-per-pk`	Minimum number of entity bean wrapper instances allowed in its pool for a given primary key.
`persistence-filename`	Path to the file where sessions are stored across restarts. Applicable to session beans.
`pool-cache-timeout`	Amount of time in seconds that an entity is to be kept in the pooled (unassigned) state. Specifying never retains the entities forever. Default: 60. Applicable to entity beans.
`subscription-name`	Subscription name of a message-driven bean.
`table`	[Required] Name of the table in the database if you're using container-managed persistence. Applicable to entity beans.
`timeout`	Inactivity timeout in seconds. If the value is zero or negative, timeouts are disabled. Applicable to session beans.
`transaction-timeout`	Transaction timeout of a message-driven bean.
`update-changed-fields-only`	If true, specifies that only changed fields should be included in SQL UPDATEs for an entity EJB. Valid values: true, false. Default: true.
`validity-timeout`	Maximum amount of time (in milliseconds) that an entity is valid in the cache (before being reloaded). Useful for loosely coupled environments where rare updates from legacy systems occur. This attribute is valid only when `exclusive-write-access=true` (the default). Applicable to entity beans.

Table C.35 Method-level Oracle AS tags

Method-level tag/Attributes	Description
`@oc4j.field-persistence-manager`	Marks a method as being a method of a custom persistence manager.
class	This tag doesn't seem to be used, but must be set in order for the method to be marked as a custom persistence manager method.
`@oc4j.field-persistence-manager-property`	If `@oc4j.persistence field-persistence-manager` is specified and there are some properties for the persistence manager, specify one or more `@oc4j.field-persistence-manager-property` tags for the persistent field.
name	[Required] Name of the property.
value	[Required] Value of the property.
`@oc4j.persistence`	Specifies Orion-specific persistence mechanisms, such as persisting primitive collections.
ejb-class-name	EJB class name.
field-persistence-manager	Fully qualified class name of a custom persistence handler for a CMP-field.
immutable	Specifies whether the field is immutable. Valid values: true, false.
persistence-name	Name of the column for single column fields or the name of the second column in the table specified in table-name.
persistence-type	Persistence type of a CMP field.
sql-type	SQL type of the persistent field.
table-name	Name of the second table to use if the field is a collection.

Orion Application Server EJB tags

Table C.36 Class-level Orion tags

Class-level tag/Attributes	Description
`@orion.bean`	All parameters of `<session-deployment/>`, `<entity-deployment/>`, and `<message-driven-deployment/>` are placed under this class-level tag.

Table C.36 Class-level Orion tags *(continued)*

Class-level tag/Attributes	Description
cache-timeout	Number of seconds before a cached instance can be timed out. Can be set to never to never time out or to 0 (zero) to never cache. Default: 60. Applicable to message-driven beans.
call-timeout	Time (long milliseconds in hex) to wait for an EJB if it's busy (before throwing a RemoteException, treating it as a deadlock). 0 equals forever and is the default. Applicable to session and entity beans.
clustering-schema	[Required] Name of the datasource used if you're using container-managed persistence. Applicable to entity beans.
connection-factory-location	[Required] JNDI location of the connection factory to use. Applicable to message-driven beans.
copy-by-value	Specifies whether to copy (clone) all the incoming/outgoing parameters in EJB calls. Set this to false if you're certain your application doesn't assume copy-by-value semantics for a speed-up. Default: true. Applicable to session and entity beans.
data-source	[Required] Name of the datasource used if you're using container-managed persistence. Applicable to entity beans.
destination-location	[Required] JNDI location of the destination (queue/topic) to use. Applicable to message-driven beans.
exclusive-write-access	Specifies whether the EJB-server has exclusive write (update) access to the database backend. If it does, it will speed up common bean operations and enable better caching. Default: true. Applicable to entity beans.
instance-cache-timeout	Amount of time in seconds that an entity is to be kept in the instance (assigned to an identity) state. Specifying never retains the entities forever. Default: 60. Applicable to entity beans.
isolation	Isolation level for database actions. Applicable to entity beans. Valid values: serializable, uncommitted, committed, repeatable_read. Default: serializable.
max-instances	Number of maximum instances to be kept instantiated or pooled. Default: infinite. Applicable to entity beans.
max-tx-retries	Number of times to retry a transaction that was rolled back due to system-level failures. Default: 0 (no retries). Applicable to session and entity beans.

Table C.36 Class-level Orion tags *(continued)*

Class-level tag/Attributes	Description
`min-instances`	Minimum number of bean instances to instantiate. The set amount will be instantiated at startup, and there will always be at least the set amount of instances active. Default: 0 (none). Applicable to message-driven beans.
`persistence-filename`	Path to the file where sessions are stored across restarts. Applicable to session beans.
`pool-cache-timeout`	Amount of time in seconds that an entity is to be kept in the pooled (unassigned) state. Specifying never retains the entities forever. Default: 60. Applicable to entity beans.
`table`	[Required] Name of the table in the database if you're using container-managed persistence. Applicable to entity beans.
`timeout`	Inactivity timeout in seconds. If the value is zero or negative, timeouts are disabled. Applicable to session beans.
`validity-timeout`	Maximum amount of time (in milliseconds) that an entity is valid in the cache (before being reloaded). Useful for loosely coupled environments where rare updates from legacy systems occur. This attribute is valid only when `exclusive-write-access=true` (the default). Applicable to entity beans.

Table C.37 Method-level Orion tags

Method-level tag/Attributes	Description
`@orion.field-persistence-manager-param`	Tags a method as being a method of a custom persistence manager.
`@orion.field-persistence-manager-property`	If `@orion.persistence field-persistence-manager` is specified and there are some properties for the persistence manager, specifies it as one or more `@orion.field-persistence-manager-property` tags for the persistent field.
`name`	[Required] Name of the property.
`value`	[Required] Value of the property.

Table C.37 Method-level Orion tags *(continued)*

Method-level tag/Attributes	Description
`@orion.persistence`	Specifies Orion-specific persistence mechanisms, such as persisting primitive collections.
`ejb-class-name`	EJB class name.
`field-persistence-manager`	Fully qualified class name of a custom persistence handler for a CMP field.
`immutable`	Specifies whether the field is immutable. Valid values: true, false.
`persistence-name`	Name of the column for single column fields or the name of the second column in the table specified in table-name.
`sql-type`	SQL type of the persistent field.
`table-name`	Name of the second table to use if the field is a collection.

Portlet tags

Table C.38 Class-level portlet tags

Class-level tag/Attributes	Description
`@portlet.portlet`	Defines a portlet class.
`description`	Description for the portlet.
`display-name`	Display name for the portlet.
`expiration-cache`	Time (in seconds) to retain the portlet's output in cache. Defaults to –1, indicating no caching.
`name`	Name of the portlet.
`@portlet.portlet-init-param`	Sets a portlet initialization parameter.
`description`	Description of the initialization parameter.
`name`	Name of the initialization parameter.
`value`	Value of the initialization parameter.
`@portlet.portlet-info`	Defines additional portlet information.
`keywords`	Comma-separated list of keywords for this portlet.
`short-title`	An abbreviated title for the portlet.
`title`	Portlet's title.

Table C.38 **Class-level portlet tags** *(continued)*

Class-level tag/Attributes	Description
@portlet.preference	Defines a portlet preference.
name	Name of the preference.
read-only	Valid values: true, false. If true, the preference may not be overridden by the user. Default: false.
value	Value of the preference. If read-only is false, the portlet user may override this value.
@portlet.preferences-validator	Defines a preferences validator for this portlet.
class	Fully qualified name of a class that implements javax.portlet.PreferencesValidator.
@portlet.security-role-ref	Defines a security role reference with the name role-name to a security role link named role-link.
description	Description of the security role reference.
role-link	Name of the role link.
role-name	Name of the role reference.
@portlet.supports	Specifies the mime-types and modes supported by the portlet.
mime-type	Valid mime-type (such as text/html).
modes	Comma-separated list of modes supported by the mime-type. The VIEW mode is a given, so only specify modes that are in addition to VIEW.

Pramati Server tags

Table C.39 **Class-level Pramati tags**

Class-level tag/Attributes	Description
@pramati.bean	Defines Pramati-specific metadata for an EJB.
is-secure	Specifies whether access to the bean is secure. Valid values: true, false.
low-activity-interval	Low activity interval for the pools.
max-pool-size	Maximum pool size.
min-pool-size	Minimum pool size.
run-as-principal	Run-as principal used to invoke methods on the EJB.

Table C.39   Class-level Pramati tags *(continued)*

Class-level tag/Attributes	Description
`session-timeout`	Specifies how long an idle session survives before timing out.
`@pramati.destination-mapping`	Provides external mapping information related to the external JMS server for message-driven bean destinations.
`conn-factory`	External connection factory.
`destination-link`	External destination (queue or topic).
`@pramati.ejb-local-ref`	Defines a local EJB reference.
`ejb-link`	EJB local name.
`ejb-ref-name`	Name of the EJB reference.
`@pramati.ejb-ref`	Defines an EJB reference.
`ejb-link`	JNDI name of the EJB.
`ejb-ref-name`	Name of the EJB reference.
`@pramati.persistence`	Indicates whether the EJB has exclusive access and updates to the EJB's table.
`exclusion-type`	Exclusion type. Valid values: exclusive, non-exclusive. exclusive indicates that the table belongs exclusively to the EJB, so the container can make optimizations based on the assumption that no other source will ever modify the table. non-exclusive indicates that the table can be accessed by means other than the EJB. Default: exclusive.
`@pramati.resource-env-ref`	Defines an environment resource reference.
`resource-env-ref-link`	Reference link.
`resource-env-ref-name`	Reference name.
`resource-env-ref-type`	Type of the reference.
`@pramati.resource-mapping`	Defines a mapping of a logical resource name to a resource on the server.
`resource-link`	Resource link.
`resource-name`	Resource name.
`resource-type`	Resource type.
`@pramati.server-session`	Defines server session pool details for a message-driven bean.
`max-messages`	Maximum messages for the server session.

Table C.39 Class-level Pramati tags *(continued)*

Class-level tag/Attributes	Description
max-pool-size	Maximum pool size.
min-pool-size	Minimum pool size.
@pramati.thread-pool	Defines specifics of the thread pool used for a message-driven bean.
max-pool-size	Maximum thread pool size.
min-pool-size	Minimum thread pool size.

Resin tags

Table C.40 Class-level Resin tags

Class-level tag/Attributes	Description
@resin.access-log	Configures the Resin web access log.
archive-format	Archive format.
class-name	Specifies a class that implements AbstractAccessLog for custom logging.
format	Format of the log messages.
id	[Required] Access log path.
rollover-period	Specifies how often the access log should be rolled over.
rollover-size	Specifies how large the access log can get before it rolls over.
@resin.auth-constraint	Defines an authorization security constraint.
description	Description of the constraint.
role-name	Role name to which authorization is granted.
@resin.browser-mapping	Defines a browser mapping.
force10	If set, forces HTTP/1.0.
regexp	Regular expression used to match the User-Agent.
@resincache-mapping	Defines a web cache mapping.
expires	Expiration of the cache.
url-pattern	URL pattern for pages that are to be cached.

Table C.40 Class-level Resin tags *(continued)*

Class-level tag/Attributes	Description
`url-regexp`	Regular expression to match URLs that are to be cached.
`@resin.chain-mapping`	Defines a servlet filter to transform the output of another servlet based on mime-type.
`mime-type`	Mime-type to match.
`servlet-name`	Name of the servlet to match.
`@resin.classpath`	Adds entries to the application-specific classpath.
`args`	Sets additional arguments to `javac` when auto-compiling.
`compile`	Enables automatic compilation of Java source code. Valid values: true, false. Default: true.
`encoding`	Character encoding to use when compiling.
`id`	Path to the directory that will contain compiled code.
`library-dir`	Location of a library directory, such as `WEB-INF/ lib`.
`source`	Sets an optional Java source code directory.
`@resin.context-param`	Sets a servlet context parameter.
`description`	Description of the parameter.
`param-name`	Name of the parameter.
`param-value`	Value of the parameter.
`@resin.error-log`	Configures the web error log.
`encoding`	Character encoding of the error log file.
`href`	File name of the log file.
`rollover-period`	Specifies how often the access log should be rolled over.
`rollover-size`	Specifies how large the access log can get before it rolls over.
`timestamp`	Specifies a format for a timestamp before each log entry.
`@resin.error-page`	Defines a page to display if the current request fails.
`error-code`	HTTP status code that triggers display of this error page.

Table C.40   Class-level Resin tags *(continued)*

Class-level tag/Attributes	Description
`exception-type`	Java exception that triggers display of this error page.
`location`	Error page to display.
@resin.form-login-config	Sets up pages for user authentication.
`form-error-page`	Error page for failed user authentication.
`form-login-page`	Login form page for user authentication.
@resin.ip-constraint	Restricts a web resource to a specific IP address.
`ip`	Authorized IP address.
@resin.jdbc-store	Configures sessions to use a JDBC backing store. The database must be specified using `@web.resource-ref`.
`blob-type`	Database type for a blob.
`data-source`	Datasource name for the table session table.
`session-timeout`	Lifespan of a session before it's cleaned up from the database.
`table-name`	Database table name for session data.
`timestamp-type`	Database type for a timestamp.
@resin.jsp	JSP configuration.
`auto-compile`	If set to false, changes in JSP files aren't auto-compiled. Valid values: true, false. Default: true.
`disable-init-log`	If true, JSP initialization and destroy aren't logged. Valid values: true, false. Default: false.
`jsp-max`	Limits the number of active JSP pages. Default: 1024
`jsp-update-interval`	Defines how often JSP files should be changed for changes. Default: the value of the `classUpdateInterval` attribute of `<resinwebxml>`.
`precompile`	Specifies whether to use precompiled JSP classes, if available. Valid values: true, false. Default: true.
`recompile-on-error`	If true, recompiles a JSP page if `java.lang.Error` is thrown. Valid values: true, false. Default: false.

Table C.40   Class-level Resin tags *(continued)*

Class-level tag/Attributes	Description
`recycle-tags`	Specifies whether tags should be recycled. Valid values: true, false. Default: true.
`require-source`	If true, Resin should check to see if the `*.jsp` file is still available (whether it's been deleted.) even if the precompiled JSP class is available. Valid values: true, false. Default: false.
`session`	Specifies whether sessions are enabled. Valid values: true, false. Default: true.
`static-encoding`	Specifies that character encoding can be precompiled. Valid values: true, false. Default: true.
`velocity`	Specifies that Velocity-style syntax is enabled. Valid values: true, false. Default: false.
`@resin.login-config`	Configures user authentication.
`auth-method`	Authentication method.
`realm-name`	Realm name.
`@resin.mime-mapping`	Defines a MIME mapping.
`extension`	Filename extension.
`mime-type`	MIME type.
`@resin.multipart-form`	Configures multipart upload capability.
`enable`	Specifies whether multipart forms are enabled.
`upload-max`	Maximum amount that can be uploaded.
`@resin.path-mapping`	Maps URLs to real paths.
`real-path`	Prefix of the real path. When used with `url-regexp`, you can use substitution variables such as $1.
`url-pattern`	Pattern to match the URL.
`url-regexp`	Regular expression to match the URL.
`@resin.security-constraint`	Used with `auth-constraint`, `ip-constraint`, and `user-data-constraint` to specify a display name for the security constraint.
`display-name`	Display name of the security constraint.

Table C.40 Class-level Resin tags *(continued)*

Class-level tag/Attributes	Description
@resin.session-config	Session configuration.
always-load-session	Specifies that session data should be reloaded from the datastore on every request. Valid values: true, false. Default: false.
always-save-session	Specifies that session data should be saved to the datastore on every request. Valid values: true, false. Default: false.
cookie-domain	Domain for session cookies.
cookie-length	Maximum length of the session cookie.
cookie-max-age	Maximum age for persistent session cookies. Default: `Integer.MAX_VALUE`.
cookie-version	Version of the cookie specification used for session cookies. Default: 1.0.
enable-cookies	Specifies whether cookies are enabled for sessions. Valid values: true, false. Default: true.
enable-url-rewriting	Specifies whether URL rewriting is enabled for sessions. Valid values: true, false. Default: true.
file-store	Specifies the use of a file store for persistence sessions.
ignore-serialization-errors	If true, ignores any values that don't implement `java.io.Serializable` when persisting a session. Valid values: true, false. Default: false.
reuse-session-id	Specifies whether a session ID can be reused, even if the session has timed out. Valid values: true, false. Default: true.
save-on-shutdown	If true, saves a session only when the application shuts down. Valid values: true, false. Default: false.
session-max	Maximum number of active sessions. Default: 4096.
session-timeout	Session timeout in minutes. Default: 30.
tcp-store	Specifies the use a distributed ring for persistent sessions.
@resin.stderr-log	Configures `STDERR` logging.
encoding	Character encoding of the log file.
href	Location of the log file.
rollover-period	Specifics how often the log is rotated.

Table C.40 Class-level Resin tags *(continued)*

Class-level tag/Attributes	Description
`rollover-size`	Specifies how large the log can get before it's rotated.
`timestamp`	Timestamp format before each log entry.
@resin.stdout-log	Configures STDOUT logging.
`href`	Location of the log file.
`rollover-period`	Specifies how often the access log should be rolled over.
`rollover-size`	Specifies how large the access log can get before it rolls over.
`timestamp`	Timestamp format before each log entry.
@resin.taglib	Describes a JSP tag library.
`taglib-location`	Location (as a resource relative to the root of the web application) where you can find the TLD file for the tag library.
`taglib-uri`	URI, relative to the location of the web.xml document, identifying a tag library used in the web application.
@resin.user-data-constraint	Indicates how data communicated between the client and container should be protected.
`description`	Description of the constraint.
`transport-guarantee`	Transport guarantee between the client and server. Valid values: NONE, INTEGRAL, CONFIDENTIAL. NONE indicates that the application doesn't require a transport guarantee. INTEGRAL indicates that data be sent between the client and server in such a way that it can't be changed in transit. CONFIDENTIAL indicates that the data be transmitted in a fashion that prevents other entities from observing the contents of the transmission.
@resin.web-resource-collection	Identifies a subset of the resources and HTTP methods on those resources within a web application to which a security constraint applies.
`description`	Description of the resource collection.
`http-method`	HTTP method to which the constraint applies. If not specified, it applies to all HTTP methods.
`url-pattern`	URL pattern of resources to which the constraint applies.

Table C.40 Class-level Resin tags *(continued)*

Class-level tag/Attributes	Description
web-resource-name	Name of the web resource to which the constraint applies.
@resin-ejb.entity-bean	Declares a Resin CMP entity bean. Requires @ejb.bean.
cache-size	Bean cache size.
cache-timeout	Bean cache timeout; default unit is second(s) if none specified.
data-source	Entity datasource.
sql-table	Database table for this entity.
@resin-ejb.entity-method	Business method configuration.
query-loads-bean	Specifies that a find or select query loads the bean rather than just the primary key. Valid values: true, false. Default: false.
resin-isolation	Caching hint for Resin. Valid values: read-only, database.
signature	Java method signature or * (for general case); mandatory at the class level.

Table C.41 Method-level Resin tags

Method-level tag/Attributes	Description
@resin-ejb.cmp-field	Specifies database column properties of a persistent field. Requires @ejb.persistent-field.
abstract-sql-type	java.sql.Types column type that's matched with the driver type map to determine the physical column type during table generation.
sql-column	Database column name.
sql-type	SQL column type used during table generation.
@resin-ejb.entity-method	Business method configuration.
query-loads-bean	Specifies that a find or select query will load the bean rather than just the primary key. Valid values: true, false. Default: false.
resin-isolation	Caching hint for Resin. Valid values: read-only, database.

Table C.41 Method-level Resin tags *(continued)*

Method-level tag/Attributes	Description
`@resin-ejb.relation`	Database configuration for persistent relations. Requires `@ejb.relation`.
order-by	Persistent field name for ordering collections in 1-n relationships (only).
sql-column	Database column.
sql-table	Database table for n-m relationships (only).

Jakarta Struts tags

Table C.42 Class-level Struts tags

Class-level tag/Attributes	Description
`@struts.action`	Defines an `Action` class and its attributes.
attribute	Name of the request-scope or session-scope attribute used to access the `ActionForm` bean, if it's different than the `name` attribute.
className	Fully qualified Java class name of the `ActionForward` subclass to use for this object.
contextRelative	Set to true if, in a modular application, the `path` attribute starts with a slash (/) and should be considered relative to the entire web application rather than the module. Valid values: true, false. Default: false.
input	Module-relative path of the action or other resource to which control should be returned if a validation error is encountered.
name	[Required] Name of the action. Must be unique within the bounds of the Struts application.
parameter	[Required] Optional parameter for the action.
path	[Required] Path the action will match.
prefix	Prefix used to match request parameter names to `ActionForm` property names.
roles	Comma-delimited list of security role names that are allowed access to this `ActionMapping` object. Since Struts 1.1.
scope	[Required] Scope of the action. Valid values: request, session, application. Default: request.

Table C.42   Class-level Struts tags *(continued)*

Class-level tag/Attributes	Description
suffix	Suffix used to match request parameter names to ActionForm property names.
unknown	Set to true if this object should be configured as the default action mapping for this module.
validate	[Required] Validation flag for the action.
@struts.action-exception	Defines the action-specific exception handling.
className	Configuration bean for this `ExceptionHandler` object. If specified, `className` must be a subclass of the default configuration bean.
handler	Fully qualified Java class name for this exception handler.
key	[Required] Key to use with this handler's message resource bundle that will retrieve the error message template for this exception.
path	Module-relative URI to the resource that will complete the request/response if this exception occurs.
scope	Context (request or session) used to access the `ActionError` object (`org.apache.struts.action.ActionError`) for this exception.
type	[Required] Fully qualified Java class name of the exception type to register with this handler.
@struts.action-forward	Defines local forwards for a Struts action class.
name	[Required] Name of the forward.
path	[Required] Path of the forward.
@struts.form	Defines a form bean and its attributes.
extends	Class the generated form must extend.
implements	Interface the generated form must implement.
include-all	Specifies whether to include all persistent fields in form. Default: false.
include-pk	Specifies whether to include primary key field in form. Default: true. If set to false, individual primary key fields can still be included.
name	[Required] Unique name for the form.

Table C.43   Method-level Struts tags

Method-level tag/Attributes	Description
@struts.form-field	Includes this property in a specific Struts form.
form-name	Name of the action form in which this field should be included. Should match the name attribute of a corresponding @struts.form tag.
@struts.validator	Defines a Struts Validator for the current setter field.
arg0resource	Resource key of argument index 0.
arg0value	Value of argument index 0.
arg1resource	Resource key of argument index 1.
arg1value	Value of argument index 1.
arg2resource	Resource key of argument index 2.
arg2value	Value of argument index 2.
arg3resource	Resource key of argument index 3.
arg3value	Value of argument index 3.
msgkey	Override key for the validator error message.
page	Specifies that only fields with a page attribute value equal to or less than the page property on the form JavaBean are processed.
type	[Required] Validator type, such as required.
@struts.validator-args	Defines arguments for the current setter field.
arg0resource	Resource key of argument index 0.
arg0value	Value of argument index 0.
arg1resource	Resource key of argument index 1.
arg1value	Value of argument index 1.
arg2resource	Resource key of argument index 2.
arg2value	Value of argument index 2.
arg3resource	Resource key of argument index 3.
arg3value	Value of argument index 3.
@struts.validator-var	Defines a Struts Validator variable.
name	[Required] Variable name.
value	[Required] Variable value.

SunONE/iPlanet tags

Table C.44   Class-level SunONE tags

Class-level tag/Attributes	Description
`@sunone.bean`	All parameters of `<session-deployment/>`, `<entity-deployment/>`, and `<message-driven-deployment/>` are placed under this class-level tag.
`cmp-mapping-properties`	[Required] Location of the persistence vendor's specific O/R database-mapping file.
`commit-option`	Optionally specifies the commit option to be used on transaction completion. Valid values: B or C (commit option A isn't supported for the SunONE Application Server 7 release). Default: B.
`destination-name`	[Required] Name of the `Queue` or the `Topic` a message-driven bean listens to.
`durable-name`	Durable name of the topic subscription.
`failover-required`	Indicates whether failover is required. Valid values: true, false.
`guid`	String that represents the globally unique ID of the EJB in question.
`iiop`	Optional element indicating if the bean is rich client enabled. Default: false.
`max-mdb-pool-size`	[Required] Maximum size of the `ServerSessionPool`.
`max-message-limit`	[Required] Maximum number of messages to load into a JMS session.
`mdb-connection-factory-password`	Password used to access a message-driven bean connection factory.
`mdb-connection-factory-user`	User used to access a message-driven bean connection factory.
`min-mdb-pool-size`	[Required] Minimum size of the `ServerSessionPool`.
`pass-by-value`	Controls use of pass-by-value/reference semantics for calls from an enterprise bean to remote interface methods in another EJB co-located in the same process. If true, pass by value is used. If false, pass by reference is used.

Table C.44   Class-level SunONE tags *(continued)*

Class-level tag/Attributes	Description
`pass-timeout`	[Required] Passivation timeout in seconds used by the container. The Administration Tool can change this value during runtime.
`read-only`	Flag specifying that this bean is read-only.
`refresh-period`	Rate at which a read-only bean must be refreshed from the datasource, in seconds. If this value is less than or equal to zero, the bean is never refreshed; if it's greater than zero, the bean instances are refreshed at the specified interval. This rate is just a hint to the container. Default: 600.
`session-timeout`	[Required] Session timeout. In seconds, according to the DTD; in minutes, according to Sun's online documentation.
`transaction-manager-type`	Transaction manager type for the component. Relevant only to version 6.5. Valid values: local, global.
`@sunone.bean-cache`	Entity bean cache properties. Used for entity beans and stateful session beans.
`cache-ide-timeout`	Optionally specifies the maximum time in seconds that a bean can remain idle in the cache. After this amount of time, the container can passivate this bean. A value of 0 specifies that beans may never become candidates for passivation. Default: 600.
`max-cache-size`	Optionally specifies the maximum number of beans allowable in cache. A value of 0 indicates an unbounded cache. In reality, there is no hard limit. The `max-cache-size` limit is just a hint to the cache implementation. Default: 512.
`removal-timeout`	Optionally specifies the amount of time in seconds a bean instance can remain idle in the container before it's removed (timeout). A value of 0 specifies that the container doesn't remove inactive beans automatically. Default: 5400. If `removal-timeout` is less than or equal to `cache-idle-timeout`, beans are removed immediately without being passivated.
`victim-selection-policy`	Optionally specifies how stateful session beans are selected for passivation. Valid values: FIFO, LRU, NRU. Default: NRU.
`@sunone.bean-pool`	Pool properties of stateless session beans, entity beans, and message-driven bean.
`max-pool-size`	Maximum number of beans in the pool. Values are from 0 to MAX_INTEGER. Default: 60.

Table C.44 Class-level SunONE tags *(continued)*

Class-level tag/Attributes	Description
`pool-idle-timeout`	Maximum time in seconds that a bean is allowed to be idle in the pool. After this time, the bean is removed. This is a hint to the server. Default: 600 seconds (10 minutes).
`resize-quantity`	Number of beans to be created if the pool is empty (subject to the `max-pool-size` limit). Values are from 0 to `MAX_INTEGER`.
`steady-pool-size`	Initial and minimum number of beans maintained in the pool. Default: 32.
@sunone.consistency	Specifies container behavior in guaranteeing transactional consistency of the data in the bean. Any one of the parameters may be used alone; `lock-when-modified` and `check-all-at-commit` can also be used together. If not present, none is assumed.
`check-all-at-commit`	Checks modified instances at commit time.
`check-modified-at-commit`	Not implemented for SunONE Application Server 7.
`lock-when-loaded`	Obtains an exclusive lock when the data is loaded.
`lock-when-modified`	Not implemented for SunONE Application Server 7.
`none`	No consistency checking occurs.
@sunone.finder	Describes the finders for CMP 1.1 with a method name and query.
`method-name`	[Required] Method name for the query field.
`query-filter`	Query filter for the CMP 1.1 finder method.
`query-params`	Optional data that specifies the query parameters for the finder method.
`query-variables`	Optional data that specifies variables in a query expression for the CMP 1.1 finder method.
@sunone.persistence-manager	Defines all the persistence manager–specific information.
`factory-class-name`	[Required] Factory class used to create new instances of a persistence manager.
`properties-file-location`	Location in a JAR file of the properties file, relative to the `METAINF/` of the JAR.

Table C.44   Class-level SunONE tags *(continued)*

Class-level tag/Attributes	Description
`@sunone.pool-manager`	Descriptor for cache pool attributes.
`commit-option`	[Required] Commit option. Valid values: COMMIT_OPTION_B, COMMIT_OPTION_C. Default: COMMIT_OPTION_C.
`free-pool-maxsize`	[Required] Maximum size of the instance free pool (in number of entries). An integer that defaults to 0. The Administration Tool can change this value during runtime.
`ready-pool-maxsize`	[Required] Maximum size of the ready cache (in number of entries). An integer that defaults to 0. The Administration Tool can change this value during runtime.
`ready-pool-timeout`	[Required] Ready pool timeout used by the container. An integer in seconds. Default: 0 (infinite). The Administration Tool can change this value during runtime.

Table C.45   Method-level SunONE tags

Method-level tag/Attributes	Description
`@sunone.fetched-with`	Specifies the fetch group configuration for fields and relationships. A field may participate in a hierarchical or independent fetch group. If the `fetched-with` element isn't present, the value none is assumed. Only one of the parameters should be specified.
`level`	Hierarchical fetch group. Fields and relationships that belong to a hierarchical fetch group of equal or lesser value are fetched at the same time. Valid values: integers greater than zero.
`named-group`	Name of an independent fetch group. All the fields and relationships that are part of a named group are fetched at the same time.
`none`	Value of true indicates that this field or relationship is fetched by itself.
`@sunone.relation`	Specifies the column pairs in the mapping of a relation. Must occur at least once, but may occur multiple times, once for each column pair.
`column`	[Required] TABLE.COLUMN for this end of the relation.

Table C.45   Method-level SunONE tags *(continued)*

Method-level tag/Attributes	Description
target	[Required] `TABLE.COLUMN` for the target end of the relation.

EAServer tags

Table C.46   Class-level EAServer tags

Class-level tag/Attributes	Description
@easerver.ejb-ref	Describes a mapping between the name of an EJB reference and the JNDI name of the referenced bean. There should be a corresponding `@ejb.ejb-ref` tag present.
ejb-ref-name	[Required] Name of an EJB reference provided by the bean developer. It should match the `ref-name` attribute of an `@ejb.ejb-ref` tag.
jaguar-link	[Required] JNDI name of the referenced EJB provided by the application assembler.
@easerver.resource-ref	Describes a mapping between the name of a resource reference and its resource. There should be a corresponding `@ejb.resource-ref` tag present.
res-link	[Required] Value of the resource provided by the application assembler. This depends on the type (`res-type`) of the resource; for example, for datasources it will be the connection cache name, and for mail sessions it will be the SMTP server name.
res-ref-name	[Required] Name of a resource provided by the bean developer. It should match the `res-ref-name` attribute of an `@ejb.resource-ref` tag.

Triactive JDO tags

Table C.47   Property-level TJDO tags

Property-level tag/Attributes	Description
@tjdo.field	Specifies JDO metadata specific to Triactive's implementation of JDO.
collection-field	Name of the `Set` field in the owner class.

Table C.47 Property-level TJDO tags *(continued)*

Property-level tag/Attributes	Description
column-length	Size limit on `String` fields. May be a specific column size (such as 80) to specify that the value must be an exact length, or a maximum length may be specified by using the max X form (such as max 80). For an unlimited size, use unlimited.
column-precision	For fields of type `java.math.BigDecimal` and `java.math.BigInteger`, specifies the precision (the total number of digits).
column-scale	For fields of type `java.math.BigDecimal` and `java.math.BigInteger`, specifies the scale (the number of digits to the right of the decimal).
element-length	Size limit on `String` elements of collection fields. May be a specific column size (such as 80) to specify that the value must be of an exact length, or a maximum length may be specified by using the max X form (such as max 80). For an unlimited size, use unlimited.
element-precision	For collection elements of type `java.math.BigDecimal` and `java.math.BigInteger`, specifies the precision (the total number of digits).
element-scale	For collection elements of type `java.math.BigDecimal` and `java.math.BigInteger`, specifies the scale (the number of digits to the right of the decimal).
key-field	For map fields, specifies the key field in the value class.
key-length	Size limit on `String Map` keys. May be a specific column size (such as 80) to specify that the value must be of an exact length, or a maximum length may be specified by using the max X form (such as max 80). For an unlimited size, use unlimited.
key-precision	For Map keys of type `java.math.BigDecimal` and `java.math.BigInteger`, specifies the precision (the total number of digits).
key-scale	For Map keys of type `java.math.BigDecimal` and `java.math.BigInteger`, specifies the scale (the number of digits to the right of the decimal).
map-field	Name of the `Map` field in the owner class.

Table C.47   Property-level TJDO tags *(continued)*

Property-level tag/Attributes	Description
owner-field	For collection fields, specifies the name of the owner field (for example, foreign-key field) in the element class of the collection. For map fields, specifies the name of the owner field in the value class.
value-length	Specifies a size limit on String Map values. May be a specific column size (such as 80) to specify that the value must be of an exact length, or a maximum length may be specified by using the max X form (such as max 80). For an unlimited size, use unlimited.
value-precision	For Map values of type java.math.BigDecimal and java.math.BigInteger, specifies the precision (the total number of digits).
value-scale	For Map values of type java.math.BigDecimal and java.math.BigInteger, specifies the scale (the number of digits to the right of the decimal).

Servlet and JSP tags

Table C.48   Class-level servlet and JSP tags

Class-level tag/Attributes	Description
@jsp.attribute	Declares the specified field to be a JSP tag attribute. This tag should be placed on getter or setter methods.
description	Optional description of the attribute.
required	[Required] Specifies whether the attribute is required.
rtexprvalue	[Required] Specifies whether the attribute is a runtime attribute.
type	[Required] Type of the attribute.
@jsp.tag	Declares the class as a class implementing a JSP tag and specifies various properties of that tag.
body-content	Body content field for the tag. Valid values: tagdependent, JSP, empty. Default: JSP.
description	[Optional] Description of the tag.
display-name	[Optional] Display name for the tag.
large-icon	[Optional] Large icon for the tag.

Table C.48   Class-level servlet and JSP tags *(continued)*

Class-level tag/Attributes	Description
`name`	[Required] Name of the JSP tag.
`small-icon`	[Optional] Small icon for the tag.
`tei-class`	Tag extra info class for the JSP tag.
`@jsp.validator-init-param`	Declares initialization parameters for the `Validator`.
`description`	[Optional] Description for the validator.
`name`	[Required] Name of the validator initialization parameter.
`value`	[Required] Value of the validator initialization parameter.
`@jsp.variable`	Declares a JSP tag variable and information on the scripting variables defined.
`class`	Name of the class of the variable. Default: java.lang.String.
`declare`	Specifies whether the variable is declared.
`description`	[Optional] Description of the variable.
`name-from-attribute`	Name of an attribute whose (translation time) value gives the name of the variable. One of `name-given` or `name-from-attribute` is required.
`name-given`	Variable name as a constant.
`scope`	Scope of the scripting variable defined. Valid values: NESTED, AT_BEGIN, AT_END.
`@web.ejb-local-ref`	Defines a local EJB reference with the specified name, type, home interface name, local interface name, link name, and description. The value of the `link` parameter must be the `ejb-name` of an enterprise bean in the same J2EE application unit.
`description`	[Optional] Description for the EJB local reference.
`home`	Home interface of the referenced EJB.
`link`	Link to the EJB.
`local`	Local interface of the referenced EJB.
`name`	Name of the EJB reference.
`type`	Expected type of the referenced enterprise bean. Valid values: Entity, Session.

Table C.48   Class-level servlet and JSP tags *(continued)*

Class-level tag/Attributes	Description
@web.ejb-ref	Defines a remote EJB reference with the specified name, type, home interface name, remote interface name, link name, and description. The value of the `link` attribute must be the `ejb-name` of an enterprise bean in the same J2EE application unit.
description	[Optional] Description for the EJB reference.
home	Home interface of the referenced EJB.
link	Link to the EJB.
name	Name or the EJB reference.
remote	Remote interface of the referenced EJB.
type	Expected type of the referenced enterprise bean. Valid values: Entity, Session.
@web.env-entry	Defines an environment entry with the specified description, name, type, and value.
description	Description of the environment entry.
name	[Required] Name of the environment entry.
type	[Required] Type of the environment entry.
value	Value of the environment entry.
@web.filter	Declares the class as a `Filter` class, with the specified name, display-name, icon, and description. Applicable to Servlet 2.3 only.
description	Description of the filter.
display-name	Display name of the filter.
icon	Icon for the filter.
name	[Required] Name for the filter. Unique within the application.
@web.filter-init-param	Declares an initialization parameter for a servlet filter.
description	[Optional] Description of the parameter.
name	[Required] Name of the initialization parameter.
value	Value for the parameter.
@web.filter-mapping	Defines the mapping for the `Filter`. Either `url-pattern` or `servlet-name` should be specified. Applicable to Servlet 2.3 only.
servlet-name	Servlet name for the filter.

Table C.48 Class-level servlet and JSP tags *(continued)*

Class-level tag/Attributes	Description
url-pattern	URL pattern the filter should match.
@web.listener	Declares the class as a `Listener` class.
@web.resource-env-ref	Defines a resource environment reference with the specified name, type, and description.
description	[Optional] Description of the resource reference.
name	[Required] Name of the resource environment reference.
type	[Required] Type of the referenced resource.
@web.resource-ref	Defines a resource reference with the specified name, type, description, authentication (auth), and scope.
auth	[Required] Authentication for the resource. Valid values: Application, Container.
description	[Optional] Description of the resource reference.
jndi-name	Physical JNDI name of the resource.
name	[Required] Name of the resource reference.
scope	Scope of the resource. Valid values: Shareable, Unshareable.
type	[Required] Type of the referenced resource.
@web.security-role	Defines a security role with the specified role name and description.
description	Description of the role.
role-name	Role name.
@web.security-role-ref	Defines a security role reference with the name `role-name` to a security role link named `role-link`.
description	Description of the role reference.
role-link	[Required] Name of the role link.
role-name	[Required] Name of the role reference.
@web.servlet	Declares the class as a servlet class, with the specified name, display name, icon, and description.
description	Description of the servlet.
display-name	Display name of the servlet.

Table C.48 Class-level servlet and JSP tags *(continued)*

Class-level tag/Attributes	Description
icon	Icon for the servlet.
jsp-file	JSP file that should be precompiled on servlet startup if `load-on-startup` is true.
load-on-startup	Integer indicating the order in which the servlet should be loaded.
name	[Required] Name of the servlet. Unique within the application.
run-as	Name of a security role to be used for the execution of the web application.
`@web.servlet-init-param`	Declares initialization parameters for the servlet with the specified parameter name, value, and description.
description	[Optional] Description of the parameter.
name	[Required] Name of the initialization parameter.
value	Value for the parameter.
`@web.servlet-mapping`	Defines the mapping for the servlet to the specified URL pattern.
url-pattern	URL pattern the servlet should match.

WebLogic tags

Table C.49 Class-level WebLogic tags

Class-level tag/Attributes	Description
`@weblogic.allow-concurrent-calls`	Specifies whether a stateful session bean instance allows concurrent method calls. Valid values: true, false. When a stateful session bean instance is currently in a method call and another (concurrent) method call arrives on the server, the EJB specification requires that the server throw a `RemoteException`. By default the EJB container follows the EJB specification. When this value is set to true, the EJB container blocks the concurrent method call and allows it to proceed when the previous call has completed.
`@weblogic.automatic-key-generation`	Installs the automatic sequence/key generation facility.
generator-name	Name of the key generator.

Table C.49 Class-level WebLogic tags *(continued)*

Class-level tag/Attributes	Description
`generator-type`	Type of generator. Valid values: ORACLE, SQL_SERVER, NAMED_SEQUENCE_TABLE.
`key-cache-size`	Size of the key cache.
@weblogic.cache	Specifies various options for the caching.
`cache-type`	Cache type. Used in `stateful-session-cache`. Valid values: NRU, LRU. Default: NRU.
`concurrency-strategy`	Specifies how the container should manage concurrent access to an entity bean. Valid values: Exclusive, Database, ReadOnly, Optimistic. Default: Database.
`idle-timeout-seconds`	Scrubs the cache (see `max-beans-in-cache`) of inactive objects after at least this many seconds. Scrubbed objects are passivated.
`max-beans-in-cache`	Maximum number of objects of this class that are allowed in memory. Objects are kept in an LRU chain, and the ones dropped from the end of the chain are passivated.
`read-timeout-seconds`	Number of seconds between `ejbLoad` calls on a read-only entity bean. If `read-timeout-seconds` is 0, `ejbLoad` is called only when the bean is brought into the cache.
@weblogic.cache-ref	Used to add an `entity-cache-ref` element to `weblogic-ejb-jar.xml`. Refers to an application-level entity cache, which can cache instances of multiple entity beans that are part of the same application. Application-level entity caches are declared in the `weblogic-application.xml` descriptor.
`cache-between-transactions`	Tells the EJB container whether to cache the persistent data of an entity bean across (between) transactions. Valid values: true, false. Default false.
`cache-name`	[Required] Application-level entity cache that an entity bean uses. An application-level entity cache is a cache that may be shared by multiple entity beans in the same application. Application-level entity caches are declared in the `weblogic-application.xml` deployment descriptor.

Table C.49   Class-level WebLogic tags *(continued)*

Class-level tag/Attributes	Description
`concurrency-strategy`	[Required] Specifies how the container should manage concurrent access to an entity bean. Valid values: Exclusive, Database, ReadOnly, Optimistic. Default: Database.
`estimated-bean-size`	Estimated average size of the instances of an entity bean in bytes. The average number of bytes of memory that are consumed by each instance.
@weblogic.clustering	Specifies various options for how an entity bean is invoked in a WebLogic cluster. Setting `home-is-clusterable` to True enables clustering for both the home and remote stubs of the entity bean.
`home-call-router-class-name`	Custom class to be used for routing home method calls. This class must implement `weblogic.rmi.cluster.CallRouter`.
`home-is-clusterable`	If True, this bean can be deployed from multiple servers in a cluster. Calls to the home stub will be load-balanced between the servers on which this bean is deployed, and if a server hosting the bean is unreachable, the call will automatically fail over to another server hosting the bean. Valid values: True, False. Default: True.
`home-load-algorithm`	Algorithm to use for load-balancing between replicas of this home. If this property isn't specified, the algorithm specified by the server property `weblogic.cluster.defaultLoadAlgorithm` is used. Valid values: RoundRobin, Random, WeightBased.
`replication-type`	Describes how to replicate stateful session beans in a cluster. Valid values: InMemory, None. Default: None.
`stateless-bean-call-router-class-name`	Custom class to be used for routing bean method calls. This class must implement `weblogic.rmi.cluster.CallRouter`. If specified, an instance of this class will be called before each method call and be given the opportunity to choose a server to route to based on the method parameters. It returns either a server name or null, indicating that the current load algorithm should be used to pick the server.

Table C.49 Class-level WebLogic tags *(continued)*

Class-level tag/Attributes	Description
`stateless-bean-is-clusterable`	Applicable only to session EJBs with a `session-type` of Stateless (see `ejb-jar.dtd`). If `home-is-clusterable` is True and this parameter is also True, calls to this bean stub will be load-balanced between all the servers on which this bean is deployed; and if a server hosting the bean becomes unreachable, the call will automatically fail over to another server hosting the bean. Valid values: True, False. Default: True.
`stateless-bean-load-algorithm`	Algorithm to use for load-balancing between replicas of this bean. If this property isn't specified, the algorithm specified by the server property `weblogic.cluster.defaultLoadAlgorithm` is used. Valid values: RoundRobin, Random, WeightBased.
`stateless-bean-methods-are-idempotent`	Set to True if the bean is written such that repeated calls to the same method with the same arguments have exactly the same effect as a single call. This allows the fail-over handler to retry a failed call without knowing whether the call completed on the failed server. Valid values: True, False. Default: False.
`@weblogic.ejb-local-reference-description`	Specifies a reference to an EJB. There must also be an `@ejb.ejb-ref` tag that points to the referenced bean. Only for WebLogic 6.1 and later.
`ejb-ref-name`	[Required] EJB reference name. This is the reference you put in the tag `@ejb.ejb-ref` with `ref-name` parameter.
`jndi-name`	[Required] JNDI name where the bean or resource will be bound in WebLogic Server. References the tag `@ejb.bean` with the `jndi-name` attribute.
`@weblogic.ejb-reference-description`	Specifies a reference to an EJB external to the current deployment package. There must also be an `@ejb.ejb-ref` tag that points to the referenced bean.
`ejb-ref-name`	[Required] EJB reference name. This is the reference you put in the tag `@ejb.ejb-ref` with `ref-name` parameter.
`jndi-name`	[Required] JNDI name where the bean or resource will be bound in WebLogic Server. References the tag `@ejb.bean with jndi-name` attribute.

Table C.49 Class-level WebLogic tags *(continued)*

Class-level tag/Attributes	Description
`@weblogic.enable-call-by-reference`	By default, EJB methods called from within the same server pass arguments by reference. This increases the performance of method invocation because parameters aren't copied. If you set `enable-call-by-reference` to False, parameters to the EJB methods are copied (passed by value) in accordance with the EJB 1.1 specification. Pass by value is always necessary when the EJB is called remotely (not from within the server). Valid values: True, False.
`@weblogic.enable-dynamic-queries`	Specifies whether dynamic queries are enabled. For WebLogic 7.0 and EJB 2.0 CMP beans only. Valid values: True, False.
`@weblogic.invalidation-target`	Specifies a read-only entity EJB that should be invalidated when this CMP entity bean has been modified.
`ejb-name`	Name of the entity EJB to be invalidated. Must be a read-only EJB and may only be specified in an EJB 2.0 CMP.
`@weblogic.lifecycle`	Specifies various options for the management of the lifecycle of stateful beans.
`passivation-strategy`	Passivation strategy for stateful session beans. Valid values: default, transaction. With the default setting, the container attempts to keep a working set of beans in the cache. With the transaction setting, the container passivates the bean after every transaction (or method call for a nontransactional invocation). Default: default.
`@weblogic.message-driven`	Specifies various options for message-driven beans.
`connection-factory-jndi-name`	JNDI name of the JMS `ConnectionFactory` that the MDB should look up to create its queues and topics. If not specified, defaultd to `weblogic.jms.MessageDrivenBean ConnectionFactory`, which must have been declared in `config.xml`.
`destination-jndi-name`	Associates a message-driven bean with a JMS queue or topic that has been deployed in the WebLogic JNDI tree.

Table C.49   Class-level WebLogic tags *(continued)*

Class-level tag/Attributes	Description
initial-context-factory	Initial `ContextFactory` that the container uses to create its connection factories. If not specified, defaults to `weblogic.jndi.WLInitialContextFactory`.
jms-client-id	JMS specification allows JMS consumers to specify an associated ID. This ID is necessary for durable subscriptions to JMS topics.
jms-polling-interval-seconds	Number of seconds between each attempt to reconnect to the JMS destination.
provider-url	URL provider to be put in the `Properties` used by the `InitialContext`. It's typically host:port and used in conjunction with `initial-context-factory` and `connection-factory-jndi-name`.
@weblogic.persistence	Specifies various options for entity beans.
db-is-shared	If False, the container assumes it has exclusive access to the bean data in the database. If True, the container assumes the bean data could be modified between transactions and reloads data at the beginning of each transaction.
delay-updates-until-end-of-tx	[Optional] Applicable to entity beans only (both container- and bean-managed). Affects when changes to a bean's state are propagated to the persistent store. If True, updates to the persistent store of all beans in the transaction are performed just before the end of the transaction. If False, the pstore update of a bean is performed at the conclusion of each method invocation. Default: "True".
finders-load-bean	[Optional] Applicable to CMP entity beans only. Affects whether the beans returned by a finder (or `ejbSelect` method) are loaded immediately into the cache before the finder method returns. Valid values: True, False.
is-modified-method-name	Applies to bean-managed persistence or EJB 1.1 container-managed persistence entity EJBs. EJB 2.0 entity EJBs don't need to implement an `is-modified-method`. The EJB container can automatically detect which fields were modified in a transaction.

Table C.49 Class-level WebLogic tags *(continued)*

Class-level tag/Attributes	Description
`@weblogic.pool`	Specifies various options for instance pooling.
`initial-beans-in-free-pool`	Initial size of the free pool of beans that WebLogic EJB maintains for every bean class.
`max-beans-in-free-pool`	Maximum size of the free pool of beans that WebLogic EJB maintains for every bean class.
`@weblogic.resource-description`	Specifies a reference to a resource. There must also be a matching `@ejb.resource-ref` tag that points to the referenced resource.
`jndi-name`	[Required] Reference to the resource.
`res-ref-name`	[Required] JNDI name from the `@ejb.resource-ref` tag.
`@weblogic.resource-env-description`	Specifies a reference to a resource. There must also be a matching `@ejb.resource-env-ref` tag which points to the referenced resource.
`jndi-name`	[Required] Reference to the resource.
`res-env-ref-name`	[Required] Name from the `@ejb.resource-env-ref`.
`@weblogic.run-as-identity-pricipal`	Specifies which security principal is to be used for the `run-as` identity. This tag is necessary if the role specified in the `run-as` element of the `ejb-jar.xml` descriptor doesn't map to a single security principal representing a `User` in the security realm. This could be true in two cases. When the role maps to multiple security principals, the `run-as-identity-principal` element must be used to specify which security principal you want to be used. When the role maps to a single security principal, that represents a `Group` in the security realm. In this case, the `run-as-identity-principal` element must be used to specify a particular `User` in the security realm.
`@weblogic.transaction-descriptor`	Specifies properties relating to transactions. Applicable to all bean types.
`trans-timeout-seconds`	Maximum duration of EJB container -initiated transactions. If the transaction takes longer then the `trans-timeout-seconds`, the Weblogic Server rolls back the transaction.

Table C.49   Class-level WebLogic tags *(continued)*

Class-level tag/Attributes	Description
`@weblogic.transaction-isolation`	Sets the transaction isolation level for all methods in the tagged class. This tag has no parameters, but instead takes as its value a parameter to the tag itself. For example: `@weblogic.transaction-isolation TRANSACTION_SERIALIZABLE`. Valid values: TRANSACTION_SERIALIZABLE, TRANSACTION_READ_COMMITTED, TRANSACTION_READ_UNCOMMITTED, TRANSACTION_REPEATABLE_READ, TRANSACTION_READ_COMMITTED_FOR_UPDATE.

Table C.50   Method-level WebLogic tags

Method-level tag/Attributes		Description
`@weblogic.field-group`		Places the CMP/CMR property into a named field group to be loaded into memory as a unit.
	`group-name`	Field group name.
`@weblogic.finder`		Defines a CMP finder query.
	`find-for-update`	If true, specifies that a `SELECT ... FOR UPDATE` should be used when performing the query. Valid values: true, false. Default: false.
	`finder-query`	Finder query.
`@weblogic.select`		Configures a selector defined by `@ejb:select`.
	`include-updates`	If True, indicates that updates made during the current transaction must be reflected in the result of the select. Valid values: True, False. Default: False.
`@weblogic.transaction-isolation`		Sets the transaction isolation level for the tagged method. This tag has no parameters, but instead takes as its value a parameter to the tag itself. For example: `@weblogic.transaction-isolation TRANSACTION_SERIALIZABLE`. Valid values: TRANSACTION_SERIALIZABLE, TRANSACTION_READ_COMMITTED, TRANSACTION_READ_UNCOMMITTED, TRANSACTION_REPEATABLE_READ, TRANSACTION_READ_COMMITTED_FOR_UPDATE.

IBM's WebSphere tags

Table C.51 Class-level WebSphere tags

Class-level tag/Attributes	Description
`@websphere.bean`	Defines the timeout period for session EJBs.
timeout	Timeout value.
`@websphere.bean-cache`	Configures the EJB cache.
activate-at	Specifies when to activate the cache. Default: TRANSACTION.
load-at	Specifies when to load the cache. Default: TRANSACTION.
`@websphere.datasource`	Defines a datasource.
jndi-name	JNDI name used to look up the datasource.
`@websphere.finder-query`	Defines a WebSphere 4.0–specific finder method query.
home	[Required] EJB interface in which the finder query is exposed. Valid values: Home, Remote. Default: Home.
name	[Required] Name of the finder method.
parms	[Required] Space-delimited list specifying parameter types of the finder method.
where-clause	[Required] WHERE clause of the finder query.
`@websphere.local-tran`	Defines a local transaction.
boundary	Boundary of the transaction. Default: BEAN-METHOD.
unresolved-action	Indicates how to handle unresolved actions in a transaction. Default: ROLLBACK.
`@websphere.mapping`	Maps a CMP entity EJB to a specific table.
table-name	[Required] Table to which the entity bean should be mapped.
`@websphere.mapping-constraint`	Defines a constraint on a table that's mapped to by a CMP entity EJB.
constraint-name	[Required] Name of the constraint.
constraint-type	[Required] Constraint type.

WebWork tags

Table C.52   Class-level WebWork tags

Class-level tag/Attributes	Description
`@webwork.action`	Defines a WebWork action class.
error	View to use in the event of an error.
input	View to use as input for the action (typically a form page).
name	Name of the action.
success	View to use upon successful completion of the action.
views	Comma-separated list of other (not input, error, or success) views.

Table C.53   Method-level WebWork tags

Method-level tag/Attributes	Description
`@webwork.command`	Defines a WebWork command method.
error	View to use in the event of an error.
input	View to use as input for the command (typically a form page).
name	Name of the command.
success	View to use upon successful completion of the command.

XDoclet tags

Table C.54   Class-level XDoclet tags

Class-level tag/Attributes	Description
`@xdoclet.merge-file`	Documents a subtask's template merge points.
description	[Required] Description of what the merge point is used for and what the merge file should contain.
file	[Required] Filename pattern of the merge file. This will either be a simple filename (such as assembly-descriptor.xml) or a filename pattern (such as ejb-env-entries-{0}.xml) and should match the file parameter of the `<XDtMerge:merge/>` template tag.

Table C.54   Class-level XDoclet tags *(continued)*

Class-level tag/Attributes	Description
relates-to	Generated file to which a given merge point relates. Helps to clarify things if a given subtask generates a number of types of file (such as a deployment descriptor and a CMP mapping file).
@xdoclet.taghandler	Declares a class to be an XDt tag handler.
namespace	[Required] Namespace (without XDt) for the tag's handler. Example: `PkTagsHandler` has `namespace=EjbPk`, and the templates look like `<XDtEjbPk:xxx/>`.

XDt template language tags

Sometimes the tasks and tags that come out of the box with XDoclet won't suffice. Sometimes you need to extend XDoclet to meet your custom code generation requirements. Or, maybe you're trying to figure out how the built-in subtasks do their job, and you're looking at the templates associated with those subtasks. In any event, you need to understand the tags that form the templates.

This appendix documents all the XDt template tags that come with XDoclet, as of XDoclet version 1.2.0.

Abstract program element namespaces

Many of the namespaces presented in this appendix share a common set of tags defined in `xdoclet.tagshandler.AbstractProgramElementTagsHandler`. When you come across a namespace that indicates that it includes abstract program element tags, refer back to this section for additional tags available in that namespace.

Table D.1   Content tags of abstract program element namespaces

Tag name/Attributes	Description
`currentToken`	Returns the current token inside `<XDtClass:forAllClassTagTokens>`.
`matchValue`	Returns the value of the match variable. The match variable serves as a variable for templates; you set it somewhere in the template and look it up somewhere else in the template.
`setMatchValue`	Sets the value of the match variable.
`value`	[Required] New value for the match pattern.
`skipToken`	Skips the current token. Returns an empty string.

Axis namespace

This namespace is implemented in `xdoclet.modules.apache.axis.ejb.AxisTags Handler`. These tags take the form of `<XDtAxis:tagName>`.

Table D.2   Content tag in the `Axis` namespace

Tag name/Attributes	Description
`serviceId`	Returns the service ID of the web service.

Antdoc namespace

This namespace is implemented in `xdoclet.modules.doc.AntdocTagsHandler`. These tags take the form of `<XDtAntdoc:tagName>`.

Table D.3   Block tags in the `Antdoc` namespace

Tag name/Attributes	Description
`forAllSubElements`	Iterates through all sub-elements.
`ifHasSubElements`	Evaluates the body if the current element has sub-elements.

Table D.4   Content tags in the `Antdoc` namespace

Tag name/Attributes	Description
`elementName`	Returns the name of the current element.

Table D.4 **Content tags in the `Antdoc` namespace** *(continued)*

Tag name/Attributes	Description
`required`	Returns Yes if the current method is tagged with `@ant.required` or No if the method is tagged with `@ant.not-required`.
`subElementDescription`	Returns the comment text of the current element.
`subElementLink`	Returns the link to the current sub-element.
`subElementName`	Returns the name of the sub-element.

BesEjbRel namespace

This namespace is implemented in `xdoclet.modules.borland.bes.ejb.Borland-RelationTagsHandler`. These tags take the form of `<XDtBesEjbRel:tagName>`.

In addition to the tags listed here, the `BesEjbRel` namespace shares all the tags contained in the `Ejb` and `EjbRel` namespaces.

Table D.5 **Block tags in the `BesEjbRel` namespace**

Tag name/Attributes	Description
`ifDoesntHaveLeftColumnName`	Evaluates the body block if the `left-column-name` attribute of `@bes.relation` isn't set.
`ifDoesntHaveLeftTableName`	Evaluates the body block if the `left-table-name` attribute of `@bes.relation` isn't set.
`ifDoesntHaveRightColumnName`	Evaluates the body block if the `right-column-name` attribute of `@bes.relation` isn't set.
`ifDoesntHaveRightTableName`	Evaluates the body block if the `right-table-name` attribute of `@bes.relation` isn't set.
`ifHasLeftColumnName`	Evaluates the body block if the `left-column-name` attribute of `@bes.relation` is set.
`ifHasLeftTableName`	Evaluates the body block if the `left-table-name` attribute of `@bes.relation` is set.
`ifHasRightColumnName`	Evaluates the body block if the `right-column-name` attribute of `@bes.relation` is set.
`ifHasRightTableName`	Evaluates the body block if the `right-table-name` attribute of `@bes.relation` is set.

Table D.6   Content tags in the `BesEjbRel` namespace

Tag name/Attributes	Description
defaultLeftColumnName	Returns the default left column name defined by the `column-name` attribute of `@ejb.persistence` on the left-hand side of the relationship.
defaultLeftTableName	Returns the default left table name defined by the `table-name` attribute of `@ejb.persistence` on the left-hand side of the relationship.
defaultRightColumnName	Returns the default right column name defined by the `primkey-field` attribute of `@ejb.bean` on the right-hand side of the relationship.
defaultRightTableName	Returns the default right table name defined by the `table-name` attribute of `@ejb.persistence` on the right-hand side of the relationship.
leftColumnName	Returns the left column name as defined by the `left-column-name` attribute of `@bes.relation`.
leftTableName	Returns the left table name as defined by the `left-table-name` attribute of `@bes.relation`.
rightColumnName	Returns the right column name as defined by the `right-column-name` attribute of `@bes.relation`.
rightTableName	Returns the right table name as defined by the `right-table-name` attribute of `@bes.relation`.

Bsf namespace

This namespace is implemented in `xdoclet.modules.apache.bsf.BsfEngine TagHandler`. These tags take the form of `<XDtBsf:tagName>`.

This namespace enables you to embed Bean Scripting Framework (BSF) templates within XDt templates by including the BSF template as the body of `<XDtBsf:generator>`.

Table D.7 Block tag in the `Bsf` namespace

Tag name/Attributes	Description
`generator`	Evaluates the body block with the BSF template engine.
`disable`	If yes, then does nothing.
`scriptengine`	[Required] BSF scripting engine to use.
`silent`	If yes, then runs in silent mode and doesn't send BSF output to XDoclet output.

Table D.8 Content tags in the `Bsf` namespace

Tag name/Attributes	Description
`clearVariables`	Clears all BSF variables.
`getVariable`	Gets the value of a BSF variable.
`default`	Default value to return if the specified variable isn't found.
`name`	[Required] Name of the BSF variable.

Castor namespace

This namespace is implemented in `xdoclet.modules.exolab.castor.ejb.Castor TagsHandler`. These tags take the form of `<XDtCastor:tagName>`.

Table D.9 Block tags in the `Castor` namespace

Tag name/Attributes	Description
`forAllClasses`	Iterates over all classes loaded by javadoc and evaluates the body of the tag for each class.

Class namespace

This namespace is implemented in `xdoclet.tagshandler.ClassTagsHandler`. These tags take the form of `<XDtClass:tagName>`. This namespace also includes abstract program element tags defined in the section "Abstract program element namespaces."

Table D.10   Block tags in the `Class` namespace

Tag name/Attributes	Description
`classOf`	Returns the not-fully qualified name of the fully-qualified class name specified in the body of this tag.
`forAllClasses`	Iterates over all classes loaded by javadoc and evaluates the body of the tag for each class. Discards classes that have an `@xdoclet-generated` class tag defined.
abstract	If true, then also accepts abstract classes; otherwise, it doesn't.
type	Specifies a type to be iterated over.
extent	Extent of the type search. Valid values: concrete-type, superclass, hierarchy. If concrete-type, then only checks the concrete type; if superclass, then also checks the superclass; if hierarchy, then searches the whole hierarchy and determines whether the class is of the specified type. Default: hierarchy.
`forAllClassTags`	Iterates over all tags of the current class with the name specified in `tagName` and evaluates the body of the tag for each method.
superclasses	If true, then also traverses superclasses; otherwise, looks up the tag in the current concrete class only.
tagKey	Tag property to be used as a unique key. This is used to avoid duplicate code due to similar tags in superclasses.
tagName	[Required] Tag name.
`forAllClassTagTokens`	Iterates over all tokens in the specified class tag with the name specified in `tagName` and evaluates the body for every token.
delimiter	Delimiter used to tokenize the tokens. Default: comma (,).
paramName	[Required] Parameter of the tag whose value is to be tokenized.
skip	How many tokens to skip on start.
superclasses	If true, then also traverses superclasses; otherwise, looks up the tag in the current concrete class only.
tagName	[Required] Name of the tag to look in.

Table D.10 Block tags in the `Class` namespace *(continued)*

Tag name/Attributes	Description
`forAllDistinctClassTags`	Iterates over all tags named according to `tagName` in a nonduplicated manner. Duplicated tags generate a warning message. Note that this tag already processes all classes; there is no need to wrap it inside a `<XDtClass:forAllClasses>` tag or any other tag that processes a group of classes.
`paramName`	Parameter name that should also be considered for uniqueness.
`tagName`	[Required] Tag to iterate over.
`ifClassTagValueEquals`	Evaluates the body if the value for the class tag equals the specified value.
`paramName`	Parameter name. If not specified, then the raw content of the tag is returned.
`paramNum`	Zero-based parameter number. It's used if the user used the space-separated format for specifying parameters.
`tagName`	[Required] Tag name.
`value`	[Required] Desired value.
`ifClassTagValueMatches`	Evaluates the body if the match variable equals with the value of the specified tag/parameter.
`default`	Default value returned if the user doesn't specify the parameter for the tag.
`superclasses`	If true, then also traverses superclasses; otherwise, looks up the tag in the current concrete class only.
`values`	Valid values for the parameter, comma separated. An error message is printed if the parameter value isn't one of the values.
`ifClassTagValueNotEquals`	Evaluates the body if the value for the class tag doesn't equal the specified value.
`paramName`	Parameter name. If not specified, then the raw content of the tag is returned.
`paramNum`	Zero-based parameter number. It's used if the user used the space-separated format for specifying parameters.
`tagName`	[Required] Tag name.
`value`	[Required] Desired value.

Table D.10   Block tags in the `Class` namespace *(continued)*

Tag name/Attributes	Description
`ifDoesntHaveClassTag`	Evaluates the body if the current class doesn't have at least one tag with the specified name.
`error`	Shows this error message if no tag is found.
`paramName`	Parameter name. If not specified, then the raw content of the tag is returned.
`paramNum`	Zero-based parameter number. It's used if the user used the space-separated format for specifying parameters.
`superclasses`	If true, then also traverses superclasses; otherwise, looks up the tag in the current concrete class only.
`tagName`	[Required] Tag name.
`ifHasClassTag`	Evaluates the body if the current class has at least one tag with the specified name.
`error`	Shows this error message if no tag is found.
`paramName`	Parameter name. If not specified, then the raw content of the tag is returned.
`paramNum`	Zero-based parameter number. It's used if the user used the space-separated format for specifying parameters.
`superclasses`	If true, then also traverses superclasses; otherwise, looks up the tag in the current concrete class only.
`tagName`	[Required] Tag name.
`ifIsClassAbstract`	Evaluates the body block if the current class is declared abstract.
`ifIsClassNotAbstract`	Evaluates the body block if the current class isn't declared abstract.
`pushClass`	Pushes the class specified by the `value` parameter to the top of the stack, making it the current class.
`value`	[Required] If `return-type` is specified, then pushes the current method return type. Otherwise, finds the `XClass` for the class name and pushes it. Valid values: return-type, some class name.

Table D.11   Content tags in the Class namespace

Tag name/Attributes	Description
`classComment`	Comment for the current class.
`no-comment-signs`	If true, then doesn't decorate the comment with comment signs. Default: false.
`classCommentTags`	Javadoc comment tags for the current class (plus `@xdoclet-generated`).
`classCommentText`	Text of the javadoc comment for the current class.
`no-comment-signs`	If true, then doesn't decorate the comment with comment signs. Default: false.
`className`	Returns the not-fully-qualified name of the current class without the package name.
`classTagValue`	Returns the value of the specified class tag.
`default`	Default value returned if the user doesn't specify the parameter for the tag.
`paramName`	Parameter name. If not specified, then the raw content of the tag is returned.
`paramNum`	Zero-based parameter number. It's used if the user used the space-separated format for specifying parameters.
`superclasses`	If true, then also traverses superclasses; otherwise, looks up the tag in the current concrete class only.
`tagName`	[Required] Tag name.
`values`	Valid values for the parameter, comma separated. An error message is printed if the parameter value isn't one of the values.
`classTagValueMatch`	
`paramName`	Parameter name. If not specified, then the raw content of the tag is returned.
`paramNum`	Zero-based parameter number. It's used if the user used the space-separated format for specifying parameters.
`tagName`	[Required] Tag name.
`firstSentenceDescription`	Return the standard javadoc of the current class.
`no-description-if-lacking`	Returns *No Description* if a comment is lacking.
`fullClassName`	Returns the fully qualified name of the current class.

Table D.11 Content tags in the Class namespace *(continued)*

Tag name/Attributes	Description
`fullSuperClassName`	Returns the fully qualified name of the superclass of the current class.
`getClassNameFor`	Returns the not-fully-qualified name of the current class without the package name.
`getFullClassNameFor`	Returns the fully qualified name of the current class with the package name.
`getFullSuperclassNameFor`	Returns the fully qualified name of the superclass of the current class.
`importedList`	Iterates over all imported classes and packages imported in the current class and returns the list. The composed string has *import* in front of each import statement, and each import is in a separate line.
`symbolicClassName`	Returns the symbolic name of the current class. For a JavaBean, it's the same as the class name.

Collection namespace

This namespace is implemented in `xdoclet.modules.util.CollectionTagsHandler`. These tags take the form of `<XDtCollection:tagName>`.

Table D.12 Block tags in the Collection namespace

Tag name/Attributes		Description
`ifContains`		Generates the contained template code if the specified collection contains the key or value passed as attributes. If the collection is a set, only the `value` attribute should be specified. If the collection is a map, the `key` attribute should be specified. If the `value` attribute is also specified, an additional check for equality is made.
	key	Key to check, if the collection is a map.
	name	[Required] Collection to operate on.
	value	Value to check, if the collection is a set. If the collection is a map, the value to check for equality.

Table D.12 Block tags in the `Collection` namespace *(continued)*

Tag name/Attributes	Description
`ifDoesntContain`	Generates the contained template code if the specified collection doesn't contain the key or value passed as attributes. If the collection is a set, only the `value` attribute should be specified. If the collection is a map, the `key` attribute should be specified. If the `value` attribute is also specified, an additional check for equality is made.
`key`	Key to check, if the collection is a map.
`name`	[Required] Collection to operate on.
`value`	Value to check, if the collection is a set. If the collection is a map, the value to check for equality.

Table D.13 Content tags in the `Collection` namespace

Tag name/Attributes	Description
`create`	Creates a new utility collection that stores template data. If a collection with the specified name already exists, an `XDocletException` is thrown.
`name`	[Required] Name for the newly created collection.
`type`	Type of the collection to create. Valid values: map, set. Default: set.
`destroy`	Destroys the specified collection. The collection must exist, or an exception will be thrown.
`name`	Collection to destroy.
`get`	Obtains one value contained in the collection. This tag applies only to map valued collections, and an XDoclet exception is thrown if the specified collection isn't a map.
`key`	[Required] Collection to operate on.
`name`	[Required] Key to retrieve.
`put`	Puts a new element into the specified collection. If the collection is a set, only the `name` and `value` attributes should be specified. If the collection is a map, the `key` value should also be specified. If the `key` is specified and the collection is a set, or if `key` isn't specified and the collection is a map, an `XDocletException` is thrown.
`key`	Key to the new value. Should be specified only if the collection is a map.

Table D.13 Content tags in the `Collection` namespace *(continued)*

Tag name/Attributes	Description
name	[Required] Name of the collection to operate on. If the collection doesn't exist, an exception is thrown.
value	[Required] Value to put into the collection.
remove	Removes an element from the specified collection. One of the `key` or `value` attributes should be specified, depending on whether the collection is a map or a set.
key	Key to remove from the map. Invalid if the collection is a set.
name	[Required] Name of the collection to operate on. If the collection doesn't exist, an exception is thrown.
value	Value to remove from the set. Invalid if the collection is a map.

Comment namespace

This namespace is implemented in xdoclet.tagshandler.CommentTagsHandler. These tags take the form of <XDtComment:*tagName*>.

Table D.14 Block tag in the `Comment` namespace

Tag name/Attributes	Description
comment	Outputs nothing. This tag is used to include comments in template files.

Config namespace

This namespace is implemented in xdoclet.tagshandler.ConfigTagsHandler. These tags take the form of <XDtConfig:*tagName*>.

Table D.15 Block tags in the `Config` namespace

Tag name/Attributes	Description
`forAllConfigParameters`	Evaluates the body for all configuration parameters with the name specified in `paramName`. It's basically used for `java.util.ArrayList`-based parameter types, and the body is evaluated for all items of the `ArrayList`.
`paramName`	[Required] Configuration parameter name. It's a parameter settable from within the build file.
`ifConfigParamEquals`	Evaluates the body if the value of the configuration parameter equals `value`.
`paramName`	[Required] Configuration parameter name. It's a parameter settable from within the build file.
`value`	[Required] Desired value.
`ifConfigParamGreaterOrEquals`	Evaluates the body if the value of the configuration parameter is greater or equal to `value`.
`paramName`	[Required] Configuration parameter name. It's a parameter settable from within the build file.
`value`	[Required] Desired value.
`ifConfigParamNotEquals`	Evaluates the body if the value of the configuration parameter is greater or equal to `value`.
`paramName`	[Required] Configuration parameter name. It's a parameter settable from within the build file.
`value`	[Required] Desired value.
`ifConfigParamNotGreaterOrEquals`	Evaluates the body if the value of the configuration parameter isn't greater or equal to `value`.
`paramName`	[Required] Configuration parameter name. It's a parameter settable from within the build file.
`value`	[Required] Desired value.
`ifHasConfigParam`	Evaluates the body if the configuration parameter specified isn't null.
`paramName`	[Required] Configuration parameter name. It's a parameter settable from within the build file.

Table D.16   Content tag in the `Config` namespace

Tag name/Attributes	Description
`configParameterValue`	Returns the value of a configuration parameter with the name `paramName`.
`paramName`	[Required] Configuration parameter name. It's a parameter settable from within the build file.

Constructor namespace

This namespace is implemented in `xdoclet.tagshandler.ConstructorTagsHandler`. These tags take the form of `<XDtConstructor:tagName>`. This namespace also includes abstract program element tags defined in the section "Abstract program element namespaces."

Table D.17   Block tags in the `Constructor` namespace

Tag name/Attributes	Description
`executeAndRestoreConstructor`	Evaluates the current block, and then restores the current constructor before continuing.
`forAllClassConstructors`	Loops through all constructors for all classes after first sorting all the constructors.
`extent`	Specifies the extent of the type search. Valid values: concrete-type, superclass, hierarchy. If concrete-type, then only checks the concrete type; if superclass, then also checks the superclass; if hierarchy, then searches the whole hierarchy and determines whether the class is of the specified type. Default: hierarchy.
`type`	Specifies a type whose constructors are to be iterated over.
`forAllConstructors`	Iterates over all constructors of the current class and evaluates the body of the tag for each constructor.
`sort`	If true, then sorts the constructors list.
`superclasses`	If true, then also traverses superclasses; otherwise, looks up the tag in the current concrete class only.
`forAllConstructorTags`	Iterates over all tags of the current constructor and evaluates the body of the tag for each constructor.
`tagName`	[Required] Tag name.

Table D.17   Block tags in the `Constructor` namespace *(continued)*

Tag name/Attributes	Description
`forAllConstructorTagTokens`	Iterates over all tokens in the current constructor tag with the name specified in `tagName` and evaluates the body for every token.
`delimiter`	Delimiter used for tokenizing the tag tokens. Default: comma (,).
`skip`	Number of tokens to skip on start.
`tagName`	[Required] Tag name.
`ifConstructorTagValueEquals`	Evaluates the body if the value for the constructor tag equals the specified value.
`paramName`	Parameter name. If not specified, then the raw content of the tag is returned.
`paramNum`	Zero-based parameter number. It's used if the user used the space-separated format for specifying parameters.
`tagName`	[Required] Tag name.
`value`	[Required] Value to check for equality.
`ifConstructorTagValueNotEquals`	Evaluates the body if the value for the constructor tag doesn't equal the specified value.
`paramName`	Parameter name. If not specified, then the raw content of the tag is returned.
`paramNum`	Zero-based parameter number. It's used if the user used the space-separated format for specifying parameters.
`tagName`	[Required] Tag name.
`value`	[Required] Value to check for equality.
`ifDoesntHaveConstructor`	Evaluates the body if the current class doesn't have a constructor with the specified `name` and `parameters`. If `parameters` isn't specified, then any constructor with the given name and any set of parameters is considered equal to the given constructor name; so, the test result is positive, and the body is evaluated.
`delimiter`	Delimiter for tokenizing the list of parameters. Default: comma (,).

Table D.17 Block tags in the `Constructor` namespace *(continued)*

Tag name/Attributes	Description
name	[Required] Name of the constructor whose existence you're checking for in the current class.
parameters	Searches for a constructor that has the exact set of parameters specified.
ifDoesntHaveConstructorTag	Evaluates the body if the current constructor doesn't have at least one tag with the specified name.
error	Shows this error message if no tag is found.
paramName	Parameter name. If not specified, then the raw content of the tag is returned.
paramNum	Zero-based parameter number. It's used if the user used the space-separated format for specifying parameters.
tagName	[Required] Tag name.
ifHasConstructor	Evaluates the body if the current class has a constructor with the specified `name` and `parameters`. If `parameters` isn't specified, then any constructor with the given name and any set of parameters is considered equal to the given constructor name; so, the test result is positive, and the body is evaluated.
delimiter	Delimiter for tokenizing the list of parameters. Default: comma (,).
name	[Required] Name of the constructor whose existence you're checking for in the current class.
parameters	Searches for a constructor that has the exact set of parameters specified.
ifHasConstructorTag	Evaluates the body if the current constructor has at least one tag with the specified name.
error	Shows this error message if no tag is found.
paramName	Parameter name. If not specified, then the raw content of the tag is returned.
paramNum	Zero-based parameter number. It's used if the user used the space-separated format for specifying parameters.
tagName	[Required] Tag name.

Table D.17   Block tags in the `Constructor` namespace *(continued)*

Tag name/Attributes	Description
`setCurrentConstructor`	Sets the current constructor.
`delimiter`	Delimiter for tokenizing the list of parameters. Default: comma (,).
`name`	[Required] Name of the constructor whose existence you're checking for in the current class.
`parameters`	Searches for a constructor that has the exact set of parameters specified.

Table D.18   Content tags in the `Constructor` namespace

Tag name/Attributes	Description
`constructorComment`	Comment for the current constructor.
`no-comment-signs`	If true, then doesn't decorate the comment with comment signs.
`constructorName`	Returns the name of the current constructor.
`constructorTagValue`	Value of the current constructor tag or one of its parameters.
`default`	Default value returned if the user doesn't specify the parameter for the tag.
`paramName`	Parameter name. If not specified, then the raw content of the tag is returned.
`paramNum`	Zero-based parameter number. It's used if the user used the space-separated format for specifying parameters.
`tagName`	[Required] Tag name.
`values`	Valid values for the parameter, comma separated. An error message is printed if the parameter value isn't one of the values.
`exceptionList`	Iterates over all exceptions thrown by the current constructor and returns a string containing definitions of all those exceptions.
`append`	Comma-separated list of exceptions that should be always appended regardless of whether the current constructor has that constructor defined.
`constructor`	Constructor name from which the exceptions list is extracted. If not specified, then the current constructor is used.

Table D.18 Content tags in the `Constructor` namespace *(continued)*

Tag name/Attributes	Description
`skip`	Comma-separated list of exceptions that should be skipped and not put into the list.
`firstSentenceDescriptionOfCurrent Constructor`	Returns the standard javadoc of the current constructor.
`getClassNameFor`	Returns the not-fully-qualified name of the current class without the package name.
`getFullClassNameFor`	Returns the fully qualified name of the current class with the package name.
`getFullSuperclassNameFor`	Returns the fully qualified name of the superclass of the current class.

Doc namespace

This namespace is implemented in `xdoclet.modules.doc.DocumentationTags Handler`. These tags take the form of `<XDtDoc:tagName>`.

Table D.19 Block tag in the `Doc` namespace

Tag name/Attributes	Description
`forAllNamespaces`	Iterates over all template namespaces registered in the `/tagmappings.properties` file and evaluates the body of the tag for each namespace.

Table D.20 Content tags in the `Doc` namespace

Tag name/Attributes	Description
`currentNamespace`	Returns the current namespace. Used in `tags_toc.xdt`.
`currentNamespaceTagsHandlerClassName`	Returns the current namespace tags handler class name. Used for `.html` files.
`namespace`	[Required] Namespace to look for the handler in.
`currentNamespaceTagsHandlerClassName AsDirStructure`	Returns the current namespace tags handler class name as a directory structure.
`namespace`	[Required] Namespace to look for the handler in.
`namespace`	Returns the current namespace name. Used in `<XDtDoc:forAllNamespaces>` only.

Table D.20 **Content tags in the** `Doc` **namespace** *(continued)*

Tag name/Attributes	Description
`namespaceFromClassName`	Returns the current namespace name from the current class name.
`namespaceTagsHandlerClassName`	Returns the current namespace tags handler class name. Used in `<XDtDoc:forAllNamespaces>` only.

Ejb namespace

This namespace is implemented in `xdoclet.modules.ejb.EjbTagsHandler`. These tags take the form of `<XDtEjb:tagName>`.

Table D.21 **Block tags in the** `Ejb` **namespace**

Tag name/Attributes	Description
`forAllBeans`	Evaluates the body block for each EJB derived from one of the three EJB types: `EntityBean`, `SessionBean`, or `MessageDrivenBean`.
`ifIsAConcreteEJBean`	Evaluates the body block if the current bean is a concrete bean. meaning the `generate` parameter of `@ejb.bean` is either not specified or equals true. Otherwise the bean is an abstract base class bean that isn't meant to be used as an EJB but rather to serve as the base for other EJBs.
`ifLocalEjb`	Evaluates the body block if the current bean is tagged to expose a local interface.
`ifNotLocalEjb`	Evaluates the body block if the current bean isn't tagged to expose a local interface.
`ifNotRemoteEjb`	Evaluates the body block if the current bean is tagged to expose a remote interface.
`ifRemoteEjb`	Evaluates the body block if the current bean isn't tagged to expose a remote interface.

Table D.22 **Content tags in the** `Ejb` **namespace**

Tag name/Attributes	Description
`beanType`	Returns the bean type: Entity, Session, or Message Driven.

Table D.22   Content tags in the `Ejb` namespace *(continued)*

Tag name/Attributes	Description
`concreteFullClassName`	Returns the fully qualified name of the current class's concrete class. This is the class that's generated and derived from the current class.
`ejbExternalRefName`	Returns the name of the external EJB reference.
`ejbName`	Returns the name of the current EJB.
`prefixWithEjbSlash`	Specifies whether to prefix the EJB name with `ejb/`. Default: false.
`ejbRefName`	Returns the name of the EJB reference.
`id`	Returns the unique ID for the current EJB.
`shortEjbName`	Returns the short version of the EJB name. Example: `foo.bar.MyBean ->MyBean, or foo/bar/MyBean ->MyBean`.
`symbolicClassName`	Returns the symbolic name of the current class. For an EJB, it's the value of `@ejb.bean`'s `name` parameter.

EjbBmp namespace

This namespace is implemented in `xdoclet.modules.ejb.entity.BmpTagsHandler`. These tags take the form of `<XDtEjbBmp:tagName>`.

In addition to the tags listed here, the `EjbBmp` namespace shares all the tags contained in the `Ejb` and `EjbEntity` namespaces.

Table D.23   Block tags in the `EjbBmp` namespace

Tag name/Attributes	Description
`forAllBmpEntityBeans`	Evaluates the body block for each EJB derived from `EntityBean` whose `type` is "BMP".
`ifEntityIsBmp`	Evaluates the body block if the current class is a BMP entity bean.
`ifUseSoftLocking`	Evaluates the body block if `@ejb.use-soft-locking` is set for the current class.

Table D.24   Content tag in the `EjbBmp` namespace.

Tag name/Attributes	Description
`entityBmpClass`	Returns the name of the generated BMP class.

EjbCmp namespace

This namespace is implemented in `xdoclet.modules.ejb.entity.CmpTagsHandler`. These tags take the form of `<XDtEjbCmp:tagName>`.

In addition to the tags listed here, the `EjbCmp` namespace shares all the tags contained in the `Ejb` and `EjbEntity` namespaces.

Table D.25   Block tags in the `EjbCmp` namespace

Tag name/Attributes	Description
`forAllCmpEntityBeans`	Evaluates the body block for each EJB derived from `EntityBean` whose `type` is "CMP".
`forAllCmpFields`	Evaluates the body block for each persistent field of the current class (if entity is CMP). Looks at superclasses as well. Searches for the getter methods that have `@ejb.persistent-field` defined.
`ifEntityIsCmp`	Evaluates the body block if the current class is a CMP entity bean.
`ifIsPersistent`	Evaluates the body if the class is tagged with `@ejb.persistence`, `@jboss.table-name`, or `@weblogic.table-name`.
`ifNotUsingCmp2`	Evaluates the body block if you aren't using EJB 2.0 or are using EJB 2.0 but CMP version 1.x.
`ifUsingCmp2`	Evaluates the body block if you're using EJB 2.0 and CMP version 2.x.

Table D.26   Content tags in the `EjbCmp` namespace

Tag name/Attributes	Description
`dbmsColumn`	Returns the dbms column. Looks for `@ejb.persistence column-name`, then for legacy app-server specific tags, and then for `propertyName` as a fallback.
`dbmsTable`	Returns the table name for the current class.
`entityCmpClass`	Returns the name of the generated CMP class.

EjbDao namespace

This namespace is implemented in xdoclet.modules.ejb.dao.DaoTagsHandler. These tags take the form of <XDtEjbDao:*tagName*>.

In addition to the tags listed here, the EjbDao namespace shares all the tags contained in the Ejb namespace.

Table D.27   Block tag in the EjbDao namespace

Tag name/Attributes	Description
ifUsingDao	Evaluates the body block if the @ejb.dao tag is present and the <dao> subtask is being used.

Table D.28   Content tag in the EjbDao namespace

Tag name/Attributes	Description
daoClass	Returns the fully-qualified DAO class name for the bean.

EjbDataObj namespace

This namespace is implemented in xdoclet.modules.ejb.entity.DataObject TagsHandler. These tags take the form of <XDtEjbDataObj:*tagName*>.

In addition to the tags listed here, the EjbDataObj namespace shares all the tags contained in the Ejb namespace.

Table D.29   Block tags in the EjbDataObj namespace

Tag name/Attributes	Description
forAllSuperSetData	Evaluates the body block for each setData method.
ifIsAggregate	Evaluates the body block if @ejb.aggregate is defined for the current getter method, denoting that the specified getter method returns an aggregated object.
ifIsNotAggregate	Evaluates the body block if @ejb.aggregate isn't defined for the current getter method.
ifIsWithDataContainer	Evaluates the body block if the @ejb.data-object container attribute is true. If it isn't defined, then the default is true.

Table D.29 Block tags in the `EjbDataObj` namespace *(continued)*

Tag name/Attributes	Description
`ifIsWithDataMethod`	Evaluates the body block if the `@ejb.data-object setdata` attribute is true. If it isn't defined, then the default is true.
`isDataContentEquals`	Evaluates the body block if the `@ejb.data-object equals` attribute equals the current class.

Table D.30 Content tags in the `EjbDataObj` namespace

Tag name/Attributes	Description
`dataMostSuperObjectClass`	Returns the data-object class name highest in the hierarchy of derived beans. Because of possible inheritance between entity beans, the type of the generated `getData` method must be that of the most super class of the current entity bean. The current `Data` class must extend the corresponding super `Data` class.
`dataObjectClass`	Returns the data-object class name for the bean.
`dataObjectClassNameFromInterfaceName`	Return the data-object class name from the interface name.
`extendsFrom`	Returns the name of the class that the data-object class extends.
`generateDataObjectClass`	Returns the name of the generated data-object class.
`parentDataObjectClass`	Returns the name of the generated data object's superclass.

EjbEntity namespace

This namespace is implemented in `xdoclet.modules.ejb.entity.EntityTags Handler`. These tags take the form of `<XDtEjbEntity:tagName>`.

In addition to the tags listed here, the `EjbEntity` namespace shares all the tags contained in the `Ejb` namespace.

Table D.31 Block tags in the `EjbEntity` namespace

Tag name/Attributes	Description
`forAllEjbSelectMethods`	Evaluates the body block for each `ejbSelect` method.

Table D.31   Block tags in the `EjbEntity` namespace *(continued)*

Tag name/Attributes	Description
`forAllEntityBeans`	Evaluates the body block for each EJB derived from EntityBean.
`ifEntity`	Evaluates the body block if the current class is of an entity type.

Table D.32   Content tags in the `EjbEntity` namespace

Tag name/Attributes	Description
`persistenceType`	Returns the persistent type of the current bean.
`reentrant`	Returns True if `@ejb.bean reentrant` is true or False otherwise. It does the case-conversion trick from true to True and false to False.

EjbFacade namespace

This namespace is implemented in `xdoclet.modules.ejb.entity.FacadeTags Handler`. These tags take the form of `<XDtEjbFacade:tagName>`.

In addition to the tags listed here, the `EjbFacade` namespace shares all the tags contained in the `Ejb` and `EjbEntity` namespaces.

Table D.33   Block tags in the `EjbFacade` namespace

Tag name/Attributes	Description
`ifUseLocalInterface`	Decides whether you have to use the bean's local interface.
`ifUseRemoteInterface`	Decides whether you have to use the bean's remote interface.

Table D.34   Content tags in the `EjbFacade` namespace

Tag name/Attributes	Description
`beanPermission`	Returns the permission specification. Inherited from the bean definition.
`beanRef`	Returns the bean reference.
`entityFacadeClass`	Returns the class name for the EJB façade.
`facadeEjbName`	Returns the facade EJB name.

Table D.34 Content tags in the `EjbFacade` namespace *(continued)*

Tag name/Attributes	Description
`jndiName`	Returns the JNDI name, if any.
`localJndiName`	Returns the local JNDI name, if any.
`remoteFacadeClass`	Returns the name of the remote façade class.
`sessionType`	Returns the session type.
`viewType`	Returns the view type.

EjbHome namespace

This namespace is implemented in `xdoclet.modules.ejb.home.HomeTagsHandler`. These tags take the form of `<XDtEjbHome:tagName>`.

In addition to the tags listed here, the `EjbHome` namespace shares all the tags contained in the `Ejb` namespace.

Table D.35 Block tags in the `EjbHome` namespace

Tag name/Attributes		Description
`forAllHomeMethods`		Iterates over all the finder methods defined in a class and superclasses.
	`superclasses`	Also traverses superclasses. If false, used in remote/local home interface templates. Default: false.
	`tagKey`	Tag property to be used as a unique key. This is used to avoid duplicate code due to similar tags in superclasses.
	`tagName`	[Required] Tag name.
`ifDoesntHavePostCreateMethod`		Evaluates the body block if the current create method's `ejbPostCreate` method doesn't exist.
`ifIsCollectionType`		Evaluates the body block if the current method's return type is either `java.util.Collection` or `java.util.Set`.
`ifIsCreateMethod`		Evaluates the body block if the current method is a create method. Create methods should have `@ejb.create-method` defined.
	`superclasses`	Also traverses superclasses. If false, used in remote/local home interface templates. Default: false.

Table D.35 Block tags in the EjbHome namespace *(continued)*

Tag name/Attributes	Description
ifIsEnumerationType	Evaluates the body block if the current method's return type is `java.util.Enumeration`.
ifIsFinderMethod	Evaluates the body block if the current method is an `ejbFind` method.
superclasses	Also traverses superclasses. If false, used in remote/local home interface templates. Default: false.
ifIsHomeMethod	Evaluates the body block if the current method is a home method. Home methods should have `@ejb.home-method` defined.
superclasses	Also traverses superclasses. If false, used in remote/local home interface templates. Default: false.
ifIsInterfaceType	Evaluates the body block if the return type of the current method is either the local or remote interface type of the current class.
ifNotRemoveMethod	Evaluates the body block if the current method isn't an `ejbRemove` method.

Table D.36 Content tags in the EjbHome namespace

Tag name/Attributes	Description
compName	Returns the `COMP_NAME`.
prefixWithEjbSlash	Specifies whether to prefix the `COMP_NAME` with `ejb/`. Default: false.
type	[Required] Specifies whether you want the JNDI name value for local or remote lookup. Valid values: remote, local.
currentExceptions	Returns the exceptions thrown by the current method.
currentMethod	Returns the name of the current method.
currentPermission	Returns the permissions of the current method.
currentSignature	Returns the signature of the current method.
currentType	Returns the return type of the current method.
ejbPostCreateSignature	Returns the appropriate `ejbPostCreate` method name for the current `ejbCreate` method.

Table D.36   Content tags in the `EjbHome` namespace *(continued)*

Tag name/Attributes	Description
extendsFrom	Returns the name of the class that the home interface extends.
finderClass	Generates a name for the finder utility class backing the current finder.
homeInterface	Returns the fully qualified local or remote home interface name for the bean, depending on the value of the `type` parameter.
type	[Required] Specifies the type of the component home interface. Valid values: remote, local.
jndiName	Returns the JNDI name.
type	[Required] Specifies whether you want the JNDI name value for local or remote lookup. Valid values: remote, local.
parameterList	Returns the parameter list for invocation.
parameterListDefinition	Returns a definition of the parameter list for the definition for the current home method.

EjbIntf namespace

This namespace is implemented in `xdoclet.modules.ejb.intf.InterfaceTags Handler`. These tags take the form of `<XDtEjbIntf:tagName>`.

In addition to the tags listed here, the `EjbIntf` namespace shares all the tags contained in the `Ejb` namespace.

Table D.37   Block tags in the `EjbIntf` namespace

Tag name/Attributes	Description
forAllInterfaceViewTypes	Evaluates the body block for each view-type of the current method.
ifIsInterfaceMethod	Evaluates the body block if the current method is an EJB local or remote interface method.
interface	[Required] Type of interface in which to check for the method's validity. Valid values: local, remote.
superclasses	Also traverses superclasses. If false, used in remote/local. Default: true.

Table D.37 Block tags in the `EjbIntf` namespace *(continued)*

Tag name/Attributes	Description
`ifIsNotInterfaceMethod`	Evaluates the body block if the current method isn't an EJB local or remote interface method.
interface	[Required] Type of interface in which to check for the method's validity. Valid values: local, remote.

Table D.38 Content tags in the `EjbIntf` namespace

Tag name/Attributes	Description
`beanClassNameFromInterfaceName`	Returns the bean implementation class name for the interface name specified as the return type of the current method or the method specified by the parameter interface (if any).
`componentInterface`	Returns the fully qualified local or remote interface name for the bean, depending on the value of the `type` parameter.
type	[Required] Specifies the type of the component interface. Valid values: remote, local.
`extendsFrom`	Returns the name of the class the home interface extends.
`interfaceMethodName`	Returns the interface method name for the current interface method.
`methodIntf`	Returns Remote if the current method has `@ejb.remote-method` defined, or Home otherwise.

EjbMdb namespace

This namespace is implemented in `xdoclet.modules.ejb.mdb.MdbTagsHandler`. These tags take the form of `<XDtEjbMdb:tagName>`.

In addition to the tags listed here, the `EjbMdb` namespace shares all the tags contained in the `Ejb` namespace.

Table D.39 Block tags in the `EjbMdb` namespace

Tag name/Attributes	Description
`forAllMDBeans`	Evaluates the body block for each EJB derived from `MessageDrivenBean`.

Table D.39   Block tags in the `EjbMdb` namespace *(continued)*

Tag name/Attributes	Description
`ifMessageDriven`	Evaluates the body block if the current class is of a message-driven bean type.
`ifNotMessageDriven`	Evaluates the body block if the current class isn't of a message-driven bean type.

Table D.40   Content tag in the `EjbMdb` namespace

Tag name/Attributes	Description
`messageDrivenClass`	Returns the name of message-driven bean class.

EjbPersistent namespace

This namespace is implemented in `xdoclet.modules.ejb.entity.Persistent TagsHandler`. These tags take the form of `<XDtEjbPersistent:tagName>`.

In addition to the tags listed here, the `EjbPersistent` namespace shares all the tags contained in the `Ejb`, `EjbEntity`, and `EjbCmp` namespaces.

Table D.41   Block tags in the `EjbPersistent` namespace

Tag name/Attributes	Description
`forAllPersistentFields`	Evaluates the body for each persistent field.
`not-pk`	If true, then evaluates only fields that aren't primary key fields.
`only-pk`	If true, then evaluate only fields that are primary key fields.
`superclasses`	Includes persistent fields of superclasses. Default: true.
`valueobject`	Evaluates only fields that are to match a specified value object name.
`ifHasAtLeastOnePersistentField`	Evaluates the body if the class has at least one persistent field.
`ifHasAtLeastOnePkField`	Evaluates the body if the class has at least one primary key field.

Table D.42   Content tags in the `EjbPersistent` namespace

Tag name/Attributes	Description
`persistentfieldList`	Returns a string containing a comma-separated list of persistent fields with their types.
superclasses	Includes persistent fields of superclasses. Default: true.
valueobject	Includes only fields that are to match a specified value object name.
`persistentfieldNameValueList`	Returns a string containing a comma-separated list of persistent fields without their types in *field-name=value* format.
superclasses	Includes persistent fields of superclasses. Default: true.
valueobject	Includes only fields that are to match a specified value object name.

EjbPk namespace

This namespace is implemented in `xdoclet.modules.ejb.entity.PkTagsHandler`. These tags take the form of `<XDtEjbPk:tagName>`.

In addition to the tags listed here, the `EjbPk` namespace shares all the tags contained in the `Ejb` namespace.

Table D.43   Block tags in the `EjbPk` namespace

Tag name/Attributes	Description
`ifDoesntHavePrimkeyField`	Processes the tag body if the `primkey-field` attribute of `@ejb.bean` on the current class isn't set.
`ifHasPrimkeyField`	Processes the tag body if the `primkey-field` attribute of `@ejb.bean` on the current class is set.
`ifHasPrimkeySetter`	Processes the tag body if the current class has defined a setter for the field specified by `@ejb.bean primkey-field`.
`ifIsPkField`	Evaluates the body if the current method is a primary key field.
`ifIsNotPrimkeyField`	Processes the tag body if the current method isn't a getter or setter for the field specified by `@ejb.bean primkey-field`.

Table D.43 Block tags in the `EjbPk` namespace *(continued)*

Tag name/Attributes	Description
`ifIsPrimkeyField`	Processes the tag body if the current method is a getter or setter for the field specified by `@ejb.bean primkey-field`.

Table D.44 Content tags in the `EjbPk` namespace

Tag name/Attributes	Description
`extendsFrom`	Returns the name of the class that the primary key class extends.
`pkClass`	Returns the name of the generated primary key class for the current class.
`pkClassForEjbJarXml`	Returns the name of the primary key class for the current class.
`pkfieldList`	Returns a string containing a comma-separated list of primary key fields with their types.
`pkfieldListFrom`	Returns a string containing a comma-separated list of primary key fields gotten from an object specified as parameter.
`primkeyField`	Returns the `primkey-field` defined for the current class.
`primkeyGetter`	Returns the getter name for the `primkey-field`.
`primkeySetter`	Returns the setter name for the `primkey-field`.

EjbRef namespace

This namespace is implemented in `xdoclet.modules.ejb.dd.EjbRefTagsHandler`. These tags take the form of `<XDtEjbRef:tagName>`.

In addition to the tags listed here, the `EjbRef` namespace shares all the tags contained in the `Ejb` namespace.

Table D.45 Block tag in the `EjbRef` namespace

Tag name/Attributes	Description
`forAllEjbRefs`	Evaluates the body block for each `@ejb.ejb-ref` defined for the EJB. One of the useful things this does is to look up the EJB using the `ejb-name` attribute of `@ejb.ejb-ref` and fill in other required information.

Table D.46 Content tags in the `EjbRef` namespace

Tag name/Attributes	Description
`ejbRefId`	Returns a unique ID for the specified `ejb-ref`. It prefixes the ID with the referring class's ID, followed by an underscore (_) and the ID of the EJB object.
`ejbRefJndiName`	Returns the name of the EJB reference.

EjbRel namespace

This namespace is implemented in `xdoclet.modules.ejb.dd.RelationTagsHandler`. These tags take the form of `<XDtEjbRel:tagName>`.

In addition to the tags listed here, the `EjbRel` namespace shares all the tags contained in the `Ejb` namespace.

Table D.47 Block tags in the `EjbRel` namespace

Tag name/Attributes	Description
`forAllRelationships`	Evaluates the body block for each relationship. Relations are denoted by `@ejb.relation` for the getter method of the CMR field.
`ifHasLeftRoleName`	Evaluates the body block if the left-hand side of the relationship has a role name.
`ifHasRelationships`	Evaluates the body block if the current class has relationships.
`ifHasRightRoleName`	Evaluates the body block if the right-hand side of the relationship has a role name.
`ifIsBidirectional`	Evaluates the body block if the current relationship is bidirectional.
`ifIsLeftMany`	Evaluates the body block if the left-hand side is a many side of a relationship.
`ifIsMany2Many`	Evaluates the body block if the current relationship is a many-to-many type, meaning both sides of the relation return `java.util.Collection` or `java.util.Set`.
`ifIsNotACollection`	Evaluates the body block if the current method's return type isn't a `java.util.Collection` or `java.util.Set`.

Table D.47 Block tags in the `EjbRel` namespace *(continued)*

Tag name/Attributes	Description
`ifIsOne2Many`	Evaluates the body block if the current relationship is a one-to-many type, meaning only one side of the relation returns `java.util.Collection` or `java.util.Set`.
`ifIsOne2One`	Evaluates the body block if the current relationship is a one-to-one type, meaning neither side of the relation returns `java.util.Collection` or `java.util.Set`.
`ifIsRightMany`	Evaluates the body block if the right-hand side is a many side of a relationship.
`ifIsUnidirectional`	Evaluates the body block if the current relationship is unidirectional.
`ifLeftCascadeDelete`	Evaluates the body block if the left-hand side of the relationship is tagged for cascade deletion.
`ifLeftNavigable`	Evaluates the body block if the left-hand side of the relationship is navigable.
`ifNotIsMany2Many`	Evaluates the body block if the current relationship *is not* a many-to-many type, meaning at least one side of the relation doesn't return `java.util.Collection` or `java.util.Set`.
`ifNotIsOne2Many`	Evaluates the body block if the current relationship *is not* a one-to-many type, meaning either both sides or neither side of the relation returns `java.util.Collection` or `java.util.Set`.
`ifNotIsOne2One`	Evaluates the body block if the current relationship *is not* a one-to-one type, meaning at least one side of the relation returns `java.util.Collection` or `java.util.Set`.
`ifRightCascadeDelete`	Evaluates the body block if the right-hand side of the relationship is tagged for cascade deletion.
`ifRightNavigable`	Evaluates the body block if the right-hand side of the relationship is navigable.

Table D.48 Content tags in the `EjbRel` namespace

Tag name/Attributes	Description
`leftEJBName`	Returns the EJB name of the left side of this relationship.

Table D.48   Content tags in the `EjbRel` namespace *(continued)*

Tag name/Attributes	Description
`leftFieldName`	Returns the name of the field on the left-hand side of the relationship.
`leftFieldType`	Returns the type of the field on the left-hand side of the relationship.
`leftMuliplicity`	Returns the multiplicity of the left-hand side of the relationship.
`leftRoleName`	Returns the security role on the left-hand side of the relationship.
`relationComment`	Returns the current relationship name in an XML comment.
`relationName`	Returns the current relationship name.
`rightEJBName`	Returns the EJB name of the right side of the relationship.
`rightFieldName`	Returns the name of the field on the right-hand side of the relationship.
`rightFieldType`	Returns the type of the field on the right-hand side of the relationship.
`rightMultiplicity`	Returns the multiplicity of the right-hand side of the relationship.
`rightRoleName`	Returns the security role on the right-hand side of the relationship.

EjbSec namespace

This namespace is implemented in `xdoclet.modules.ejb.dd.SecurityTagsHandler`. These tags take the form of `<XDtEjbSec:tagName>`.

In addition to the tags listed here, the `EjbSec` namespace shares all the tags contained in the `Ejb` namespace.

Table D.49   Block tag in the `EjbSec` namespace

Tag name/Attributes	Description
`forAllSecurityRoles`	Evaluates the body block for each `@ejb.permission` defined in the class level or method level.

Table D.50   Content tag in the `EjbSec` namespace

Tag name/Attributes	Description
`securityRoleName`	Returns the current security role name set by the containing `<XDtEjbSec:forAllSecurityRoles>`.

EjbSession namespace

This namespace is implemented in xdoclet.modules.ejb.session.SessionTags Handler. These tags take the form of <XDtEjbSession:*tagName*>.

In addition to the tags listed here, the EjbSession namespace shares all the tags contained in the Ejb namespace.

Table D.51   Block tags in the `EjbSession` namespace

Tag name/Attributes	Description
`forAllSessionBeans`	Evaluates the body block for each EJB derived from `SessionBean`.
`forAllStatefulSessionBeans`	Evaluates the body block for each EJB derived from `SessionBean` that's stateful.
`forAllStatelessSessionBeans`	Evaluates the body block for each EJB derived from `SessionBean` that's stateless.
`ifNotStatefulSession`	Evaluates the body block if the current class isn't of a stateful session bean type.
`ifNotStatelessSession`	Evaluates the body block if the current class isn't of a stateless session bean type.
`ifStatefulSession`	Evaluates the body block if the current class is of a stateful session bean type.
`ifStatelessSession`	Evaluates the body block if the current class is.of a stateless session bean type.

Table D.52   Content tag in the `EjbSession` namespace

Tag name/Attributes	Description
`sessionClass`	Returns the name of the generated session class.

EjbUtilObj namespace

This namespace is implemented in xdoclet.modules.ejb.lookup.LookupUtil TagsHandler. These tags take the form of <XDtEjbUtilObj:*tagName*>.

In addition to the tag listed here, the EjbUtilObj namespace shares all the tags contained in the Ejb namespace.

Table D.53   Content tag in the EjbUtilObj namespace

Tag name/Attributes	Description
utilClass	Returns the fully qualified utility class name for the bean.

EjbValueObj namespace

This namespace is implemented in xdoclet.modules.ejb.entity.ValueObject TagsHandler. These tags take the form of <XDtEjbValueObj:*tagName*>.

In addition to the tags listed here, the EjbValueObj namespace shares all the tags contained in the Ejb namespace.

Table D.54   Block tags in the EjbValueObj namespace

Tag name/Attributes	Description
forAllAggregates	Evaluates the body block for all aggregate relationships.
forAllComposes	Evaluates the body block for all compose relationships.
forAllRelations	Evaluates the body block for all relationships.
forAllSuperSetValue	Evaluates the body block for all value objects of the current class's ancestor classes.
forAllValueObjects	Evaluates the body block for all value objects defined for the current class.
ifGeneratePKConstructor	Evaluates the body block if a constructor for a primary key is to be generated.
ifIsAbstractValueObject	Evaluates the body block if the abstract attribute of @ejb.value-object is true.
ifNotIsAbstractValueObject	Evaluates the body block if the abstract attribute of @ejb.value-object isn't true.
ifUsingValueObject	Evaluates the body block if the <valueobject> subtask is being used.

Table D.55 Content tags in the `EjbValueObj` namespace

Tag name/Attributes	Description
`concreteCollectionType`	Type of the constructor for aggregates or compositions.
`currentAggregateName`	Returns the name of the current aggregate relationship.
`currentAggregateType`	Returns the type of the current aggregate relationship.
`currentRelationBeanClass`	Returns the class name of the current relationship bean.
`currentValueObjectAttribute`	Returns the value of the current value object attribute.
`currentValueObjectClass`	Returns the class name of the current value object.
`currentValueObjectMatch`	Returns the match name of the current value object.
`extendsFrom`	Returns the name of the class the value object class extends.
`valueMostSuperObjectClass`	Returns the data-object class name highest in the hierarchy of derived beans. Because of possible inheritance between entity beans, the type of the generated `getData` method must be that of the most super class of the current entity bean. The current `Data` class must extend the corresponding super `Data` class.
`valueObjectClass`	Returns the fully qualified name of the value object class.
`valueObjectImplements`	Returns interfaces that are to be implemented by the value object class.
`valueObjectMatch`	Returns the current value object's `match` value.
`valueObjectName`	Returns the current value object name as specified in the `name` attribute of `@ejb.value-object`.

Externalizer namespace

This namespace is implemented in `xdoclet.modules.externalizer.Externalizer-TagsHandler`. These tags take the form of `<XDtExternalizer:tagName>`.

Table D.56 Block tag in the `Externalizer` namespace

Tag name/Attributes	Description
`forAllFieldTags`	Evaluates the body for all field tags. Works only in the context of the `<externalizer>` subtask.

Table D.57 Content tags in the `Externalizer` namespace

Tag name/Attributes	Description
`bundleKey`	Current resource bundle name, to be called by the `<translator>` subtask.
`key`	Key.
`value`	Value.

Field namespace

This namespace is implemented in `xdoclet.tagshandler.FieldTagsHandler`. These tags take the form of `<XDtField:tagName>`. This namespace also includes abstract program element tags defined in the section "Abstract program element namespaces."

Table D.58 Block tags in the `Field` namespace

Tag name/Attributes	Description
`forAllFields`	Iterates over all fields of the current class and evaluates the body of the tag for each field.
`sort`	If true, then sorts the list of fields.
`superclasses`	If true, then also traverses superclasses; otherwise, looks up the tag in the current concrete class only.
`forAllFieldTags`	Iterates over all tags of the current field and evaluates the body of the tag for each field.
`tagName`	[Required] Tag name.
`forAllFieldTagTokens`	Iterates over all tokens in the current field tag with the name `tagName` and evaluates the body for every token.
`delimiter`	Delimiter used to tokenize the tag tokens. Default: comma (,).
`skip`	Number of tokens to skip on start.
`tagName`	[Required] Tag name.

Table D.58 Block tags in the Field namespace *(continued)*

Tag name/Attributes	Description
ifFieldTagValueEquals	Evaluates the body block if the tag value equals the specified value.
paramName	Parameter name. If not specified, then the raw content of the tag is use.
tagName	[Required] Tag name.
value	[Required] Value to compare for equality.
ifHasFieldTag	Evaluates the body if the current field has at least one tag with the specified name.
error	Shows this error message if no tag is found.
paramName	Parameter name. If not specified, then the raw content of the tag is used.
paramNum	Zero-based parameter number. It's used if the user used the space-separated format for specifying parameters.
tagName	[Required] Tag name.

Table D.59 Content tags in the Field namespace

Tag name/Attributes	Description
fieldComment	Comment for the current field.
no-comment-signs	If true, then doesn't decorate the comment with comment signs.
fieldName	Returns the name of the current field.
fieldTagValue	Iterates over all field tags with the specified tagName for the current field, probably inside a `<XDtField:forAllFieldTags>` body.
default	Default value returned if the user doesn't specify the parameter for the tag.
paramName	Parameter name. If not specified, then the raw content of the tag is returned.
paramNum	Zero-based parameter number. It's used if the user used the space-separated format for specifying parameters.
tagName	[Required] Tag name.

Table D.59 Content tags in the `Field` namespace *(continued)*

Tag name/Attributes	Description
`values`	Valid values for the parameter, comma separated. An error message is printed if the parameter value isn't one of the values.
`fieldType`	Returns the type of the current field.
`firstSentenceDescriptionOfCurrentField`	Return the standard javadoc of the current field.
`getClassNameFor`	Returns the not-fully-qualified name of the current class without the package name.
`getFullClassNameFor`	Returns the fully qualified name of the current class with the package name.
`getFullSuperclassNameFor`	Returns the fully qualified name of the superclass of the current class.

Hibernate namespace

This namespace is implemented in `xdoclet.modules.hibernate.HibernateTags Handler`. These tags take the form of `<XDtHibernate:tagName>`.

Table D.60 Block tags in the `Hibernate` namespace

Tag name/Attributes	Description
`forAllSubclasses`	Iterates over all classes loaded by javadoc that are direct subclasses of the current class, and evaluates the body of the tag for each class. It discards classes that have an XDoclet-generated class tag defined.
`ifHasCompositeId`	Renders the template if the ID is composite.
`ifHasPrimitiveId`	Render the template if the ID is primitive.

Table D.61 Content tags in the `Hibernate` namespace

Tag name/Attributes	Description
`dataSource`	Datasource JNDI name extractor.
`dialect`	SQL dialect extractor.
`getCurrentMappingElement`	Returns the current mapping element as set by `<XDtHibernate:setCurrentTag>`.

Table D.61 Content tags in the `Hibernate` namespace *(continued)*

Tag name/Attributes	Description
`getCurrentTag`	Returns the current tag as set by `<XDtHibernate:setCurrentTag>`.
`getFileName`	Returns the full path of the Hibernate file for the current class.
`jndiName`	Configured JNDI name.
`logMapping`	Prints the name of the current class to the console.
`mappingList`	Comma-separated list of hibernate mappings.
`roleAttribute`	Gets the attribute used for collection property names in this version of Hibernate (`role` or `name`).
`serviceClassName`	Gets the name of the class that implements the `SessionFactory` as an MBean in this version of Hibernate.
`serviceName`	Returns the configured service name.
`setCurrentTag`	Sets the current tag and mapping element.
`mappingElement`	[Required] Mapping element.
`name`	[Required] Name of the current tag.

I18n namespace

This namespace is implemented in `xdoclet.tagshandler.TranslatorTagsHandler`. These tags take the form of `<XDtI18n:tagName>`.

Table D.62 Content tag in the `I18n` namespace

Tag name/Attributes	Description
`getString`	Returns a localized text string.
`arguments`	[Optional] List of arguments to be substituted for any placeholders ({0}, {1}, and so on) in the resource value string.
`bundle`	Base name of the resource bundle to use, such as xdoclet.modules.ejb (corresponding to `modules/ejb/src/xdoclet/modules/ejb/resources/Messages.properties`). Default: xdoclet.
`delimiter`	Delimiter used in the `arguments` parameter. Default: comma (,).
`resource`	[Required] Resource key to look up in the bundle.

Id namespace

This namespace is implemented in `xdoclet.tagshandler.IdTagsHandler`. These tags take the form of `<XDtId:tagName>`.

Table D.63   Content tags in the `Id` namespace

Tag name/Attributes	Description
`id`	Generates an ID attribute based on the given tag values. This is used for generating ID attributes for XML elements.
paramNames	[Required] Comma-separated list of parameter names. The list is ordered: a preferred parameter comes before another parameter that's less important. If the parameter exists, its value is taken and used as the `id` value.
tagName	[Required] Tag from which the value of the ID is calculated.
`prefixedId`	Generates an ID attribute based on the given prefix. This is used for generating ID attributes for XML elements.
prefix	[Required] Tag from which the value of the ID is calculated.

Info namespace

This namespace is implemented in `xdoclet.modules.doc.info.InfoTagsTagsHandler`. These tags take the form of `<XDtInfo:tagName>`.

Table D.64   Body tags in the `Info` namespace

Tag name/Attributes	Description
`forAllClassTags`	Iterates over all tags of the current class with the name `tagName` and evaluates the body of the tag for each method.
superclasses	If true, then also traverses superclasses; otherwise, looks up the tag in the current concrete class only.
tagName	[Required] Tag to iterate over.
tagKey	Attribute name to look for in addition to the specified tag.

Table D.64   Body tags in the `Info` namespace *(continued)*

Tag name/Attributes	Description
`forAllConstructorTags`	Iterates over all tags of the current constructor and evaluates the body of the tag for each constructor.
`superclasses`	If true, then also traverses superclasses; otherwise, looks up the tag in the current concrete class only.
`tagName`	[Required] Tag to iterate over.
`forAllFieldTags`	Iterates over all tags of the current field and evaluates the body of the tag for each field.
`superclasses`	If true, then also traverses superclasses; otherwise, looks up the tag in the current concrete class only.
`tagName`	[Required] Tag to iterate over.
`forAllMethodTags`	Iterates over all tags of the current method and evaluates the body of the tag for each method.
`superclasses`	If true, then also traverses superclasses; otherwise, looks up the tag in the current concrete class only.
`tagName`	[Required] Tag to iterate over.
`ifTagCountNotZero`	Evaluates the body block if the current level has at least one tag.
`level`	[Required] The level to check for tags. Valid values: all, package, whole-class, class, field, constructor, method.

Table D.65   Content tags in the `Info` namespace

Tag name/Attributes	Description
`classTagValue`	Returns the value of a current class tag or one of its attributes.
`default`	Default value returned if the user doesn't specify the parameter for the tag.
`paramName`	Parameter name. If not specified, then the raw content of the tag is returned.
`paramNum`	Zero-based parameter number. It's used if the user used the space-separated format for specifying parameters.
`superclasses`	If true, then also traverses superclasses; otherwise, looks up the tag in the current concrete class only.

Table D.65   Content tags in the Info namespace *(continued)*

Tag name/Attributes	Description
tagName	[Required] Tag name.
values	Valid values for the parameter, comma separated. An error message is printed if the parameter value isn't one of the values.
constructorTagValue	Value of the current constructor tag or one of its parameters.
default	Default value returned if the user doesn't specify the parameter for the tag.
paramName	Parameter name. If not specified, then the raw content of the tag is returned.
paramNum	Zero-based parameter number. It's used if the user used the space-separated format for specifying parameters.
tagName	[Required] Tag name.
values	Valid values for the parameter, comma separated. An error message is printed if the parameter value isn't one of the values.
fieldTagValue	Returns the value of the current field tag or one of its attributes.
default	Default value returned if the user doesn't specify the parameter for the tag.
paramName	Parameter name. If not specified, then the raw content of the tag is returned.
paramNum	Zero-based parameter number. It's used if the user used the space-separated format for specifying parameters.
tagName	[Required] Tag name.
values	Valid values for the parameter, comma separated. An error message is printed if the parameter value isn't one of the values.
methodTagValue	Returns the value of a method tag or one of its values.
default	Default value returned if the user doesn't specify the parameter for the tag.
paramName	Parameter name. If not specified, then the raw content of the tag is returned.

Table D.65   Content tags in the Info namespace *(continued)*

Tag name/Attributes	Description
paramNum	Zero-based parameter number. It's used if the user used the space-separated format for specifying parameters.
tagName	[Required] Tag name.
values	Valid values for the parameter, comma separated. An error message is printed if the parameter value isn't one of the values.
projectname	Returns the current project name.
rootlink	Returns a path back to the source root relative to the current package's path.
tagCount	Returns the number of tags at the specified level.
level	[Required] Level to check for tags. Valid values: all, package, whole-class, class, field, constructor, method.

JavaBean namespace

This namespace is implemented in xdoclet.modules.java.javabean.JavaBean TagsHandler. These tags take the form of <XDtJavaBean:*tagName*>.

Table D.66   Content tags in the JavaBean namespace

Tag name/Attributes	Description
beanClass	Returns the configured bean class name or the current class name.
capitalizeClassTag	Capitalizes the first letter of a class tag. Example: countToken => CountToken.
getBeanInfoClassFor	Returns the name of the BeanInfo class.
getterPrefix	Returns the getter prefix according to the class tag that contains a class.

JBEjbRel namespace

This namespace is implemented in xdoclet.modules.jboss.ejb.JBossRelation TagsHandler. These tags take the form of <XDtJBEjbRel:*tagName*>.

In addition to the tags listed here, the JBEjbRel namespace shares all the tags contained in the Ejb and EjbRel namespaces.

Table D.67 Body tags in the `JBEjbRel` namespace

Tag name/Attributes	Description
forAllLeftForeignKeys	Iterates over all foreign keys on the left-hand side of the relationship.
forAllRightForeignKeys	Iterates over all foreign keys on the right-hand side of the relationship.
ifHasRelationTableAttribute	Evaluates the body block if the specified attribute of `@jboss.relation-table` is set.
paramName	[Required] Attribute name.
ifIsForeignKeyMapping	Evaluates the body block if the `style` attribute of `@jboss.relation-mapping` is set to foreign-key.
ifIsRelationTableMapping	Evaluates the body block if the `style` attribute of `@jboss.relation-mapping` is set to relation-table.
ifLeftHasFK	Evaluates the body block if the left-hand side of the current relationship has a foreign key declaration tag (`@jboss.relation`/`@jboss.target-relation`).
ifLeftHasFKConstraint	Evaluates the body block if the left-hand side of the current relationship has a foreign key constraint.
ifLeftHasReadAhead	Evaluates the body block if the left-hand side of the current relationship has a read-ahead strategy.
ifLeftHasReadAheadEagerLoadGroup	Evaluates the body block if the left-hand side of the current relationship has a read-ahead strategy of eager-load-group.
ifLeftHasReadAheadPageSize	Evaluates the body block if the left-hand side of the current relationship has a read-ahead strategy of page-size.
ifNotIsForeignKeyMapping	Evaluates the body block if the `style` attribute of `@jboss.relation-mapping` isn't set to foreign-key.
ifNotIsRelationTableMapping	Evaluates the body block if the `style` attribute of `@jboss.relation-mapping` isn't set to relation-table.
ifNotLeftHasFK	Evaluates the body block if the left-hand side of the current relationship doesn't have a foreign key declaration tag (`@jboss.relation`/`@jboss.target-relation`).

Table D.67 Body tags in the `JBEjbRel` namespace *(continued)*

Tag name/Attributes	Description
`ifNotRightHasFK`	Evaluates the body block if the right-hand side of the current relationship doesn't have a foreign key declaration tag (`@jboss.relation/@jboss.target-relation`).
`ifRightHasFK`	Evaluates the body block if the right-hand side of the current relationship has a foreign key declaration tag (`@jboss.relation/@jboss.target-relation`).
`ifRightHasFKConstraint`	Evaluates the body block if the right-hand side of the current relationship has a foreign key constraint.
`ifRightHasReadAhead`	Evaluates the body block if the right-hand side of the current relationship has a read-ahead strategy.
`ifRightHasReadAheadEagerLoadGroup`	Evaluates the body block if the right-hand side of the current relationship has a read-ahead strategy of eager-load-group.
`ifRightHasReadAheadPageSize`	Evaluates the body block if the right-hand side of the current relationship has a read-ahead strategy of page-size.

Table D.68 Content tags in the `JBEjbRel` namespace

Tag name/Attributes	Description
`fkColumn`	Returns the foreign-key column of the current relationship.
`leftFKConstraint`	Returns the foreign-key constraint on the left-hand side of the current relationship.
`leftReadAheadEagerLoadGroup`	Returns the eager load group name of the left-hand side of the current relationship.
`leftReadAheadPageSize`	Returns the page size of the left-hand side of the current relationship.
`leftReadAheadStrategy`	Returns the read-ahead strategy of the left-hand side of the current relationship.
`relatedPKField`	Returns the primary key field name of the related EJB in the current relationship.
`relationTableAttribute`	Returns the value of the specified attribute of `@jboss.relation-table`.
`paramName`	[Required] Attribute name.

Table D.68   Content tags in the `JBEjbRel` namespace *(continued)*

Tag name/Attributes	Description
`rightFKConstraint`	Returns the foreign-key constraint on the right-hand side of the current relationship.
`rightReadAheadEagerLoadGroup`	Returns the eager load group name of the right-hand side of the current relationship.
`rightReadAheadPageSize`	Returns the page size of the right-hand side of the current relationship.
`rightReadAheadStrategy`	Returns the read-ahead strategy of the right-hand side of the current relationship.

JBoss namespace

This namespace is implemented in `xdoclet.modules.jboss.ejb.JBossTagsHandler`. These tags take the form of `<XDtJBoss:tagName>`.

In addition to the tags listed here, the `JBoss` namespace shares all the tags contained in the `Class` namespace.

Table D.69   Body tags in the `JBoss` namespace

Tag name/Attributes	Description
`ifHasDVC`	Evaluates the body if at least one of the classes has a `@jboss.dvc` tag; otherwise doesn't.
`ifMethodTagMatchesClassTag`	Evaluates the body if the tag specified by `param` is present on both the class and the method.
param	[Required] Tag to match.

JBossWeb namespace

This namespace is implemented in `xdoclet.modules.jboss.web.JBossWebTagsHandler`. These tags take the form of `<XDtJBossWeb:tagName>`.

In addition to the tags listed here, the `JBossWeb` namespace shares all the tags contained in the `Class` namespace.

Table D.70   Body tags in the `JBossWeb` namespace

Tag name/Attributes	Description
`forAllEjbRefs`	Evaluates the body for all classes tagged with `@jboss.ejb-ref-jndi` and the `ref-name` attribute.

Table D.70   Body tags in the `JBossWeb` namespace *(continued)*

Tag name/Attributes	Description
`forAllResourceEnvRefs`	Evaluates the body for all classes tagged with `@jboss.resource-env-ref` and the `resource-env-ref-name` attribute.
`forAllResourceRefs`	Evaluates the body for all classes tagged with `@jboss.resource-ref` and the `resource-ref-name` attribute.

Jdo namespace

This namespace is implemented in `xdoclet.modules.jdo.JdoTagsHandler`. These tags take the form of `<XDtJdo:tagName>`.

Table D.71   Body tags in the `Jdo` namespace

Tag name/Attributes	Description
`forAllClassesInPackage`	Iterates through all the classes in the current package.
`forAllPackages`	Iterates through all packages, and generates the template if the `@jdo.persistence-capable` tag is present in at least one class in the package.
tagName	[Required] Tag name that must be present in at least one class in the package in order for the template to be generated.
`forAllVendorExtensions`	Iterates through all vendor extension tags at the specified level.
level	[Required] Level of vendor extension tags to iterate through. Valid values: array, class, collection, field, map.

Table D.72   Content tag in the `Jdo` namespace

Tag name/Attributes	Description
`vendorExtension`	Returns the XML configuration for the current vendor extension.

JMX namespace

This namespace is implemented in xdoclet.modules.jboss.jmx.JMXTagsHandler.
These tags take the form of <XDtJMX:*tagName*>.

In addition to the tag listed here, the JMX namespace shares all the tags contained in the Class namespace.

Table D.73   Content tag in the JMX namespace

Tag name/Attributes	Description
managedAttributeType	Returns the type of the current property. This tag is used in the context of <XDtProperty:forAllPropertiesWithTag tagName=jmx.managed-attribute>.

Jmx namespace

This namespace is implemented in xdoclet.modules.jmx.JMXTagsHandler.
These tags take the form of <XDtJmx:*tagName*>. This namespace also includes abstract program element tags defined in the section "Abstract program element namespaces."

Table D.74   Body tags in the Jmx namespace

Tag name/Attributes	Description
forAllIndexedConstructorParams	Evaluates the body block for all @jmx.managed-constructor-parameter tags.
forAllIndexedMethodParams	Evaluates the body block for all @jmx.managed-operation-parameter tags.
ifHasAttributeDescription	Evaluates the body block if the current method has the description attribute of @jmx.managed-attribute set.
ifIsGetterMethod	Evaluates the body block if the current method is a getter method.
ifIsSetterMethod	Evaluates the body block if the current method is a setter method.

Table D.75   Content tags in the Jmx namespace

Tag name/Attributes	Description
`constructorSignature`	Returns the signature of the current constructor.
`indexedConstructorParamValue`	Returns the value of the specified tag parameter on the current constructor.
paramName	[Required] Parameter name.
tagName	[Required] Tag name.
`indexedMethodParamValue`	Returns the value of the specified tag parameter on the current method.
paramName	[Required] Parameter name.
tagName	[Required] Tag name.
`mbeanName`	Returns the value of the `name` attribute of `@jmx.mbean`.

MVCSoft namespace

This namespace is implemented in xdoclet.modules.mvcsoft.ejb.MVCSoftTags Handler. These tags take the form of <XDtMVCSoft:*tagName*>.

Table D.76   Body tags in the MVCSoft namespace

Tag name/Attributes	Description
`forAllAliases`	Iterates over all the key aliases specified in the `key-aliases` attribute of `@mvcsoft.relation`.
`forAllQueryMethodParams`	Iterates over all parameters of the current query method.
`forEachRoleMapping`	Iterates over each role defined in the `key-aliases` attribute of `@mvcsoft.relation`.
`forNestedFaultGroups`	Iterates over each nested fault group.
`forSingleRoleMapping`	Iterates over a single role mapping.
`ifHasSortDirection`	Evaluates the body block if the sort direction is set.

Table D.77   Content tags in the MVCSoft namespace

Tag name/Attributes	Description
`colName`	Returns the current column name.
`keyFieldName`	Returns the name of the current field.
`methodParamType`	Returns the type of the current method parameter.
`nestedFaultGroups`	Returns a semicolon-separated list of nested fault groups.
`roleName`	Returns the current role name.
`sortDirection`	Returns the sort direction.

Mavenplugin namespace

This namespace is implemented in `xdoclet.modules.maven.MavenpluginTagsHandler`. These tags take the form of `<XDtMavenplugin:tagName>`.

In addition to the tags listed here, the `Mavenplugin` namespace shares all the tags contained in the `Antdoc` namespace.

Table D.78   Body tags in the Mavenplugin namespace

Tag name/Attributes	Description
`forAllTasks`	Iterates over all tasks.
`ifIsAConfigParam`	Evaluates the body block if the current sub-element is an XDoclet configuration parameter (`xdoclet.ConfigParameter`).
`ifIsAFileSet`	Evaluates the body block if the current sub-element is a fileset.
`ifIsANestedElement`	Evaluates the body block if the current sub-element is a nested element.
`ifIsASubTask`	Evaluates the body block if the current sub-element is a subtask.
`ifIsNotAFileSet`	Evaluates the body block if the current sub-element isn't a fileset.
`ifIsNotANestedElement`	Evaluates the body block if the current sub-element isn't a nested element.
`ifIsNotASubTask`	Evaluates the body block if the current sub-element isn't a subtask.

Table D.79   Content tags in the `Mavenplugin` namespace

Tag name/Attributes	Description
`nestedElementName`	Returns the current nested element name.
`nestedElementType`	Returns the type of the current nested element.

Merge namespace

This namespace is implemented in `xdoclet.tagshandler.MergeTagsHandler`. This tag takes the form of `<XDtMerge:tagName>`.

Table D.80   Body tag in the `Merge` namespace

Tag name/Attributes	Description
`merge`	Merges the contents of the file designated by the `file` parameter and evaluates the body if the file isn't found. It searches for the file in the directory specified by the `mergeDir` configuration parameter.
`file`	[Required] Path to the file to be merged. The value of this parameter can have {0} in it; if so, {0} is replaced with the current class name, and system searches for the file in the `mergeDir+packageName` directory. {0} is used in cases where you want to define and merge a file for each class.
`generateMergedFile`	If true, also processes the merged file; otherwise, only merges it and doesn't process it. Default: true.

Method namespace

This namespace is implemented in `xdoclet.tagshandler.MethodTagsHandler`. These tags take the form of `<XDtMethod:tagName>`. This namespace also includes abstract program element tags defined in the section "Abstract program element namespaces."

Table D.81   Body tags in the `Method` namespace

Tag name/Attributes	Description
`executeAndRestoreMethod`	Evaluates the current block, and then restores the current method before continuing.

Table D.81   Body tags in the Method namespace *(continued)*

Tag name/Attributes	Description
forAllClassMethods	Loops through all methods for all classes after first sorting all the methods.
extent	Specifies the extent of the type search. Valid values: concrete-type, superclass, hierarchy. If concrete-type, then only checks the concrete type; if superclass, then also checks superclasses; if hierarchy, then searches the whole hierarchy and determines whether the class is of the specified type. Default: hierarchy.
type	Specifies a type whose methods are to be iterated over.
forAllMethods	Iterates over all methods of the current class and evaluates the body of the tag for each method.
sort	If true, then sorts the methods list.
superclasses	If true, then also traverses superclasses; otherwise, looks up the tag in the current concrete class only.
forAllMethodTags	Iterates over all tags of the current method and evaluates the body of the tag for each method.
tagName	[Required] Tag name.
forAllMethodTagTokens	Iterates over all tokens in the current method tag with the name tagName and evaluates the body for every token.
delimiter	Delimiter used to tokenize the method tag tokens. Default: comma (,).
skip	Number of tokens to skip on start.
tagName	[Required] Tag name.
ifDoesntHaveMethod	Evaluates the body if the current class doesn't have a method with the specified name and parameters. If parameters isn't specified, then any method with the given name and any set of parameters is considered equal to the given method name; so, the test result is positive, and the body is evaluated.
delimiter	Delimiter used to tokenize parameters. Default: comma (,).
name	[Required] Name of the method whose existence you're checking for in the current class.

Table D.81   Body tags in the Method namespace *(continued)*

Tag name/Attributes	Description
parameters	Searches for a constructor that has the exact set of parameters specified.
ifDoesntHaveMethodTag	Evaluates the body if the current method doesn't have at least one tag with the specified name.
error	Shows this error message if no tag is found.
paramName	Parameter name. If not specified, then the raw content of the tag is returned.
paramNum	Zero-based parameter number. It's used if the user used the space-separated format for specifying parameters.
tagName	[Required] Tag name.
ifDoesntReturnVoid	Evaluates the body block if the current method doesn't return void.
method	Method name whose return type is checked. If not specified, then the current method is used.
ifHasMethod	Evaluates the body if the current class has a method with the specified name+parameters. If parameters isn't specified, then any method with the given name and any set of parameters is considered equal to the given method name; so, the test result is positive, and the body is evaluated. This method doesn't change the current method to the one specified.
delimiter	Delimiter used to tokenize parameters. Default: comma (,).
name	[Required] Name of the method whose existence you're checking for in the current class.
parameters	Searches for a constructor that has the exact set of parameters specified.
ifHasMethodComment	Evaluates the body if the current method has a comment.
ifHasMethodTag	Evaluates the body if the current method has at least one tag with the specified name.
error	Shows this error message if no tag is found.
paramName	Parameter name. If not specified, then the raw content of the tag is returned.

Table D.81   Body tags in the Method namespace *(continued)*

Tag name/Attributes	Description
paramNum	Zero-based parameter number. It's used if the user used the space-separated format for specifying parameters.
tagName	[Required] Tag name.
ifIsAbstract	Evaluates the body block if the current method is abstract.
method	Method name whose abstractness is evaluated. If not specified, then the current method is used.
ifIsGetter	Evaluates the body if the value for the method tag equals the specified value.
paramName	Parameter name. If not specified, then the raw content of the tag is returned.
paramNum	Zero-based parameter number. It's used if the user used the space-separated format for specifying parameters.
tagName	[Required] Tag name.
ifIsNotAbstract	Evaluates the body block if the current method isn't abstract.
method	Method name from which the exceptions list is extracted. If not specified, then the current method is used.
ifIsNotOfType	Evaluates the body block if the current method's return type isn't of the specified type.
type	[Required] Type to check for.
ifIsOfType	Evaluates the body block if the current method's return type is the specified type.
type	[Required] Type to check for.
ifIsPublic	Evaluates the body block if the current method is public.
ifIsSetter	Evaluates the body if the value for the method tag equals the specified value.
paramName	Parameter name. If not specified, then the raw content of the tag is returned.
paramNum	Zero-based parameter number. It's used if the user used the space-separated format for specifying parameters.

Table D.81 **Body tags in the** `Method` **namespace** *(continued)*

Tag name/Attributes	Description
tagName	[Required] Tag name.
ifMethodNameEquals	Evaluates the body if the method name is equal to the specified value.
name	[Required] Method name.
ifMethodNameNotEquals	Evaluates the body if the method name is equal to the specified value.
name	[Required] Method name.
ifMethodTagValueEquals	Evaluates the body if the value for the method tag equals the specified value.
paramName	Parameter name. If not specified, then the raw content of the tag is returned.
paramNum	Zero-based parameter number. It's used if the user used the space-separated format for specifying parameters.
tagName	[Required] Tag name.
ifMethodTagValueNotEquals	Evaluates the body if the value for the method tag doesn't equal the specified value.
paramName	Parameter name. If not specified, then the raw content of the tag is returned.
paramNum	Zero-based parameter number. It's used if the user used the space-separated format for specifying parameters.
tagName	[Required] Tag name.
ifReturnsVoid	Evaluates the body block if the current method returns void.
method	Method name whose return type is checked. If not specified, then the current method is used.
setCurrentMethod	Evaluates the body if the current class has a method with the specified name+parameters. If parameters isn't specified, then any method with the given name and any set of parameters is considered equal to the given method name; so, the test result is positive, and the body is evaluated. This method changes the current method to the one specified.
delimiter	Delimiter used to tokenize parameters. Default: comma (,).

Table D.81   Body tags in the Method namespace *(continued)*

Tag name/Attributes	Description
name	[Required] Name of the method whose existence you're checking for in the current class.
parameters	Searches for a constructor that has the exact set of parameters specified.

Table D.82   Content tags in the Method namespace

Tag name/Attributes	Description
currentMethodName	Returns the current method's name.
exceptionList	Iterates over all exceptions thrown by the current method, and returns a string containing definition of all those exceptions.
append	Comma-separated list of exceptions that should always be appended regardless of whether the current method has that method defined.
method	Method name from which the exceptions list is extracted. If not specified, then the current method is used.
skip	Comma-separated list of exceptions that should be skipped and not put into the list.
firstSentenceDescriptionOfCurrent Method	Return the standard javadoc of the current method.
getClassNameFor	Returns the not-fully-qualified name of the current class without the package name.
getFullClassNameFor	Returns the fully qualified name of the current class with the package name.
getFullSuperclassNameFor	Returns the fully qualified name of the superclass of the current class.
getterMethod	Returns the getter method name for the current method by prefixing the method name with the proper getter prefix.
getterPrefix	Returns the *get* or *is* getter prefix part of the current method. Returns an empty string if the method doesn't start with either of the two getter prefixes.
methodComment	Comment for the current method.
no-comment-signs	If true, then doesn't decorate the comment with comment signs.

Table D.82 Content tags in the Method namespace *(continued)*

Tag name/Attributes	Description
methodName	Returns the name of the current method.
methodNameWithoutPrefix	Returns the name of the current method without the first three characters. Used for cases where you need the method name without the *get*/*set* prefix.
methodTagValue	Returns the value of a method tag or one of its values.
default	Default value returned if the user doesn't specify the parameter for the tag.
paramName	Parameter name. If not specified, then the raw content of the tag is returned.
paramNum	Zero-based parameter number. It's used if the user used the space-separated format for specifying parameters.
tagName	[Required] Tag name.
values	Valid values for the parameter, comma separated. An error message is printed if the parameter value isn't one of the values.
methodType	Returns the return type of the current method.
modifiers	Returns the modifiers for the current method.
propertyName	Returns the property name extracted from the current method name. Removes any getter/setter prefix from the method name and decapitalizes it.
setterMethod	Returns the setter method name for the current method by prefixing the method name with *set* and removing the getter method's *get* or *is* prefix, if any.

MockObject namespace

This namespace is implemented in xdoclet.modules.mockobjects.MockObject TagsHandler. These tags take the form of <XDtMockObject:*tagName*>.

In addition to the tags listed here, the MockObject namespace shares all the tags contained in the Parameter namespace.

Table D.83 Body tags in the MockObject namespace

Tag name/Attributes	Description
forAllExceptions	Iterates over all the exceptions for the current method.

Table D.83   Body tags in the `MockObject` namespace *(continued)*

Tag name/Attributes	Description
`ifThrowsException`	Evaluates the body block if an exception is thrown by the current method.

Table D.84   Content tags in the `MockObject` namespace

Tag name/Attributes	Description
`currentException`	Returns the current exception.
`mockClass`	Returns the mock class name for the current class.
`parameterTypeList`	Iterates over all parameters in the current method and returns a string containing the types of all those parameters.
`forConstructor`	If true, then iterates over all parameters in the current constructor.
`uniqueMethodName`	Returns a `String` with the current method using the supplied template as boilerplate.
`template`	[Required] Boilerplate template for the unique method name.
`uniqueMethodNameAndParam`	Returns a `String` with the current method concatenated with the parameter types using the supplied template as boilerplate.
`template`	[Required] Boilerplate template for the unique method name.
`unwrap`	Tag for unwrapping a simple type out of its object counterpart.
`name`	[Required] Name of the object.
`type`	[Required] Object type.
`wrap`	[Required] Tag for wrapping a simple type in its object counterpart.
`name`	[Required] Name of the object.
`type`	[Required] Object type.

Module namespace

This namespace is implemented in `xdoclet.modules.doc.ModuleTagsHandler`. These tags take the form of `<XDtModule:tagName>`.

Table D.85 Body tag in the `Module` namespace

Tag name/Attributes	Description
`forAllModules`	Iterates over all modules.

Table D.86 Content tag in the `Module` namespace

Tag name/Attributes	Description
`moduleName`	Name of the current module.

Package namespace

This namespace is implemented in `xdoclet.tagshandler.PackageTagsHandler`. These tags take the form of `<XDtPackage:tagName>`. This namespace also includes abstract program element tags defined in the section "Abstract program element namespaces."

Table D.87 Body tags in the `Package` namespace

Tag name/Attributes	Description
`forAllPackages`	Iterates over all packages loaded by the javadoc. Subsequent calls to `forAllClasses` will only iterate over the classes in the current package.
abstract	If true, then also accepts abstract classes also; otherwise it doesn't.
extent	Specifies the extent of the type search. Valid values: concrete-type, superclass, hierarchy. If concrete-type, then only checks the concrete type; if superclass, then also checks the superclass, if hierarchy, then searches the whole hierarchy and determines whether the class is of the specified type. Default: hierarchy.
type	Specifies a type whose packages should be iterated over.

Table D.88 Content tags in the `Package` namespace

Tag name/Attributes	Description
`getClassNameFor`	Returns the not-fully-qualified name of the current class without the package name.

Table D.88 Content tags in the `Package` namespace *(continued)*

Tag name/Attributes	Description
`getFullClassNameFor`	Returns the fully qualified name of the current class with the package name.
`getFullSuperclassNameFor`	Returns the fully qualified name of the superclass of the current class.
`packageName`	Returns the current package name. If you're in the context of a package iteration, this is the name of the current package. If you're in the context of a class iteration without a package iteration, returns the name of the current class's package.
`packageNameAsPath`	Returns the current package name as a path.
`packageNameAsPathFor`	Returns the current package name as a path.
`packageOf`	Returns the not-fully-qualified package name of the fully qualified class name specified in the body of this tag.

Parameter namespace

This namespace is implemented in `xdoclet.tagshandler.ParameterTagsHandler`. These tags take the form of `<XDtParameter:tagName>`. This namespace also includes abstract program element tags defined in the section "Abstract program element namespaces."

Table D.89 Body tags in the `Parameter` namespace

Tag name/Attributes	Description
`forAllConstructorParams`	Iterates over all parameters of the current constructor and evaluates the body of the tag for each method.
`forAllMethodParams`	Iterates over all parameters of the current method and evaluates the body of the tag for each method.
`forAllParameterTypes`	Gets the value of the parameter specified by the `paramName` of the current tag, and, assuming the value has the format of a typical method definition, extracts from it the parameter types and evaluates the body for each parameter type. The current parameter type can be accessed as `<XDtParameter:currentToken/>`. Also gives back the parameter name as `<XDtParameter:currentName/>`.
`paramName`	[Required] Parameter name that its value is used for extracting parameter types out of it.

Table D.89 Body tags in the `Parameter` namespace *(continued)*

Tag name/Attributes	Description
`ifHasParams`	Evaluates the body of the tag if the current method/constructor has parameters.
`forConstructor`	If true, then looks for parameters of the current constructor instead of the current method.

Table D.90 Content tags in the `Parameter` namespace

Tag name/Attributes	Description
`currentName`	Returns the name of the parameter currently being iterated.
`getClassNameFor`	Returns the not-fully-qualified name of the current class without the package name.
`getFullClassNameFor`	Returns the fully qualified name of the current class with the package name.
`getFullSuperclassNameFor`	Returns the fully qualified name of the superclass of the current class.
`methodParamDescription`	Returns the comment text associated with the `ParamTag` for the current `Parameter`.
`methodParamName`	Returns the name of the current method parameter. The current method parameter is set inside an `<XDtParameter:forAllMethodParams>` tag in each iteration.
`methodParamType`	Returns the type of the current method parameter. The current method parameter is set inside an `<XDtParameter:forAllMethodParams>` tag in each iteration. Don't forget to add array dimensions (if any).
`parameterList`	Iterates over all parameters in the current method and returns a `String` containing definitions of all those parameters.
`forConstructor`	If true, then looks for parameters of the current constructor instead of the current method.
`includeDefinition`	If true, then includes the parameter type of parameters in the composed string.

Property namespace

This namespace is implemented in `xdoclet.tagshandler.PropertyTagsHandler`. These tags take the form of `<XDtProperty:tagName>`. This namespace also includes abstract program element tags defined in the section "Abstract program element namespaces."

Table D.91   Body tags in the `Property` namespace

Tag name/Attributes	Description
forAllPropertiesWithTag	Evaluates the body block for each property of the current MBean. You can specify whether superclasses are also examined with the `superclass` attribute. Finds properties with getter, setter, or both. The getter and setter should use the JavaBean naming convention. Only methods with the supplied tag are considered in looking for properties.
superclasses	Includes properties of superclasses. Default: true.
tagName	[Required] Required tag for methods to be considered a getter or setter. For example, `jmx:managed-attribute`.
ifHasGetMethodWithTag	Looks for a get method based on the attribute name from the current method, sets the current method to that get method, and applies the template if found. This is used to look for getters for MBean-managed attributes. The get method found may be the current method.
tagName	[Required] Required tag for methods to be considered a getter or setter. For example, `jmx:managed-attribute`.
ifHasSetMethodWithTag	Looks for a set method based on the attribute name from the current method, sets the current method to that set method, and applies the template if found. This is used to look for setters for MBean-managed attributes. The set method found may be the current method.
tagName	[Required] Required tag for methods to be considered a getter or setter. For example, `@jmx.managed-attribute`.
ifHasParamWithTag	Determines if there is a get or set method with the required tag for the current property that also has the requested parameter.
paramName	Parameter name. Required for property parameter values. The content of the tag is returned.

Table D.91 Body tags in the `Property` namespace *(continued)*

Tag name/Attributes	Description
tagName	[Required] Tag name required for a getter or setter to belong to a property.

Table D.92 Content tags in the `Property` namespace

Tag name/Attributes	Description
getClassNameFor	Returns the not-fully-qualified name of the current class without the package name.
getFullClassNameFor	Returns the fully qualified name of the current class with the package name.
getFullSuperclassNameFor	Returns the fully qualified name of the superclass of the current class.
paramValueWithTag	Looks for a get or set method with the required tag for the current property that also has the requested parameter, and returns the value of the requested parameter if present.
default	Default value to return if the parameter isn't tagged with the requested tag.
paramName	Parameter name. Required for property parameter values. The content of the tag is returned.
tagName	[Required] Tag name.
propertyTypeWithTag	Returns the type for the current property with tag by looking for a getter, then a setter.
tagName	[Required] Required tag for methods to be considered a getter or setter. For example, `@jmx.managed-attribute`.

Resin namespace

This namespace is implemented in `xdoclet.modules.caucho.ResinWebTagsHandler`. These tags take the form of `<XDtResin:tagName>`.

Table D.93 Body tag in the `Resin` namespace

Tag name/Attributes	Description
forAllCurrentTagParams	Iterates over all parameters of the current javadoc tag.

Table D.94   Content tags in the `Resin` namespace

Tag name/Attributes	Description
`parameterAsElement`	Writes the current javadoc parameter as an XML element of the form *Parameter=value*. If the parameter maps to a non-empty value in the attributes, the value is used as the XML element name instead of the javadoc parameter name.
`parameterAsInitParam`	Writes the current javadoc parameter as an element or an initialization parameter, depending on the tag attributes; if the parameter name is contained in the attributes, the element form is used; otherwise the `init-param` form is used.
`parameterAsXml`	Writes the current javadoc parameter as an XML element.
`parameterName`	Returns the current javadoc parameter name.
`parameterValue`	Returns the current javadoc parameter value.
`sourceComment`	Writes an XML comment indicating the current method or class name.

ResinEjb namespace

This namespace is implemented in `xdoclet.modules.caucho.ResinEjbTagsHandler`. These tags take the form of `<XDtResinEjb:tagName>`.

In addition to the tags listed here, the `ResinEjb` namespace shares all the tags contained in the `Ejb` and `EjbRel` namespaces.

Table D.95   Body tags in the `ResinEjb` namespace

Tag name/Attributes	Description
`ifHasLeftOrderBy`	Evaluates the body if the left side of the relationship is many and the `order-by` parameter of the `@resinejb.relation` method-level tag is defined.
`ifHasLeftSqlColumn`	Evaluates the body if the left side of the relationship is single and the `sql-column` parameter of the `@resinejb.relation` method-level tag is defined.
`ifHasRightOrderBy`	Evaluates the body if the right side of the relationship is many and the `order-by` parameter of the `@resinejb.relation` method-level tag is defined.

Table D.95   Body tags in the `ResinEjb` namespace *(continued)*

Tag name/Attributes	Description
`ifHasRightSqlColumn`	Evaluates the body if the right side of the relation-ship is single and the `sql-column` parameter of the `@resinejb.relation` `method-level` tag is defined.
`ifHasSqlTable`	Evaluates the body if either side of the current relation is many and the `sql-table` parameter of the `@resinejb.relation` `method-level` tag is defined.

Table D.96   Content tags in the `ResinEjb` namespace

Tag name/Attributes	Description
`leftOrderBy`	Returns the `order-by` for the left side of the cur-rent relation, if applicable.
`leftSqlColumn`	Returns the `sql-column` for the left side of the current relation, if applicable.
`rightOrderBy`	Returns the `order-by` for the right side of the current relation, if applicable.
`rightSqlColumn`	Returns the `sql-column` for the right side of the current relation, if applicable.
`signatureFromMethod`	Returns the signature of the current method in a form suitable for the `/resinejb/enterprise-beans/entity/method/signature` element.
`sqlTable`	Returns the `sql-table` of the current relation-ship, if any.

Soap namespace

This namespace is implemented in `xdoclet.modules.apache.soap.ejb.SoapTags Handler`. This tag takes the form of `<XDtSoap:tagName>`.

Table D.97   Content tag in the `Soap` namespace

Tag name/Attributes	Description
`serviceId`	Returns the service ID of the web service.

StrutsForm namespace

This namespace is implemented in xdoclet.modules.apache.struts.Struts
FormTagsHandler. These tags take the form of <XDtStrutsForm:*tagName*>.

In addition to the tags listed here, the StrutsForm namespace shares all the
tags contained in the Ejb namespace.

Table D.98 Body tags in the **StrutsForm** namespace

Tag name/Attributes	Description
forAllFormFields	Evaluates the body for all fields included in form generation.
ifUseMethodInForm	Evaluates the body if the method belongs in a given form.

Table D.99 Content tags in the **StrutsForm** namespace

Tag name/Attributes	Description
strutsFormClass	Return the class name for the current class.
strutsFormName	Returns the name of the current form.

SunONE namespace

This namespace is implemented in xdoclet.modules.sun.sunone.ejb.SunONE
TagsHandler. These tags take the form of <XDtSunONE:*tagName*>. This namespace
also includes the abstract program element tags defined in the section "Abstract
program element namespaces."

Table D.100 Content tags in the **SunONE** namespace

Tag name/Attributes	Description
generateGUID	Returns a 32-byte GUID generator (Globally Unique ID).
getClassNameFor	Returns the not-fully-qualified name of the current class without the package name.
getFullClassNameFor	Returns the fully qualified name of the current class with the package name.
getFullSuperclassNameFor	Returns the fully qualified name of the superclass of the current class.

TagDef namespace

This namespace is implemented in xdoclet.tagshandler.TagDefTagsHandler. This tag takes the form of <XDtTagDef:*tagName*>.

Table D.101 Content tag in the `TagDef` namespace

Tag name/Attributes	Description
`tagDef`	Defines a template tag handler for a template tag to `TemplateEngine`.
handler	[Required] Template tag handler fully qualified class name. This class implements the namespace tags. It should be a public class with a no-argument public constructor, and it should extend xdoclet.XDocletTagSupport.
namespace	[Required] Template namespace name. Example: `Merge`, if you were to define template namespace `Merge` this way.

Type namespace

This namespace is implemented in xdoclet.tagshandler.TypeTagsHandler. These tags take the form of <XDtType:*tagName*>.

Table D.102 Content tags in the `Type` namespace

Tag name/Attributes	Description
`ifIsNotPrimitive`	Evaluates the body block if the value isn't of a primitive type.
value	[Required] String containing the type name.
`ifIsNotPrimitiveArray`	Evaluates the body block if the value isn't of a primitive array type.
value	[Required] String containing the type name.
`ifIsNotPrimitiveOrString`	Evaluates the body block if the value is of a primitive type or `String`.
value	[Required] String containing the type name.

Table D.102 Content tags in the `Type` namespace *(continued)*

Tag name/Attributes		Description
`ifIsNotOfType`		Evaluates the body block if the entity isn't of the specified type.
	`extent`	Specifies the extent of the type search. Valid values: concrete-type, superclass, hierarchy. If concrete-type, then only checks the concrete type; if superclass, then also checks the superclass; if hierarchy, then searches the whole hierarchy and determines whether the class is of the specified type. Default: hierarchy.
	`type`	[Required] Type you're checking against.
	`value`	[Required] Valid values: class, return-type. If class, then check the current class's type; if return-type, then check the current method's return type.
`ifIsOfType`		Evaluates the body block if the entity is of the specified type.
	`extent`	Specifies the extent of the type search. Valid values: concrete-type, superclass, hierarchy. If concrete-type, then only checks the concrete type; if superclass, then also checks the superclass; if hierarchy, then searches the whole hierarchy and determines whether the class is of the specified type. Default: hierarchy.
	`type`	[Required] Type you're checking against.
	`value`	Valid values: class, return-type. If class, then checks the current class's type; if return-type, then checks the current method return type. Default: class.
`ifIsPrimitive`		Evaluates the body block if the value is of a primitive type.
	`value`	[Required] String containing the type name.
`ifIsPrimitiveArray`		Evaluates the body block if the value is of a primitive array type.
	`value`	[Required] String containing the type name.
`ifIsPrimitiveOrString`		Evaluates the body block if the value is of a primitive type or `String`.
	`value`	[Required] String containing the type name.

Table D.103   Content tag in the `Type` **namespace**

Tag name/Attributes	Description
`typeWithoutDimensions`	Returns the type specified with the `type` parameter without dimensions.
type	[Required] Specifies the type to return without dimensions. So, the value `String[][]` will be returned as `String`.

Validator namespace

This namespace is implemented in `xdoclet.modules.apache.struts.Struts ValidatorTagsHandler`. These tags take the form of `<XDtValidator:tagName>`. This namespace also includes abstract program element tags defined in the section "Abstract program element namespaces."

Table D.104   Block tags in the `Validator` **namespace**

Tag name/Attributes	Description
`forAllFieldArgs`	Iterates over all arguments for the current field.
`forAllFields`	Iterates the body for each field of the current form requiring validation.
`forAllForms`	Iterates over all Struts form beans and evaluates the body of the tag for each class.
`ifArgIsForType`	Evaluates the body if the current argument is a validator-specific argument.
`ifArgIsResource`	Evaluates the body if the current argument is a resource key.
`ifArgIsValue`	Evaluates the body if the current argument is an inline value rather than a resource key.
`ifFormHasFields`	Evaluates the body if the form has fields requiring validation.
`ifNoArg0`	Evaluates the body if no `arg0` is specified.

Table D.105   Content tags in the `Validator` **namespace**

Tag name/Attributes	Description
`argIndex`	Current argument index number (0 to 3).
`argName`	Current argument name. Valid only if the argument is for a specific validator type.

Table D.105 Content tags in the `Validator` namespace *(continued)*

Tag name/Attributes	Description
`argValue`	Current argument value, which is either an inline value or resource key.
`fieldName`	Returns the current fields name.
`formName`	Gets the name attribute for the `<form>` element in the XML descriptor. This should be the `path form` attribute if this is a `ValidatorActiorForm` or the `name` attribute otherwise.
`generateGUID`	Returns a 32-byte GUID generator (Globally Unique ID).
`getClassNameFor`	Returns the not-fully-qualified name of the current class without the package name.
`getFullClassNameFor`	Returns the fully qualified name of the current class with the package name.
`getFullSuperclassNameFor`	Returns the fully qualified name of the superclass of the current class.
`validatorList`	Returns a comma-separated list of the specified validator types.

Velocity namespace

This namespace is implemented in `xdoclet.modules.apache.velocity.Velocity EngineTagHandler`. These tags take the form of `<XDtVelocity:tagName>`.

This namespace enables you to embed Velocity templates within XDt templates by including the Velocity template as the body of `<XDtVelocity:generator>`.

Table D.106 Block tag in the `Velocity` namespace

Tag name/Attributes		Description
`generator`		Evaluates the body block with the Velocity template engine. If the `silent=yes` attribute is set, then the Generator won't produce any output, but the template will run. If the `disable=yes` attribute is set, then the Velocity template won't run.
	`disable`	If yes, then does nothing.
	`silent`	If yes, then runs in silent mode; Velocity output isn't sent to XDoclet output.

Table D.107   Content tags in the `Velocity` namespace

Tag name/Attributes	Description
`clearVariables`	Clears all Velocity variables.
`getVariable`	Gets a value of a Velocity variable from the context. Example: `<XDtTemplateEngines:getVelocityVariable name=numMethods default=0 />`.
`default`	Default value to return if the specified variable isn't found.
`name`	[Required] Name of the Velocity variable.

Web namespace

This namespace is implemented in `xdoclet.modules.web.WebTagsHandler`. These tags take the form of `<XDtWeb:tagName>`.

Table D.108   Block tags in the `Web` namespace

Tag name/Attributes	Description
`forAllEnvEntries`	Processes the tag body for each `@web.env-entry` tag in all source files. Look at `forAllEjbRefs` for some notes about the behavior of this tag.
`forAllEjbLocalRefs`	Processes the tag body for each `@web.ejb-local-ref` tag in all source files. Look at `forAllEjbRefs` for some notes about the behavior of this tag.
`forAllEjbRefs`	Processes the tag body for each `@web.ejb-ref` tag in all source files. Note that this tag already iterates over all available sources; it should *not* be enclosed by a `<XDtClass:forAllClasses>` tag or any other tag that process classes. This tag doesn't process tags with duplicated name attributes. If such tags occur, only the first tag is processed, and further tags only emit a warning message.
`forAllResourceEnvRefs`	Processes the tag body for each `@web.resource-env-ref` tag in all source files. Look at `forAllEjbRefs` for some notes about the behavior of this tag.

Table D.108 Block tags in the Web namespace *(continued)*

Tag name/Attributes	Description
forAllResourceRefs	Processes the tag body for each @web.resource-ref tag in all source files. Look at forAllEjbRefs for some notes about the behavior of this tag.
forAllSecurityRoles	Processes the tag body for each @web.security-role tag in all source files. Look at forAllEjbRefs for some notes about the behavior of this tag.

WebWork namespace

This namespace is implemented in xdoclet.modules.webwork.WebWorkTagsHandler. These tags take the form of <XDtWebWork:*tagName*>.

Table D.109 Content tags in the WebWork namespace

Tag name/Attributes	Description
commandName	Returns the command name from the name of the current method.
javadocHtmlFile	Returns the path to the HTML file in the javadoc pointing to the action class.

WlEjbRel namespace

This namespace is implemented in xdoclet.modules.bea.wls.ejb.WlEjbRelTagsHandler. These tags take the form of <XDtWlEjbRel:*tagName*>.

Table D.110 Body tags in the WlEjbRel namespace

Tag name/Attributes	Description
ensureColumnMapTagsRight	Makes sure the column-map tags are on the right side and target-column-map tags are on the left.
forAllLeftColumnMaps	Iterates over all column maps on the left-hand side of the current relationship.
forAllRightColumnMaps	Iterates over all column maps on the right-hand side of the current relationship.
ifHasKeyColumn	Evaluates the body block if the current EJB has a primary key field.

Table D.110 **Body tags in the** `WlEjbRel` **namespace** *(continued)*

Tag name/Attributes	Description
`ifHasLeftGroupName`	Evaluates the body block if the left-hand side of the current relationship has a group name.
`ifHasRightGroupName`	Evaluates the body block if the right-hand side of the current relationship has a group name.

Table D.111 **Content tags in the** `WlEjbRel` **namespace**

Tag name/Attributes	Description
`foreignKeyColumn`	Returns the name of the foreign key column.
`joinTableName`	Returns the name of the join table for a many-to-many relationship.
`keyColumn`	Returns the name of the key column.
`leftGroupName`	Returns the left group name.
`rightGroupName`	Returns the right group name.

Xml namespace

This namespace is implemented in `xdoclet.tagshandler.XmlTagsHandler`. These tags take the form of `<XDtXml:tagName>`.

Table D.112 **Content tags in the** `Xml` **namespace**

Tag name/Attributes	Description
`publicId`	Returns the DTD's public ID for an XML template.
`schema`	Returns the schema for an XML template.
`systemId`	Returns the DTD's system ID for an XML template.

The future of XDoclet

A virtue of any good software system is that it continues to evolve to meet new demands and to reflect new insights and lessons learned by the development team. XDoclet is no exception. Already it has evolved from generating only EJB deployment descriptors to satisfying the code-generation needs of a variety of other frameworks and technologies. Experience gained with the javadoc prompted the XDoclet team to develop their own XJavaDoc API for parsing Java source code for tags.

In this appendix, we'll give you a glimpse of what the future holds for XDoclet and show how you can help shape that future.

XDoclet 2: code-generation revisited

Even as we're writing this book, the XDoclet team is moving XDoclet through to its next major evolution: XDoclet 2. Although XDoclet 2 is still in an alpha stage, we're starting to get a fairly clear picture of what it will look like and how it will differ from the XDoclet we've spent the last dozen chapters discussing.

Let's explore the new features and changes being cooked up by the XDoclet 2 team.[1]

Introducing Generama

Before you can understand XDoclet 2, you must know about Generama. Generama is a truly general-purpose code generation engine. Like XDoclet, Generama can generate practically any code your project needs. However, unlike XDoclet, Generama isn't limited to doclet tags in Java source code to provide its metadata.

On the receiving end, Generama takes metadata given to it by a metadata provider. Metadata providers are responsible for collecting metadata from a source and packaging it to be consumed by Generama. Metadata providers are pluggable components, enabling Generama to take its metadata from a variety of sources. For example, you may have a metadata provider that parses XMI (XML metadata interchange) files to accumulate metadata for Generama. Or you may use a metadata provider that examines a database schema to provide metadata for Generama.[2] The source of the metadata isn't important as long as there is a metadata provider that can give it to Generama.

On the generation end, Generama uses template plugins to generate code. Currently, Generama has two template plugins: a Jelly plugin for generating XML code and a Velocity plugin for generating non-XML code.

So, why is Generama important to XDoclet 2? As you'll soon see, XDoclet 2 is based on Generama.

XDoclet 2 and Generama

Looking closely at XDoclet 2, you'll find that there isn't much to it. In fact, at the time when we're writing this appendix, XDoclet 2 is made up of only seven classes (not counting unit tests).

---

[1] At the time of this writing, XDoclet 2 is still very early in alpha development. Although we're getting a pretty good idea of how XDoclet 2 will look, much of the information presented in this appendix is subject to change as development of XDoclet 2 continues.

[2] This could be the approach taken by the Middlegen project.

Much of the functionality of XDoclet 2 is the same functionality as found in Generama. Therefore, XDoclet 2 is based on Generama. In fact, XDoclet 2 *is* Generama with a QDox[3] metadata provider pre-registered.

Using the <xdoclet> task

Although XDoclet 2 is decoupled from Ant, Ant (and Ant's Jakarta cousin, Maven) is still a likely mechanism for launching XDoclet. Unlike XDoclet 1.2, which comes with a sizeable collection of Ant tasks, XDoclet 2 has only one task: <xdoclet>. Listing E.1 shows <xdoclet> being used to generate EJB files.

Listing E.1   Generating EJB artifacts with XDoclet 2

```
<xdoclet>
  <fileset dir="${pom.build.sourceDirectory}">          Select
    <include name="**/beans/*.java"/>                   metadata
  </fileset>                                             source files     Register
                                                                         utility
  <component classname="org.xdoclet.plugin.ejb.EjbUtils"/>    ◁┘  class

  <component                                       Generate remote
    classname=                                           interfaces
      "org.xdoclet.plugin.ejb.interfaces.RemoteInterfacePlugin"
    destdir="${basedir}/target/test-output"/>

  <component                                        Generate local
    classname=                                          interfaces
      "org.xdoclet.plugin.ejb.interfaces.LocalInterfacePlugin"
    destdir="${basedir}/target/test-output"/>

  <component                                             Generate
    classname=                                           deployment
      "org.xdoclet.plugin.ejb.descriptor.EjbJarXmlPlugin"  descriptor
    destdir="${basedir}/target/test-output/META-INF"/>
</xdoclet>
```

What's interesting is that <xdoclet> has no subtasks. But without subtasks, what generates code? Notice that the sub-elements of <xdoclet> include several <component> elements. The <component> element is used to register a plugin with XDoclet. Under

---

[3]   QDox is the replacement for XJavaDoc. It was chosen over XJavaDoc because it's faster and has an easier API. For more information on QDox, visit the QDox project site at http://qdox.codehaus.org.

the covers, XDoclet (and more accurately, Generama) is based on PicoContainer,[4] an *inversion of control* container.

It's not important for you to fully understand inversion of control to use XDoclet. It's sufficient to know that each of the plugins may or may not require some other component(s) in the container to get their work done, and that the container will provide those components to the plugins (instead of the plugins asking for the components). In the case of listing E.1, each plugin requires an instance of `org.xdoclet.plugin.ejb.EjbUtils`. When XDoclet starts up the plugin, XDoclet is required to give the plugin an instance of `EjbUtils`, or the plugin can't proceed to generate code. This is why, in addition to the plugin classes, you must also register the `EjbUtils` class with the `<xdoclet>` task.

Tagging code with metadata

Tagging a class with metadata hasn't changed significantly between XDoclet 1.2 and XDoclet 2. For example, tagging a method for inclusion in an EJB's generated local interface may look like this:

```
/**
 * @ejb.interface-method
 *     view-type="local"
 */
public void doSomething() {
...
}
```

However, although the syntax for tagging hasn't changed, don't assume that the same set of tags and attributes will be available in XDoclet 2. The plugin authors may decide to deprecate, remove, or rename tags and attributes, rendering the old tags and attributes unusable.

Fortunately, as someone who uses XDoclet, you have a voice within the XDoclet community and can help steer the direction of XDoclet—perhaps deciding which tags carry over from XDoclet 1.2 to XDoclet 2. Here's how you can plug yourself into the XDoclet development process.

Getting involved with XDoclet

One of the great things about open-source software is that you don't have to settle for what comes out of the box. If you need a feature, you can add it yourself. If a

---

[4] To learn more about PicoContainer, visit http://picocontainer.org.

bug is causing you grief, you can fix it yourself. There's no need to wait for the next release to get what you want. You're in control.

As an open-source project, XDoclet is no different. If you see an opportunity to improve the XDoclet code base, then you're invited to do so. And if you think other XDoclet users will find your improvements useful, you can contribute your changes to the project for consideration in future versions of XDoclet.

A question that is frequently asked on the XDoclet mailing lists is how to contribute to the project. If you're interested in contributing, this appendix will give you the basics on how to get involved.

XDoclet team structure

Developers involved with XDoclet fall into one of three levels of involvement:

- *Users* accept XDoclet as is and play no role in shaping it other than perhaps suggesting features or reporting bugs.

- *Contributors* are users who see opportunities to improve XDoclet and don't want to wait for someone else to make the changes. They either have a feature they want added or they see a bug in JIRA (XDoclet's issue-tracking system) and volunteer to fix it. Anyone who has an interest in contributing can do so by posting patches to JIRA (more on that later).

- *Committers* are contributors who have authorization to directly commit changed code into CVS. To establish some order and to prevent changes from being haphazardly committed to the XDoclet code base, only committers are allowed to commit changes directly to CVS. Becoming a committer involves establishing a record of making significant contributions to XDoclet as a contributor and then being nominated and voted in by other committers.

Subscribing to the mailing lists

Regardless of the level of involvement you're interested in, we strongly recommend that you subscribe to one or more of the mailing lists pertaining to XDoclet. There are three XDoclet mailing lists:

- *xdoclet-announce* is used to announce XDoclet news. This mailing list sees the fewest posts, because a moderator approves all posts prior to publication to make certain they're legitimate XDoclet announcements.

- *xdoclet-user* is where XDoclet users can post questions about how to use XDoclet or some of its features. Other users, including members of the XDoclet team, answer these questions. If you have a "how to" question, this is the mailing list to send it to.

- *xdoclet-devel* is where XDoclet contributors and committers exchange thoughts and ideas that shape future XDoclet releases. In addition, any updates to JIRA issues or commits to CVS are posted to xdoclet-devel.

To subscribe to one of these mailing lists, send an email with *SUBSCRIBE* in the subject line to one or more of the following e-mail addresses:

- xdoclet-announce@sourceforge.net
- xdoclet-user@sourceforge.net
- xdoclet-devel@sourceforge.net

You can also view archived posts to these lists by visiting the following URLs:

- http://www.mail-archive.com/xdoclet-announce@lists.sourceforge.net
- http://www.mail-archive.com/xdoclet-user@lists.sourceforge.net
- http://www.mail-archive.com/xdoclet-devel@lists.sourceforge.net

Accessing the source code from CVS

XDoclet's source-code is kept in a CVS repository at SourceForge. Using the standard command-line CVS client, you can anonymously access the XDoclet CVS repository as follows (when prompted for a password, press the Enter key):

```
% cvs -d
  :pserver:anonymous@cvs.xdoclet.sourceforge.net:/cvsroot/xdoclet
  login
```

Now you can check out XDoclet:

```
% cvs -z3 -d
  :pserver:anonymous@cvs.xdoclet.sourceforge.net:/cvsroot/xdoclet
  co xdoclet-all
```

If you plan to build XDoclet, then you also need XJavaDoc. You can check out XJavaDoc using the following CVS incantation:

```
% cvs -z3 -d :pserver:anonymous@cvs.xdoclet.sourceforge.net:/cvsroot/
  xdoclet co xjavadoc
```

Building XDoclet

Now that you've checked out the source code from CVS and perhaps made some changes, you'll want to build XDoclet to test your changes. XDoclet's source code comes with an Ant build file for building its binaries. If you aren't using Ant yet (and you should be—everything in this book depends on it!), then refer to appendix A for details on how to install it.

Building XJavaDoc

If you've checked out XJavaDoc's source code from CVS as described earlier, you can build it by changing into XJavaDoc's base directory and running Ant:

```
% ant
```

Building all of XDoclet

If you've made changes to XDoclet's core, or if you've never built XDoclet from scratch before, you need to do a full build of XDoclet. To build XDoclet in its entirety, change into XDoclet's base directory and run Ant:

```
% ant
```

The files that result from building XDoclet are placed in a directory called `target` under XDoclet's base directory. The JAR files that define XDoclet are placed in `target/lib`. To use these JAR files when you build your projects with XDoclet, change your build files to use this directory when you use `<taskdef>` to define XDoclet tasks. For the examples presented in this book, that means changing the `xdoclet.lib.dir` variable to point to the `target/lib` directory.

One of the last steps in the full build is to generate HTML documentation for XDoclet and its modules. This process uses another open-source tool called Maven to generate the documentation. If you haven't installed Maven, you'll get errors when Ant reaches this point in the build. That's OK if you don't care about building the documentation. But if you also want to build the documentation, you need to download and install Maven. You can get Maven from http://maven.apache.org.

Building only the modules

Building XDoclet in its entirety is a lengthy process. Even if you've only made changes to a single template or task class, the build can still take several minutes to complete.

Fortunately, the full XDoclet build relies on several individual `build.xml` files within each module's directory. This makes it possible to test simple changes by performing a build on a single module at a time without having to wait for the full-blown build.

For example, suppose you've just made an enhancement to `mx4j-mbean-description.xdt`, the template file used by the `<mx4jdescription>` subtask. You're eager to test the enhancement, and you don't want to wait for a complete build. To perform a build on only the MX4J module, navigate to the `modules/mx4j` folder and run Ant from there. In a matter of seconds (rather than minutes), a new MX4J module will be built and ready for you to use.

Building the HTML documentation

Occasionally, you may want to change the documentation of an XDoclet task or tag, or you may have developed a new task or tag that needs to be documented. Even though doing a full build of XDoclet (with Maven installed) will generate the HTML documentation anew, you may want to build only the documentation. For example, if you've changed the documentation but you haven't changed any code, a complete build is unnecessary.

If you have Maven installed, you can build the HTML documentation for XDoclet by running the following line from XDoclet's base directory:

```
% maven site:generate
```

After a few minutes, the new documentation will be available in the `target/docs` directory.

Tracking issues in JIRA

Bugs and improvement ideas for XDoclet are tracked in an issue-tracking system called JIRA. The XDoclet JIRA can be accessed at http://opensource.atlassian.com/projects/xdoclet/.

As an XDoclet user, you can browse submitted issues in JIRA. If you're registered as a JIRA user, you can also report bugs and submit feature requests.

If you've made a change to the XDoclet code, then you can contribute your changes by following these steps:

1   Build and test your changes on your local machine. This may sound like an obvious step, but forgetting it can cause a lot of headaches for other XDoclet users.

2   Create a patch. From the XDoclet root directory, you can create a patch using CVS:

```
% cvs -q diff -b -u -N > patch.diff
```

3   If an applicable issue in JIRA doesn't already exist, create one.

4   Attach your patch to the JIRA issue.

Unless you're submitting a new file that doesn't already exist in CVS, don't attach complete files to JIRA issues. You should always attach patches for existing code.

Once a patch is attached to an issue in JIRA, an XDoclet committer can come along and apply the patch to the code base for future builds of XDoclet.

recommended reading

Alur, Deepak, John Crupi, and Dan Malks. *Core J2EE Patterns: Best Practices and Design Strategies,* 2d ed. Upper Saddle River, NJ: Prentice Hall, 2003.

Fowler, Martin, David Rice, Matthew Foemmel, Edward Hieatt, Robert Mee, and Randy Stafford. *Patterns of Enterprise Application Architecture.* Boston: Addison-Wesley, 2002.

Gallardo, David, Ed Burnette, and Robert McGovern. *Eclipse in Action.* Greenwich, CT: Manning, 2003.

Hatcher, Erik, and Steve Loughran. *Java Development with Ant.* Greenwich, CT: Manning, 2003.

Herrington, Jack. *Code Generation in Action.* Greenwich, CT: Manning, 2003.

Husted, Ted, Cedric Dumoulin, George Franciscus, David Winterfeldt, and Craig R. McClanahan. *Struts in Action.* Greenwich, CT: Manning, 2002.

Massol, Vincent, and Ted Husted. *JUnit in Action.* Greenwich, CT: Manning, 2003.

Roman, Ed, Scott W. Ambler, and Tyler Jewell. *Mastering Enterprise JavaBeans.* New York: Wiley, 2001.

Sullins, Benjamin G., and Mark B. Whipple. *EJB Cookbook.* Greenwich, CT: Manning, 2003.

———. *JMX in Action.* Greenwich, CT: Manning, 2002.

index